WHAT MAKES A PHILOSOPHER GREAT?

This book is inspired by a single powerful question. What *is* it to be great as a philosopher? No single grand answer is presumed to be possible; instead, rewardingly close studies of philosophical greatness are developed. This is a scholarly yet accessible volume, blending metaphilosophy with the long history of philosophy and traversing centuries and continents. The result is a series of case studies by accomplished scholars, each chapter trying to understand and convey a particular philosopher's greatness:

- Lloyd P. Gerson on Plato
- Karyn Lai on Zhuangzi
- David Bronstein on Aristotle
- Jonardon Ganeri on Buddhaghosa
- Jeffrey Hause on Aquinas
- Gary Hatfield on Descartes
- Karen Detlefsen on Du Châtelet
- Don Garrett on Hume
- Allen Wood on Kant (as a moral philosopher)
- Nicholas F. Stang on Kant (as a metaphysician)
- Ken Gemes on Nietzsche
- Cheryl Misak on Peirce
- David Macarthur on Wittgenstein

This also serves a larger philosophical purpose. Might we gain increased clarity about what philosophy *is* in the first place? After all, in practice we individuate philosophy partly through its greatest practitioners' greatest contributions.

The book does not discuss every philosopher who has been regarded as great. The point is not to offer a definitive list of The Great Philosophers, but, rather, to learn something about what great philosophy is and might be, from illuminated examples of past greatness.

Stephen Hetherington is Professor of Philosophy at the University of New South Wales. His publications include *Epistemology's Paradox* (1992), *Good Knowledge, Bad Knowledge* (2001), *How to Know* (2011), and *Knowledge and the Gettier Problem* (2016).

"What is the difference between a merely good philosopher and a great one? Lists of the great (and usually dead) philosophers presuppose an answer to this question but it's far from obvious what the answer is. The distinguished contributors to this terrific volume advance our understanding of what great philosophy is and explain the greatness of some of the greatest philosophers."

Quassim Cassam, *University of Warwick*

"An impressive assembly of scholars, each a top expert on their subject, addresses the title question of the volume. A fascinating collaboration, in which the contrasts will no doubt illuminate no less than the agreements."

Ernest Sosa, *Rutgers University*

WHAT MAKES A PHILOSOPHER GREAT?

Thirteen Arguments for
Twelve Philosophers

Edited by Stephen Hetherington

NEW YORK AND LONDON

First published 2018
by Routledge
711 Third Avenue, New York, NY 10017

and by Routledge
2 Park Square, Milton Park, Abingdon, Oxon, OX14 4RN

Routledge is an imprint of the Taylor & Francis Group, an informa business

© 2018 Taylor & Francis

The right of Stephen Hetherington to be identified as the author of the editorial material, and of the authors for their individual chapters, has been asserted in accordance with sections 77 and 78 of the Copyright, Designs and Patents Act 1988.

All rights reserved. No part of this book may be reprinted or reproduced or utilised in any form or by any electronic, mechanical, or other means, now known or hereafter invented, including photocopying and recording, or in any information storage or retrieval system, without permission in writing from the publishers.

Trademark notice: Product or corporate names may be trademarks or registered trademarks, and are used only for identification and explanation without intent to infringe.

Library of Congress Cataloging-in-Publication Data
Names: Hetherington, Stephen Cade, editor.
Title: What makes a philosopher great? : Thirteen arguments for twelve philosophers / edited by Stephen Hetherington.
Description: New York : Routledge, [2018] | Includes bibliographical references and index.
Identifiers: LCCN 2017030195| ISBN 9781138936157 (hbk) | ISBN 9781138936164 (pbk) | ISBN 9781315676999 (ebk)
Subjects: LCSH: Philosophers.
Classification: LCC B72 .W49 2018 | DDC 109.2—dc23
LC record available at https://lccn.loc.gov/2017030195

ISBN: 978-1-138-93615-7 (hbk)
ISBN: 978-1-138-93616-4 (pbk)
ISBN: 978-1-315-67699-9 (ebk)

Typeset in Bembo
by Apex CoVantage, LLC

CONTENTS

Contributors	*vii*
Preface and Acknowledgments	*ix*

1 Philosophical Greatness: Introducing the Very Idea   1
   Stephen Hetherington

2 Plato, Platonism, and the History of Philosophy   12
   Lloyd P. Gerson

3 Zhuangzi's Suggestiveness: Skeptical Questions   30
   Karyn Lai

4 Aristotle as Systematic Philosopher: Essence, Necessity, and Explanation in Theory and Practice   48
   David Bronstein

5 Attention to Greatness: Buddhaghosa   67
   Jonardon Ganeri

6 Aquinas's Complex Web   86
   Jeffrey Hause

7 Descartes as a Great Philosopher: Comprehensive Physics, Methodological Systematicity, and Mechanistic Embodiment   104
   Gary Hatfield

8 Émilie Du Châtelet on Women's Minds and Education 128
   Karen Detlefsen

9 What's So Great About Hume? 148
   Don Garrett

10 Is Kant a *Great* Moral Philosopher? 169
   Allen Wood

11 'How Is Metaphysics Possible?': Kant's Great Question
   and His Great Answer 187
   Nicholas F. Stang

12 Nietzsche, This Time It's Personal 211
   Ken Gemes

13 What Makes Peirce a Great Philosopher? 227
   Cheryl Misak

14 Wittgenstein's Un-Ruley Solution to the Problem
   of Philosophy 246
   David Macarthur

Index *267*

CONTRIBUTORS

David Bronstein, Associate Professor of Philosophy, Georgetown University

Karen Detlefsen, Associate Professor of Philosophy and Education, University of Pennsylvania

Jonardon Ganeri, Global Network Professor of Philosophy, New York University

Don Garrett, Professor of Philosophy, New York University

Ken Gemes, Professor of Philosophy, Birkbeck College, University of London

Lloyd P. Gerson, Professor of Philosophy, University of Toronto

Gary Hatfield, Adam Seybert Professor in Moral and Intellectual Philosophy, University of Pennsylvania

Jeffrey Hause, Michael W. Barry Professor of Philosophy, Creighton University

Stephen Hetherington, Professor of Philosophy, University of New South Wales

Karyn Lai, Associate Professor of Philosophy, University of New South Wales

David Macarthur, Associate Professor of Philosophy, University of Sydney

Cheryl Misak, Professor of Philosophy, University of Toronto

Nicholas F. Stang, Assistant Professor of Philosophy, University of Toronto

Allen Wood, Ruth Norman Halls Professor of Philosophy, Indiana University, Bloomington

PREFACE AND ACKNOWLEDGMENTS

The idea for this book arose, like many an idea, in the back of a taxi. I was in Taipei with Michael Slote and Chienkuo (Michael) Mi. Michael Slote and I were being hosted by Soochow University, courtesy of Michael Mi. Michael Slote was telling us about a paper of his—'Kant for Anti-Kantians', in his book *Essays on the History of Ethics* (New York: Oxford University Press, 2010). In that paper, Michael describes 'some contributions that Kant made to ethics that even an anti-Kantian like myself ought to accept and acknowledge' (p. 101). This struck me as being a step toward understanding why Kant was *great* as a moral philosopher: Michael Slote was telling us how even those philosophers who would never call themselves Kantians about moral philosophy have learned from Kant—and have learned not merely interesting details, but potentially fundamental moves. Hearing this, I made one of those mental leaps so beloved by so many philosophers: I generalized, swiftly and optimistically—in this case, from Kant on moral philosophy to philosophers in general. Let's think about philosophical greatness as such, if possible (I thought, enthusiastically).

Inescapably, this is a speculative book. I do not—for even one moment—claim that it is bound to reveal, clearly and incontestably, what philosophical greatness is, if indeed there is any such quality in the first place. But I do—for more than one moment—believe that the idea of philosophical greatness is a tantalizing one. Wouldn't it be *grand* to gain some sense of what philosophical greatness is, if indeed it does or could exist? Shouldn't we at least try to gain that sense, if we are at least to examine or test the hypothesis that philosophical greatness ever is or could be manifested?

The book is not intended to be discussing every philosopher with some claim to being great. Perhaps there are great philosophers *beyond* the people discussed in this book. And I am confident that not everyone will agree that every philosopher discussed here is great. No matter; I have sought a suggestive sample of several *prima facie* candidates for philosophical greatness. Here is that sample, courtesy of some excellent contemporary scholars.

Andy Beck at Routledge was vital to this book's existence and development. He was enthusiastic and constructive, offering excellent suggestions for shaping the book. The same is true of Routledge's three anonymous reviewers. And welcome editorial assistance was provided by Vera Lochtefeld (Routledge) and Lindsay Yeates (University of New South Wales).

1
PHILOSOPHICAL GREATNESS

Introducing the Very Idea

Stephen Hetherington

1. Philosophy as Such

In understanding something's nature—whatever it *is*, within itself, more or less fundamentally—we typically need to understand at least something of whatever it *could* be. This might encompass ways in which various sorts of circumstance would constrain that something's functioning, but might also envisage what it could be when *free* of circumstantial encumbrances. This can allow us to contemplate what the something would be like at its *best*—in its fullest flowering, at its most pure, its potentiality fully displayed. Sometimes, this will even allow us to imagine how the something could achieve a form of *greatness*.

I do not know whether, for example, the property of being a welder is like that. But many people across the centuries have suspected that being a philosopher includes this sort of potential—for a kind of greatness. Thus, already we confront the question of whether philosophy—at least as practised—*is* ever like that. More concretely, are *individual* philosophers—the advocates, creators, and communicators of philosophy—ever great in their philosophical guises? To answer that question would be to take a step toward understanding what philosophy even is in the first place.[1] The inherent nature of This Thing Called Philosophy might encompass *the very best* that someone could be as a philosopher—what we could call *philosophical greatness*.

What would that involve? It is natural, in answering this, to want to think about some actually great philosophers. Can we do this? *Are* there any great philosophers? Western philosophy and Chinese philosophy have been with us for around 2,500 years (see the book's chapters on Plato, on Aristotle, and on Zhuangzi), and Indian philosophy for perhaps 3,000 years (see the chapter on Buddhaghosa): is that long enough for philosophy to have given us flesh-and-blood manifestations of philosophical greatness? Let us begin the book with some optimism about that. After which, I conjecture, a focus upon these philosophers could be our best possible guide to the heart of philosophy—to what, *most* fundamentally, it is. Here is another conjecture: perhaps philosophy at its greatest is philosophy at its most deeply *distinctive* from other forms of thought (and maybe philosophy in general would be philosophy by being enough *like* philosophy at its greatest).

2. Philosophical Writing

Even a great sportsperson is generally great only for parts of his or her career. Might a great philosopher not *always* be great, even while working on his or her philosophy? If so, maybe any discussion of philosophical greatness should focus on greatness as such—the property itself, if there is one. This property would be *instantiated*, at least sometimes, by the occasional philosopher. A great philosopher would be one who gives us some great philosophical *work*. This would be a real achievement, even when it is a mere segment of the person's entire philosophical effort.

That thinking can be extended. Might it be that just part of even an individual book—a chapter here, a section there—is what makes that book great, thereby making the book's author a great philosopher? Are great philosophical *moments* what we must notice—and treasure?

That question's aptness suggests that we should focus on greatness in pieces of philosophical *writing*—on either individual pieces or larger bodies of it. This is not to deny that a philosopher could be great in speech or in thought. Maybe Socrates, most famously, was great in speech (and never in his own writing, nonexistent as it was). Maybe, indeed, the greatest philosophical thoughts have never appeared in writing—never will. All of that is possible. As philosophers seeking to understand philosophical greatness, though, we must reach for our best possible *evidence* of it. The best evidence that has persisted across centuries is some of the philosophical writing that is our past, is still our present, is even perhaps our future.

3. The Philosophical Image

A few years ago, I edited an anthology (Hetherington 2013) of philosophy readings, directed mainly at students. My aim was not simply to bring together—and to write introductions for each individual item in—a group of excellent pieces of philosophy (67 of them, as it transpired). I sought a unifying or motivating theme for the collection—one that could convey to an introductory reader something illuminating, even if generic, about what philosophy is. This led me to the idea of what I called *the philosophical image*—as potentially a distinct way of looking at the world, life, and beyond.

My intention was to complement one of Wilfrid Sellars's contributions to twentieth-century philosophy—his distinction (1963) between *the manifest image* and *the scientific image*. Think of how the world appears to a person when she confronts it without clearly scientific views in mind: this is the manifest image for her. Contrast that with how the world appears to a person once her gaze is scientifically tutored, once she possesses that sort of awareness of what is 'really' there 'behind' the manifest image: this is the scientific image for her. Now ask this: where does philosophy fit into that distinction (seemingly a philosophical one anyway)? Is philosophy an element within common sense, for instance—perhaps cleaving closely to the manifest image, as a way of organizing without radically reshaping those 'intuitive' worldly appearances? Is philosophy instead a subtle and possibly conceptual element within the scientific image, maybe an unacknowledged yet nevertheless animating commitment permeating those overtly scientific details? Or is philosophy something further, perchance a blend of common sense and science? In introducing the anthology's readers to philosophy, I left open those various options. I wrote, simply and programmatically, of *the philosophical image*.

Implicitly, I was asking readers to hold in mind the following question (also raised above, in section 1) when engaging with that book's readings:

> Might there be something unique about philosophy? Are there distinctively philosophical questions or answers?

We may now complicate that question a little further. Are there distinctively *great* philosophical questions or answers? In being distinctive, do they convey a purely philosophical image—whatever this is—so that in this sense all other philosophical efforts can usefully be measured against them? In being great, would those questions and answers be ones against which all other philosophical efforts are to be measured? Those questions lead again to this one (that also ended section 1). Are most pieces of philosophy by most philosophers only philosophy *at all* by being lesser manifestations of whatever—if anything—is most distinctive and formative of the philosophical image?

4. Knowledge

Those are abstract questions. Where should we begin, if we are to render them—along with potential answers—in more specific terms?

We can start with the following examples of how someone might advert—mixedly—to the greatness of a piece of philosophical writing:

- 'So much in her book is false—one mistaken view after another. Oddly, though, the result is still great philosophy.'

- 'Careless thinking is scattered throughout his work—large steps taking us far beyond what the evidence strictly supports. Yet there is something great about what he has produced.'
- 'No one could sensibly believe what she is claiming in her book: it is clearly counter-intuitive. How does the book manage, even so, to be great philosophy?'

If these sorts of remarks make sense, note that they collectively concern what most philosophers standardly regard as among the typically formative elements of *knowledge*.[2] On traditional philosophical conceptions, a person's knowledge—a particular piece of knowledge on her part—is a belief of hers. But it is more than a belief. It is also *true*, and somehow it is *well supported* in a way—such as by resting on good evidence (maybe evidence of its being embedded within an extensive and systematically coherent interweaving of beliefs)—pointing toward its being true. Accordingly, a philosopher might naturally regard a particular belief's being true, supported by good reasoning, and not clearly counter-intuitive as at least part of what makes the belief knowledge. However, in the preceding hypothetical examples we are being told of the *absence*, respectively, of truth, of reasoning, or of intuitively sensible belief. So, if some or all of those imagined comments make sense, do we have a recipe for *denying* that philosophically great writing would always need to be knowledge, let alone great knowledge?

That is a question with wider resonance. Catherine Elgin (1988) has argued—in one of contemporary epistemology's wittiest papers—that philosophical theories of knowledge often ignore clearly admirable intellectual qualities or virtues, such as breadth or sensitivity of thought.[3] Many contemporary college or university administrators apparently derive professional satisfaction from telling the waiting world about how their institutions are an integral component of 'the knowledge economy'. Suppose, for argument's sake, that philosophers employed in those colleges or universities typically say that philosophical knowledge is among their professional goals. But also suppose, still for argument's sake, that philosophers typically wish their professional writing to have breadth, sensitivity, and so forth. And let us suppose for the moment that the latter intellectually admirable qualities would—while the attaining of knowledge would not—be essential to some writing's being philosophically great. Then which of philosophical knowledge and philosophical greatness should be *preferred* by a university administrator, as the result of encouraging the institution's philosophers? And which of those alternatives *would*, in general, be preferred by the administrator? Suppose that the eighteenth-century German philosopher Immanuel Kant (discussed in two of this book's chapters) was giving voice to little if any actual knowledge in his monumental 1781 book, *Critique of Pure Reason*. If this had been his only 'research output' (to use a term in vogue within universities these days), would he *not* have been great—if knowledge is part of philosophical greatness? Is even philosophical greatness—if it need not include the emergence of knowledge—out of place within universities? Or might it be that philosophical greatness *is* intrinsically tied to the production of knowledge—so that it must include some belief(s) being true, well-reasoned, and so forth?

5. No Philosophical Greatness?

We should not lose sight of a contrary possibility—that no writing *has* been philosophically great. Various philosophers have been *called* 'great'. Is that linguistic history decisive, though? We can expand that question into the following ones. If we follow enough philosophers from earlier generations in calling a piece of philosophical writing 'great', is it *therefore* great? If most future philosophers will likewise deem that piece of philosophical writing to be great, does this suffice for its being great—then and/or now?

Those questions cluster around this further one. Is philosophical greatness something about which we should, in effect, be metaphysical *realists*? By that, I mean this:[4]

> Is philosophical greatness a real property? Is it at least indirectly so—a real property that is only ever manifested *in virtue of some other* real property or properties being manifested (and not merely in virtue of a term such as 'philosophically great' being applied by enough pertinent people)?

A metaphysical realist might assure us that one of those options does obtain: philosophical greatness is 'out there, in reality'—even if rarely so, since almost no philosopher achieves greatness.[5] In contrast, a metaphysical *anti*-realist about philosophical greatness might say that all there really is in that respect is the *appearance* of such greatness within the world: for example, there would merely be people *saying* (believing, writing, etc.) that some work is philosophically great. In this sense, the anti-realist is saying that there is nothing *objective* about philosophical greatness: there are *opinions*, even considered and shared ones, converging on a view of some particular book, for instance, as philosophically great; there is nothing more to the book's *being* philosophically great. A metaphysical realist about philosophical greatness would reply that there *is* something objective in a piece of writing's being philosophically great: philosophical greatness is real—hence, someone could be genuinely *mistaken* when deeming a particular philosophy book to be less than great.[6]

6. Originality

In assessing whether there could be a real property of being philosophically great, we need to think about what such a property would encompass. Presumably, further properties will be mentioned when we ponder the nature of that first proposed property. We will be asking whether, for example, some properties are such that to instantiate one or more of them is *enough* to make a piece of writing philosophically great—even if no particular one of them is *necessary* to the writing's being philosophically great. Or are there unequivocally necessary recurring features of *any* piece of writing's being philosophically great?

Consider originality. We may assume, for the sake of immediate argument, that any piece of great philosophical writing is original in some one or more ways. Yet in *what* ways would it be original? As this book's chapters show, possibly there is no single adequate answer to that question, applicable uniformly to the philosophers discussed here. Still, is there a *range* of properties of which the following is true?

- At least one of them is instantiated whenever the property of being philosophically original is instantiated by a piece of writing. But no specific one of them is always needed—or indeed sufficient—if the property of being philosophically original is to be instantiated. (Call these *Individual-Originality-constituting* properties.)

That is a beginning. But would even that structure be inadequate until it talks also of grades or degrees of originality? Some pieces of philosophy, we usually believe, are *more* original than others in various respects. Presumably, philosophical greatness would be present only when some threshold of originality is reached—so that a piece of philosophy, such as a book, is original *enough* in virtue of its features. We would need to ask about how *well* any one or more of those Individual-Originality-constituting properties is being instantiated, and how *many* of them are being instantiated, by the book in question if it is to be philosophically original.

Can we make this discussion slightly less gestural? Here are some candidate Individual-Originality-constituting properties:

- *Using new concepts* or *new theses*. Philosophers routinely profess to be articulating new concepts or theses, ones of philosophical pith and import, ones that are needed if we are to understand or solve some pressing philosophical challenge. A new philosophical thesis could say less, or it could say more: a lengthy one might amount to a theory—a new theory. Some new theories stand out—somehow—even among other new ones. Note, incidentally, that a new philosophical thesis might be presented as a hypothesis rather than a result, as new possibilities are conceived of and perhaps tested: sometimes, 'new' means 'something new to ponder'.
- *Using new reasoning*. Philosophers generally provide argumentation—reasoning—in explicating their concepts. Naturally, they do so when testing or supporting their theses. Disparate individuals and traditions approach this differently. Within this book, contrast—dramatically—so many with so many: for instance, compare

Zhuangzi with Aristotle with Aquinas with Descartes with . . . with Peirce with Wittgenstein. Reasoning has the capacity to be original in many ways, especially when subtle or complex. Even in noticing previously overlooked details while elaborating a widely accepted thesis, originality could be present.

- *Displaying new 'reach' and notable boldness.* Someone might be the first to recognize the philosophical *potential* in some concept, thesis, or reasoning. She might then 'stay with' that concept, thesis, or reasoning longer than others do or would—exploring further that philosophical hinterland, travelling more extensively and revealingly within its boundaries than others have done. Even after a thesis has become a philosophical commonplace, someone might—distinctively—espy its extended philosophical significance. There is something original in doing so. We might regard such a tendency as an originality of philosophical *character*: remaining longer with an idea than other philosophers do so can be intellectual boldness; and—occasionally—this originality could be manifesting philosophical greatness, if the idea itself is philosophically great.
- *Posing new questions.* Permeating all of this—the new concepts, theses, reasoning, and boldness—are philosophical *questions*. Old questions seen anew; new questions seen . . . at all. Philosophy is nothing without questions—overt or hidden. Even then, there are questions, and there are questions. Do great philosophers ask great questions? Do great philosophers ask questions that lesser philosophers do not even see? In the nineteenth century, Arthur Schopenhauer—for many, a great philosopher himself—said this (1974: 4):

> The two promising requirements for philosophizing are first that we have the courage to make a clean breast of a question, and secondly that we become clearly conscious of everything that is *self-evident* in order to comprehend it as a problem.

In a similar spirit (without overtly mentioning questions), Schopenhauer also offered this (1966: 391):

> Talent is like the marksman who hits a target which others cannot reach; genius is like the marksman who hits a target, as far as which others cannot even see.

7. Influence

Many possible criteria for being philosophically great can thus be thought of as aspects of being philosophically original. What, though, of being philosophically influential? Is this a greatness-constituting property? Is it at least good, or even excellent, evidence of being philosophically great?

We know, it seems, that sometimes a person's distinctive talent or contribution is not widely recognized or acknowledged within his or her lifetime. Even once it is widely accepted as significant, it might no longer have influence: by then, it could receive respect, even veneration, without inspiring changes in doctrinal or methodological direction by future thinkers or investigators. Is the same true of links between being philosophically great and being philosophically influential? Might some great work of philosophy be professionally inert, lacking wider influence at a given time among practising philosophers? Could that be true of it forever? At any rate, could such a fate befall that particular work of philosophy for centuries? Perhaps so: it has happened at times even to some who are featured in this book. Sweeping social factors (such as sexism among those with relevant social power) can coalesce to prevent someone's originality from having marked influence—indeed, any influence at all—among other philosophers during, or even long after, his or her lifetime.

Certainly, a metaphysical *realist* about philosophical greatness (an approach envisaged in section 5) should be open to that possibility; for this metaphysical realist allows that in principle someone's philosophical work could have been actually great without being widely acknowledged as being so. For instance, the metaphysical realist about philosophical greatness has the conceptual option of saying that there has been *actually* great philosophical writing by women that was undervalued due to those authors being women. Some contemporary philosophers are paying increasing attention to this phenomenon (see the chapter on Émilie Du Châtelet), and such attention is welcome in at least three ways. First, it can accord individuals a respect that might—and should—have been accorded before now. Second, it enriches our sense of philosophy's potential—how philosophy has been great, hence how it can be great. Third, it is conceptually salutary: it reminds us not to assume that actual historical influence is always deserved influence—or that an actual lack of historical influence is always a deserved lack.

Maybe we could conceive of the issue by adapting a famous distinction from Thomas Kuhn (1962). His domain was the history of science. But what, for philosophers, has been his most influential idea is more broadly evocative and applicable. It is suggestive of one possible aspect of what might demarcate great philosophy from non-great philosophy. Kuhn's distinction was between scientific *paradigms* and *normal* science. The former fundamentally underlie and guide the latter: each period of normal science (for a given research area) unfolds within the methodological and conceptual scope of a guiding paradigm for how to think scientifically about that area's issues. Occasionally, under internal stresses and strains, an existing paradigm buckles; in principle, a new one can emerge.[7] Now, does great *philosophical* work stand to lesser— even very good—philosophical work in ways akin to how a new paradigm within a branch of scientific thought stands to correlatively normal science? Is philosophical greatness *paradigm*-creating philosophy? Or—on a metaphysically realist construal of it—is philosophical greatness whatever *should* be, or whatever *deserves* to be, paradigm-creating, regardless of whether philosophers are ever actually influenced by it in ways that lead to new philosophical paradigms being in place as normal philosophical inquiry flows onwards?

8. The Philosophical Image, Again

The preceding sections have been discussing, schematically and programmatically, a few factors that might help to shape an idea of philosophical greatness. Let us close the chapter with a question about what *kind* of property philosophical greatness would be.

Suppose that philosophical greatness would be like scientific greatness (a comparison that we might have in mind when pondering the previous section's invocation of Kuhn on paradigms). Such an assimilation could prompt us to say that philosophers are always seekers, at least partly so, of literal truth. This might suggest that philosophical greatness would be tied at least partly to features of philosophical truths, such as associated aspects of their originality; and so we asked whether philosophical greatness must be manifested in philosophical knowledge. But we might also wonder whether philosophical greatness would ever be more akin to *artistic* greatness. For example, does Ludwig Wittgenstein's greatness resemble what some would regard as Jackson Pollock's—in the interweaving of patterns of order beneath layers of apparent chaos? Does Friedrich Nietzsche call to mind Vincent van Gogh, each of them capturing a wild, almost manic, beauty of spirit in their representations of living and of reality? What of Zhuangzi—with his multi-perspectival playfulness, Pablo-Picasso-like in its apparent simplicity of 'line'? And so on.

Alva Noë (2015: 73) argues that art is 'a philosophical practice': it reorganizes how we see. It 'investigates or exposes by destabilising' (ibid.). Is philosophy, in turn, art? Is philosophy art in words? Is great philosophy like that? Is great philosophy great art in words? This is not quite Noë's view. Rather, he says (ibid.: 133), 'Art and philosophy are both species of a common genus: they are . . . reorganizational practices'—reorganizational 'of ourselves' (ibid.: 138). If Noë is right, philosophy is at least more *like* art than most philosophers seem to treat it as being.

Those comments are merely suggestive in this setting, and there might already be one potentially important disanalogy. Does philosophy seek results, ones answerable to truth—descriptive and literal truth? Would philosophical results thereby need to admit of being tested—able to be measured against a wider world, perhaps even falsified—as scientific results are, *but* as artistic results are not? Most philosophers seem to believe so, although this does not entail that such a belief—even by being about their own practice—would be correct. The capacity for philosophical theories to be tested is more restricted, even at best, than is so for scientific theories or observations. This is partly why section 2 introduced the idea of the philosophical image: not only was I not presuming that philosophy fits ultimately within either the manifest image or the scientific image; I was taking seriously the possibility that, somehow, philosophy *is* an image. If it is, then greatness in philosophy could literally *be* a kind and degree of artistic greatness.

That is a speculation—a philosophical speculation about the nature of philosophy. It is a thought seeking further thought. Or it is a gesture toward a sketch toward a study toward a detail toward a preliminary philosophical image. It is nothing more at this stage. No matter; this book will help us in that respect. It will supply further marks, lines, shades, tones, and so forth. Its chapters will assist us to reflect more deeply—and philosophically—upon what, if anything, is involved in a piece of philosophy's being great. This is metaphilosophy: it introduces us to some philosophy *of* philosophy.[8]

Notes

1 Maybe it is something quite puzzling, many-headed. The quest for such understanding continues (e.g. Smith 2016).
2 Note also how they reflect a conception of greatness as able to encompass flaws and limitations: to be great at X is not to be unimprovably, let alone flawlessly, excellent at X. Here is the nineteenth-century artist Camille Pissarro (in a letter to his son Lucien, of May 5, 1891), writing about some paintings, *Sunsets*, in an exhibition by his contemporary, Claude Monet (Patin 1993: 137):

> They seemed to me filled with light, undoubtedly the work of a master. But since, for our own instruction, we must go beneath the surface, I asked myself what could be lacking. It's hard to make this out: the lack is certainly not one of exactness or harmony, more of execution, of a calmer, less ephemeral way of seeing. The colours are pretty rather than strong, the draughtsmanship fine but drifting, particularly in the backgrounds. Nevertheless he's a very great artist!

3 And such as originality—a quality to be discussed in the next section.
4 Like most else within philosophy, the term 'metaphysical realist' is debated. For an overview, see Devitt (1991).
5 Even when it does occur, might it be somewhat intangible or surprising, or at least very far from obvious? In a story from the time of the Warring States, the Taoist Lieh Tzu tells of a man said to have the exceedingly rare ability to know when a horse is *great* (a 'super-horse', in another translation, too charming to omit: 'an animal which could run a thousand miles a day without leaving tracks and without raising dust' [Leys 2011: 29]). Sent by the Duke of Qin to find such a horse, the man reported success. Asked by the Duke to describe the horse, the man deemed it 'a yellow mare'. But when the horse, when presented to the Duke, was a black stallion. The Duke was outraged; his adviser—his retiring horse-breeder—was delighted. How so?

> It is even better than I had hoped. . . . He has completely transcended judging a horse by its appearance and sees only its inner nature. When he looks at the horse

he does not see a male or female or what color it is but looks instead to its very essence. In this way he can see the potential for greatness in a horse.

And yes, it proved to be 'the greatest horse [that the Duke] had ever seen' (Towler 2007: 18).
6 In accord with this chapter as a whole, of course, these remarks are introductory. For a sophisticated—and somewhat skeptical—discussion of the idea of a great philosopher, see Shapiro (2016).
7 This is a simplified portrayal of Kuhn's distinction. For more detailed guidance, see Godfrey-Smith (2003: chs. 5, 6).
8 I am grateful to Parveen Seehra for comments on a draft of this chapter.

References

Devitt, Michael. 1991. *Realism and Truth*, 2nd edn., Princeton: Princeton University Press.
Elgin, Catherine Z. 1988. The Epistemic Efficacy of Stupidity, *Synthese* 74: 297–311.
Godfrey-Smith, Peter 2003. *Theory and Reality: An Introduction to the Philosophy of Science*, Chicago: University of Chicago Press.
Hetherington, Stephen (ed.) 2013. *Metaphysics and Epistemology: A Guided Anthology*, Malden, MA: Wiley-Blackwell.
Kuhn, Thomas S. 1962. *The Structure of Scientific Revolutions*, Chicago: University of Chicago Press.
Leys, Simon 2011. *The Hall of Uselessness: Collected Essays*, Collingwood: Black Inc.
Noë, Alva 2015. *Strange Tools: Art and Human Nature*, New York: Hill and Wang.
Patin, Sylvie 1993 (1991). *Monet: The Ultimate Impressionist*, trans. A. Roberts, London: Thames and Hudson.
Schopenhauer, Arthur 1966 (1844). *The World as Will and Representation*, vol. 2, trans. E.F.J. Payne, New York: Dover.
Schopenhauer, Arthur 1974 (1851). On Philosophy and Its Method, in *Parerga and Paralipomena: Short Philosophical Essays*, vol. 2, trans. E.F.J. Payne, Oxford: Clarendon Press: 3–20.
Sellars, Wilfrid F. 1963. Philosophy and the Scientific Image of Man, in *Science, Perception and Reality*, London: Routledge & Kegan Paul: 1–40.
Shapiro, Lisa 2016. Rewriting the Early Modern Philosophical Canon, *Journal of the American Philosophical Association* 2: 365–83.
Smith, Justin E.H. 2016. *The Philosopher: A History in Six Types*, Princeton: Princeton University Press.
Towler, Solala 2007 (2005). *Tales from the Tao: The Wisdom of the Taoist Masters*, rev. edn., London: Duncan Baird.

2

PLATO, PLATONISM, AND THE HISTORY OF PHILOSOPHY

Lloyd P. Gerson

1. Introduction

I respectfully decline to take the predictable approach to the topic of this book as it pertains to my subject, Plato. That approach would begin with a citation of Whitehead's endlessly quoted remark in *Process and Reality* that the history of European philosophy is nothing but a series of footnotes to Plato. QED, as it were. I am also going to eschew the patronizing acknowledgment of Plato as a most 'edifying' philosopher, great to the extent that the positive content of his philosophy is ignored and his high-minded intellectualism is embraced.[1] My alternative approach is actually somewhat more ambitious. I aim to show that the history of philosophy contains four streams: (a) Platonism, (b), anti-Platonism (which I will call 'Naturalism'), (c) various concessions made by Platonists to anti-Platonists, and (d) various concessions made by anti-Platonists to Platonists. If this is true, or even close to being true, then Plato's greatness is of an order of magnitude somewhat beyond that of anyone else treated in this book. In the first part of this chapter, I shall try to say what I think (a) and (b) are. In the second part of the chapter, I shall try to illustrate (c) and (d). My conclusion will mirror the position of the late Richard Rorty to the effect that Platonism is, in fact, identical with systematic (as opposed to edifying) philosophy and that, accordingly, to reject the one is necessarily to reject the other.[2] The history of philosophy is not, like the bad tragedies that Aristotle disdained, a series of disconnected intellectual 'episodes'. It is, rather, the history of the arguments of those who do, and those who do not, regard philosophy as a source of knowledge independent of the natural sciences. The 'concessions' that I mentioned are, for the most part, strategic attempts to 'have one's cake and eat it, too.' As richly confirmed by the history of philosophy itself, the latent inconsistencies contained in any attempt to be a Platonist and a little bit of an anti-Platonist, or an anti-Platonist and a little bit of a Platonist, do not remain latent for long.

2. Ur-Platonism

I shall not take time here to argue what I have elsewhere argued at length, namely, that Plato was a Platonist.[3] I am going to assume that he was. The issue is of some importance because if one believes that Platonism as a historical construct has little or nothing to do with Plato himself, then assuming that one wants to proclaim Plato's greatness, one is going to approach the matter in a way vastly different from the way I am proceeding. When I speak of Platonism, I shall speak of the philosophy found in the dialogues and recorded and adumbrated by Aristotle and the rest of the indirect tradition. If one rejects that testimony and that tradition—as many would certainly do—then the Plato that remains is so different from the Plato that I shall be discussing that one of us should in all decency designate his subject as 'Plato' rather than Plato. This being my chapter, I shall exercise my right to refer to Plato, not his analogue.

Traditionally, the early history of ancient philosophy has been received as an inchoate amalgam of empirical science, or merely observation, and speculative philosophy. For example, Anaximander's thinking about the shape of the universe or the origin of human life is reported alongside his postulation of a first principle of all, 'the *apeiron*', out of which all things come by a vortex motion. The separation of philosophy and science is variously attributed to Parmenides, to Plato, or to Aristotle. All reasonable choices, although it is rare to find attempts to locate precisely the demarcation. A measure of Plato's greatness is that we can locate at least one plausible place in the dialogues where this demarcation is made and one precise method for separating philosophy from science. As we shall see, Plato did not only conceive of the philosophical position known now as Platonism, but he showed why Platonism, properly understood, is philosophy and as such stands apart from the natural sciences.

The matrix out of which Plato's Platonism arises is the array of philosophical positions unequivocally rejected in the dialogues. I have called this 'Ur-Platonism'. These are principally five in number.

First, Plato rejects both moderate nominalism and the extreme nominalism of the Eleatics.[4] Moderate nominalism, sometimes said to be supported by Antisthenes, holds, roughly, that predication is impossible because a thing is nothing but itself, whereas predication supposes that it is also something else. But moderate nominalism at least presumes that it is possible for there to be a multiplicity of things, all of which can only be named. By contrast, the extreme nominalism of the Eleatics maintains that there is only one thing, being, which cannot even be named since that would entail the existence of two things (being and the name).

Second, Plato rejects materialism, the view that the only things that exist are three-dimensional bodies and their properties; however, these properties are explained causally in relation to the bodies.[5] The principal arguments against materialism, to which I shall return at length, are that 'higher' cognition would not be possible if we, that is, human beings, were material entities in the above sense, and that the samenesses and differences among things cannot satisfactorily be accounted for unless immaterial entities are postulated to exist. Stated thus, it is evident that the reason for rejecting nominalism is that in fact sensible things do have properties and hence can be the same as other sensible things without being identical with them. The existence of the phenomenon of sameness in (numerical) difference is thus a crucial premise in at least one of the arguments for the falsity of materialism.

Third, Plato rejects mechanism, which I define as the principal of causal closure within the sensible world.[6] In *Phaedo*, he attributes mechanism to Anaxagoras, who was no doubt not alone in holding this view. Plato argues that no explanation for any sensible phenomenon that presupposes the truth of materialism can be adequate. Thus, mechanism and materialism are in Plato's mind inextricably connected, although it is not difficult to imagine the possibility of an occasionalist position that insists on causal closure at the same time as postulating the existence of immaterial entities.

Fourth, Plato rejects skepticism. That is, he rejects the view that *epistēmē* is impossible.[7] *Epistēmē* is an infallible mental state; it is the *ne plus ultra* of cognition. Plato does not reject the possibility of true belief or even of justified true belief. However, Plato argues that these would not be possible if it were not the case that *epistēmē* is possible for us. Since infallible mental states are possible only if we are immaterial entities, and since *epistēmē* is only of immaterial entities, the connection between his rejection of skepticism and his rejection of nominalism and materialism is clear.

Fifth and finally, Plato rejects relativism.[8] He rejects it both in its ethical and in its epistemological form, in both cases attributing the position to Protagoras. Relativism is the view that, as Protagoras said, man is the measure of all things, of what is that it is and of what is not that it is not. The rejection of relativism by Plato should be understood not merely as the affirmation of the objectivity of truth and of moral value, but also of their universality. Objectivity does not entail the rejection of relativism, since what is objectively good or true for (or about) someone, even if it conflicts with what that individual believes to be good or true, does not entail that the same thing is good or true for (or about) someone else.

These elements or building blocks of Plato's Platonism are not for him logically unconnected. This connection is implied by the positing of an unhypothetical first principle of all, which Plato calls 'the Idea of the Good'. This superordinate first principle of all is the cause of the existence and essence of the Forms, and of their knowability.[9] It is much else, as we shall see, but here I want to concentrate on how the postulation of such a principle connects the five 'anti's of Ur-Platonism.

In the famous 'autobiography' of Socrates in *Phaedo*, we have Socrates describing his younger self as in search of the sort of ultimate explanations of natural phenomena that constituted the currency of 'pre-Socratic' philosophy. In particular, Socrates describes his disillusionment with the works of Anaxagoras who, we learn, promised to show how some sort of divine intellect explains why things are as they are. In fact, when the explanation was actually delivered, divine intellect is not aduced to do any honest explanatory work: all the work is done by the interaction of *homoiomeres*, continuous lumps of every conceivable material containing bits of very other. Things were named according to the preponderance of one element over the rest. The details of Anaxagoras's theory are not important here. But, in response to him, Socrates claims to have taken a new approach, 'a second voyage' (*deuteron ploun*) to explanation (*aitia*), one that first offers a 'simple' hypothesis of participation in a Form as an explanation for the presence of a property. The simple hypothesis of a Form is to be tested for its consequences, and discarded if these consequences are contradictory. When an account of the hypothesis is needed, another 'higher' hypothesis is to be given until 'something adequate' (*ti hikanon*) is achieved.

There is, unfortunately, a considerable and portentous controversy regarding the nature of this 'adequate' explanation. On the one hand, some have taken it to refer to any hypothesis or Form that is uncontestable in its explanatory role. On the other hand, and throughout antiquity, the 'something adequate' refers implicitly to the *unhypothetical* first principle of all of *Republic*, the Idea of the Good.[10] To my mind, the historical evidence, including Aristotle's testimony, makes it overwhelmingly likely that Plato means the latter.[11] It is difficult to see how the Idea of the Good can be the explanation for the existence and essence of Forms and yet not be the ultimate explanatory principle here sought. But this point will only have force if we focus on the very notion of explanatory adequacy here at play. For it will turn out that the distinctiveness of Plato's Platonism depends on his account of explanatory adequacy and his claim that this is not to be found in natural science.

3. Platonic Explanations

The inadequacy of explanations of the sort provided by Anaxagoras and others consists in the fact that these failed explanations appeal to what we may call 'physical factors'. Thus, in the simple cases mentioned in the dialogue, Helen's beauty is supposed to be explained by her color or shape, and so on; something being taller than something else is explained by the relative quantity of material in the two things. The explanation for Socrates sitting in prison as opposed to fleeing is supposed to be the disposition of his limbs and muscles, and so on. By contrast, Socrates will insist that Helen is beautiful because she participates in the Form of Beauty, while something is taller than something else because it participates in the Form of Tallness. And Socrates is sitting because he wills to sit, it being assumed that what everyone wills is their own good. It is clear from the text that Forms are aduced not as an addition to an explanatory framework but rather as the sole explanation in each case.[12] At the same time, there is no suggestion that the preceding 'naturalistic' pseudo-explanations are not necessary conditions for the true explanations of natural phenomena.[13] The reason why these necessary conditions are not explanations at all is that they will be identical to the necessary conditions for the presence of the opposite of that which they claim to explain.[14] Thus, the very quantity that supposedly makes one thing taller than another is also the quantity that makes it shorter than something else. The sole explanatory adequacy of a Form is related to a specific *explanandum*, namely, the existence of a property, whether it be 'beautiful' or 'large' or 'sitting in a certain position'. It depends entirely upon the assumption that to say something is beautiful or large is to say something that is possibly true and therefore different from saying that it is ugly or small. Of course, Forms have no explanatory relevance to what the nominalist claims is true, that is, that things cannot have properties. If things cannot have properties, then there is no real difference between saying that something is alive and that it is dead or even, perhaps somewhat more controversially, that it exists or doesn't exist. This seems a rash position to maintain, which of course does not make it false. And yet Plato more or less wants to contend that the possibility of philosophy as a source of knowledge independent of the natural sciences depends entirely on the manifest falsity of the position.

Explanatory adequacy in a Platonic framework means first of all that the explanation is not susceptible to the preceding counterexamples, that is, that the explanation will also be adequate for explaining the presence of the opposite property. Accordingly, the *explanans* must be of a different order of existence from the *explanandum*. By this, I mean that the existence of sensible properties or, more broadly, 'states of affairs' can only be explained by that which is non-sensible. Here is what I mean. Suppose that a quantity x is aduced as the explanation for something having the property of being larger than something else, say, the quantity of being 1.78 meters in height. That quantity is itself a sensible property that is either (a) identical with the property of being taller than something else, in which case it is obviously no explanation at all, or else (b) itself in need of an explanation for its being the property that explains the original property. But (b) faces the problem that the property of being 1.78 meters in height is no less an explanation for the same thing being shorter than something else. This seems to be an endemic problem with putative explanations for sensible properties by sensible properties, since, *ex hypothesi*, (b) is different from the property of being taller than, in which case there is nothing about it as such that prevents it being the explanation for the presence of the opposite property. In general, if a hunk of material, uncharacterizable by a particular property, is aduced as the explanation for the presence of that property, there seems to be no way to simultaneously distinguish that hunk of material from the property and to locate in it the adequate explanation for the presence of that property. The examples given in the dialogue are of 'opposites', but the point is generalizable to include any putative 'intrinsic' properties. Thus, a proposed explanation in physical terms actually explains nothing, where an explanation is supposed to yield understanding.

Perhaps the best way to characterize the hypothetical explanation for the existence of a property is that it is the truthmaker for the proposition, for example, that Helen is beautiful. There is an ambiguity in the postulation of such a truthmaker between the Form itself and the fact that something participates in it. I am inclined to think that the Form itself is the hypothesis, but it differs little if we say that hypothesizing the Form as the *explanans* is elliptical for hypothesizing that participation in the Form is the *explanans*.

I take it that the vague phrase 'something adequate' indicates that a real truthmaker is not itself in need of the same sort of explanation that the truthmaker is postulated as providing for the existence of a sensible property here and now. An argument analogous to the argument that leads Plato to maintain that only non-sensibles or intelligibles could be adequate explanations for sensibles leads him to maintain that intelligibles, that is, Forms, cannot be adequate explanations for the intelligibility that sensible properties themselves possess. As Socrates insists, not only is it true that Largeness itself will never admit Smallness, but the largeness in us will never admit smallness.[15] His point is that the singular identity of the Form of Largeness is what an instance of that Form possesses, albeit in a diminished or compromised state. Why, though, cannot the Form itself be the adequate explanation for the instance?

The answer to this question is not explicitly given in *Phaedo*. For that we need to turn to *Parmenides*, where in the dialectical exercise of Part Two, we learn that, if a 'one' exists, it must partake of *ousia*, in which case there is a distinction within that one, between it and its *ousia*.[16] That this is a distinction between the existence and the essence of a Form is confirmed by *Republic*, where we learn that both the existence and essence of a Form are provided by the Idea of the Good.[17] So, the reason why a Form cannot be the truthmaker or ultimate explanation for the presence of a sensible property is that the Form itself cannot do this unless it participates in the essence that its name names. The participation of the one Form of Beauty in the essence of Beauty is a necessary condition for the Form of Beauty being the truthmaker for the truth of the sentence 'Helen is beautiful.' So, it is not 'adequate' to make the Form or Beauty the truthmaker even if it is the case that whatever *is* the truthmaker could not be this if not for the instrumentality of the Form of Beauty.[18]

To claim that the ultimate explanation for the truth of the sentence 'Helen is beautiful' is the Form of Beauty is analogous to claiming that the ultimate explanation for a window being broken is that a ball hit it. An ultimate explanation is a *per se*, not a *per accidens*, cause. But a *per se* cause is not itself in need of the same sort of explanation as that which it is aduced to provide. In this case, the participation of the Form of Beauty in the nature or essence of Beauty is itself a case of the same sort of explanation that the hypothesis of the Form of Beauty was supposed to provide. But the *Republic* passage tells us that the existence of a Form participating in an essence is not self-explanatory.

Nothing in the dialogues tells us why the necessary and eternal existence of a Form is not self-explanatory. *If* the Idea of the Good gives existence and essence to the Forms, we can understand why their necessary existence is, nevertheless, contingent or non-self-explanatory. But why should we suppose that this is the case? The Idea of the Good also gives truth and knowability to the Forms.[19] I take it that 'truth' here is 'ontological truth', that is, a property of being that makes it available to our intellects, in which case the truth and the knowability of Forms are properties very close together. The Idea of the Good is required because to discover the truth that Anaxagoras sought, but failed, to find is to know ultimate explanations or truthmakers. And the existence of a Form of, say, Beauty is only knowable if that Form is a composite of existent and essence—that is, knowing it consists in knowing the essence of that which is distinct from its essence. Knowing what Beauty is would not be possible if Beauty did not exist, or if the essence of Beauty were not distinct from the separated existence of the Form. And not only is the essence of Beauty distinct from the Form, but the entire array of essences that make up the intelligible world are distinct from each other yet necessarily connected. For the Form of Beauty could not be known if Beauty were not self-identical and different from other Forms and partaking of Being.

Is this whole complex array of intelligible entities self-explanatory? It is not, according to Plato, because something could not be self-identical and different from something else unless its self-identity were compromised. By this, I mean that it does not have perfect self-identity; otherwise, it would not have the property of being different from another. But compromised self-identity is only recognizable as such in relation to perfect self-identity. And that is exactly what the postulated first principle of all, 'beyond existence and essence', is supposed to be.

In the superordinate and absolutely incomposite Idea of the Good, we do have a logical and non-arbitrary stopping-point for explanation. As we learn from the Divided Line passage in *Republic* that follows immediately after the introduction of the Idea of the Good, it is not possible to grasp the role in explanation that the Forms have, without recourse to this first principle of all.[20]

In sum, to know the *aitia* for the truth of a sentence about the sensible world, one must know the truthmaker for that sentence. But the putative truthmaker that a Form is cannot itself be the real truthmaker because no Form has the uncompromised identity that a truthmaker must have, that is, the *per se* identity of an unequivocal *aitia*. Only the unhypothetical first principle of all can be the real truthmaker or ultimate explanation for any true sentence here below.

Plato uses the term *philosophia* for an intellectual desire for wisdom, which he identifies with the highest possible cognitive achievement, namely, knowledge (*epistēmē*). This desire is fulfilled in the activity sharply demarcated from all natural sciences as 'dialectic'.[21] Dialectic is a sort of mental seeing or understanding of the intelligible world in its articulated structure. Although there are no grounds for supposing that, for Plato, philosophy aims for anything other than this, it is certainly true that knowledge, once attained, is applicable to the sensible world. That is, the technological and the practical are not dissolved but are subordinated, and are shunned only to the extent that they purport to be the wisdom that they can never be.

What Plato meant by mental seeing or understanding may be briefly set forth in three steps. The first step is actually 'pre-dialectical', so to speak, and is essential to all thinking, whether philosophical or not. It involves a grasp of material identity, that is, the grasp that two or more things, albeit different, are the same in some respect. For example, there is the mental seeing that the two sides of an equation are the same or that the person standing before me now is the same as the person standing before me yesterday. Or, again, the referent of the subject of a proposition is the same as the referent of the predicate attributing to the subject some property or other. Second, in the beginning of dialectic itself, there is the grasp of the self-identical nature in virtue of which there is a material identity. This grasp must be distinguished from the representation of it as, for example, the representation of the number that is identical in the two sides of the equation. This is true even if it is the case that there is no such grasp without representation. Third, there is the mental seeing of the material identity of all the possible objects of understanding that explain all possible material identities. Dialectic includes both the second and third steps, using representations all of the way but without being identified with them. As Plato emphasizes, only when the third stage is reached is explanatory adequacy attained. Dialectic is the substance of philosophy. To reject philosophy is to reject dialectic as Plato outlined it.

That rejection is, however, quite costly. For the commitment to representationalism as a *substitute* for understanding is not only to homogenize all cognition—human and animal—but to homogenize cognitional and non-cognitional representation. Let us suppose that this, despite its oddness, is true. But mustn't we also then suppose that we understand that, say, rule following or the application of representations, is the same in humans and in machines? If the chess-playing machine follows rules that determine outputs on the basis of represented inputs, then the naturalist, whether a Rortyan or not, would have to maintain that the human chess-player is doing the same thing. That is, he must have an understanding of the material identity of the functionality of the two 'systems'. That understanding, if it is real, is neither empirical knowledge nor is it, counter to the present hypothesis, identical to any representation of the understanding, linguistic or otherwise.

Forswearing the possibility of understanding or explaining material identity and hence the reality of the latter is, of course, radically nominalistic in just the way that Plato thought that Heraclitean flux theory was. I do not offer this as a *reductio* of the naturalist's position, since some naturalists will simply embrace the position and others will seek to relativize material identities according to, say, linguistic conventions; for example, if two things look the same according to a conventional way of identifying things, then we count this as a material identity. But surely to count two or more things as the same and so as materially identical requires that we understand what it means to be the same while at least being numerically different. And understanding what it would mean for two things to be the same requires that we understand that there is an identity underlying the difference, hence material *identity*. That seems to amount to a lot of understanding occurring in someone who claims to deny the possibility of understanding.

Of course, if one concedes the possibility of understanding, one can continue to maintain that there is understanding only in the natural sciences. This is what I called earlier 'pre-dialectic'. Among the most refined of the Naturalists who want to make the most minimal possible concession to Platonism or systematic philosophy,[22] 'understanding' is the *deus ex machina*. Here, it seems appropriate to refer to Aristotle's remark that a philosophical argument against the possibility of philosophy fails to impress. But to acknowledge the possibility of understanding—however that understanding may be represented, to ourselves or to others—is to set one on the road back to explanation and the Platonic argument for the radical distinction between conditions and causes, and to the identification of philosophy as the desire for knowledge of the latter.

4. The First Principle of All

Plato insists that there must be an unhypothetical *aitia* of all. Without it, philosophy—that is, dialectic—would be impossible. In *Republic*, Plato calls this principle the Idea of the Good. But it is a spectacular loss for students of the history of philosophy—and, indeed, if I am right, for students of the very possibility of philosophy—that a reliance on the dialogues alone for understanding Plato's Platonism makes this claim practically unintelligible. The claim that there should be a first principle of all, however it is described, is readily understandable. The claim that it is the Idea of the Good is not. And it is for this reason that modern students of Plato and the history of philosophy have, especially in the English-speaking world, mostly missed or forgotten the systematic nature of Plato's Platonism and again, if I am right, why Richard Rorty was largely correct in identifying philosophy with Platonism. For philosophy, as a source of knowledge independent of the natural sciences, is about explanation in the manner sketched earlier. There is no explanation, however, no explanation independent of the purported explanations in the natural sciences, without an unequivocally self-identical and hence unique first principle of all. The complaint made by Aristotle and many others to the effect that postulation of Forms as *aitiai* amounts merely to a reduplication of the essences found in things is correct. But the problem is not with Forms; the problem is with the supposed claim that Forms are the genuine *aitiai*. If one were to adduce a Form as *aitia* alongside sensible *aitiai*, and to claim that they are jointly a necessary and sufficient explanation, this would constitute a fatal concession to anti-Platonism or to Naturalism. For, on this basis, it is easy to see how the Form can drop out of the explanation altogether. Only if the first principle of all is the *aitia* and sensibles are demoted to the status of mere necessary conditions is the authentic Platonic position preserved.

Aristotle confirms the analysis of the argument in *Phaedo* that Forms are not ultimate principles. He reports that Plato identified the Forms as Numbers and derived them from the real first principle of all, the One that, along with the Indefinite Dyad, is the ultimate explanation for everything.[23] How the Indefinite Dyad is supposed to be related to the One is, to say the least, a vexed question in the history of philosophy. I shall have a bit more to say about it toward the end of this chapter. But the revelation that the Good is the One, although far from transparent, can, as we shall see presently, go a long way toward elucidating both the systematic structure of Plato's Platonism and the role of the first principle of all in connecting together all the elements of Ur-Platonism. It is apparently Plato's intuition that intelligible structure, or simply intelligibility, is essentially a mathematical concept, not of course mathematical in the sense of arithmetic or geometry, but in the logically prior sense of ordering.[24] This intuition is shared, for example, by Bertrand Russell and Alfred North Whitehead in *Principia Mathematica*, with the crucial difference that for Plato logic is not independent of metaphysics but rather is derived from it. Hence, explanation is expanded beyond the mathematical to the ontological.

The need to posit a unique first principle of all that is 'beyond *ousia*' follows from the explanatory exigency that such a principle be absolutely simple. That is why no Form can fulfill this role. I take it that the salient feature of the One is its absolute simplicity or undividedness. Aristotle, the most famous Platonist after Plato, emphatically endorsed the need for an absolutely simple first principle of all, although he rejected Plato's claim that this principle must be beyond *ousia*. Instead, he claimed that such a principle could be *ousia* and absolutely simple if it is identified with pure self-reflexive thinking. Later Platonists from Plotinus to Proclus rejected this attempt, with the argument that thinking is essentially intentional, in which case the distinction between thinking and object(s) of thinking—even if this object be the thinking itself—cannot be effaced and absolute simplicity is lost. It was left for later Platonists, mostly those influenced by Christianity, to try to show that thinking could be somehow understood to preserve absolute simplicity.

An absolutely simple principle is most definitely not a Form-Number since Forms, as we have seen, are not absolutely simple. But it can be the principle of Number in the sense that Numbers are distinct manifestations of undividedness, that is, unity. For the One or Good to be the principle that explains the array of undivided Numbers it must be virtually all of these, approximately in the sense in which 'white' light is virtually the color spectrum or in which a mathematical function is virtually its domain and range. Presumably, the reason for reducing Forms to Numbers is that Numbers (including ratios or proportions) are purely intelligible or transparent. There is nothing in them in principle unavailable to the intellect.[25] By contrast, everything here below, including all large and beautiful things, must contain an element of that which is in principle non-intelligible, what Aristotle will designate as matter and will claim is knowable only by analogy. Thus, the identification of philosophy with knowledge of the purely intelligible and its absolutely first principle of all decisively sets philosophy apart from natural science, which, insofar as it is committed to the study of things that are changeable, is committed to understanding that which is not purely understandable. The Indefinite Dyad is the principle of unintelligibility in the things whose limited intelligibility is ultimately explained by the One.

From a Platonic perspective, the irremovable problem for anti-Platonism and its presumption that knowledge is found exclusively in the natural sciences is that there can really be no knowledge of the objects of natural science. This does not mean that there can be no cognition of them—the position of Pyrrhonian or extreme skepticism, rejected by Plato—but that the cognition that there is cannot in principle eliminate the non-intelligible element in the sensible world. This is not a problem for the Platonist who views cognition of sensibles as derivative and as dependent on cognition of that which is purely intelligible. It is a problem for those who think that in the canons of natural science the *ne plus ultra* of cognition is reached by rational belief. What Plato saw or claimed to see was that rational belief is only possible when it rests on the knowledge of intelligibles. Since so-called empirical knowledge can in principle only aspire to being rational belief, its subordination to philosophy is manifest.

The unique, absolutely simple, first principle of all connects the five doctrines that comprise the foundation of Platonism, what I have called 'Ur-Platonism'. It connects them by showing how the rejection of nominalism, materialism, mechanism, relativism, and skepticism amounts to the rejection of non-philosophical explanatory frameworks. The five 'ism's are all principles of Naturalism or anti-Platonism, requiring that the explanations that compose wisdom are all natural scientific ones. The rejection of the five must be set within a positive metaphysical framework to see why ultimate explanations or wisdom cannot be naturalistic. This is what the postulation of the Idea of the Good or the One is meant to do. Of course, one can reject one or another of the five; but, without showing how that rejection enables a superior explanation, the rejection is, as Hegel might say, one barren assertion up against another. Indeed, I would suggest that Plato believed that, without the unifying first principle of all, explanations that purport to be preferable to naturalistic explanations are, in fact, no such thing. Without the first principle, characterized such as to provide an ultimate explanation, the mere insistence on immaterial souls or Forms as explanatorily relevant cannot be other than wheels turning nothing or than empty simulacra of real explanatory entities. To suppose that it is adequate to substitute a Form of Largeness for some sensible quantity as an explanation for something's being large is to invite a variety of replies, all of which amount to an accusation of irrelevance, with the least unsympathetic being Aristotle's, to the effect that immanent formal causality will do all the explanatory work that a separate Form purports to do but fails to do. The crux of the issue, then, is not whether naturalistic explanations are better or worse than non-naturalistic explanations, but whether or not naturalistic explanations are ultimate or real explanations at all as opposed to being mere *sunaitiai*—that is, accompaniments to, or auxiliaries of, real explanations.

5. Platonism vs. Naturalism

The best documented polar opposite of Platonism in antiquity is Atomism, whether that be the version found among its first-generation proponents or that of its most famous later defender, Epicurus. Democritus may well be an unnamed object of criticism in Plato's *Timaeus*, in which case the two principal criticisms of Atomism there are, first, that at most Atomism can offer *sunaitiai* of sensible phenomena and, second, that Atomism can attain only to true belief, never intellection. For true belief is, in principle, without an account.[26] I take it that the absence of an account means that Atomism cannot offer ultimate explanations, but must rather be content with offering *sunaitiai*. Although Forms and the Demiurge are the central factors in the explanations that *Timaeus* provides, Plato alludes twice to the first principle or principles of all.[27] Of particular significance is that, when the Demiurge acts to instill intelligibility in the sensible world, he does this with 'shapes' and numbers', that is, by the use of (solid) geometry and arithmetic.[28] Thus, all that is susceptible of ultimate explanation is mathematical, and the ultimate explanations themselves must culminate in the One and the Indefinite Dyad.

The Stoics provide the stellar example in antiquity of an attempt to maintain a principled Naturalism while at the same time making concessions to Platonism. The Stoics' principled materialism comes into conflict with their two most important concessions to Platonism: the possibility of knowledge and the existence of finality or purpose in nature. As we saw earlier, Plato rejected skepticism regarding the possibility of infallible cognition of reality. And, as we also saw, this position was not sustainable without the additional claims that the intellect is immaterial and that only immaterial reality is knowable. Therefore, it is all the more remarkable that the Stoics, without deviating from materialism, wanted to maintain the infallibility of knowledge. The easiest way to see why this is so is to consider the Pyrrhonian Sceptic Sextus Empiricus, whose argument against all dogmatism embraces Stoicism. Sextus argued that, unless there is infallible cognition, there is no difference between rational and irrational belief. That is, to put it simply, what would distinguish rational from irrational belief would be the fulfillment of some evidentiary criterion. But there is no such thing as evidence that is not entailing evidence. If there is no such thing as entailing evidence—undoubtedly an extremely strong requirement for evidence—then there is no such thing as evidence, and the supposed distinction between rational and irrational belief is effaced. Only infallible knowledge could provide entailing evidence, just the evidence that a universal true proposition provides for a particular instantiation of it. The Stoics were so keen to maintain the high standard of infallible cognition because, without it, there would be no difference between a rational life and an irrational life, insofar as lives are governed, in part, by beliefs. But, for Stoicism, the ideal is a rational life, in which one is perfectly in line with the reason that permeates nature. So, Stoics could not see how to defend their fundamental insights about human life without defending a mode of cognition that, based on their materialist principle, does not seem to be really defensible.

Human rationality is an ideal because of the naturalistic assumption of the underlying continuity of nature. The rationality according to which the universe operates is natural necessity, and the Stoics urge human beings to align themselves with this. But human rationality in action is essentially goal-directed or teleological. Even the universal propositions in practical syllogism are normative. So, aligning ourselves with nature means aligning ourselves with a providential deity of some sort. It is tempting to *identify* providence with necessity and to locate all the normativity in the notion of providence with necessity itself as a standard, deviation from which is never desirable. But, apart from the massive amount of evidence that the Stoics did not in fact take this deflationary view of providence, the prominence of the virtue of justice in Stoic ethics alone should lead us to resist this easy elision. But from where does the normativity contained in the notion of justice come? For Plato, it comes ultimately from the Idea of the Good. For the Stoics, the universality of justice and its desirability can have no other foundation than in natural necessity, which is to say that they have no foundation at all. A consistent naturalism would strip Stoicism of its epistemology and ethics, without which the metaphysics would disintegrate into not much more than an unsupported amalgam of materialism, mechanism, relativism, skepticism, and nominalism.

The history of philosophy up until roughly the seventeenth century is largely the history of Platonism, that is, various disputes within Platonism and amongst Platonists. Occasionally, such as in the case of Antiochus of Ascalon, efforts were made to incorporate authentic Stoic doctrine into Platonism, but such syncretism is almost impossible to understand at the level of principle. It is worth noting, however, that Stoic psychological analysis and the personal probity of a number of Stoic figures were much admired among Platonists. It is not infrequent that philosophers holding contradictory principles can arrive at identical conclusions regarding practical matters, in part because the principles are usually underdetermining for the solution to particular problems, and in part because the conclusion is reached not as a deduction from principles but rather from 'bottom-up' experience. Many Stoics were keen observers of human nature. It is just that, for Platonists, the practical conclusions they derived from their observations were ultimately inconsistent with their principles.

Beginning in the seventeenth century, those whose fidelity to Platonism did not amount to much more than nominal or weak acceptance of a Christianized first principle of all began to engage with the new physics. I would identify the idea of empirical knowledge as especially crucial in breaking apart the nexus of elements in Ur-Platonism and as paving the way for multiple compromises with Naturalism. The various efforts to provide criteria for empirical knowledge—a Skeptical project of the third century BCE—implicitly severed the connection between cognition and infallibility and thus any grounds for a rejection of materialism. It seems that efforts like those of John Locke to account for knowledge within a materialistic framework at the same time as affirming an immaterial first principle were open to obvious criticisms, including of course those of Skepticism but also those of hardcore materialists. For without entailing criteria for empirical knowledge claims, there were no firm grounds for resisting a reduction of the study of knowledge to a branch of ethology, that is, environmental response. But then there is no reason to resist mechanism either. I presume that, with the compromise with materialism, attempts to resist relativism and nominalism (with something like divine ideas), were open to obvious refutation. For if the first principle of all is identified with the Christian deity, and if this is rejected on evidential grounds, then the basis for resisting relativism and nominalism is lost. All of this must have seemed obvious to David Hume.

Ever since Hume, his dream of integrating the science of man within the natural sciences has been the blueprint of naturalists. For many of these, a naturalistic account of intentionality or consciousness or morality or free choice seems imminent or just over the horizon. Occasionally, otherwise respectable naturalists obliquely suggest that there may not be such naturalistic accounts available. It is not my intention here either to criticize or to defend any of these suggestions. I simply want to emphasize that, if one has a clear conception of what Platonism and anti-Platonism are, it is not too difficult to see that compromises or concessions by the former to the latter or by the latter to the former are not going to be very persuasive.

6. Platonism and Philosophy

Returning to the central theme of this paper and to the insights of Richard Rorty, it may now be somewhat easier to see the point of what, on the surface, is his extraordinary identification of philosophy with Platonism. The idea that philosophy is an activity, the fundamental assumption of which is that there is a source of knowledge independent of the natural sciences, is precisely what Plato proclaims in Socrates's 'autobiography' in *Phaedo*. Recognizing this, Rorty recoiled from Platonism. Accordingly, he recoiled from any *compromise* with Platonism or anything that might be dubbed 'liberal' Platonism. For opening the door even a bit means admitting to the principled inadequacy of natural science as a source of knowledge. Indeed, as we have seen, the result is even more radical: for Plato, at any rate, to admit a source of knowledge independent of the natural sciences is at a stroke to subordinate the natural sciences to that knowledge. This is not, we should be clear, a problem about due humility in scientific exploration. After all, a Platonist like Aristotle insisted on the *dignity* of the natural sciences, especially biology. Rather, it is a problem about the claim of the natural sciences to any sort of real knowledge. As Rorty saw, and as those who were generally supportive of his arguments saw to their evident dismay, his arguments against Platonism could also be used against the natural sciences themselves as sources of knowledge. To the Platonist, it looks like Rorty's reasons for rejecting Platonism or philosophy undercut the only possible basis for that rejection, namely, that the source of genuine knowledge is found in the natural sciences. This genuine knowledge has as its aim 'attaining truth', as Plato put it.[29] But, for this to be intelligible, we need a criterion of 'truth attainment', and that criterion is not easily found in a 'Humean' account of human nature.[30]

Rorty was very much the inheritor of a naturalistic position going back ultimately to the Stoics but already ubiquitous by the seventeenth century, namely, the idea that all knowledge must be representational. Since there is no neutral criterion for distinguishing among true or correct representations and their opposites, there is in fact no such thing as knowledge. Hence, the mental seeing or understanding that I referred to earlier is supposed to be impossible.

The identification of Platonism with philosophy, in particular with *systematic* philosophy, is strikingly evident in the extent to which those committed to anti-Platonism or naturalism are willing to go to deny the existence of anything that might even appear to be a concession to Platonism. Supposedly naturalistic accounts of the self, consciousness, intentionality, rationality, and morality strain credulity, particularly when these accounts amount to the denial of what is self-evident. It seems ironic that the typical complaint that there is no scientific evidence for the existence of the immaterial sits uneasily alongside the denial of abundant evidence for the existence of phenomena that cannot be explained naturalistically. Is the existence of an immaterial mind really less plausible than the denial of the existence of consciousness or intentionality? Or is the existence of the eternal truths of mathematics refuted by an ungrounded commitment to empirical knowledge?

The position that the understanding of the above phenomena or features of our world must be reductive in nature must conflate condition with cause or explanation. I take it that this is an essential property of this sort of reductionism, although I have no space to argue the point here. If you can locate all the sufficient conditions for, say, consciousness, you have explained it because all the sufficient conditions jointly constitute the necessary condition.[31] Plato's argument, as we saw, is that no conjunction of conditions constitutes a cause or explanation.

It may be argued that reserving the terms 'cause' or 'explanation' for that which is not reducible to necessary and sufficient conditions is arbitrary. Perhaps the only explanations there are consist of necessary and sufficient conditions, and searching for something else is quixotic at best, like the quest of the alchemist or astrologer for 'understanding'.

Because of his insistence on what we might choose to call 'extra-conditional' explanations and because of his identification of philosophy with the search for these, Plato and Platonism today exist beyond the pale of acceptable Naturalism. Those who dare to dally in those forbidden fields seem forever tainted when they return to civilization. A dalliance is typically taken as a betrayal. And rightly so, since if, say, intentionality cannot possibly be explained naturalistically, what is the naturalistic explanation for this impossibility? If instead of 'impossibility' one simply pronounces a secular mystery, how does this differ from a withdrawal altogether from the task of explanation? The point is not that everything is explicable. Rather, the point is that the hetero-explicable must find its explanation in the auto-explicable; otherwise, there is no explanation at all. The spectrum of human ways of being in the world ranges from those who, almost like cats, find everything auto-explicable ('that is just the way things are') to those who seek to broaden the scope of the hetero-explicable and so to shrink the scope of the auto-explicable. What Plato and what *soi-disant* Platonists saw clearly, and what naturalists are in principle incapable of seeing, is that something like a singularity could not meet the conditions for auto-explicability. The principal condition for that is simplicity. Only the incomposite could be auto-explicable. If, though, a singularity exists, it must be internally composite, that is, composed of an existent with a nature. So, it is not auto-explicable. There is nothing about what it is that entails *that* it is, in which case the nature does not explain the existence.

What sets Plato apart from all the other great philosophers discussed in this book is that he first articulated the vision of what philosophy is, and that all subsequent philosophers either operated strictly within the framework of that vision or else began to seek out various sorts of compromises with Naturalism. All of these philosophers—even most of the compromisers—embraced what the late Norman Kretzmann called 'a top-down metaphysics', although I doubt very much whether there is such a thing as a 'bottom-up metaphysics'. If indeed there is no such thing, any attempt to construct the latter just lapses into Naturalism or idle speculation where no knowledge could possibly be forthcoming. It is unfortunate for philosophy today that most naturalists assume—and not without some reason—that abandoning naturalism means embracing some religious as opposed to philosophical position. This is, I suppose, the explanation for the fact that Platonism is, albeit indirectly, habitually associated with a position that is anti-natural science. But nothing could be further from the truth. Still, philosophy, identified with Platonism, is not in principle incompatible with religion because it is committed on philosophical grounds to the existence of the immaterial—indeed, to its explanatory pre-eminence. It seems to me that the simplest way to profess Plato's greatness is to insist on the identification of Platonism with philosophy by showing that the rejection of the former is perforce the rejection of the latter.

Notes

1 See Rorty (1979: 5) on the distinction between 'systematic' and 'edifying' philosophy. It is the former that Rorty wants to reject as hopelessly outdated. It seems to me that much admiration for Plato is based on the supposedly edifying nature of his dialogues, especially those in which the figure of Socrates is prominent.
2 See Rorty (1999: xii) on the 'dualisms' that constitute Platonism or philosophy, at least as traditionally conceived. These include appearance/reality, matter/mind, made/found, and sensible/intellectual. Other important 'Platonic dualisms' rejected by Rorty are knowledge/belief, cognitional/volitional, and subject/object. See Rorty's response to McDowell (2000: 124).
3 See my (2013: ch. 1).
4 See *Sophist* 244B–245E, 251E–252A. For Antisthenes, see Aristotle's *Metaphysics* 5.27.1024b32–34 and 8.3.1043b23–27.
5 See *Sophist* 246E–248A.
6 See *Phaedo* 95A4–102A9.
7 See *Phaedo* 72E3–78B3 for the so-called Recollection Argument.
8 See *Theaetetus* 184B–186E for the refutation of Protagoras.
9 See *Republic*, especially 509B5–9.
10 See *Republic* 510B7.
11 See Aristotle, *Metaphysics* A 6.
12 See *Phaedo* 100D4–5: 'nothing makes something beautiful other than the presence of Beauty or association with it or however this is to be expressed.' Also 99A4–5, where Socrates says that it would be 'exceedingly absurd' to count as causes or explanations those that are offered by Anaxagoras. At *Timaeus* 51D3–52A4, Plato says that (even) *true* belief has no account (*alogon*). I take it that this is the identical point.
13 Cf. 95E8–96A1, 8–10; 97B3–7, C7. The things that are *conditiones sine quibus non* are here distinguished sharply from causes or explanations.
14 See *Phaedo* 101A5–B2.
15 See *Phaedo* 102D6–7. Cf. 103B5.
16 See *Parmenides* 142B5–6.
17 See *Republic* 509B6–7.

18 The instrumentality of Forms in relation to the first principle of all needs to be distinguished from the *conditiones sine quibus non* in the sensible world, but there is no space here for the analysis of this distinction.
19 See *Republic* 508D10, 509B5–6.
20 At *Republic* 511B2–C2, the necessity for dialectic of ascending to the unhypothetical first principle of all is made explicit. Thus, the connection with being unhypothetical and being sufficient is clear.
21 The word 'dialectic' comes from the ordinary Attic Greek word for 'having a conversation' (*dialegesthai*) and indicates the back and forth of rational communication. It is important to appreciate that Plato viewed his systematic philosophy as continuous with such conversation, even though his system concludes to the aforementioned counter-intuitive 'dualisms'.
22 By equating Platonism with systematic philosophy, I am once again echoing Rorty's point alluded to at the beginning of this chapter. A self-declared systematic philosophy that is anti-Platonic is in fact always an attempt at a *rapprochement* between Platonism and Naturalism.
23 See Aristotle, *Metaphysics* A 6, 988a8–14; cf. N 4, 1091b13–15.
24 See Descartes's postulation of a *Mathesis universalis*, a general science that explains all the points that can be raised concerning order and measure, irrespective of the subject matter.
25 Plato is emphatic that this does not conflate mathematics with philosophy, although he very clearly thinks that mathematics is the best preparation for philosophy. Mathematics is not philosophy because it does not seek out ultimate explanations.
26 See *Timaeus* 51E2–3. At D7, the materialism of naturalists in general is the salient feature of their position.
27 See *Timaeus* 48C2–6, 53D4–7. These are clear references to the One and the Indefinite Dyad.
28 See *Timaeus* 55B5.
29 See *Theaetetus* 186C–D. The verb *tuchein* ('attaining' or 'hit upon') in Greek emphasizes discovery as opposed to invention and excludes any 'constructivist' notion of truth.
30 Hence, Rorty's 'turn' to pragmatism that, as he himself acknowledged, is essentially Protagorean relativism, for each person is the 'measure' of what works for him.
31 Here, we need to understand type and not token, although that is not always the case.

References

Gerson, Lloyd 2013. *From Plato to Platonism*, Ithaca, NY: Cornell University Press.
McDowell, John 2000. Towards Rehabilitating Objectivity, in *Rorty and His Critics*, ed. R. Brandom, Oxford: Blackwell: 109–28.
Rorty, Richard 1979. *Philosophy and the Mirror of Nature*, Princeton: Princeton University Press.
Rorty, Richard 1999. *Philosophy and Social Hope*, London: Penguin Books.

3

ZHUANGZI'S SUGGESTIVENESS

Skeptical Questions

Karyn Lai

1. Introduction

The *Zhuangzi*, a fourth-century BCE Chinese text, makes light of the charged debates of its day.[1] It playfully casts doubt on entrenched practices and beliefs, raising open-ended questions that engage readers, in the form of 'Is it like this? Or is it not like this?' It uses stories about ordinary life, and fantasy dialogues between animals, to unsettle the familiar. Many of the extant texts from this time—the Warring States period in China (475–221 BCE)—reflect the views of those in official life. The *Zhuangzi* challenged proposals for settling the unrest of this time. Zhuangzi did not contest doctrine with doctrine but caricatured other traditions, particularly the Confucian[2] and the Mohist,[3] mischievously calling their representatives 'cramped scholars' and comparing them to a summer insect with which one cannot discuss ice.[4] The *Zhuangzi*'s doubt is compelling because it expresses disagreement with not only the content of the proposals, but also the attitudes that accompanied their promulgation. Apart from its lighthearted repartee, does the *Zhuangzi* itself offer more weighty considerations? I propose that its models of mastery prompt a serious re-examination of the institutional and personal resources required for a good life, an insight that is still relevant today. This account of the *Zhuangzi*'s views begins, in section 2, with a discussion of its skeptical questions and their implications. Section 3 explores responsiveness in the *Zhuangzi*, an indispensable element of a person's engagement with the world. The final section examines some examples of mastery and considers how these ancient models of craftsmanship are relevant in the contemporary world.

2. *Zhuangzi's* Skeptical Questions

From the perspective of the *Zhuangzi*, the other thinkers sought to prove others wrong in order to establish the strength of their own proposals. They seemed dazed, bound by a covenant, 'like an arrow or a crossbow pellet, certain that they are the arbiters of right and wrong. They cling to their position as though they had sworn before the gods, sure that they are holding on to victory' (3/2/11–12).[5] In response, Zhuangzi emphasizes the limits of understanding. This is articulated in a number of ways in the text. We examine two specific concerns expressed through its stories. The first, a conversation between 'Toothless' and Wang Ni, wonders about the use of language to express the vast plurality of views in the world. A second issue relates to the limitations of individual perspectives, reflected in a conversation between two little creatures whose grasp of the world is constrained by their physiological makeup. These two issues draw attention to the misguided nature of the political discourse of the time. The thinkers believed, first, that their assertions about right and wrong were properly grounded in knowledge and, second, that what they individually held to be correct was applicable for everyone else. We examine these issues now.

In a conversation with Toothless (Nie Que) about knowledge, Wang Ni responds to each question with a rhetorical question, until he gets to a point where he turns the tables by posing questions about some assumptions that underlie knowledge-claims:

> [Nie Que] asked Wang Ni, 'Do you know what all things agree in calling right?'
> 'How would I know that?' said Wang Ni.
> 'Do you know that you don't know it?'
> 'How would I know that?'
> 'Then do all beings know nothing?'
> 'How would I know that? However, I will try to say something about this. How can we know that when I say I know something, it is not actually not-knowing? How can we know that when I say I don't know something, it is not actually knowing?'
> *(6/2/64–6; adapted from the translation by Watson [1968: 45])*

The conversation continues, with Wang Ni using examples of different choices by different species, of habitats, foods, mating partners, and appreciation of aesthetic and moral standards, to demonstrate variance in the preferences and habits of these creatures:

> Now let me ask *you* some questions . . . Monkeys pair with monkeys, deer go out with deer, and fish play around with fish. Men claim that

> [Mao Qiang] and Lady Li were beautiful, but if fish saw them they would dive to the bottom of the stream, if birds saw them they would fly away, and if deer saw them they would break into a run. Of these four, which knows how to fix the standard of beauty for the world? The way I see it, the rules of benevolence and righteousness and the paths of right and wrong are all hopelessly snarled and jumbled. How could I know anything about such discriminations?
>
> (6/2/66–70; trans. Watson [1968: 45–6])[6]

At first glance, Wang Ni's remarks may seem to suggest relativism. However, I propose that the text is more sophisticated. It does not propose multiple truths or values, all of which are acceptable or correct. The problem here is an epistemological one: Wang Ni asks how he, or anyone else, could justify the distinction between right and wrong in epistemological terms. In other words, the issue here is not one of *choice* (between different views) but of *justification* (of one's own position). In the previous passage, Wang Ni specifies that the problem relates to assertions (*yan* 言, saying), or claims to knowledge. Why are assertions a particular problem? In the *Zhuangzi*'s view, some of the debaters attempted to determine the winner of their debates (*bian* 辯, disputation) by arguing about right and wrong (*shi* 是, *fei* 非). By *proclaiming* their doctrines, each with a specific 'bundle' of values (of right and wrong), they believed that they were expressing what *was* the case. The Confucians *claimed* they were right, as did the Mohists; so, they resorted to disputation to resolve their disagreement. Wang Ni's concern is this: how do we know that what a person says is the case is in fact the case? His question is not merely rhetorical, nor is he saying that knowledge-claims are always indefensible. In the preceding passage, his first question, about claims to knowledge, is followed immediately by its converse, about claims that one *does not know*. Wang Ni's agnostic questions suggest that he is grappling with the lack of a reliable method to determine the claims about knowledge. They highlight the problematic connection—or lack of it—between assertions of knowledge, and (the possession of) knowledge, a connection that the other thinkers took for granted in their attempts to prove that they were correct. Elsewhere in the same chapter, the *Zhuangzi* wonders about the use of debate to settle disputes: should an arbiter be appointed? But if the point of the debate is to establish a perspective-free stance to determine who is correct, how do we ensure that the arbiter holds such a view, or whether it is even possible for anyone to have such a stance (7/2/84–90)?[7]

The second issue concerns the limitations of individual perspectives. This complicates the questions we have just considered. According to the *Zhuangzi*, one reason for being less certain about what we know is that our understanding is constrained by a range of factors. It presents a story about two little creatures, a cicada and a dove, which fail to fathom how a giant bird, Peng, could sweep across the sky when all that they can see is the forest surrounds they are familiar with. In the *Zhuangzi*'s characteristically playful style, giant Peng, who has transformed from a tiny fish called Kun (meaning 'spawn'), has a back like Mount Tai and wings that spread like clouds (1/1/1–2). The cicada and dove dwell on Peng's situation:

> The cicada and the little dove laugh at this, saying, 'When we make an effort and fly up, we can get as far as the elm or the sapanwood tree, but sometimes we don't make it and just fall down on the ground. Now how is anyone going to go ninety thousand li^8 to the south!'
> *(1/1/8–9; trans. Watson [1968: 30])*

The little creatures are aware that their own capacities are limited in comparison to those of Peng. They know that they can only fly as far as a tall tree, sometimes even not succeeding in doing so. But the rhetorical question at the end of their conversation is revealing: it demonstrates how their personal embodied experience is not only limited, but *limiting*. They cannot imagine a scenario different from theirs, and this makes them incredulous that a being like Peng is even possible. The text has other images that evoke the same idea, amongst them the frog who lived in the dilapidated well, enjoyed the comforts provided by his environment, and who enthusiastically invited the giant sea turtle of the Eastern Sea to come into the well to see all of this for himself. But, of course, the turtle's right knee was stuck fast at the mouth of the well (45/17/69–74). The well-frog's perspective is irreducibly lodged, as he believes that his habitat is the right one for him, and for everyone else.

Earlier, we saw how the *Zhuangzi* characterizes the misguided ambitions of the thinkers, believing that they were party to a covenant to determine right and wrong. In this imagery, the thinkers were taking their task far too seriously, believing that it was their responsibility to *pronounce* right and wrong. Language was an important component of their promulgation of norms. The *Zhuangzi* takes their earnestness to task, using features of language ironically to describe the insularity of their points of view. It uses indexical referents, 'this' and 'that', to highlight the inability of these thinkers to imagine anything beyond their immediate experience:

> There is nothing that is not 'that' and there is nothing that is not 'this.' Things do not know that they are the 'that' of other things; they only know what they themselves know.
> *(4/2/27; adapted from the translation by Chan [1963: 182])*

The *Zhuangzi* uses the indexical term 'that' (*bi*) to denote distance from the self. Correspondingly, the perspective of 'I' or 'this' is also indexical. An unreflective individual does not know there are 'those' perspectives, nor is he aware of what things might look like from *there*, rather than *here*. Tragically, because we do not understand the indexicality of our own point of view, 'our rights and wrongs end up charioteering us around . . . [w]e try to control others, using ourselves as the regulating standard' (64/23/64; trans. Ziporyn [2009: 101]). Two aspects of this epistemological oversight bother Zhuangzi. The first is the belief of the debating thinkers that their views are fixed and once-and-for-all solutions to social disorder. The second is that their individual perspectives are universalizable.

What do the *Zhuangzi*'s skeptical questions amount to? As noted previously, the *Zhuangzi* seems to advocate relativism when it relates the different preferences and interest of the animals. Chad Hansen proposes that the *Zhuangzi*'s view be characterized as 'perspectival relativism' (1983b: 44–6). On this view, each assertion, including one's own, is made from a particular perspective. The point in the *Zhuangzi* is neither to shed one's perspective (for these are irreducible) nor is it to hold a view that is the simple sum of all perspectives. For Hansen, the text avoids the self-defeating characteristic of relativism because the vision that the *Zhuangzi* proposes does not claim to be more 'natural' than any other perspective. However, it is a 'metaperspective . . . a perspective on the plurality of perspectives', which has both epistemological and ethical aspects (Hansen 1992: 284). A person who holds this meta-perspectival view has a more flexible approach, understanding that others might have important insights from where they sit. Such a person would also have a more tolerant attitude (Hansen 2003: 153).

There are a number of problems with the relativist thesis. First, it requires that the *Zhuangzi* itself holds commitments to each of the views expressed in Wang Ni's account—that they are true or real—as well as elsewhere in the text. There is, however, no such explicit or firm statement of its commitments, especially in light of the way in which the text poses scenarios to rouse doubt rather than certainty. Second, the relativist thesis cannot accommodate the suggestion that the *Zhuangzi* has normative commitments. The text advocates models of mastery, intended as a challenge to the then-dominant picture of official life. The skill masters, such as the wheelwright Bian, the expert swimmer, the bellstand carver, and the cicada catcher (some of them are discussed in section 4) embody the text's positive visions of the Way (*dao*), as proposed by Philip Ivanhoe (1993, 1996).[9] Lee Yearley incorporates religious elements—which he terms 'intraworldly mysticism'—in his reading of the text, whereby the daemonic person transcends many aspects of this-worldly life but nevertheless maintains engagement with it (1982, 1983, 1996).[10] Harold Roth similarly promotes a normative mystical vision in the *Zhuangzi*, although—being more focused on Daoist religious practices—he emphasizes the quality of the experience in terms of psychological tranquility, attained through meditative contemplation (1991, 1999).

One element of Hansen's analysis is insightful: it brings out the way in which the *Zhuangzi* is a unique text. He suggests that the *Zhuangzi* holds a 'metaperspective'. While disagreeing with Hansen that the meta-perspective is bound up with commitments to each perspective, the view here highlights the nature of the *Zhuangzi*'s engagement with the doctrinal disputes. Zhuangzi's meta-perspective sets it apart from existing discourse, whose argumentative method was to debunk doctrine with doctrine. This method relied on the clarification of objective terms of reference in language, and according to which a winner is decided upon (7/2/84–92; see Lai 2006). The *Zhuangzi* demonstrates its refusal to engage in these debates, simply by pointing out the insularity of the other thinkers' perspectives, and their unfounded assumption that these were universally held. It is at this level that it uses doubt to unsettle the thinkers' commitment to their doctrines, instead of offering yet another doctrine. Lisa Raphals (1996) suggests that chapter 2 of the text (the chapter in which epistemological issues feature most prominently)[11] uses doubt to question prevailing assumptions about knowledge. This account proposes that the *Zhuangzi* was not denying the possibility of knowledge but was, more importantly, highlighting the place of doubt. At this point, we need to return to the then urgent debates to consider the viability of the *Zhuangzi*'s position in light of the unrest during the Warring States. If we accept that individual perspectives are insular, what *can* be done to address the unrest?

3. Thinking From Lodging-Places, and Responsiveness

In the way that the *Zhuangzi* portrays the animals in the passages cited earlier, we are made aware of the 'lodged' nature of each of their perspectives. What is only an indexical resting point is assumed to be permanent, and not *simply* a resting point. Stories like these speak to readers by asking them *temporarily* to lodge within these views in order to experience and understand the nature of the limitations. One way to understand the place of the different perspectives is to take Zhuangzi not as a theoretician (e.g. viewing the perspectives along relativist vs. monist lines) but rather as someone whose ideas are shaped by observations of the world and who in that sense thinks more like an empiricist.[12] This is a novel interpretation of the *Zhuangzi*; to date, discussions on this topic— we have seen some—tend to focus on the issue of the *Zhuangzi*'s commitment to relativism or to perspectivism (e.g., Ivanhoe 1993; Connolly 2011).

If we proceed with the argument that the *Zhuangzi*'s view is based on an empirical approach, then we could say that each of these lodged perspectives is irreducible and non-universalizable. An empirically focused thinker would embrace plurality quite differently from how a relativist would. A relativist would accept that each view is true for the person whose 'truth' it is. By contrast, as a thinker who attends to empirical observations, Zhuangzi's concern would not so much be whether each view is *true*, but whether it is *legitimate*: the well-frog's view that his well is Paradise-like is legitimate, as is a fish's, which prefers a habitat in water to one up in the trees. (Indeed, both the fish and the frog have no choice, so it seems.) However, as readers of the text, we have an opportunity that is not available to them: we have the ability to lodge temporarily in the scenarios presented in the text. When we do so, we provisionally consider different perspectives by imagining how comfortable the frog and the fish are, respectively, in their given environments. In doing so, we come to *agree* with the text that the human, the monkey, the fish, and the deer have different preferences and thrive in different conditions.[13] Yet these animals, like the summer insect used to represent the cramped scholars, simply cannot see beyond their own preferences. The point that Wang Ni makes about our (lack of) understanding of knowledge-claims derives its significance in part from readers' agreement with the legitimacy of each of the different preferences. From an empirical perspective, these examples are real: they are real in the sense that a monkey's experience is *just like that*, and a human's experience is *just like this*. We may never see the fish's preferences like 'this', but we can attempt to imagine it by lodging, temporarily, *there*. To be able to lodge temporarily in others' perspectives is to be sage-like:

> The sage recognises a 'this', but a 'this' which is also 'that', a 'that' which is also 'this'. . . . A state in which 'this' and 'that' no longer find their opposites is called the pivot of *dao*. When the pivot is fitted into the centre of the ring, it can respond endlessly. Its 'yea' is limitless and its 'nay' too is limitless. So I say, the best thing to use is illumination.
>
> *(4/2/29–31; adapted from the translation by Watson [1968: 40])*

Here, again, the language of indexicals is used to highlight different perspectives. However, unlike the previously cited passage, this offers a solution to indexicality. In this passage, the *Zhuangzi* seems implicitly to accept indexicality as a given. Then, rather than dwell on it as a problematic issue, the text proposes how indexicality can be dealt with: the sage recognizes that what one individual takes as 'this', another takes as 'that'. The sage takes his position at the center of the swiveling pivot, responding to the different perspectives *and* not being bound by any one of them. He engages—limitlessly—with different perspectives because he is not permanently lodged in any one of them. The metaphor of illumination (*ming* 明) suggests that the *Zhuangzi* does not promote a Way that stands among the other doctrines, at the level of first-order doctrines.[14] To illuminate is to cast light on, and not to add to, the plethora of existing doctrines. From the vantage point of the pivot, the sage understands that each doctrine is proposed from some individual's lived reality and therefore he does not uncritically accept them as true.[15] Yet he sees them as equal, since they all have the feature of indexicality (which helps to explain the title of chapter 2, 'Discussion on Making Things Equal'). According to this interpretation, the point of the *Zhuangzi*'s engagement with the other thinkers is not to voice another opinion by deciding on who is right and who is wrong, but rather, in a more sophisticated way, to point out the shortcomings of all of them.[16]

In the pivot metaphor, the text suggests a different approach from the ones that were available then. Imagination plays a central role, where readers are encouraged to consider alternative ways of viewing things. Yet the *Zhuangzi* is not simply committed to plurality for its own sake. Distinctively, it offers a way for human communication and interactions to proceed in spite of the limits of knowledge and what may be shared through language. The idea of responsiveness (*ying* 應) is fundamental in illumination: the sage's responsiveness on the pivot is qualitatively different from the responses given by the 'cramped scholars'. First, it recognizes the constraints of others' as well as its own positions, as each is a lodged position. Second, building on this recognition, the sage lodges temporarily in another's position, seeing from that position—in the way we lodge in the fish's, the monkey's, or the little bird's perspective. In this way, the text prompts readers to lodge, just like the sage does, in the different perspectives. The text is not simply *telling* readers that there are varied perspectives, or what these perspectives *are like*; rather, it is getting them to imagine and *to see for themselves* what it might be like to have a lodged view. The sage's responsiveness is marked by the efficacy in the way he moves and lodges in different perspectives. In doing so, his engagements are limitless, as, indeed, are the perspectives held by different individuals. His responses are limitless because he is not stuck within a single perspective. In contrast, although the other thinkers are saying something—they are making assertions, just like chirping fledglings do (4/2/24)[17]—are they fully responsive to the situation at hand? Their responses reflect their ingrained ways of thinking, not unlike the standard responses of those who subscribe to the same doctrine. A response of this kind is task- or context-insensitive and is better described as a conditioned reflex.

These considerations support the chapter's interpretation of Zhuangzi's approach as an empirically grounded one, an approach with important implications for how the text is interpreted. The particularities matter and, because they do, a standardized reflex will not suffice. Here, we need to ask the question of what this means in practice: how should an official respond to the existing unrest?

In a passage where Confucius is presented as a spokesperson for the *Zhuangzi*'s thinking, he speaks with his favored disciple, Yan Hui, who had decided that he was going to take up office with the Prince of Wei. The prince had a notorious reputation for treating his people appallingly (8/4/1–9/4/24). The details of the conversation are interesting, as there is remarkable acuity in the way the Confucian project and the Confucian master and disciple are portrayed here. Yan Hui seeks the permission of his master, Confucius, to undertake this mission; and Yan Hui's decision to take up office in Wei was a principled response to the Confucian master's teaching, that one should serve where help is most needed. An important element of the Confucian solution to the unrest lay in the hands of capable officials to positively influence their superiors (e.g., *Analects* 4.26, 19.10).[18] In this conversation, instead of encouraging this noble pursuit, Confucius dissuades Yan Hui, saying 'you will probably go and get yourself executed, that's all' (trans. Watson [1968: 54]). In the course of the conversation, Yan Hui demonstrates that he has already devised a multi-pronged strategy, to be 'inwardly direct, outwardly compliant, and [to do his] work through the examples of antiquity' (ibid.: 56). To be inwardly direct is to follow Heaven; to be outwardly compliant is to fulfill the ways of humanity (Yan Hui talks about fulfilling the ritual proprieties expected of a minister) and to draw on the normative authority of tradition in criticizing wrongdoing. Confucius disparages Yan Hui's plans (ibid.: 57):

> Goodness, how could *that* do? You have too many policies and plans and you haven't seen what is needed. You will probably get off without incurring any blame, yes. But that will be as far as it goes. How do you think you can actually convert him? You are still making the mind[-heart] your teacher!

In Confucian terms, Yan Hui has prepared himself well for the task. His mind-heart[19] is attuned to Confucian commitments and he demonstrates due thoughtfulness about them in his plans. However, the Zhuangzian Confucius accuses Yan Hui of having too many plans and policies, especially as he has not encountered the situation as yet. Yan Hui's conditioned and context-insensitive plans will obscure what he might actually encounter in his service of the Prince of Wei. To fail to see beyond one's lodged perspective is the fundamental malaise gripping the debating thinkers. Sharp lines are drawn between what is right and wrong, missing out on the many possibilities, of what is perhaps 'partly right' or 'partly wrong', as well as others in-between.[20] For each cramped scholar, every other perspective is 'that' or, more simply, just 'not this'. The problem, as the *Zhuangzi* sees it, is as follows:

> It is by establishing definitions of what is 'this', what is 'right', that boundaries are made. Let me explain what I mean by boundaries. There are right and left, then there are classes of things and ideas of the proper responses to them, then there are roles and disputes, then there are competitions and struggles . . . Wherever debate shows one of two alternatives to be right, something remains undistinguished and unshown.
>
> *(5/2/55–8; trans. Ziporyn [2009: 16])*

The text highlights the complacency of those who believe that they hold and articulate what is correct. Bolstered by misplaced confidence in the correctness of their views, they fail to see what is remaindered in their pre-determined distinctions. Instead of attending to the situation, they make their decisions on the basis of what they already know to be correct. The conviction that they are correct, and the determination with which they promote their views, beget blindness to what falls beyond the sights of their doctrines. In response to such unfounded confidence, the *Zhuangzi* advocates doubt, perhaps better described as a lack of certainty. In the final section, we consider what it means to be attentive to situations and how such responsiveness may be cultivated.

4. Doubt, A-certainty, and Mastery

The *Zhuangzi*'s questions sow seeds of doubt on quarrels about values, and on assertions about their correctness ('Of these three creatures, then, which one knows the proper place to live?' (6/2/67; trans. Watson [1968: 66]). In the literature, its hesitations have sometimes been described in terms of 'skepticism' and it is therefore important to understand how the text comes across in this way. How do elements in the *Zhuangzi* compare, for example, with the doubt of the ancient Skeptics? It may be, as Steve Coutinho has pointed out, that the aim of Zhuangzi's doubt is to increase awareness of fallibilism, quite unlike the epistemic attitudes (e.g., of ataraxy) in ancient Skepticism (2004: 66). Coutinho's point—about not drawing similarities across the two traditions on slender threads[21]—prompts us to consider more carefully the finer details of the comparisons. Perhaps, as suggested by Paul Kjellberg, the text does not deny the possibility of knowledge but simply questions it. On this basis, the *Zhuangzi* advocates skepticism not of a 'dogmatic' nature, but instead an 'aporectic' one (1996: 20). For Kjellberg, the text is focused on practice—philosophical practice— using 'therapeutic' arguments to generate uncertainty. Another account, proposed by Eric Schwitzgebel, distinguishes between a 'philosophical skeptic' and 'skeptic in the everyday sense'. Schwitzgebel recommends that the *Zhuangzi*, belonging to the latter kind, promotes open-mindedness, 'putting somewhat less faith than is standard in one's own and others' beliefs' (1996: 91). This has important moral outcomes, Schwitzgebel suggests, engendering receptiveness to new evidence and tolerance of people with different beliefs.

These characterizations of the *Zhuangzi*'s skepticism highlight some of its different effects. Nevertheless, they converge on one point—that doubt in the *Zhuangzi* addresses attitudes such as open-mindedness, acceptance of fallibilism, and uncertainty. It is important to capture the attitudinal focus of Zhuangzi's epistemology, but we should understand this in light of the text's concerns about the nature of knowledge. I propose that *lack of certainty*, or *a-certainty*, best describes the text's hesitations. The text is not simply advocating open-mindedness as a measure to stimulate greater tolerance of difference, for it does not accept that any of the doctrines are 'correct', given their constraints. It is critically aware of fallibilism, but it says more: it is eye-opening first to lodge in the well-frog's perspective, and then in the giant sea turtle's perspective. It seems to uphold uncertainty, but its underlying concern is not that the sage should be *un*-certain. Clearly, the text does not seek to promote the nagging and perhaps debilitating doubt that can sometimes accompany uncertainty. The *Zhuangzi* speaks out against aspects of certainty, manifest in the thinkers' views, in two different ways. The first relates to their views on the nature of knowledge (that it is indubitable), which leads to the aggravated debates in order to determine one correct doctrine. For the *Zhuangzi*, the search for knowledge *qua* certainty is misdirected.

The second problem is one of epistemological attitude. The thinkers' false confidence—the certainty that they are correct—drives the desire to promulgate their entrenched standards. From this angle, every situation a cramped scholar encounters is assessed according to his fixed standard of right and wrong. It is this situation against which Confucius speaks when he accuses Yan Hui of having already devised plans and policies prior to taking up office. In Yan Hui's approach, when a person encounters a new situation, it is simply another opportunity to rehearse the all-too-familiar. Closure on an issue has been attained prior to the encounter, guiding and constraining how a person responds in a particular situation. Such certainty leaves no room for a person to focus on, and respond to, the significant particularities of the matter at hand. By contrast, responsiveness requires openness to situations, not closure to them.

In the remainder of this discussion, I dwell on some models of mastery proposed in the *Zhuangzi*, where responsiveness is critical. Unlike the standard discourse of its time, the text upholds a contrarian model of excellence, using examples of the mastery of people skilled in ordinary activities including swimming, ferrying, cicada-catching, butchering, and wheelmaking. The skillfulness of these experts rests in their attentiveness to salient features of their respective activities: although cultivated, their actions are not habitual. Each particular instance of the same activity can throw up contingent, yet important, factors: steering a ferry successfully in choppy waters requires cognizance of the nature of the waves one encounters at that moment *and* the skills to handle the particular ferry, just as awareness of burls in a piece of wood, *and* the skills to work with them to make a wheel, are aspects of mastery in carpentry. Flexibility, rather than certainty about outcomes or products, is a mark of mastery. This is not to say that the *Zhuangzi*'s skill masters have no goals, or that there are no evaluative criteria for measuring success; it is to say that mastery is understood not simply in terms of outcomes. For Zhuangzi, mastery is multifaceted. It is manifest in performance,[22] centering on how a person executes a task (adroitly, or excellently, or clumsily, or unsystematically, etc.), while also considering resources, circumstantial constraints, or enablers, as well as the outcomes or products of her action. How is this notion of performance expressed in the text? Consider the case of the bell stand carver, Qing, who makes magnificent bell stands at which people marvel. The Marquis of Lu, one of the onlookers, asks Qing about his skill. Qing's mastery begins with the selection of the wood he works with. He says that he fasts so that his 'skill is concentrated and the outside world slides away' (50/19/57–8; trans. Ziporyn [2009: 82]). Qing continues,

> Then I enter into the mountain forests, viewing the inborn [Heavenly] nature of the trees. My body arrives at a certain spot, and already I see the completed bell stand there; only then do I apply my hand to it. Otherwise I leave the tree alone.
>
> *(50/19/58–9; brackets inserted by author; trans. Ziporyn [ibid.])*

Qing turns wonderful bell stands, not only because he handles the chisel and wood-carving tools well, but because he understands what he is working with, in making each bell stand. Quite a few of the *Zhuangzi*'s examples, like this one, highlight the responsiveness of the master to the situation that he encounters. Unlike the Confucian Yan Hui, who plans to turn the Prince of Wei toward his own ingrained Confucian ways, the skill master stories emphasize the depth of the master's engagement with the task, approaching it without superimposing preconceived notions of what ought to be done. The *Zhuangzi* points out how the responsive actions of the skill masters are unique in each case as they are actions taken spontaneously, in response to each scenario: they leave no footprints or traces (*ji* 跡; 41/16/11–17, 52/20/29–35, 58/22/30–3). In contrast, the tendency of the other thinkers is to impose a primarily norm-guided life to quell the unrest. From the *Zhuangzi*'s point of view, it would be regrettable if its models of mastery were to be taken as authoritative and normative, for that would reduce responsiveness to certainty.

Therefore, Zhuangzi's skill masters need to 'forget' a norm-driven approach in order to be responsive. The mastery stories state explicitly that the masters have forgotten many aspects of conventional life. For example, wood-carver Qing has had to fast to reach the state where he is able appropriately to select the wood that he can work with to craft into bell stands. In doing so, he has (progressively) forgotten: 'praise or reward, rank or salary . . . honor or disgrace . . . skill and clumsiness', and even that he has four limbs or a body, 'as if the royal court has ceased to exist' (50/19/56–57). Similar themes of absorbed attentiveness are also part of the butcher and cicada-catcher stories, as is the theme of forgetting, especially in a famous passage of 'sitting and forgetting' (17/6/89–93). The sage in the *Zhuangzi* 'forgets' a range of matters, including 'worldly learning' (Cook 2003: 76), 'sense perception' and 'bodily awareness' (Roth 2003: 18), 'propositional knowledge' (ibid.: 28–9), and even the self.[23] For example, Butcher Ding is no longer led by sight, so that he is able to attend to each particular ox as each is different—and yet he carves each one masterfully, so that he has not sharpened his knife in 19 years (7/3/2–8/3/12). The masters lack certainty prior to the encounter—even though Qing has carved many bell stands, and Ding has dressed many head of oxen—for each encounter with *this* tree or *this* ox throws up new details and they do not assume that they already know what is at stake.

Why was this model of mastery so important to Zhuangzi? The *Zhuangzi* was dissatisfied with existing approaches to government and their underlying assumptions. In response, it did not offer another doctrine but instead looked to excellence in ordinary life, appealing to paradigms that were accessible to the greater majority. In doing so, it challenged elitist discourses and pictures of ideal life upheld by those in office. From Zhuangzi's perspective, their doctrines reflected the lodged perspectives of their lives, failing to see a variety of views and the differences between them. Their rigidity, fueled by their certainty in the correctness of their doctrine, meant that they could not respond adequately to contingencies, manifold needs, and shifting contexts—features of life in the Warring States period, a time of great instability. Placed within its context, the *Zhuangzi* is significant because it challenged the status quo, using doubt to unsettle the *complacency* of those who believed they were irrefutably correct. But this is only one factor in its significance as a philosophical text. Importantly, in its use of accessible stories and imagery instead of proclamation, the *Zhuangzi* disputed both the other thinkers' beliefs and their methods of justification. Zhuangzi effectively *entraps* the other thinkers, using them as figures, or using creatures to represent them, in its stories. In doing so, it draws them in to engage with the doubts it raises in its scenarios.

For us today, the *Zhuangzi*'s challenge to understand the insularity of perspectives remains. It invites readers to imagine what it feels like to *see* from a number of different perspectives. The text, realistically, does not ask us permanently to transcend our own perspectives or to uphold a view that inclusively takes in all perspectives (if indeed that is possible). In place of abstractly derived norms, it focuses on a person's engagement with situations, promoting a more tentative approach to knowledge (one that is more conducive to mastery). This shifts the paradigm of knowledge and action to responsiveness. In its pictures of skill mastery, the *Zhuangzi* resists habitual, context-insensitive reflexes and makes the case for an empirically grounded philosophy whose central themes are those of spontaneous and efficacious action.[24] Beyond the intellectual enjoyment of hopping into different perspectives, and the aesthetically charming pictures of mastery, the *Zhuangzi* offers an approach to life that is attuned to the practicalities of a rich and diverse world.

Notes

1 The *Zhuangzi* and the *Laozi* have traditionally been grouped as belonging to one tradition, the Lao-Zhuang Daoist tradition. Wing-tsit Chan believes that the *Hou Hanshu* (*History of the Later Han Dynasty*) makes this association (1963: 178). Traditionally, it was also held that the *Laozi* was compiled earlier than the *Zhuangzi* and, as they stand in that relation, that the *Laozi* is less sophisticated and the *Zhuangzi* represents mature and developed Daoism. There are problems with the traditional views on the text. First, sections of the *Laozi* have a probable date of composition later than the *Zhuangzi*. Second, the extant *Zhuangzi* comprises 33 chapters, after a major revision of the 52-chapter text by Guo Xiang (d. 312 CE). Guo Xiang appears to have edited out 19 chapters of that text. The extent of Guo Xiang's editing of the text is not insignificant, and it is not possible fully to determine its impact on the 52-chapter *Zhuangzi* (Knaul 1985). The discussion in this chapter uses the name of the text, *Zhuangzi*, and the name of its alleged author, Zhuangzi, interchangeably for stylistic reasons. Phrases such as 'Zhuangzi believed that' indicate that the source of the idea is to be found in the *Zhuangzi*. It is not the intention to suggest that Zhuangzi was the author of all of the ideas in the extant text.

2 The Confucian tradition is named after its alleged founder, Confucius (551–469 BCE). The tradition is typically characterized by its utopic ideal of benevolent government, which would lead by exemplary conduct, instilling in the people a sense of propriety in their relational interactions (Lai 2017: ch. 2).

3 Mohism is named after Mozi (480?–390? BCE), leader of a group that proposed an altruistic ethic (*jianai*: impartial concern) marked by equal concern of each person for everyone else. The Mohists conceived of morality in terms of a standard applicable to all, much like the standards with which some of them might have been familiar in craftsmanship (e.g., use of the plumb line). Mohist doctrine competed with Confucian ideals: its view of *jianai* may be construed as an attempt to anchor moral values independently of the courts and its officials (Lai 2017: chs. 4, 6).
4 'Jo of the North Sea said, "You can't discuss the ocean with a well frog—he's limited by the space he lives in. You can't discuss ice with a summer insect—he's bound to a single season. You can't discuss the Way with a cramped scholar—he's shackled by his doctrines. Now you have come out beyond your banks and borders and have seen the great sea—so you realize your own pettiness. From now on it will be possible to talk to you about the Great Principle" (42/17/5–8; trans. Watson [1968: 175–6]).
5 References to sections of the *Zhuangzi* follow the numbers of the Harvard-Yenching concordance (*Zhuangzi Yinde*).
6 In citations I have, where necessary, altered transliterations of Chinese terms and names to the standard Pinyin for consistency. All other markings of text (e.g., italics) are the author's or translator's, unless otherwise specified.
7 See Lai (2006) for a detailed discussion of disputation and adjudication.
8 A *li* (里) measured approximately a third of a mile.
9 Ivanhoe notes, '[i]n his examples of skilful individuals, Zhuangzi completely abandons the perspectivist argument and reveals the foundation of his normative vision' (1993: 652).
10 I suggest that the 'state' to which Yearley refers is in fact better described as a way of life that brings together its ethical, religious, political, social, and psychological dimensions.
11 The title of this chapter is 'Discussion on Making Things Equal' ('Qiwu Lun'; trans. Watson 1968).
12 In fact, it seems strange for Hansen to assert, for example, both that Chinese philosophy had no place for abstractions, on the one hand, and that the *Zhuangzi* holds a meta-perspectival view, on the other. On the topic of abstractions, Hansen writes:

> I would like to argue for the claim that no Chinese philosophical system of the classical period in China was committed to the existence of or had roles for abstract (universal) entities in any of the traditionally important ways that Western semantics, epistemology, ontology, or philosophy of mind had roles for abstractions. (1983a: 37–8)

It would seem sensible, in light of this remark, to follow the view I propose here—that, on the topic of perspectives, Zhuangzi was an empiricist.
13 Steve Coutinho contends that the *Zhuangzi*'s scepticism is very much a 'distant relative' of ancient Greek scepticism (with which I agree). The point I make about readers' agreement with the examples is taken from Coutinho's discussion, although his point is about the *Zhuangzi*'s knowledge-claims. Coutinho writes, 'Unlike the ancient Sceptics, Zhuangzi makes many knowledge claims—indeed, he makes several such claims, on which his argument depends . . . Zhuangzi does not shy away from claiming to know such things' (2004: 66).
14 In this way, the proposal here is similar to Hansen's characterization of the *Zhuangzi*'s view as a meta-level and second-order thesis.
15 Some have argued that the illuminated position is one from which the sage sees a fundamental unity of opposites (e.g., Radice 2001: 33). Together with Wai Wai Chiu, I have argued against Radice's interpretation: we have presented a detailed argument

for viewing illumination as a higher-order stance and not simply as one that aggregates across different doctrinal positions (Lai and Chiu 2013).
16 I believe this is why it seems to many interpreters of the *Zhuangzi* that its doubt does not generate the anxiety that we might sense in some versions of skepticism. Angus Graham describes the *Zhuangzi*'s doubt in the follow way, in a phrase that has been cited numerous times in the literature: 'there is no vertigo in the doubt' (1989: 186). For discussions of the *Zhuangzi*'s position in relation to the debates of the day, see Wong (2005) and Lai (2006).
17 The context of this question is as follows:

> Words are not just wind. Words have something to say. But if what they have to say is not fixed, then do they really say something? Or do they say nothing? People suppose that words are different from the peeps of baby birds, but is there any difference, or isn't there? What does [*dao*] rely upon, that we have true and false? What do words rely upon, that we have right and wrong? How can the Way go away and not exist? How can words exist and not be acceptable? When the Way relies on little accomplishments and words rely on vain show, then we have the rights and wrongs of the Confucians and the [Mohists]. What one calls right the other calls wrong; what one calls wrong the other calls right. But if we want to right their wrongs and wrong their rights, then the best thing to use is [illumination]. (4/2/23–7; adapted from the translation by Watson [1968: 39])

18 The *Analects* is a text closely associated with the early Confucian tradition. It comprises short conversations that Confucius was supposed to have had with a range of people, including his followers. *Analects* 19.10 presents one of Confucius's followers, Zixia, saying this:

> Only once exemplary persons (*junzi* 君子) have won the confidence (*xin* 信) of the common people do they work them hard; otherwise, the people would think themselves exploited. Only once they have won the confidence of their lord do they remonstrate with him; otherwise, their lord would think himself maligned. (19.10; trans. Ames and Rosemont [1998: 220])

This conversation captures the difficulties of the roles of the officials, negotiating between the ruler and the people while maintaining their personal moral commitments. Many of the conversations in Book Four of the *Analects* dwell on how Confucian officials should adhere to their principles.
19 The character *xin* (心) refers to both cognitive and emotional capacities and therefore is most often translated 'mind-heart' in English language literature. Thinkers belonging to the Confucian tradition emphasized the cultivation of the mind-heart in such a way that one's sensibilities and desires were attuned to Confucian commitments such as benevolence (*ren* 仁). For example, Mencius emphasized that the mind-heart that would not be moved or distracted (*budong xin* 不動心) once it had been cultivated. See Shun (1997) and Chan (2002).
20 The discussion of these positions is as follows:

> Suppose you and I argue. If you beat me instead of my beating you, are you really right and am I really wrong? If I beat you instead of your beating me, am I really

right and are you really wrong? Or are we both partly right and partly wrong? Or are we both wholly right and wholly wrong? (7/2/84–6; trans. Chan [1963: 189–90])

See Lai (2006) on the nature of debate and adjudication.
21 Coutinho writes,

> I am not sure that the similarities between the two are sufficient to outweigh the differences . . . I do concede that, once it is pointed out, the *family resemblance* between Zhuangzi and the ancient Sceptics is unmistakable, but it is, surely, at most a family resemblance of a distant relative. (2004: 66)

22 There might be a tendency to interpret performance as a process or occurrence *additional to* knowledge. The suggestion here, however, is that performance *is* knowledge. This understanding of performance takes from Ryle's views on knowing and thinking. Ryle writes (1979: 24):

> To X, thinking what one is doing, is not to be doing both some X-ing and some separately do-able Y-ing. It is to be X-ing under a variety of qualifications, such as X-ing on purpose, with some tentativeness, some vigilance against some known hazards, some perseverance and with at least a modicum of intended or unintended self-training. It is to X intentionally, experimentally, circumspectly and practisingly, and these by themselves are not additional things that he is doing or might be doing.

Chris Fraser (2009) explores notions of agency and performance.
23 The characterization of 'self' or 'no self' in the *Zhuangzi* is a fairly prominent line in *Zhuangzi* studies. Christian Jochim (1998) is wary of these representations, describing the various positions in detail and presenting arguments against the view that *Zhuangzi* advocates a 'no self' theory.
24 The actions or responses of the skill masters in the various stories have often been characterized in terms of spontaneity (see, for example, Graham 1983 and Kupperman 1996). The Zhuangzi's ideas and argumentative style continue to generate discussions in epistemology and action theory, especially in considerations of attention, spontaneity, and efficacy (Wu 1982; Jullien 1999, 2004; Slingerland 2003; Bruya 2010a, 2010b).

References

The Analects of Confucius: A Philosophical Translation 1998, trans. Roger Ames and Henry Rosemont Jr., New York: Ballantine.
Bruya, Brian 2010a. The Rehabilitation of Spontaneity: A New Approach in Philosophy of Action, *Philosophy East and West* 60: 207–50.
Bruya, Brian 2010b. *Effortless Attention: A New Perspective in the Cognitive Science of Attention and Action*, Cambridge, MA: MIT Press.
Chan, Alan K. L. (ed.) 2002. *Mencius: Contexts and Interpretations*, Honolulu: University of Hawai'i Press.
Chuang-Tzu: The Inner Chapters 2001, trans. Angus C. Graham, Indianapolis: Hackett.
The Complete Works of Chuang Tzu 1968, trans. Burton Watson, New York: Columbia University Press.

Connolly, Tim 2011. Perspectivism as a Way of Knowing in the *Zhuangzi*, *Dao* 10: 487–505.
Cook, Scott 2003. Harmony and Cacophony in the Panpipes of Heaven, in *Hiding the World in the World: Uneven Discourses on the Zhuangzi*, ed. Scott Cook, Albany: State University of New York Press: 64–87.
Coutinho, Steve 2004. *Zhuangzi and Early Chinese Philosophy: Vagueness, Transformation and Paradox*, Aldershot: Ashgate.
Fraser, Chris 2009. Action and Agency in Early Chinese Thought, *Journal of Chinese Philosophy and Culture* 5: 217–39.
Graham, Angus C. 1983. Taoist Spontaneity and the Dichotomy of 'Is' and 'Ought', in *Experimental Essays on the Chuang-tzu*, ed. Victor H. Mair, Honolulu: University of Hawai'i Press: 3–23.
Graham, Angus C. 1989. *Disputers of the Tao: Philosophical Argument in Ancient China*, La Salle, IL: Open Court Press.
Hansen, Chad 1983a. *Language and Logic in Ancient China*, Ann Arbor: University of Michigan Press.
Hansen, Chad 1983b. A *Tao* of *Tao* in Chuang-tzu, in *Experimental Essays on Chuang-tzu*, ed. Victor H. Mair, Honolulu: University of Hawai'i Press: 24–55.
Hansen, Chad 1992. *A Daoist Theory of Chinese Thought*, New York: Oxford University Press.
Hansen, Chad 2003. "The Relatively Happy Fish," Asian Philosophy, 13.2/3: 145–64.
Ivanhoe, Philip 1993. Zhuangzi on Skepticism, Skill, and the Ineffable *Dao*, *Journal of the American Academy of Religion* 61: 639–54.
Ivanhoe, Philip 1996. Was Zhuangzi a Relativist?, in *Essays on Skepticism, Relativism and Ethics in the Zhuangzi*, ed. Philip Ivanhoe and Paul Kjellberg, Albany: State University of New York Press: 196–214.
Jochim, Christian 1998. Just Say No to 'No-Self' in Zhuang Zi, in *Wandering at Ease in the Zhuangzi*, ed. Roger Ames, Albany: State University of New York Press: 35–74.
Jullien, François 1999. *The Propensity of Things: Toward a History of Efficacy in China*, trans. Janet Lloyd, New York: Zone Books.
Jullien, François 2004. *Treatise on Efficacy: Between Western and Chinese Thinking*, Honolulu: University of Hawai'i Press.
Kjellberg, Paul 1996. Sextus Empiricus, Zhuangzi, and Xunzi on 'Why Be Skeptical', in *Essays on Skepticism, Relativism and Ethics in the Zhuangzi*, ed. Philip Ivanhoe and Paul Kjellberg, Albany: State University of New York Press: 1–25.
Knaul, Livia 1985. Kuo Hsiang and the *Chuang Tzu*, *Journal of Chinese Philosophy* 12: 429–47.
Kupperman, Joel 1996. Spontaneity and the Education of the Emotions, in *Essays on Skepticism, Relativism and Ethics in the Zhuangzi*, ed. Philip Ivanhoe and Paul Kjellberg, Albany: State University of New York Press: 183–95.
Lai, Karyn L. 2006. Philosophy and Philosophical Reasoning in the *Zhuangzi*: Dealing with Plurality, *Journal of Chinese Philosophy* 33: 365–74.
Lai, Karyn L. 2017. *Introduction to Chinese Philosophy*, 2nd. ed. Cambridge, UK: Cambridge University Press.
Lai, Karyn L. and Chiu, Wai 2013. *Ming* in the *Zhuangzi Neipian*: Enlightened Engagement, *Journal of Chinese Philosophy* 40: 527–43.
Radice, Thomas 2001. Clarity and Survival in the *Zhuangzi*, Asian Philosophy 11: 33–40.
Raphals, Lisa 1996. Skeptical Strategies in the *Zhuangzi* and *Theaetetus*, in *Essays on Skepticism, Relativism and Ethics in the Zhuangzi*, ed. Paul Kjellberg and Philip Ivanhoe,

Albany: State University of New York Press: 26–49. Reprinted, with minor revisions, from *Philosophy East and West* 44 (1994): 501–26.

Roth, Harold D. 1991. Psychology and Self-Cultivation in Early Taoistic Thought, *Harvard Journal of Asiatic Studies* 51: 599–650.

Roth, Harold D. 1999. *Original Tao: Inward Training* (Nei-yeh) *and the Foundations of Taoist Mysticism*, New York: Columbia University Press.

Roth, Harold D. 2003. Bimodal Mystical Experience in the 'Qiwulun' Chapter of the Zhuangzi, in *Hiding the World in the World: Uneven Discourses on the* Zhuangzi, ed. Scott Cook, Albany: State University of New York Press: 15–32.

Ryle, Gilbert 1979. Adverbial Verbs and Verbs of Thinking, in *On Thinking*, ed. Konstantin Kolenda, Oxford: Basil Blackwell: 17–32.

Schwitzgebel, Eric 1996. Zhuangzi's Attitude toward Language and His Skepticism, in *Essays on Skepticism, Relativism and Ethics in the* Zhuangzi, ed. Philip Ivanhoe and Paul Kjellberg, Albany: State University of New York Press: 68–96.

Shun, Kwong-Loi 1997. *Mencius and Early Chinese Thought*, Stanford, CA: Stanford University Press.

Slingerland, Edward 2003. *Effortless Action: Wu-wei as Conceptual Metaphor and Spiritual Ideal in Early China*, New York: Oxford University Press.

A Source Book in Chinese Philosophy 1963, trans. Wing-tsit Chan, Princeton: Princeton University Press.

Wong, David B. 2005. Zhuangzi and the Obsession with Being Right, *History of Philosophy Quarterly* 22: 91–107.

Wu, Kuang-Ming 1982. *Chuang Tzu: World Philosopher at Play*, New York: Crossroad Publishing Company and Scholars Press.

Yearley, Lee 1982. Three Ways of Being Religious, *Philosophy East and West* 32: 439–51.

Yearley, Lee 1983. The Perfected Person in the Radical Chuang-Tzu, in *Experimental Essays on Chuang-Tzu*, ed. Victor H. Mair, Honolulu, Hawai'i: University of Hawai'i Press: 125–39.

Yearley, Lee 1996. Zhuangzi's Understanding of Skillfulness and the Ultimate Spiritual State, in *Essays on Skepticism, Relativism and Ethics in the* Zhuangzi, ed. Philip Ivanhoe and Paul Kjellberg, Albany: State University of New York Press: 152–82.

Zhuangzi: The Essential Writings with Selections from Traditional Commentaries 2009, trans. Brook Ziporyn, Indianapolis: Hackett.

Zhuangzi Yinde 《莊子引得》 (*A Concordance to Zhuangzi*) 1956, ed. Ye Hong, 洪業主編, Harvard-Yenching Institute Sinological Index Series, Supplement #20 (哈佛燕京學社引得特刊第20號, 哈佛燕京學社引得編纂處), Cambridge, MA: Harvard University Press.

4

ARISTOTLE AS SYSTEMATIC PHILOSOPHER

Essence, Necessity, and Explanation in Theory and Practice

David Bronstein

1. Introduction

That Aristotle was a great philosopher is beyond question. He wrote at great length and in great depth about every major area of philosophy. His works have influenced countless philosophers through the centuries right up to today. The history of philosophy since Plato may be a series of footnotes to Plato (Whitehead 1978: 39), but no figure has shaped their content more than Aristotle. The question is not whether he was a great philosopher but only whether he or Plato was the greatest.

Still, what might an argument for Aristotle's greatness as a philosopher look like? There are of course many ways to go, but my approach will be to highlight the *systematic* nature of his thinking—by which I mean its high degree of unity, consistency, and coherence. Systematicity is one of the ways in which Aristotle might be thought to be superior to Plato, whose works, as later Platonists showed, was systematizable but not yet systematic. It's not systematicity alone that made Aristotle great; rather, it is that, combined with the depth of his ideas, the rigor with were which he defended them, the astonishing variety of domains across which he applied them, and their continued relevance to philosophy today. In this chapter I hope to illustrate in some small way all of these features of his thinking, with systematicity as the guiding thread.

In the *Metaphysics* Aristotle says that Socrates 'sought the universal in ethical matters and fixed thought for the first time on definitions' (987b1–4).[1] Aristotle is evidently referring to Socrates's practice, as represented in Plato's dialogues, of pursuing the 'what is it?' (*ti esti*) question about the virtues. My claim is that one way of appreciating Aristotle's greatness is by seeing that he pursued the 'what is it?' question more systematically, more fruitfully, and across a wider range of domains than any other philosopher in history. Appreciating this feature of Aristotle's thought requires seeing that, in his view, answering the 'what is it?' question is the same as answering the 'why is it?' question—that defining and explaining, seeking something's essence and seeking its cause, are somehow the same.

Philosophy, for Aristotle, begins in wonder that things are so and ends in wonder that they could be otherwise (*Metaphysics* 982b12–983a21). We move from the first state to the second by pursuing the explanations[2] of the phenomena that initially provoke our wonder: the incommensurability of the diagonal of the square with its side (*Metaphysics* 983a15–16), the speed and voracity of dolphins (*History of Animals* 591b30), and so on. The explanations we aim to provide start from first principles, which are 'the unexplained explainers' (Lennox 2010: 352) in a given domain. These first principles include definitions, which Aristotle takes to be statements of the essences of certain basic kinds of thing.[3] For example, the best (but not the only) sorts of explanation in biology start from the definitions of animal kinds. This is why philosophy ends in a state of wonder that things could be otherwise: once we grasp the causal explanations of the phenomena that initially provoke our wonder, we understand that they occur as they do, not by chance, but because of the essences of the objects they involve. We understand that things must be as they are because of what they essentially are, and therefore nothing would surprise us more, Aristotle says, than if things should turn out otherwise (*Metaphysics* 983a11–21).

My main thesis is that Aristotle's sustained commitment to essence-based explanation provides a clear and compelling example of the systematic nature of his thinking. I shall first argue that in the *Posterior Analytics* Aristotle developed the Socratic 'what is it?' question into a deep and powerful philosophical theory of the connections among essence, necessity, and explanation. I shall then argue that in his practice of essence-based explanation in his biological works, especially the *Parts of Animals*, Aristotle implemented this theoretical program. In other words, my aim is to show that one of Aristotle's greatest achievements as what we would now call a philosopher—the theory of science put forward in the *Posterior Analytics*—is systematically connected to one of his greatest achievements as what we would now call a scientist—the causal explanations of animal kinds put forward in the biological works.[4] I say 'what we would now call' a philosopher and a scientist because, for Aristotle, these are different aspects of one and the same activity: the pursuit of wisdom sparked by our sense of wonder at the world.

2. The Socratic Background

Aristotle inherited from Socrates via Plato the 'what is it?' question. Although Socrates is rarely satisfied with his interlocutors' answers, it is clear what he is looking for: in stating, for example, what virtue is, Socrates wants his interlocutor to identify the one feature because of which all and only virtuous things are so.[5] As he says in the *Meno* (72c6–d1):

> The same is true in the case of the virtues. Even if they are many and various, all of them have one and the same form which makes them virtues, and it is right to look to this when one is asked to make clear what virtue is.[6]

We can discern three conditions here: an extensional condition (the answer must apply to all and only virtuous things); a unity condition (it must identify a single feature or unified group of features shared by all and only virtuous things); and a causal condition (it must identify the cause because of which all and only virtuous things are so). So, for Socrates, it is not enough that an answer to the question 'what is virtue?' identify necessary and sufficient conditions for anything's being virtuous; it must also identify the unified causal grounds of anything's being so. That these two requirements are different is brought out in the *Euthyphro* (9e–11b), where Socrates rejects Euthyphro's definition of piety as what is loved by the gods, by arguing that something is pious if and only if, but not *because*, it is loved by the gods.

Aristotle accepts these conditions on successful answers to the 'what is it?' question and develops them into a theory of scientific explanation. I shall work my way toward this theory, starting with a general overview of Aristotle's philosophy of science. The main thought at which we are driving is that an essence—what we seek when we ask the 'what is it?' question—is the cause of the object of which it is the essence in a strikingly rich and interesting way.

3. The Four Causes

In the *Posterior Analytics* Aristotle says that to seek what something is (the essence) and to seek why something is (the cause) are the same.[7] Aristotle, as is well-known, thinks that there are four different types of cause one should mention in answering the 'why?' question (*Physics* 2.3 and 2.7). For example, if we want to explain why a certain statue of Aphrodite exists, we should mention the material cause, which is the matter (say, bronze) of which it is made; the formal cause, which is its shape or form; the efficient cause, which is the sculptor who made it (or perhaps the art of sculpting that she possesses); and the final cause, which is the end or purpose for the sake of which she made it. When we move from artifacts to natural objects, Aristotle thinks that the formal, efficient, and final causes often coincide (*Physics* 198a24–7). The formal cause of a human being, for example, is the essence specified in its definition: say, being a rational animal. The efficient cause, according to Aristotle's theory of biogenesis, is the father who transmits the human form and essence, which he possesses, to the matter provided by the mother and thereby produces an offspring. The final cause is the good performance of the function specified in the human essence: living a flourishing life of rational activity. Although all three causes often coincide, it is clear that the ground of their unity is the formal cause, the essence. For, in our example, it is in virtue of this that the father is able to produce an offspring (provided other conditions are met, of course) and that the human end is what it is. In addition, Aristotle thinks that form or essence is the cause of matter and not vice versa: natural objects have the material properties that they have because of their essences; they do not have the essences that they have because of their material properties. In other words, and as we shall now see in more detail, Aristotle's theory privileges formal causation—that is, essence-based causal explanation.[8] Or, again, the 'what?' and the 'why?' questions are for him tightly interlinked.

4. Subjects and Properties

Aristotle's scientific inquirer pursues the 'what?' and 'why?' questions about certain objects. Central to Aristotle's philosophy of science is the distinction between two types of object: subjects and properties. In the *Categories* (2a35–2b7), Aristotle indicates that everything that exists is either a 'primary substance' or a property of one. Primary substances are individuals, such as Socrates and this horse, that are subjects of properties and not properties of any subject. A property, unlike a primary substance, depends for its existence on at least one other object: namely, the primary substance(s) of which it is a property. Primary substances are grouped into nested natural kinds, which I shall call 'subject-kinds': for example, Socrates is a member of the human species, which belongs in the genus animal, which belongs in the category of substance.

The objects about which the Aristotelian scientist asks the 'what?' and 'why?' questions are the subject-kinds of which primary substances are members, and not the primary substances themselves, and certain properties of these subject-kinds. For example, the Aristotelian scientist is interested in questions such as 'what is a human being?' and 'why do all human beings have two legs?' and not 'what is Socrates?' or 'why does Socrates have two legs?' The properties of interest to scientists are the *necessary* properties of subject-kinds: for example, triangle's property of having interior angles equal to the sum of two right angles and human being's property of having two legs. For Aristotle, a property can belong necessarily to a subject-kind without belonging to all of the individual members of that subject-kind. For example, having two legs is a necessary property of the kind *human being* but human beings have two legs only, as Aristotle says, 'for the most part' (*Posterior Analytics* 1.30). This is true of the subject-kinds studied by the natural sciences, such as biology. By contrast, the necessary properties of the subject-kinds studied by the mathematical sciences, such as geometry and astronomy, belong to all of their individual members without exception. What makes a kind's property necessary, as we shall see in a moment, is not whether it belongs to all of the kind's individual members but rather its connection to the kind's essence.

5. Per Se Accidents

So far, we have seen that the Aristotelian scientist is interested in subject-kinds and their necessary properties and that these are the objects about which she asks the 'what?' and 'why?' questions. To understand Aristotle's theory of science, we also need to see that he draws a further distinction within the necessary properties of a subject-kind between those that belong to it essentially and those that do not. In other words, while most philosophers today regard all necessary properties of an object as essential properties of it, Aristotle disagrees: all essential properties of a subject-kind are necessary properties of it, but not all necessary properties of a subject-kind are essential properties of it (*Posterior Analytics* 1.4 and 1.6). Aristotle calls the necessary but non-essential properties of a subject-kind its 'per se accidents' (*Posterior Analytics* 75b1, 83b19–20). (Traditionally, they are also called 'necessary accidents' and 'propria'.) For example, Aristotle thinks that the following are both necessary properties of triangle: being a three-sided closed plane figure and having interior angles equal to the sum of two right angles. However, he thinks that the first is an essential property of triangle and the second is a per se accident. Similarly, being a rational animal is an essential property of human being and being capable of speech is a per se accident (let's suppose).[9]

Furthermore, Aristotle thinks that the essential properties of a subject-kind are *causes* of all of its per se accidents, while they themselves do not have causes (*Posterior Analytics* 1.2–6, 2.13 (96b15–25), *Metaphysics* 1025a30–3). Triangles have interior angles equal to the sum of two right angles *because* they are three-sided closed plane figures; human beings are capable of speech *because* they are rational animals. Thus, the per se accidents of a subject-kind S are those necessary properties of S that belong to it not as part of its essence but because of it. On the other hand, the essential properties of S—those properties that constitute the essence and that we find when we successfully answer the question 'what is S?'—are those necessary properties of S that are causes of other properties (the per se accidents) but do not themselves have causes: they are the uncaused causes, the unexplained explainers. Thus, the per se accidents of a subject-kind are among the explananda in a science and its essential properties are among the primary explanantia.

6. Cause, Essence, and Necessity

Aristotle has a deep and powerful view about the connections among essence, necessity, and explanation, one that was historically influential, especially in the medieval period, and continues to influence philosophical debates today in at least two different ways. First, some contemporary philosophers have taken up Aristotle's view that central to the concept of essence is its role as the cause or explanation of other properties of the object of which it is the essence.[10] Second, Aristotle thinks that something is a necessary property of a subject-kind *because* it belongs to it either as part of its essence or because of it. He therefore differs from the majority of contemporary philosophers, but has also inspired the view of a minority of them, in making essence conceptually prior to necessity:[11] he understands what it is for a property to be necessary in terms of what it is for a property to be essential (and not vice versa).[12] And, as I shall now explain, he understands what it is for a property to be essential in terms of what it is for a property to be a cause (and not vice versa)—but a cause in a different way than we have seen so far. So, while essence is conceptually prior to necessity, cause is conceptually prior to essence. Here conceptual priority tracks metaphysical priority: what makes it the case that a property is necessary is its connection to essence, and what makes it the case that a property is essential is that it is a certain sort of cause.

Aristotle's view of the connection between essence and cause is captured by his oft-repeated slogan in the *Posterior Analytics* that to seek and know what something is is to seek and know why it is.[13] The thought that the essence of an object is a cause—that the what and the why are somehow the same—was already present, as we saw above, in Socrates's pursuit of the 'what is it?' question. Knowing what virtue is will allow us, among other things, to explain why any particular virtuous thing is so. Aristotle accepts this requirement on essence, but he goes considerably further. For when he says that what a subject-kind is, is the same as why it is, he means, in the first instance, that the essence of a subject-kind is the cause because of which it is *the very thing that it is*.[14] Indeed, this is what makes it the case that an essential property is such: it is one of the things in virtue of which the subject-kind of which it is an essential property is the very thing that it is. As such, an essence is causally prior to the subject-kind of which it is the essence. So it's not that a subject-kind and its essence are identical (for then something would be prior to itself, which is impossible), and it's not only that the essence gives us necessary and sufficient conditions for anything's being a member of that subject-kind (although it does do that). Aristotle's thought is that a subject-kind and its essence are distinct entities that stand to each other in an intrinsic and primitive causal relation: the essence is the cause in virtue of which the subject-kind is just what it is; the essence *makes* the subject-kind just what it is.

In order to appreciate the complexity and sophistication of Aristotle's position, we need to distinguish carefully among three different ways in which the essence of a subject-kind is a cause—three different ways in which the what and the why are the same. Consider the following three claims, each of which captures a distinct causal role that Aristotle assigns to the essence E of a subject-kind S:

1. E is the cause in virtue of which all and only Ss are so.
2. E is the ultimate cause of all of S's per se accidents.
3. E makes S the very thing that it is.

The causal role Socrates attributes to essences is captured by 1. Aristotle attributes not only the two additional causal roles captured by 2 and 3, he also thinks that 3 is primary, for it is that in virtue of which the other two hold.

Suppose, for example, that being a rational animal is the human essence. Aristotle's view, expressed by 3, is that being a rational animal is what makes the natural kind *human being* the very thing that it is. It's true that being a rational animal is the cause of the fact that any individual human being is one—but that is the claim expressed by 1, not by 3. That the two thoughts are distinct can be seen from the fact that 3 is explanatorily prior to 1: it's because E makes S the very thing that it is, that E is the cause in virtue of which all and only Ss are so; it's not because E is the cause in virtue of which all and only Ss are so, that E makes S the very thing that it is. For example, it's because being H_2O makes the natural kind *water* the very thing that it is, that being H_2O is the cause in virtue of which any token instance of water is so; it's not because being H_2O is the cause in virtue of which any token instance of water is so, that being H_2O makes the natural kind *water* the very thing that it is.

Crucially, the same holds true for the relationship between 2 and 3. It's because E makes S the very thing that it is, that E is the ultimate cause of all of S's per se accidents. It's not because E is the ultimate cause of all of S's per se accidents, that E makes S the very thing that it is. For example, suppose that human beings are capable of speech because they are rational animals. It's because human beings are made what they are by being rational animals, that being a rational animal is the cause of their capacity for speech. It's not because being rational animals is the cause of their capacity for speech, that humans are made what they are by being rational animals.

Here it is useful to distinguish between an epistemological and ontological criterion for being an essence. It's true that if E is the ultimate cause of all of S's per se accidents, then this is very strong evidence that E is S's essence and thus that E makes S the very thing that it is.[15] But it doesn't follow that E is S's essence and the cause that makes S the very thing that it is *because* E is the ultimate cause of all of S's per se accidents. Aristotle's view has it the other way around.

In sum, Aristotle has a powerful and still relevant account of the connections among essence, necessity, and explanation. A subject-kind's essential properties include some but not all of its necessary properties, the remainder of which (the per se accidents) belong to it not as part of its essence but because of it. In addition, the causal connection between a subject-kind's essence and its per se accidents holds true because of the prior and more fundamental connection between the subject-kind and its essence. In other words, Aristotle's theory includes a compelling thesis about the *fundamentality* of essence. Some necessary properties of an object are more fundamental than others because they are the causes of the others; and these more fundamental necessary properties—the essential ones—enjoy this priority over the others because they stand in a prior and more fundamental relation to the object of which they are the essence: that of making the object just what it is.

7. Demonstration

For Aristotle, the essence of a subject-kind is both explanatorily basic and explanatorily powerful: there is no cause because of which it belongs to the subject-kind of which it is the essence, and it is among the causes because of which other properties (the per se accidents) belong to it. The Aristotelian scientist's main activity is seeking the causes of a subject-kind's per se accidents with the goal of explanatorily linking these necessary but non-essential properties to the kind's necessary and essential ones.

Aristotle's technical term for this activity is 'demonstration' (*apodeixis*). A demonstration is a sound deductive argument in which the premises state the causal explanation of the fact stated in the conclusion (*Posterior Analytics* 1.2). More specifically, a demonstration is a syllogism that proves that a property belongs to one of the subject-kinds studied by a science and reveals the cause of its belonging. These demonstrable properties of a subject-kind are its per se accidents.[16]

In the *Posterior Analytics* Aristotle discusses two main types of demonstration: in the first, the cause of the connection between the subject-kind and the property is an essential fact about the subject-kind; in the second, the cause is an essential fact about the property. Here is an example of a demonstration of the first type:[17]

(A) Being non-twinkling in the night sky belongs to all (B) celestial bodies that are near the earth
(B) Being a celestial body that is near the earth belongs to all (C) planets
(A) Being non-twinkling in the night sky belongs to all (C) planets

And here is an example of a demonstration of the second type:[18]

(A) Thunder belongs to all (B) atmospheric fire-quenchings
(B) Atmospheric fire-quenching belongs to all (C) clouds
(A) Thunder belongs to all (C) clouds[19]

In each case, the middle 'B' term signifies the cause of the connection between the items signified by the major (property) 'A' and minor (subject) 'C' terms:

planets are non-twinkling because they are near the earth; thunder occurs in the clouds because of atmospheric fire-quenching. In the first demonstration, being near the earth is an essential property of the subject, planet. In the second, being such as to involve atmospheric fire-quenching is an essential property of the property, thunder.

The fact that in the second demonstration the cause is an essential property of the property points to a crucial part of Aristotle's theory: demonstrable properties—the per se accidents—themselves have essences, these essences are the causes because of which they belong to their subject-kinds, and these causes are represented as the middle terms in demonstrations of the second type. As Aristotle says, 'the middle term is a definitional account of the major term, which is why all the sciences come about through definition' (*Posterior Analytics* 99a21–3). These will be important thoughts for us in the remainder of this chapter.

But, first, a caveat. Although the two types of demonstration differ according to whether the cause is an essential property of the subject-kind or of the demonstrable property, not all premises of demonstrations are definitional. (Recall that a definition, for Aristotle, is a statement of the essence of a thing.) For some premises may be demonstrable (and no definitional proposition is demonstrable) and others may be indemonstrable but not definitional. In the former case, Aristotle may think that the propositions are demonstrated from premises, at least some of which are definitional. The first (i.e., major) premise of the first demonstration and the second (i.e., minor) premise of the second may be examples of demonstrable premises of this type. I return to this in the next section.

8. Aristotle's Theory of Essence-Based Explanation

It is not immediately clear, however, how the claims I presented in the previous section fit together. For it seems as though Aristotle is committed to the view that the cause because of which a per se accident belongs to its subject-kind is both the essence of the subject-kind (as in the first type of demonstration) and the essence of the per se accident (as in the second). But since a subject-kind and any of its per se accidents are distinct objects with different essences, it seems as though each per se accident has two causes. And this raises the worry of causal over-determination. Put differently, in the *Posterior Analytics* Aristotle seems committed to the following two claims:

(i) Each per se accident P of a subject-kind S belongs to S because of S's essence.
(ii) Each per se accident P of a subject-kind S belongs to S because of P's essence.

I now wish to show that the two claims are not only consistent with each other, but they combine to form a coherent and compelling theory of scientific explanation.

For Aristotle, (i) should be understood to mean that the essence of a subject-kind is *a* cause and the *ultimate* cause of all of its per se accidents, but not necessarily the *only* cause, and (ii) should be understood to mean that the essence of a per se accident is *a* cause and the *proximate* cause because of which it belongs to its subject-kind, but not necessarily the *only* cause. Together, the two claims should be understood to mean that a per se accident belongs to its subject-kind because of a chain of causes in which the per se accident's essence and the subject-kind's essence are the crucial links.

Take thunder. The demonstration indicates that the proximate cause of the fact that there is thunder in the clouds is that there is atmospheric fire-quenching in the clouds. However, this cannot be the full causal story. Atmospheric fire-quenching must be either an essential property of clouds or a demonstrable property of them. Since it seems obvious that it is not essential, it must be demonstrable. So there is some cause because of which there is atmospheric fire-quenching in the clouds. Aristotle's commitment to (i) indicates that this cause is either an essential property of the clouds or an additional demonstrable property (a per se accident) of them. If it is essential, the causal chain has ended in a way consistent with (i). If the property is demonstrable, Aristotle's commitment to (i) indicates that the causal chain will eventually end in some essential property of the clouds. Since thunder belongs to the clouds because of thunder's essence, which belongs to the clouds either directly or indirectly because of the clouds' essence, thunder belongs to the clouds indirectly because of the clouds' essence. The essences of thunder and of the clouds are, respectively, the proximate and ultimate causes because of which thunder belongs to the clouds.[20] Aristotle, then, is not committed to causal over-determination but rather to the transitivity of essence-based causal explanation: if P belongs to S directly because of P's essence, and P's essence belongs to S directly or indirectly because of S's essence, then P belongs to S indirectly because of S's essence.[21]

Aristotle's approach to essence-based causal explanation reveals an important aspect of his account of the connection between essence and necessity. The per se accidents of a subject-kind are not logical consequences of its essence.[22] From the fact that human beings are essentially rational animals, it doesn't follow logically that they are capable of speech; from the fact that triangles are essentially three-sided closed plane figures, it doesn't follow logically that they have interior angles equal to the sum of two right angles. The core of Aristotle's theory is his claim that the essences of subject-kinds are explanatorily basic and explanatorily powerful. However, Aristotle recognizes that these essences *alone* cannot account for all of the per se accidents. His thought, then, is that, while facts about the essences of subject-kinds are explanatorily powerful, they are not *all* powerful. In order for a subject-kind's essence to link up with its per se accidents, other facts are needed. We can see Aristotle's systematic commitment to essence-based explanation in his claim that at least some of these other facts are facts about the essences of the per se accidents themselves.

9. Putting Theory Into Practice: *Parts of Animals*

I have argued that in the *Posterior Analytics* Aristotle presents a powerful and influential theory of the connections among essence, necessity, and explanation. The theory's central features are as follows:

1. There is a distinction between a subject-kind's necessary, essential properties and its necessary, non-essential ones—the 'per se accidents'.
2. The essence of a subject-kind is the ultimate cause of all of its per se accidents.
3. Each per se accident has an essence and this is the proximate cause because of which it belongs to its subject-kind.

I now want to argue that Aristotle's commitment to these claims is more than theoretical: he systematically implements them in his scientific works. I shall use the *Parts of Animals* as an illustration. I shall first argue that in the introductory sections of the text Aristotle distinguishes between the essential properties of an animal kind and certain necessary but non-essential properties, and that he thinks that the essences of the animal kinds are explanatorily powerful in the way we would expect, given the theory of the *Posterior Analytics*. I shall then argue that in the rest of the work it becomes clear that these essences are not *all* powerful. The ideal form of explanation to which the *Parts of Animals* aspires is one in which a certain part (for example, the lung) is shown to belong to a certain kind of animal both because of the animal's essence and because of the part's essence. More specifically, in the simplest form of explanation, an animal of a certain kind K, in virtue of its essence E, requires a part that performs function F, and it is the essence of a certain part P to perform F, from which it follows that the Ks have P.

In *Parts of Animals* 1.1 Aristotle outlines three modes of explanation that he will use (640a33–b1):

> Hence it would be best to say that, (a) since this is what it is to be a human being (*tout' ēn to anthrōpō(i) einai*), because of this it has these things; for it cannot be without these parts. If one cannot say this, one should say the next best thing, i.e. either that (b) in general it cannot be otherwise, or that (c) at least it is good thus.[23]

The following is a plausible reconstruction of the three modes of explanation Aristotle outlines.[24] The two central concepts involved are essence and necessity.

The first mode of explanation, which I've labeled (a), involves what Aristotle calls 'conditional necessity': if an animal of kind K with essence E is (to come) to be, then it must (come to) have material parts P_1, P_2, and so forth. For example, if a human being is (to come) to be and a human being is essentially capable of perception (among other things), then it must (come to) have such-and-such sense-organs. Human beings have such-and-such sense-organs by (conditional) necessity because they are essentially capable of perception. This is a teleological mode of explanation that involves essence and necessity.[25]

The second mode of explanation, which I've labeled (b), involves what commentators call 'material necessity': an animal of kind K has material part P because P is an effect necessitated by interactions among materials present during the animal's generation, and P is neither conditionally necessary for the animal to (come to) be nor serves a function beneficial to it. For example, Aristotle thinks that the horns of deer are useless (663a8–11) and even harmful (which is why shedding them is beneficial, 663b12–14). However, they are materially necessary: in virtue of being large bony animals, a surplus of earthen material accumulates during their generation and 'flows of necessity to the animal's upper region' where it becomes horns (663b29–35). This is a non-teleological mode of explanation that involves necessity but not essence.

Finally, there is the mode of explanation (labeled (c)) that appeals to the good: an animal of kind K has part P because P contributes to the well-being of the Ks, which is determined by their essence E, although P is not conditionally necessary for the Ks to be E. For example, Aristotle thinks that the kidney is present in animals that have it 'not because of [conditional] necessity, but for the sake of the good and doing well' (670b23–4). In particular, the kidney helps the bladder better perform its function (670b24–7). Since the kidney is there for the sake of the bladder, which is there by conditional necessity (670b32–a9), the explanation of the kidney goes back to the essence of the animals that have it, even though, again, it is not conditionally necessary. So this is a teleological mode of explanation that involves essence but not necessity.[26]

In our passage, Aristotle indicates that the 'best' mode of explanation, which he also calls 'the mode of demonstration . . . in natural science' (639b30–640a2; see also 642a6–13), involves conditional necessity. This is the type of necessity that attaches to those of an animal's material parts that are required on the condition that the animal exist and achieve a certain end or fulfill a certain function, which end or function is specified in the animal's definition and is thus identical to or at least part of the animal's essence. What should strike us in light of our discussion of the *Posterior Analytics* is that Aristotle here invokes the distinction between the essence of an animal kind and those necessary properties that belong to it not as part of its essence but because of it. That is, the conditionally necessitated material parts of an animal kind are among its per se accidents. Aristotle indicates, then, that the best mode of explanation in biology is to show that a given animal kind must have a given part because of that animal kind's essence.

However, we cannot move immediately from the essence of an animal kind to its material parts. For those parts, like per se accidents in general, are not logical consequences of the essence. Other explanatory principles are needed. What the *Posterior Analytics* leads us to expect is that these other explanatory principles will include the essences of the parts themselves. This expectation is richly met by Aristotle's practice of explanation in the *Parts of Animals*. Indeed, references to the essences of animal *kinds* are relatively rare in the explanatory sections of the work (books 2–4).[27] Much more abundant are references to the essences of animal *parts*.[28] Aristotle's principal question about each part is: what is it? Here, as in the *Posterior Analytics*, the 'what is it?' question is equivalent to the 'why is it?' question—that is, it is equivalent to the question 'why does this part belong to the animal kind(s) to which it characteristically belongs?' In addition, the 'what?' and 'why?' questions for each part are answered by specifying the part's function (*ergon*): what it does, how it contributes to the realization of the animal's essence and (therefore) to the animal's well-being. What I hope to show by way of two examples is, as I said above, that the ideal form of explanation to which *Parts of Animals* 2–4 aspires is one in which both the essence of the animal kind and the essence of the part are causes.

10. First Example: Flesh

Aristotle's discussion of flesh offers a relatively straightforward illustration of this pattern of explanation. He says:

> Next we need to examine the other uniform parts, and first of all flesh, in those animals which have flesh, and its analogue in the other animals. This is clear even from our account; for we define animal by the possession of perception, and primary in this account is the primary mode of perception. This is touch, and it is of touch that such a part is the sense-organ. (653b19–24)

Since all animals are essentially perceivers, and the basic mode of perception of which all perceivers are capable is touch, and all modes of perception require a sense-organ, animals require a sense-organ for touch. And since flesh (or its analogue) is essentially the sense-organ for touch, Aristotle concludes that all animals have—as a matter of conditional necessity, in order for them to be the very things that they are—flesh (or its analogue).[29]

So, flesh (or its analogue) belongs to all animals both because of what animals essentially are and because of what flesh essentially is. The essence of flesh explains, in turn, other features of it, including its material nature as soft tissue. For flesh has the material properties required for it to fulfill its function. This is crucial: for Aristotle, flesh has the material properties that it has because it is essentially the sense-organ for touch; it is not essentially the sense-organ for touch because it has the material properties that it has. This follows from Aristotle's commitment to the causal priority of form over matter, or, as we might say, the primacy of essence-based causal explanation: in general, animals have the material properties that they have because of their essences; it's not the case that animals have the essences that they have because of their material properties (645b14–21).

11. Second Example: The Lung

The following passage about the lung provides a second and somewhat more complex illustration of Aristotle's approach (668b33–669a6):

> A certain kind of animal has a lung because it is a land-dweller. For it is necessary for its heat to be cooled, and the blooded animals must be cooled from without; for they are hotter. (Those that are not blooded are able to cool themselves by their inborn breath.) And it is necessary for cooling from without to be either by water or by air. This is why none of the fish have a lung, but instead of this gills, as has been said in the works on respiration; for fish cool themselves by means of water, while the breathers do so by means of air, which is why all the breathers have a lung.

Aristotle's aim is to explain why a certain nameless kind of animal has a lung. Let's call them 'animals of kind *K*'. Aristotle mentions two properties that belong essentially to the *K*s and that feature in the explanation of why they have a lung: they are land-dwellers and they are blooded. A few lines later, he mentions the function (and thus the essence) of the lung: to be an instrument for breathing (669a13). These facts combine to form the following explanation. The *K*s, being essentially blooded, are, in virtue of blood's hot nature, necessarily hot (670a20–1). And since animals cannot survive if they become excessively hot, animals that are essentially blooded require, as a matter of conditional necessity, a means of being cooled from outside. Since the *K*s are, in addition, essentially land-dwelling, the only means of external cooling available to them is taking in and expelling air—that is, breathing. (By contrast, the blooded water-dwellers—i.e., the fish—cool themselves by means of water, using instead of the lung the functionally analogous part—gills.) And since, finally, the lung is essentially an instrument for breathing, animals of kind *K* have, as a matter of conditional necessity, a lung. So the lung is a conditionally necessitated per se accident of animals of kind *K*, an accident that belongs to them both because of essential facts about the *K*s and because of essential facts about the lung. This is the *Posterior Analytics* theory in action. Aristotle's explanation relies on several premises that do not obviously express essential facts about animal kinds or their parts. But this, too, is consistent with the approach we see recommended in the *Posterior Analytics*: facts about essences are primary explainers in a science, but they are not the only ones.

Aristotle's explanation of the lung also illustrates his thesis about the fundamentality of essence. It's because being a blooded land-dweller is the essence of animals of kind K that being a blooded land-dweller is a cause of the fact that animals of kind K have a lung. It's not because being a blooded land-dweller is a cause of the fact that animals of kind K have a lung that being a blooded land-dweller is the essence of animals of kind K.

The presence of the lung has certain downstream causal consequences that can be traced back to the essence of the animals of kind K. Here, too, we can see the *Posterior Analytics* theory in action. Aristotle's explanation of the epiglottis in *Parts of Animals* 3.3 is a striking example. Animals with a lung require, as a matter of conditional necessity, a windpipe and a larynx in order for air to be transported to and from the lung in inhalation and exhalation (664a17–35). Now, air enters the body through the mouth, but so does food. In addition, because of the position of the heart and lung—a position explained in a conditionally necessary manner by their respective functions (and perhaps by other principles too) (665a10–26)—the gut is at some distance from the mouth (664a24–6). This creates a need for the esophagus, which has to be behind the larynx and windpipe (664b2–4), again because of the position of the heart and lung (665a10–26), and whose essential function is to be the channel through which nourishment moves from the mouth to the gut (664a20–1). So the esophagus is, we might say, indirectly conditionally necessitated by the essences of the animal kinds that have them, plus other relevant facts.[30] But then, because the esophagus is behind the windpipe, and because the mouth is the place where both air and food enter, there is a risk that, if the animal inhales while taking in nourishment, the food will slip into the windpipe, producing coughing and choking (664b20–32). This creates (again in an indirectly conditionally necessary manner) the need for the epiglottis, whose function is to compensate for 'the inefficiency of the position of the windpipe' by ensuring that food passes over it and enters the esophagus (665a7–9). So Aristotle's explanation moves from (1) the essence of animals of kind K, to (2) the lung, to (3) the larynx and windpipe, to (4) the esophagus, to (5) the epiglottis.[31] Since the explanation starts with the essence of the relevant animal kind, and since the explanation *only* starts with that essence and also at each step includes, but is not restricted to, essential facts about the parts that are explained, the promise of the *Posterior Analytics* seems richly fulfilled.

12. Conclusion

I have argued that Aristotle presents and puts into practice a deep, powerful, and influential theory of the connections among essence, necessity, and explanation. Two features of this theory are worth highlighting in closing. First, there is the conceptual and metaphysical priority of essence over necessity and explanation over essence: what makes it the case that a property of an object is necessary is that it belongs to it as part of or because of its essence; and what makes it the case that a property is essential is that it is one of the things in virtue of which the object is the very thing that it is. Second, there is the explanatory power of essences: an object's necessary properties include certain non-essential 'per se accidents' each of which belongs to the object because of both the object's essence and the per se accident's essence. The first feature has influenced contemporary attempts at providing a non-modal analysis of the concept of essence.[32] The second feature has influenced current debates about the nature of essential properties.[33] In addition, Aristotle's implementation of this theory in scientific practice is a paradigm of what we might call 'applied philosophy'. The theory and the practice have been hugely, but largely separately, influential in the histories of philosophy and science. I have argued that they are systematically interconnected. This evidence of Aristotle as a systematic philosopher is striking—and it is only the beginning.

Notes

1 Ross's translation in Barnes (1984).
2 Throughout this paper I use 'explanation' in a metaphysically loaded way for a real, mind-independent, causal relation between real, mind-independent things. I sometimes use 'causal explanation' to bring this out. I also use 'explanation' for the activity of providing explanations in this metaphysically loaded sense (e.g., 'Aristotle's practice of explanation').
3 This is worth emphasizing: the primary sense of 'definition' for Aristotle is not a statement of the meaning of a word but rather a statement of the essence of a thing (*Posterior Analytics* 93b29, *Topics* 101b38–102a1).
4 The connections between Aristotle's theory of science in the *Posterior Analytics* and his practice of science in the biological works is the subject of vigorous debate among scholars. See, e.g., Barnes (1975); Gotthelf and Lennox (1987); Lloyd (1996); Charles (2000); Lennox (2001b); Leunissen (2010); and Gotthelf (2012a).
5 By 'virtuous things' I mean the particular virtues (justice, wisdom, etc.), virtuous persons, and virtuous actions.
6 Grube's translation in Cooper and Hutchinson (1997).
7 See especially 2.2 and 2.8.
8 For a recent and interesting examination of Aristotle's theory of the formal cause, see Ferejohn (2013).
9 I limit my discussion of necessary properties to what Aristotle regards as essential properties and per se accidents and omit discussion of generic or logical (and apparently trivial) necessities such as being self-identical or being such that there are infinitely many prime numbers, for Aristotle seems to show no interest in them. What he could or should say about them is a different matter that I cannot take up here.
10 See, e.g., Brody (1967, 1972) and Gorman (2005, 2014). According to Brody (1967: 445), 'it is the properties that we use in explaining other properties that are said to be essential'. According to Gorman, an essential property is a property of an object that is not 'explained' (2005) or 'supported' (2014) by any other property of that object and is thus 'foundational' (2014); in addition, Gorman thinks that essential properties will normally explain other properties (but, he adds, this is not required by his account). (Note that Brody's and Gorman's essence-bearers are particular objects whereas Aristotle's are natural kinds.) These philosophers agree with Aristotle in another important

respect: although explaining other properties is central to being an essential property, Aristotle denies that this gives us the answer to the question 'what makes it the case that a property is essential?' Aristotle, Brody, and Gorman all offer different answers to this question. As I state in the main text, Aristotle's answer is that the property is one of the things in virtue of which the object of which it is a property is the very thing that it is. Kung (1977) and Charles (2000) provide useful comparisons between Aristotle's theory and contemporary forms of essentialism. Their interpretations of Aristotle differ significantly from each other and from mine.

11 See Fine (1994) for a seminal and self-consciously Aristotelian attempt to understand modality in terms of essence (and not vice versa). See Koslicki (2012) for an excellent comparison of Fine's and Aristotle's views. The interpretation of Aristotle that I present in the main text has much in common with Koslicki's reading of him.

12 This needs qualification: my claim is that Aristotle understands what it is for a *certain kind of* property to be necessary in terms of what it is for a property to be essential—namely, the kind of property that belongs to a subject-kind and whose belonging to that subject-kind is of scientific interest or admits of scientific knowledge. Aristotle does not, in general, define necessity in terms of essence or reduce necessity to essence. For example, in *Metaphysics* 5, his philosophical lexicon, he discusses the different senses of 'necessary', and none of them has to do with essence (1015a20–b15). For an important study of the connections between necessity and essence in Aristotle's logic, see Malink (2013).

13 See especially 2.2 and 2.8. Since, as we saw earlier, there are four different ways of answering the 'why?' question (material, formal, efficient, and final), the slogan should be taken to mean that answering the 'what?' question involves identifying the privileged type of cause among the four—the formal cause.

14 See *Posterior Analytics* 2.2 (90a9–11): 'the cause of the substance (*tēn ousian*) being not this or that but without qualification . . . is the middle term.' The rest of 2.2 makes it clear that 'the middle term' is the essence. So Aristotle thinks that the essence of a substance (subject-kind) is the cause of its 'being not this or that but without qualification'. For a substance (subject-kind) to be 'without qualification', I take it, is for it to be the very thing that it is.

15 See *De Anima* 402b16–403a2.

16 In fact, the per se accidents of a subject-kind are only a subset of its demonstrable properties. For Aristotle likely places an extensional requirement on per se accidents such that P is a per se accident of S only if P belongs to all and only S, and he does not place this requirement on all demonstrable properties. However, for my purposes in this paper we can safely ignore this complication. All of the examples of demonstrable properties that I discuss can plausibly be taken to be per se accidents.

17 See *Posterior Analytics* 1.13.

18 See *Posterior Analytics* 2.8.

19 The second premise and conclusion should be understood to mean that all clouds are susceptible to having atmospheric fire-quenching and thus thunder in them, not that all clouds actually have these things in them at all times.

20 But what about the case where the proximate cause of the per se accident is the essence of the subject-kind, as it seems to be the in first type of demonstration? Aristotle is not clear on this issue, so I can here offer only a few speculative remarks. First, it is important to see that, in the first type of demonstration, the subject-kind's essential property or properties signified by the middle term need not be all of its essential properties. Second, in the second type of demonstration, the per se accident's

essential property or properties signified by the middle term need not be all of its essential properties. (I here ignore any worries that talk of 'properties of properties' might present for Aristotle's theory.) This leaves room for the following possibility: a per se accident *P* belongs to a subject-kind *S* because of some cause *C* that is an essential property both of *P* and of *S*, and *C* is neither the only essential property of *P* nor the only essential property of *S*. (If *A* and *B* are distinct types of object, then *A* and *B* cannot share all of their essential properties in common. A subject-kind and any of its per se accidents are distinct types of object.) That is, in the demonstrations of interest, the subject-kind and the per se accident share at least one and not all of their essential properties in common, and this overlap is the cause because of which the property belongs to the subject. These demonstrations thus mark the meeting point between the essences of the two types of object. If this is right, then it might be that what I have been calling the first type of demonstration should rather be regarded as a species of the second type of demonstration. I plan to develop this line of thought in future work.

21 I defend this interpretation in more detail in Bronstein (2016).
22 Koslicki (2012) argues that this is one of the principal ways in which Aristotle's view differs from Kit Fine's.
23 All translations of the *Parts of Animals* are from Lennox (2001a), occasionally altered without comment. I have also relied on his indispensable commentary.
24 There is a disagreement about how best to interpret this passage: see Cooper (1987); Leunissen (2010); and Gotthelf (2012b). My interpretation comes closest to Leunissen's.
25 See also *Parts of Animals* 639b21–30. Henceforth, all references to Aristotle are to this work.
26 It should be noted that Aristotle's explanations of animal parts are often highly complex and can involve aspects of all three modes of explanation at once: parts that are conditionally necessary also serve the good of the animal, and such parts, in addition to those that merely serve the good and are not conditionally necessary, may be explained partly in terms of material necessity.
27 See Gotthelf (2012b) for a useful discussion of the relevant passages.
28 See, e.g., 648a21, 651b17–19, 652a21–3, 654b4–5, among many other passages.
29 Aristotle's considered view seems to be that flesh is the medium for touch and the sense-organ is contained within it; see 653b24–30, with Lennox's commentary (2001a: 213). This complication need not concern us here.
30 Hence I am inclined to disagree with Lennox's verdict that 'no teleological explanation of the oesophagus is provided' (2001a: 252).
31 This is misleading: Aristotle thinks that not all animals with a lung have an epiglottis, only those that are, in addition, hairy-skinned and neither hard-scaled nor feathered (664b22–5). He says, 'In those that are hard-scaled or feathered, in place of the epiglottis the larynx contracts and opens, in the way that the epiglottis closes and opens up in other animals' (664b25–7). As Aristotle goes on to explain, the connection between being hard-scaled or feathered and lacking an epiglottis is not accidental (664b36–665a6). If these are essential properties of the relevant animals, which they may very well be, then his explanation of the absence of the epiglottis in the animals of kind *K* that lack it would seem to be as thoroughly essence-based as his explanation of the presence of the epiglottis in the animals of kind *K* that have it.
32 See note 10.
33 See note 9.

References

Barnes, Jonathan 1975. Aristotle's Theory of Demonstration, in *Articles on Aristotle, Vol. I: Science*, ed. J. Barnes, M. Schofield, and R. Sorabji, London: Duckworth: 65–87.
Barnes, Jonathan 1984. *The Complete Works of Aristotle*, two vols., Princeton: Princeton University Press.
Brody, Baruch A. 1967. Natural Kinds and Real Essences, *Journal of Philosophy* 64: 431–46.
Brody, Baruch A. 1972. Towards an Aristotelian Theory of Scientific Explanation, *Philosophy of Science* 39: 20–31.
Bronstein, David 2016. *Aristotle on Knowledge and Learning: The Posterior Analytics*, Oxford: Oxford University Press.
Charles, David 2000. *Aristotle on Meaning and Essence*, Oxford: Clarendon Press.
Cooper, John M. 1987. Hypothetical Necessity and Natural Teleology, in *Philosophical Issues in Aristotle's Biology*, ed. A. Gotthelf and J.G. Lennox, Cambridge: Cambridge University Press: 243–74.
Cooper, John M. and Hutchinson, D.S. (eds.) 1997. *Plato: Complete Works*, Indianapolis: Hackett.
Ferejohn, Michael 2013. *Formal Causes: Definition, Explanation, and Primacy in Socratic and Aristotelian Thought*, Oxford: Oxford University Press.
Fine, Kit 1994. Essence and Modality, *Philosophical Perspectives* 8: 1–16.
Gorman, Michael 2005. The Essential and the Accidental, *Ratio* 18: 276–89.
Gorman, Michael 2014. Essentiality as Foundationality, in *Neo-Aristotelian Perspectives in Metaphysics*, ed. D. Novotny and L. Novak, New York: Routledge: 119–37.
Gotthelf, Allan 2012a. *Teleology, First Principles, and Scientific Method in Aristotle's Biology*, Oxford: Oxford University Press.
Gotthelf, Allan 2012b. Notes towards a Study of Substance and Essence in Aristotle's *Parts of Animals* II–IV, in *Teleology, First Principles, and Scientific Method in Aristotle's Biology*, Oxford: Oxford University Press: 217–40.
Gotthelf, Allan and Lennox, James G. (eds.) 1987. *Philosophical Issues in Aristotle's Biology*, Cambridge: Cambridge University Press.
Koslicki, Kathrin 2012. Essence, Necessity, and Explanation, in *Contemporary Aristotelian Metaphysics*, ed. Tuomas E. Tahko, Cambridge: Cambridge University Press: 187–206.
Kung, Joan 1977. Aristotle on Essence and Explanation, *Philosophical Studies* 31: 361–83.
Lennox, James G. 2001a. *Aristotle: On the Parts of Animals I–IV*, translated with commentary, Oxford: Clarendon Press.
Lennox, James G. 2001b. *Aristotle's Philosophy of Biology: Studies in the Origins of Life Science*, Cambridge: Cambridge University Press.
Lennox, James G. 2010. Bios and Explanatory Unity in Aristotle's Biology, in *Definition in Greek Philosophy*, ed. David Charles, Oxford: Oxford University Press: 329–55.
Leunissen, Mariska 2010. *Explanation and Teleology in Aristotle's Science of Nature*, Cambridge: Cambridge University Press.
Lloyd, G.E.R. 1996. *Aristotelian Explorations*, Cambridge: Cambridge University Press.
Malink, Marko. 2013. *Aristotle's Modal Syllogistic*, Cambridge, MA and London: Harvard University Press.
Whitehead, Alfred North 1978. *Process and Reality: An Essay in Cosmology*, New York: Free Press.

5
ATTENTION TO GREATNESS
Buddhaghosa

Jonardon Ganeri

1. How Does a Philosopher Get to Be Great?

This is not the first time I have had occasion to reflect on the question of what makes a philosopher great. I was once asked, in the course of a job interview in a philosophy department, if I *really* believed that there were philosophers in the Indian tradition as great as Plato or Kant. Being young and naïve, I set about answering by providing a description of the philosophical accomplishments of one or two cases. That was, of course, a very ineffective way to handle the question, because what the question really asked was, 'Were there any Indian philosophers who could be counted as great according to standards of greatness defined for and within the European philosophical tradition?' It was like being asked whether India had great composers, the presupposition being that to be a great composer one has to compose symphonies. Evidently, the quest for a classical Indian musician who happened to spring on the world a great symphony is likely to be forlorn, and the comparable quest in the realm of philosophy is no less quixotic. The question, moreover, sought to ensnare me in a trap, one that consists in the following vicious dilemma: either Indian philosophers are making comparable philosophical discoveries to Western philosophers, with comparable philosophical tools and techniques, or else they are not. If the first, then there is no need to study them, since the tools and discoveries are already to hand; if the second, there is no point in studying them, since what they are doing is not philosophy as 'we' understand it. In responding as I did, I merely impaled myself on the first horn of this dilemma.

A greater degree of sensitivity to the issues than I encountered among my erstwhile colleagues in philosophy was manifest in a recent symposium in Berlin entitled 'Globalizing the Classics'. In Oxford, the Classics are known as 'Greats', and the question 'What makes a philosopher great?' mutates into the question, 'What makes something a classic?' The Oxford classicist Edith Hall has offered an answer, speaking about this very topic in her Gaisford Lecture at the University of Oxford on June 4, 2015 (Hall 2015). Hall laments the fact that the provision of education in the classics in Britain is now highly polarized, with the classics (she means, of course, the Greek classics) exalted in private schools and elite colleges but utterly ignored in the state system and in the majority of universities outside Oxbridge. Hall argues that the classics are too special to be ghettoized, but she is more than conscious that the topic of the exceptionalism of Greek classicism is deeply tendentious. She says this (2015):

> The question has become painfully politicised. Critics of colonialism and racism tend to play down the specialness of the ancient Greeks. Those who maintain that there was something identifiably different and even superior about the Greeks, on the other hand, are often die-hard conservatives who have a vested interest in proving the superiority of 'Western' ideals and in making evaluative judgements of culture. My problem is that I fit into neither camp. I am certainly opposed to colonialism and racism, and have investigated reactionary abuses of the classical tradition in colonial India and by apologists of slavery all the way through to the American Civil War. But my constant engagement with the ancient Greeks and their culture has made me more, rather than less, convinced that they asked a series of questions which are difficult to identify in combination amongst any of the other cultures of the ancient Mediterranean or North Eastern antiquity.

One might think that, in order to reach the conviction that the Greeks are this special, Hall would have had to spend time engaging with the non-Greek classical civilizations of India and China, about which there is not a single word in her entire lecture, although she feels confident enough to venture that 'none of these peoples produced anything quite equivalent to Athenian democracy, comic theatre, philosophical logic, or Aristotle's *Nicomachean Ethics*.' Let me let that pass, though, because what she does say is more interesting. Hall acknowledges that many recent advances in scholarship about the cultures of the Ancient Near East have called into question the idea that the ancient Greeks were special. These advances 'have revealed how much the Greeks shared with and absorbed from their predecessors and neighbours . . . they reveal the Greek "miracle" to have been one constituent in a continuous process of intercultural exchange'. She accepts that 'taken singly, most Greek achievements can be paralleled in the culture of at least one of their neighbours': the Babylonians knew Pythagoras's theorem; the Phoenicians created the phonetic alphabet; the Hittites, also highly literate, developed chariot technology; the Egyptians, *medicina*, based on empirical experience; and so on for Mesopotamia, the Levant, Persia, and Asia Minor. Summing up the situation, she says this:

> Some scholars have gone so far as to ask whether the Greeks came up with anything new at all, or whether they merely acted as a conduit through which the combined wisdom of all the civilisations of the eastern Mediterranean was disseminated across the territories conquered by Alexander the Great, before arriving at Rome and posterity. Others have seen sinister racist motives at work [and have] claimed, with some justification, that northern Europeans have systematically distorted and concealed the evidence showing how much the ancient Greeks owed to Semitic and African peoples rather than to Indo-European 'Aryan' traditions.

Then in what does the special greatness of the Greeks consist? Hall's answer is as follows:

> I do not deny that the Greeks acted as a conduit for other ancient peoples' achievements. But to function successfully as a conduit, channel, or intermediary is in itself to perform an exceptional role . . . Taking over someone else's technical knowledge requires an opportunistic ability to identify a serendipitous find or encounter, excellent communicative skills, and the imagination to seek how a technique, story or object could be adapted to a different linguistic and cultural milieu . . . Of course the Greeks were not by nature or in potential superior to any other human beings, either physically or intellectually . . . But that does not mean they were not the right people, in the right place, at the right time, to take up the human baton of intellectual progress for several hundred years.

There is, again in this comment, a certain blindness to the relay races already being run in China and India. But what I find fascinating is that the best efforts of contemporary classical scholarship to unearth that unique feature that made Greek civilization great has ended up concluding that their exceptionalism was in how well they made use of the ideas and innovations of others. Hardly exceptional enough, one would have thought, to justify Macaulay declaring that one shelf of Greek classics was of greater value to humanity than the entirety of Sanskrit literature combined.

There is an entirely comparable discussion to be had about the concept of a philosophical great. One does not need to look very far for philosophers who are willing to endorse a version of the exceptionalist position—indeed, that was the presupposition behind the question I was asked in my interview, a presupposition I was too young and naïve to challenge directly. The more sincere, among the philosophers, will perhaps be willing to concede, as Hall does, that much of what makes European philosophy exceptional consists in its borrowings and reworkings of borrowed ideas. If that was true in the ancient world, how much more so in the early modern, when, thanks to colonialism, Europeans were certainly 'in the right place, at the right time' to make wholesale appropriations of the intellectual innovations of others. During the period of the British colonial occupation of India, the dominant impression that the British left in the minds of Indian intellectuals was of the British as being a profoundly unphilosophical people. The Benares-based scholar James R. Ballantyne spoke of 'the impression, here yet too prevalent, that the Europeans, though capital workers in brass and iron, had better leave the discussion of things intellectual to those whose land was the birth-place of philosophy' (1859: 150). Wholesale looting of Indian ideas, without due citation, was the norm. Let me give one example. It is difficult to establish the exact influence that Indian ideas about logic may have had on the British logicians George Boole and Augustus De Morgan, although there is evidence of a line of transmission through a fellow member of the Royal Society, the brilliant Indologist and translator of Indian philosophical and mathematical texts, Henry T. Colebrooke. The absence of any mention of Indian philosophy in the philosophical work of John Stuart Mill, son of the author of the colonial manifesto *A History of British India*, James Mill, and himself an administrator in the East India Company, is quite striking; for he was in correspondence with Ballantyne, who had by then translated works in Indian logic, several of which contain accounts of a method of agreement and difference strikingly similar to Mill's own. It is more or less certain, too, that Mill read or even attended Colebrooke's famous lecture of 1827 (Colebrooke 1837), in which he described the emergentist philosophy of mind of the Indian materialist school of the Cārvāka thinker Bṛhaspati, a great philosophy that modern historians now trace back to Mill. Colebrooke's work enjoyed in general an extremely wide circulation—even Hegel had some of his writings, and his translations of Sanskrit texts about mathematics were, as I have mentioned, well-known to De Morgan and Boole. It is striking now how many of the ideas that were to find a place in British Emergentism are already available in that text—Mill, for example, using the example of chemical change to illustrate his idea of a 'heteropathic law' in *A System of Logic* (1843). It seems likely that Mill, a person whose duties as a senior official of the East India Company included correspondence with Colebrooke, and who belonged with him to a circle of London literati based around the Royal Society, had heard Colebrooke's lecture, or read it when it was published in 1837, the very time when he was working on *A System of Logic*. I cannot help but wonder whether the Indian materialist Bṛhaspati did not, after all, have a role in the emergence of British emergentism.

I say all of this only to prepare the ground for a definition of greatness in philosophy that does not rest on false presuppositions about European exceptionalism and universalism. If one asks, of a philosopher from India or China, Africa, or Mesoamerica, what makes them great, one had better not simply try to situate their philosophical accomplishments on a scale from Plato to Parfit.

One more reason why this would be a quixotic enterprise: thinkers like Plato and Kant have been the subject of a vast philosophical industry of interpretation, especially perhaps in the last hundred years. What we think of when we think of Kant is thus the output of a great collaboration by many of the best resourced academics of the last century. No Indian or Chinese or African thinker has benefited correspondingly from well-funded study on an industrial scale. So, if we compare what is associated with the name tags 'Plato' and 'Gaṅgeśa', we are comparing the output of a great intellectual apparatus with the humble offerings of a few scholars—hardly a good way to answer the question 'Which one is great?'

I propose, then, to speak to the question by inquiring, instead, into the extent to which a thinker—whatever the source of their ideas—transforms the philosophical landscape in which they work. To count as a great, a philosopher must draw on a past intellectual history, rethink it, modify and adapt it in such a way that the landscape is irrevocably altered; indeed, in such a way that any later thinker cannot help but look back on the past as it was before that thinker as, if not antiquated, then at least as meaningful only in terms of the rearticulation that has now been provided. In the European tradition, Kant is a standout example of a philosopher who is great according to my definition; indeed, he more or less explicitly describes himself as great in such terms with his distinction between pre-critical and critical philosophy. In Sanskritic India, a list of standout examples would include such radical reinterpreters of the Buddha as Nāgārjuna and Dignāga, game-changers in the logic of inquiry like Jayanta and Gaṅgeśa, freelance philosophers such as Jayarāśi and Śrīharṣa, not to mention 'great souls' (*mahātma*) like M.K. Gandhi and K.C. Bhattacharyya (see Ganeri 2017). I will, however, turn my attention to a philosopher who was trained in the Sanskrit tradition but who chose to write outside it: his name is Buddhaghosa.

2. Buddhaghosa

The fifth-century philosopher Buddhaghosa has been described as possessing 'one of the greatest minds in the history of Buddhism' (Heim 2014: 4). A cosmopolitan intellectual, Buddhaghosa moved between India and Sri Lanka, between Sanskrit and Pāli, between Hinduism and Buddhism, in search of a fundamental theory of mind. Buddhaghosa's ideas would influence conceptions of the human throughout South and Southeast Asia for a millennium and a half, and they continue to do so today. Their philosophical significance, moreover, is global in reach. As with every intellectual genius, Buddhaghosa stood on the shoulders of giants. As with every Indian intellectual genius, he prefers to say that he is merely hitching a ride. The truth is somewhere in the middle—a man of great brilliance, he owed the opportunity to be brilliant to those who had fired and fueled his intellect, in this case the Sinhāla commentators whose lost works he claims to summarize. One might fairly say that his writings are the distillation of a thousand years of observation and reflection in the context of a research program initiated by Śākyamuni the Buddha himself. They are more than that, though: they are also testimony to a true innovator, a pioneer, and a creative thinker. Having reviewed rival hypotheses of three of his predecessors, he wonders who is right and he answers, pointedly, 'Nobody: we should accept what is right in the claims of each' (*Fount* 287). He was an innovator, and self-consciously so, sometimes openly declaring that he was going beyond anything that can be found in the older commentaries, even acknowledging that his new thoughts had not yet gone far enough. Excellent studies of Buddhaghosa's life, affiliations, role as author and commentator, and general intellectual project have been made (Endo 2008; Collins 2009; Gethin 2012; Heim 2014, 2017), and here I will focus exclusively on his philosophy. Many of his original ideas are in commentaries on the canonical Abhidhamma-piṭaka, especially his *Fount of Meaning* (*Atthasālinī*, his commentary on the *Dhammasaṅgaṇī*) and *Dispeller of Delusion* (*Samoha-vinodanī*, his commentary on the *Vibhaṅga*)—and perhaps he permitted himself a little greater philosophical license there than in his manual, the *Path of Purification* (*Visuddha-magga*), a synthetic and comprehensive description of the Buddhist path, or in 'his' synoptic commentaries on the Sutta-piṭaka (the Majjhima-, Saṃyutta-, Aṅguttara-, and Dīgha-Nikāya *aṭṭhakathā*s).

To Buddhaghosa, it was evident that the study of the human mind is a common human affair. Acknowledging that open questions remain, he called on others to do the same, saying of one such extension,

> This is just a sketch. An in-depth understanding of this question of the [function of consciousness] is only to be gained on the strength of one's selection after considering views, one's estimation of reasons, one's preferences and credences, learning and testimonial reports.
>
> *(Fount 74)*

Some writers on Buddhaghosa have felt it necessary to try to demonstrate that all of his ideas are *already* in earlier works, not merely in the early Sinhāla commentators, but in the canonical Abhidhamma itself—a project somewhat akin to arguing that all of Plotinus is already in Plato. Another trend, in tension with the first, has been to assume that every conceptual development is an instance of philosophical progress, historians and historiographers claiming that the ideas of the Buddhist philosophers who came after Buddhaghosa—the 'Buddhist epistemologists' like Dignāga and Dharmakīrti, for example, or the Madhyamaka philosophy of Candrakīrti—render obsolete Buddhaghosa's own theories (I will say more about Dignāga later). Neither trend does justice to his greatness. It is, for example, only because of Buddhaghosa's spirit of open inquiry that the question recently posed by Theravāda Buddhist modernizers like the Burmese activist and Nobel Laureate Aung San Suu Kyi, the question whether Buddhism has the resources to articulate distinctive conceptions of human rights grounded in non-Kantian understandings of dignity, can hope for an answer.

In the works of Buddhaghosa, we find a philosophy of mind completely free from the grip of the picture that has captivated—and enslaved—speculation about the mind in the west: the picture of the mind as 'mediational', the picture that Charles Taylor describes—using the first person plural to aggregate deep trends of thought in the Western world—as 'a big mistake operating in our culture, a kind of operative (mis)understanding of what it is to know, which has had dire effects on both theory and practice in a host of domains' (2013: 61). What is clear is how thoroughly Buddhaghosa is distanced from a 'mediational' picture of the relationship between mind and world, which has it that reality is taken up by way of an inner self performing mental operations on internal representations. In what follows, I will give three examples of Buddhaghosan greatness. I will claim that we can legitimately speak of him as the founder of a distinct stance in philosophy, as Analytical Philosophy and Phenomenology are stances. I will show how he transforms an ancient metaphor in order to provide a new understanding of human agency. And I will demonstrate that he has a sophisticated analysis of human beings in relation to one another, a theory of our engagement with each other in the social world.

3. Buddhaghosa's Attentionalism

Attentionalism, as I will call the stance that lends attention centrality in explanatory projects in philosophy, encourages us to rethink many central concepts in the philosophy of mind from an attention-theoretic perspective. It is a policy, not a proposition; a body of guidelines as to how to think about the mind. Van Fraassen says that 'a philosophical position can consist in a stance (attitude, commitment, approach, a cluster of such)' (2002: 48), and the idea is helpfully elaborated by Anjan Chakravartty (2004: 175), who comments that

> a stance is a strategy, or a combination of strategies, for generating factual beliefs. A stance makes no claim about reality, at least directly, It is rather a sort of epistemic 'policy' concerning which methodologies should be adopted in the generation of factual beliefs . . . Stances are not themselves propositional; they are guidelines for ways of acting. One does not believe a stance in the way one believes a fact. Rather one commits to a stance, or adopts it.

Buddhaghosa's Attentionalism is strikingly on display in the organizational structure of his most famous work, *The Path to Purification*. The whole book takes the overt form of a sustained reflection on the meaning of a single quotation from the Canon: 'Cultivate attention, bhikkhus; a bhikkhu who attends knows things as they are' (*samādhiṃ, bhikkhave, bhāvetha; samāhito, bhikkhave, bhikkhu yathābhūtaṃ pajānāti*, S iii.13). The book begins and ends with this quotation, and its contents are substantially devoted to exploring the meaning of this one statement. What is put forward here is an application of a general epistemic principle: that attention is, in normal circumstances, sufficient for knowledge. The application in question speaks of a particular sort of attention, expert absorbed attention (*samādhi*), and a particular sort of knowledge, insight (*paññā*) into fundamental moral truths. Much is to be said about the varieties of attention, about what expertise consists in and how it is cultivated, about the relationship between attention, perceptual experience, consciousness, knowledge, and truth. Buddhaghosa's discussion of the nature of consciousness and attention is indeed of unparalleled brilliance. Conscious perceptual experience is a form of active involvement with the world, while cognitive processes transform the mind's first acknowledgments into fully intentional thought. There is no self as controlling agent of thinking, believing, and feeling. Attention instead is what explains the activity of thought and mind.

Yet it is striking that there is no single word in Pāli or Sanskrit for English 'attention', and from Buddhaghosa's perspective the search for something that can be called the essence of attention is a mistake. Buddhaghosa's view is rather, as we might put it, that there are many kinds of attention. These kinds of attention are put to work to explain perception, memory, testimony, self-awareness, empathy, and end-of-life experience, and they are all, Buddhaghosa further claims, fundamentally grounded in the embodied sense modalities. He is against representations and so against representationalism, and he dispenses with an earlier perceptual model of introspection, but he is in favor of the inseparability of intentional content and phenomenal character. In his treatment of the cognitive processes of attentional capture, he anticipates the concept of working memory, the idea of mind as a global workplace, subliminal orienting, and the thesis that visual processing occurs at three levels. He is unlike nearly every other Buddhist philosopher in that he discusses episodic memory and knows it as a reliving of experience from one's personal past; but he blocks any reduction of the phenomenology of temporal experience to the representation of oneself as in the past. The alternative claim that episodic memory is a phenomenon of attention is one that he develops with greater sophistication than has been done elsewhere. He attentional analysis of empathy, our ability to know the minds of others, is similarly innovative. He agrees with the ancients, and with thinkers like Simone Weil and Iris Murdoch who have drawn inspiration from them, in claiming that moral attention—the settling on what is good (i.e., wholesome, *kusala*) and the shunning of what is bad (*akusala*)—is a distinct ethical virtue. At the end of life, he says, one attends to that which has given one's life its significance.

Buddhaghosa's Attentionalism is a stance distinct from the stances of Phenomenology and Analytical Philosophy, and should not be conflated with either. His attention-theoretic approach brings important new options to the table in contemporary philosophy of mind and cognitive science, providing new directions to recent work on the pervasiveness of the mental, embodied cognition, cognitive phenomenology, intersubjectivity, and the experience of time. Two large bodies of data about attention are available to an aspiring Attentionalist today: first, the rich experimental studies of contemporary cognitive psychology—and it has been argued that attention is, of all cognitive functions, the most thoroughly studied—and second, Buddhaghosa's treatment of the information that emerged as a result of meticulous Buddhist observation of the human mind's structure and functioning in the first 1,000 years after the Buddha lived.

4. Human Agency

That the Buddhist denial of 'self' (*atta*) is a denial of the specific notion of self as origin of willed directives is hinted at by canonical passages such as this:

> People are intent on the idea of 'I-making' and attached to the idea of 'other-making'. Some don't realise this, nor do they see it as an arrow. But to one who, having extracted this arrow, sees, [the thought] 'I am doing,' doesn't occur, [the thought] 'Another is doing' doesn't occur.
>
> *(Udāna 6.6)*

An identification of self with control, and the rejection of it, is more exactly formulated in another key canonical text, the *Sutta on the Definition of No-Self*, which has the Buddha declaring of intending, and indeed of any constituent of a mental life, that

> intending is nonself. For if, bhikkus, intending were self . . . it would be possible to have it of intending, 'Let my intending be thus; let my intending not be thus'. . . . But because intending is nonself . . . it is not possible to have it of intending, 'Let my intending be thus; let my intending not be thus'.
>
> *(S.iii.66–7; M.i.230–3)*

Here, an equivalence is affirmed between the denial of self and the denial of voluntariness or volition in intention. The Buddha's leading argument against a conception of self as the agent of mental (and physical) acts is that every constituent of a mental life is subject to change, and 'Is what is impermanent, suffering, and subject to change fit to be regarded thus: "This is mine, this I am, this is my self?"' (S.iii.67). It may help to imagine, as fictional genealogy, the conception having arisen by taking as primary an account of distanced control and transferring it to the case of self-control. For indeed, in such texts as the *Bhagavad-gītā*, human beings are portrayed as remotely governed, a divine agent responsible for all of their apparently autonomous acts: 'O Arjuna, the Lord resides in the heart-area of all beings, making all beings revolve through his magical power [as if they were] mounted on a machine' (*Bh.Gī.* 18.61). Madhūsudana explains the phrase 'mounted on a machine' (*yantrārūḍhāni*) as meaning 'just like a magician who causes the completely non-independent wooden human forms, etc., to revolve, seated on a machine, etc., moved by a rope'. The idea of an inner agent whose intentions causes actions comes into being when the magician or puppeteer in this depiction of distal control is simply internalized: the self is now an inner magician pulling the strings that cause the human body to move. Saṃkara's comments on *Bh.Gī.* 4.13 can be read as straightforwardly rejecting the causal theory of action while allowing room for some conception of self other than an agentive one. In fact it is harmless enough to refer to overt actions as having an agent because there is the physical human being to stand in that role, but at the moment when we offer the same description of mental actions, the rejected 'Authorship View' of self materializes as if from nowhere (Peacocke 2007, 2014).

A debunking genealogy of the origins of this theory of human agency helps to loosen its grip. A human being is not like a drone, with a detached if now internalized control center, but is instead more like a self-driving vehicle whose various complex perceptual, motor, and planning systems enable it to navigate its environment. There is no driver, no charioteer, no inner magician; rather, there is a complex of mutually interacting components. It is in order to articulate this alternative model that Buddhaghosa appropriates but transforms the metaphor of the machine. He expresses the idea that human beings are without inner originators of mental action, by likening them to mechanical dolls or marionettes, which seem, but only seem, as if they are animated from within:

> Just as a mechanical doll (*dāru-yanta*) is empty (*suñña*), soulless (*nijjiva*), and undirected (*nirīhaka*), and while it walks and stands merely through the combination of strings and wood, yet it seems as if it had direction and occupation (*savyāpāra*); so too, this minded body (*nāma-rūpa*) is empty, soulless and undirected, and while it walks and stands merely through the combination of the two together, yet it seems as if it had direction and occupation.
>
> *(Path 594 [xviii.31])*

The point of the analogy is not, of course, to deny that human beings have intentions in and for action (*cetanā*); and, when it is said that intentional action is like the movement of a mechanical doll, the point is not that our actions are entirely mechanical and automatic, but is instead that, just as the marionette's movements seem—but only seem—as if produced by an inner directing self within, so likewise do ours. In fact, they are not: they are simply the bodily aspect of an intention in action, the intention itself embodied. The metaphor of the marionette is introduced only to resist that of the charioteer:

> There isn't some sort of self inside that does the bending and stretching [when one sits up] . . . there is no self of any kind inside which puts on the robe [when one puts on a robe] . . . there is no self of any kind inside which does the eating [when one eats].
> (*Dispeller* 258–62)

Agent causalism and the Authorship View are clearly identified as the target: 'There is no agent (*kattā*) or author (*kāretā*) who says, "Let you be the untasked state, you be sense-door instruction, you be seeing, you be receiving, you be examining, you be determining, you be running"' (*Fount* 271–2).

There is an alternative both to imagining that all human action must have its origin in a detached agent and its intentions and depicting human beings as entirely passive, deterministically propelled by efficient causation, and that is to understand that mindedness, notably attention, is already an activity. 'Is there such a thing as action? Yes. Is there such a thing as the author of action (*karmakārako*)? No, that cannot be truly said,' the *Kathāvatthu* succinctly puts it, continuing, 'Is action one thing, the author of it something else? No, that cannot be truly said' (*Kathāvatthu* 53). One need not deny that it is possible, as a matter of grammatical convention, to speak of an 'author' of experiencing whenever there is an experience, or an 'author' of acting whenever there is an action. In Indo-European languages, at least, one can always reformulate the description of an activity ('the flowing of water') in a subject-predicate grammatical form ('the water flows'). Yet the move from the grammatical truism that, for every activity there is something we can designate as its 'agent', to the claim that there is a single agent of every action is clearly fallacious (technically, it is known as a quantifier-shift fallacy). Buddhists make the point by saying that the agentive construction is simply an idiomatic way of speaking, an 'accessory locution' (*sasambhāra-kathā*), like 'His bow shot him', meaning '*An arrow* from his bow shot him,' or as the phrase 'on seeing a visible object with the eye' is idiomatic for 'on seeing a visible object with a moment of visual awareness' (*Path* 20; cf. Karunadasa 2010: 147). Similarly, commonplace attributions of agency to physical objects ('the knife cuts well'; 'the washing machine has nearly finished its cycle') are neither problematic nor exciting.

It would evidently be quite wrong to conclude from his appeal to the marionette simile that Buddhaghosa's view is that a mental life is entirely passive. Rather, a quite different account of the distinction between activity and passivity is put forward. Mental activity is described first as a conscious 'bending' (*namana*) of mind onto world, which 'bending' consists in being in conscious concomitance (*cetasika*) with the intentionality of the mental (*citta*) (*Path* 527 [xvii.48], 588 [xviii.4]; *Dispeller* 136). Active mindedness (*nāma*) includes attentional selecting (overt or covert focusing on one from among a group of leaves in the field of awareness), attentional placing (centering one leaf by excluding others), attentional rehearsing (repeating a number one has been given while looking for a piece of paper, or an image of a leaf that has gone out of view so as to identify it when it reappears), and attentional effort (a 'straining' that substitutes for will). Other ways by which mind 'bends' onto world include felt evaluating (for a pain is not a brute happening but is instead an evaluation of something as harmful and a corresponding shrinking away), cognitively assigning mental labels to enable identification or recognition (seeing Ānanda as 'Ānanda'), and preserving the boundaries of an experience in relation to others. Accompanying, and in *some* sense prior to, all of these activities is the activity of becoming 'in touch' with the world, a minimally active operational intentionality, a perceptual presence to the world that hovers in a grey area between active intentionality and embodied passivity (*rūpa*), where passivity has to be understood in terms of the notion of being 'molested' (*rūpana*) by the world's causal influence. These are the activities that go on inside intentional consciousness, but none is rightly thought of as the voluntary performance of an agent. If 'bending' onto the world is a modulation of conscious intentionality, another notion of mental activity is also available, one that consists in 'tasking' the mind through the activation of a variety of cognitive psychological modules (*mano-dhātu*). Such activities include subliminal orienting, constructing a sensory field, perceptually processing a stimulus to identify spatial boundaries and object category, late attentional gate-keeping, and the 'running' (*javana*) of working memory. This is a psychological or cognitive scientific notion of mental activity at a level underneath that of conscious thought. The most minimal such activity is the sending of an instruction (*āvajjana*; 'turning toward') to a sensory system to turn on or open up, a subliminal orienting toward a stimulus. Untasked thought (*bhavaṅga*, the rest or default state) is now what is to be described as 'passive'; the content of the default state consists in a residue of 'innate' autobiographical semantic information.

In order to appreciate the greatness of Buddhaghosa's approach to human agency, it may be helpful to compare it with a contrasting appeal to the marionette metaphor in a recent book by Peter Carruthers. He puts the idea as follows (2015b, summarizing his 2015a):

> In this manner our conscious minds are continually under the control of our unconscious thoughts. We [unconsciously] decide what to pay attention to, what to remember, what to think of, what to imagine, and what sentences to rehearse in inner speech. There is control, of course, and it is a form of self-control. But it is not control by a conscious self. Rather what we take to be the conscious self is a puppet manipulated by our

unconscious goals, beliefs, and decisions. Who's in charge? Well, we are. But the 'we' who are in charge are not the conscious selves we take ourselves to be, but rather a set of unconsciously operating mental states. Consciousness does make a difference. Indeed, it is vital to the overall functioning of the human mind. But a controlling conscious self is an illusion.

Carruthers's 'conscious self' is what we are calling the Authorship View of Self or the 'mythological monad of practical reason', and he agrees that it is an illusion. Yet Carruthers's position is instructively distinct from the one to be defended by Buddhaghosa. He argues that control mechanisms are only unconscious, and that they consist in the operations of working memory. This, though, has the counter-intuitive effect of rendering intentional action unconscious: 'beliefs, goals, and decisions are never conscious. Rather, these states pull the strings in the background, selecting and manipulating the sensory-based contents that do figure in consciousness . . . we are under the illusion that the decision is a conscious one' (ibid.); 'all decisions are unconscious, resulting from competitive interactions among goals, desires, information, and/or action plans' (2015a: 237). So, when Carrutthers describes the conscious mind as a marionette, what *he* means is that its strings are pulled by subpersonal-level operations. Paraphrased in Buddhist terminology, Carruthers's picture has it that the only way for mindedness to be active is in the activation of cognitive modules, and that this activity is causally determinative of apparent conscious activity. What this shows is that Carruthers is committed to the Authorship View, with its claim that the only way for conscious thought to be autonomous is for it to be authored. Buddhaghosa avoids this commitment by drawing a careful distinction between the two notions of minded activity mentioned earlier. In terms of the marionette metaphor, the whole point is that one must not make the mistake of thinking that the control mechanisms pulling the strings have to be subpersonal causal determinants: there are other sorts of determinative interdependencies between the conscious concomitants that modulate intentional awareness, the various 'consciousness-level' factors that actively contribute to being in a conscious intentional state, and that jointly operate together as a single system. Our conscious mental lives are controlled neither from *outside* nor from *below*: their autonomy is *sui generis*.

5. Empathy: Awareness of Others

Empathy relates to a person's ability to comprehend the intentions, emotions, and other states of mind of another, to assume what can be called a 'second-personal' view in which others appear not merely as bodies but as embodied 'you's. The term 'empathy' is used here as a translation of the German *Einfühlung* (Zahavi 2010: 289), meaning the idea of an ability to acknowledge others as others, and in that sense to understand others, rather than the idea of concern or care for others: 'Whereas empathy has to do with a basic understanding of expressive others, sympathy adds care or concern for the other' (Zahavi 2008: 516). Empathy, in this sense, is an awareness *of* the mental state of another while sympathy is a concern *for* their mental state. Such an ability has standardly been interpreted as consisting either in the individual's possession of a theory of mind that enables them to attribute states of mind in virtue of the other's behavior (so-called theory-theory), or else as involving a simulation of the other's states of mind by mirroring or imagining them as one's own. Much of the contemporary discussion in social cognition concerns the respective merits of theory-theory and simulation. Recently, an interesting third proposal has been put forward, that empathy has to do rather with the direct acquaintance of another's attitudes in and through their bodily expression (Gallagher 2005; Zahavi 2007, 2008, 2010; Gangopadhyay 2014). Zahavi finds the view anticipated in Max Scheler's (1954: 260) remark that

> we certainly believe ourselves to be directly acquainted with another person's joy in his laughter, with his sorrow and pain in his tears, with his shame in his blushing, with his entreaty in his outstretched hands . . . If anyone tells me that this is not 'perception' . . . I would beg him to . . . address the phenomenological facts.

According to this analysis, empathy consists in a type of perception of others' mental lives. Empathy is 'our ability to access the mind of others in their bodily and behavioural expressions' (Zahavi 2008: 522). Note that Zahavi prefers to speak of 'experiential access' rather than 'perception', perhaps reflecting discomfort with Scheler's idea that empathy is literally a perceptual skill.

Buddhaghosa's analysis is radically different: what he says is that social cognition is a proprietary kind of attention. Prior to theoretical understanding of others as minded beings there is a form of embodied intersubjective engagement in which the other's embodied actions serve to enable direct attention to them as intentional others. In Buddhaghosa's embodied approach to social cognition, perception of the other's bodily deportment does not constitute experiential access to their state of mind but rather enables a proprietary sort of attention to it. The idea is that there is a way in which a conscious being disposes itself, which serves to 'intimate' the mental state within. It is not the consciousness-endowed body as such, but a very particular change of mode, which endowment with consciousness enables, by which the body is kept firm, held up, and moved. Buddhaghosa states that the distinctive movement of the eyes is an *intimation* of a person's intention to look (*Dispeller* 356). The intimation can be called an instrumental bodily act (*kāyika-karaṇa*). One does not just see the intimation in another's posture and movement; one notices the other's intentions through the embodied intimation:

What does it intimate? One [kind of] bodily instrumentality; for someone standing in the eye's focus lifts up a head or a foot or shifts the head or an eyebrow. Now this mode of [comportment of] the hand, etc., is cognizable by the eye; but the intimation is not cognizable by the eye, it is cognizable only by the mind. For by means of the eye one only sees colours excited by the alteration in the hand, etc., but one knows the intimation by means of late attentional gate-keeping [lit. mind-door cognizance] cognizing that 'He seems to be doing such and such'.

(Fount 83)

A certain bodily comportment, a 'stiffening, alteration, and movement of the body', when attended to in a certain way, falls under the description 'He seems to be beckoning me.' A possible reading of these comments is that they simply formulate the standard argument that the mental states of others can be inferred from their observable physical behavior. Some support for that reading indeed comes from the examples that Buddhaghosa employs: the door of a wine shop bears a flag, and people know 'There is wine here'; the tree moves about, and people know 'There is wind'; the fish let out bubbles, and people know 'There are fish in the water'; and, from the tangle of leaves, grass, and rubbish, people know 'There was a flood' (*Fount* 83). One can easily read these comments as pointing to acts of inference, from an observed sign to something else that is mentally deduced (*mano-viññeya*). Yet that reading is a mistake. For Buddhaghosa has been very careful and circumspect in his formulation of the claim. He has said that one sees a displacement in the body, and one then ascribes to another an intention, with a thought process not itself caused by perceptual processing. Here the attribution of an intention has exactly the same cognitive profile as the cases we reviewed before, such as thinking of a past event *because of having seen* it before, with one's thought process triggered by some current cue. Likewise, here one attributes an intention *because of having seen* the bodily comportment. So, we should describe the claim as being that social cognition is attention to others' states of mind, with one's perception of their behavior serving not as a reason but as a cause. You raise your aim and, through that, my attention is drawn to your intention to beckon me.

If this is right, then Buddhaghosa's account of our ability to be aware of the mental states of others is that their bodily demeanor enables us to attend to their intentions, wishes, preferences, and so on. Posture and movement are attention-enabling, rather than inference-enabling, conditions in our consciousness of others' minds. Moreover, given that we are not thinking of such states as 'inner entities', and given that Buddhaghosa always ties the contents of consciousness to the sense modalities, what we should say is that our thought about another's intention or desire consists in a peculiar manner in which we attend due to their bodily posture and demeanor. That way of attending just is what it is to entertain the thought, 'He wants me to do this.'

6. Buddhaghosa's Legacy

A way to gain an appreciation of a philosopher's greatness is to compare them with great successors. Dignāga (480–540 CE) is a Buddhist philosopher who spent his working life in the Buddhist university of Nālandā, one of the most impressive institutions of higher education in South Asia—indeed, in its time, in the world. Dignāga owed much to internal dialogue with a contemporary of his, the grammarian-cum-philosopher Bhartṛhari. His disciple Dharmakīrti would go on to reinvent Dignāga's innovation and adapt it to the needs of new Buddhist communities in ways of which Dignāga himself may not have imagined, most notably by giving it an idealist inflection. Dignāga's break-through work was decisive in shaping the next period of Indian philosophy, a cosmopolitan Age of Dialogue in Sanskrit that runs at least until the transitioning of Buddhists like Kamalaśīla to Tibet. An emerging scholarly consensus agrees in identifying Dignāga as marking the beginning of a new era in Indian philosophical thought, some scholars emphasizing his theoretical innovations and others his transformation of discursive practice (Lusthaus 2002: 363; McCrea 2013: 129–30). Dignāga's new citational and critical practices were swiftly adopted by his opponents. As important as these shifts in doctrinal formulation and discursive practice was the transformation that Dignāga achieved in ways of reasoning, with a movement away from an epistemic localism to a rule-based universalism. Now, too, the precise formulation of definitions of key philosophical concepts takes center-stage as constitutive of philosophical practice, rival definitions of what purports to be a single concept locking horns in contexts of philosophical debate. Rapidly, this became the hallmark of philosophical activity in a broad Sanskrit cosmopolis that was to endure for centuries and whose geographical borders spread well beyond the subcontinent.

From a point of view centered on Buddhaghosa, however, Dignāga is to be held to account for introducing into the history of Buddhist philosophy of mind not only the Myth of Mediation but also the Myth of the Given, 'the fatal dichotomy between a supposedly brutely given, nonconceptual sensory content and free, rationally articulated belief' (Carman 2013: 167), by reducing the role of concepts to that of pawns in the game of inference, with his celebrated redefinition of perceptual experience as that which is free from conceptual construction. One could say, in very general terms, that Sanskritic discourse about mind began with Dignāga to become sharply polarized between advocates of an experiential and phenomenological approach and proponents of a conceptualist and normative approach. The greatness of Buddhaghosa, we can now appreciate, is that it talks about the mind without this polarization, and it searches for a theory in which the claims of the experiential and the normative are respected in equal measure. If the ambition of a theory of mind is to account for the unity that exists between the demands of experience and of reason, then this is the literature in which an answer is most likely to found.

Perhaps, indeed, this is another mark of greatness—that the work of a great philosopher can withstand the vicissitudes of philosophical fashion, and always threatens a return.

Buddhaghosa's influence on the development of Buddhist philosophy in Sri Lanka, Burma (Myanmar), Cambodia, Laos, and Thailand has been and continues to be immense. Important innovations do certainly occur in these countries after him, in the work of Ānanda, Dhammapāla$_1$, Dhammapāla$_2$, and Anuruddha, as well as in nineteenth-century Burmese reinventions that are also in part responses to British colonial occupation. In fact, from the fifth to the eighth century a vast Hindu and Theravāda intellectual civilization spread throughout Southeast Asia, the full story of which has yet be chronicled (a beginning is made in Guy 2014), but one in which Buddhaghosa was surely a defining intellectual presence. I began by suggesting that, to count as a great, a philosopher must draw on a past intellectual history, rethink it, and adapt it in such a way that the landscape is irrevocably altered—indeed, in such a way that any later thinker cannot help but look back on the past as it was before that thinker as, if not antiquated, then at least as meaningful only in terms of the rearticulation that has now been provided. Buddhaghosa drew on an already very rich philosophical landscape, based on a thousand years of analysis and reflection on the thought of the Buddha, which he transformed into a new theory of the human subject, of persons as living entities with a characteristic capacity for attention. I think that's pretty great.

References

Ballantyne, James R. 1859. On 'Logic' and 'Rhetoric', in *Christianity Contrasted with Hindu Philosophy*, ed. James R. Ballantyne, London: J. Madden: Appendix C, 150.

Buddhaghosa (*Dispeller*). *Dispeller (Sammoha-vinodanī)*: Ñāṇamoli, Bhikkhu 1996. trans. *The Dispeller of Delusion (Sammohavinodanī)*, 2 vols., Revised for publication by L. S. Cousins, Nyanaponika Mahāthera, and C.M.M. Shaw, Oxford: Pāli Text Society.

Buddhaghosa (*Fount*). *Fount (Attha-sālinī)*: (1) Ñāṇamoli, Bhikkhu (ms.). trans. *The Fount of Meaning (Atthasālinī) by Buddhaghosa Ācariya*, Island Hermitage Library, Dodandūwa, Partially typed, partially handwritten, ms. on *Asl.* 36–114. (2) Nyānaponika, Bhikkhu 2005 (1942). trans. *Darlegung der Bedeutung (Atthasālinī)*, edited for publication by Sven Bretfeld and Rainer Knopf, Oxford: Pāli Text Society. (3) Tin, Pe Maung 1920. trans. *The Expositor (Atthasālinī): Buddhaghosa's Commentary on the Dhammasangaṇī, the First Book of the Abhidhamma Piṭaka*, two vols., Oxford: Pāli Text Society.

Buddhaghosa (*Path*). *Path (Visuddhimagga)*: Ñāṇamoli, Bhikkhu 1991. trans. *The Path of Purification: Visuddhimagga by Bhadantācariya Buddhaghosa*, 5th edn., Kandy: Buddhist Publication Society.

Carman, Taylor 2013. Conceptualism and the Scholastic Fallacy, in *Mind, Reason, and Being-in-the World: The McDowell-Dreyfus Debate*, ed. Joseph K. Schear, Abingdon: Routledge: 165–77.

Carruthers, Peter 2015a. *The Centred Mind: What the Science of Working Memory Shows Us about the Nature of Human Thought*, Oxford: Oxford University Press.

Carruthers, Peter 2015b. Who's in Charge Anyway? URL = http://blog.oup.com/2015/08/whos-in-charge-conscious-mind

Chakravartty, Anjan 2004. Stance Relativism: Empiricism versus Metaphysics, *Studies in the History and Philosophy of Science, Part A* 35: 173–84.

Colebrooke, H. T. 1837. *Miscellaneous Essays*, 2 vols., London: W. H. Allen.

Collins, Stephen 2009. Remarks on the *Visuddhimagga*, and Its Treatment of the Memory of Former Dwelling(s) (*pubbenivāsānānussati*), *Journal of Indian Philosophy* 37: 499–532.

Endo, Toshiichi 2008. Buddhaghosa's Role as a Commentator: Faithful Translator or Critical Editor?, *Buddhist Studies* 36: 1–37.

Gallagher, Shaun 2005. *How the Body Shapes the Mind*, Oxford: Oxford University Press.

Ganeri, Jonardon 2017. Freedom in Thinking: The Immersive Cosmopolitanism of Krishnachandra Bhattacharya, in *The Oxford Handbook of Indian Philosophy*, New York: Oxford University Press: 718–36.

Gangopadhyay, Nivedita 2014. Embodiment and Empathy: Current Debates in Social Cognition, *Topoi* 33: 117–27.

Gethin, Rupert 2012. Was Buddhaghosa a Theravādin? Buddhist Identity in the Pāli Commentaries and Chronicles, in *How Theravāda Is Theravāda? Exploring Buddhist Identities*, ed. Peter Skilling, Jason Carbine, Claudio Cicuzza, and Santi Pakdeekham, Chiang Mai: Silkworm Press: 1–63.

Guy, John (ed.) 2014. *Lost Kingdoms: Hindu-Buddhist Sculpture of Early Southeast Asia*, New York: Metropolitan Museum of Art.

Hall, Edith 2015. The Gaisford Lecture: Pearls before Swine? The Past & Future of Geek, University of Oxford. URL = www.podcasts.ox.ac.uk/gaisford-2015-lecture-pearls-swine-past-future-greek

Heim, Maria 2014. *The Forerunner of All Things: Buddhaghosa on Mind, Intention, and Agency*, New York: Oxford University Press.

Heim, Maria 2017. Buddhaghosa on the Phenomenology of Love and Compassion, in *The Oxford Handbook of Indian Philosophy*, ed. Jonardon Ganeri, New York: Oxford University Press: 171–89.

Karunadasa, Yakupitiyage 2010. *The Theravāda Abhidhamma: Its Inquiry into the Nature of Conditioned Reality*, Hong Kong: Centre of Buddhist Studies, University of Hong Kong.

Lusthaus, Dan 2002. *Buddhist Phenomenology: A Philosophical Investigation of Yogācāra Buddhism and the* Ch'eng wei-shih lun, Abingdon: Routledge.

McCrea, Lawrence 2013. The Transformations of Mīmāṃsā in the Larger Context of Indian Philosophical Discourse, in *Periodization and Historiography of Indian Philosophy*, ed. Eli Franco, Vienna: De Nobili Research Library: 127–44.

Mill, John Stuart 1843. *A System of Logic, Ratiocinative and Inductive*, two vols., London: John W. Parker.

Peacocke, Christopher 2007. Mental Action and Self-awareness (I), in *Contemporary Debates in Philosophy of Mind*, ed. Brian P. McLaughlin and Jonathan D. Cohen, Oxford: Blackwell: 358–76.

Peacocke, Christopher 2014. *The Mirror of the World: Subjects, Consciousness, and Self-Consciousness*, Oxford: Oxford University Press.

Scheler, Max F. 1954. *The Nature of Sympathy*, trans. Peter Heath, London: Routledge & Kegan Paul.

Taylor, Charles 2013. Retrieving Realism, in *Mind, Reason, and Being-in-the World: The McDowell-Dreyfus Debate*, ed. Joseph K. Schear, Abingdon: Routledge: 61–90.

van Fraassen, Bas C. 2002. *The Empirical Stance*, New Haven, CT: Yale University Press.

Zahavi, Dan 2007. Expression and Empathy, in *Folk Psychology Re-Assessed*, ed. Daniel D. Hutto and Matthew Ratcliffe, Dordrecht: Springer: 25–40.
Zahavi, Dan 2008. Simulation, Projection and Empathy, *Consciousness and Cognition* 17: 514–22.
Zahavi, Dan 2010. Empathy, Embodiment and Interpersonal Understanding: From Lipps to Schutz, *Inquiry* 53: 285–306.

6

AQUINAS'S COMPLEX WEB

Jeffrey Hause

1. Introduction

Although Thomas Aquinas (1224/5–1272) did write several works of philosophy, most of his vast opus is more accurately classified as theology.[1] Nevertheless, he is a deeply philosophical theologian, studied as much in our own day by philosophers as by theologians. Both fields rightly claim him as their own. As a Dominican friar dedicated to preaching and teaching, Aquinas strove to lead people in virtuous Christian lives. However, he did so in his writings through powerful, rigorous argument of the sort that contemporary analytic philosophy strives for but does not always achieve.

There can be no doubt that his work has been influential. He was frequently read and cited in the Middle Ages and into the Renaissance, even though in some circles his thought was considered dangerous. Interest in Aquinas surged in Catholic intellectual circles in the nineteenth century thanks to Pope Leo XIII's encyclical, *Aeterni Patris* (1879), which urged the study of Aquinas in particular to revitalize Christian philosophy. In the twentieth century, a wider array of philosophers found in Aquinas a profound resource for their work in action theory, philosophy of law, ethics, and metaphysics. Among these philosophers, many identify themselves as Thomists of one variety or another.

It is harder to articulate what makes Aquinas a *great* philosopher. Some scholars would point to his most important philosophical innovations, such as these:

- The real distinction between *esse* (the actuality of being) and *essentia* (essence);
- The account of transcendentals, which forms one basis of Aquinas's ethics and aesthetics;

- The development of analogy as a way of understanding positive predication statements about God;
- A theory of human action that offers plausible explanations of intention, choice, inconstancy, and incontinence.

Although these count as major contributions to the field of philosophy, I will pass over them because scholars have been treating them intelligently and articulately over the course of seven centuries. I will instead approach Aquinas from a different angle.

What strikes anyone reading large chunks of Aquinas's work is the incessant flow of rigorous argument, informed by prodigious learning and charitable interpretation of others' thought, leading to an original philosophical and theological vision of astounding depth and scope. Today, scholars tend to borrow piecemeal from Aquinas to do philosophy of religion, action theory, ethics, or philosophy of law; and that borrowing is testimony to his enduring importance. However, it also obscures much of what is really great in his work—the way in which he weaves together disparate elements from various sources and traditions to establish his conclusions. What is most remarkable, however, is the way in which his findings in ethics, psychology, metaphysics, and so on mutually support each other. What Aquinas offers us is therefore one of the grandest philosophical systems in the history of philosophy. In this brief chapter, I will therefore focus on three such cases as representative of the many that can be adduced in favor of Aquinas's greatness as a philosopher: one in which he draws on metaphysics and philosophical anthropology, one in which he builds a distinctively Christian account on an Aristotelian one, and finally the pedagogical project that serves to unify the whole of Aquinas's wide-ranging *Summa theologiae*.

2. The Unicity of Substantial Forms

One measure of influence in philosophy is the role that a philosopher plays in originating or terminating a discussion, tasks requiring innovative analyses, the imaginative application of new models, or new insight into what is most salient. Aquinas did not terminate as many debates as he had wanted to terminate, most notably the debate over demonstrations of the world's eternity; but he did bring some to a bright and clear ending, such as the debate over the power that constitutes our capacity of free choice.

One argument that Aquinas originated concerns the number of substantial forms that material things have. While others had addressed this question before, no one before Aquinas had so clear-sighted a grasp of what is at stake in the answer. He was the first to show how this issue is tied to important topics at the heart of Aristotelian physics and metaphysics: the nature of matter, the individuation of substances and accidents, substantial unity, and identity over time. The debate that Aquinas originated would push medieval philosophers over centuries to articulate clearer and more plausible accounts of hylomorphism, and we can trace a line of influence from pluralism about substantial forms to the emerging dualism of early modern philosophy.[2]

In order to understand Aquinas's innovation, we need to keep in mind some details of the Aristotelian metaphysical landscape in which he is working. The first is Aquinas's hylomorphism—namely, that all material substances are composites of form and matter. Aquinas explains form and matter as correlative principles. Matter serves as a substratum for form, which is a property that actualizes the matter. They are thus related as potentiality to actuality. Aquinas calls the most fundamental matter 'prime matter'; it is the basic stuff that underlies the forms that actualize it, resulting in composite substances. Prime matter itself has no form or actuality of any sort. It therefore cannot exist by itself, not even by divine power, but only in a composite with the form that inheres in it. Accordingly, it is not a basic stuff that *has* potentiality for substantial form. Rather, it *is* by nature pure potentiality for substantial form. Hence, when prime matter loses its old form and gains a new one—for instance, when we run an electrical current through water and we create hydrogen and oxygen—the substratum that persists through the change has no actuality except what is imparted to it by form. The old substance is entirely destroyed and the new substances are generated.[3]

It is not just any form, but only substantial forms, that actualize prime matter. Substantial forms make a thing to be, absolutely speaking, and the composite of a substantial form and prime matter is a substance—the most fundamental sort of being. Aquinas's paradigms for substance are organisms as well as inanimate natural kinds. The substantial form of maple tree, cat, or gold actualizes prime matter in ways distinctive of each sort of substance, endowing it with its essential characteristics and organizing it into whatever integral parts it may have. However, over and above this first tier of composition, we find a further tier. After all, substances have further characteristics beyond those that are essential to them. A cat may have black or white fur, and a tree might be small or large. These further properties or 'accidents' do not form a compound with prime matter; they do so only with already existing substances. Rather than making a thing to be absolutely, as substantial forms do, accidental forms make a substance to be thus and so (ST I 76.4c). Beulah's substantial form makes her to be a cow, giving her all of those characteristics essential to bovinity. Her accidental forms make her to be black and white, stubborn, and strong.

A thing might have any number of accidental forms. But how many substantial forms can or must a thing have? Many of Aquinas's predecessors and contemporaries had no clear answer to this question, while others maintained that substances, including human beings, were composites of more fundamental substances.[4] Aquinas is the first to offer an unambiguous argument for what has come to be called the 'unicity' of substantial forms: the view that each substance has just one substantial form. Aquinas arrives at this view by considering the unity that all substances show, which we can see most clearly from the lives of animals and human beings. He repeatedly points to the ways in which the human body, vegetative powers, senses, passions, will, and intellect interact. Our vegetative and sensory powers depend on the body, but the intellect in turn requires sensory cognition in order to abstract intelligible representations or likenesses and put them to work in reasoning. Our passions may be acts of sensory appetites, and therefore a feature of our lives we share with non-human animals. In humans, however, sensory appetites are responsive to rational considerations, and in this way we extend rational control over our lives even to our passions. In fact, many virtues consist in the rational habituation of our sensory appetite. We take sensory pleasure in certain sorts of lives and activities because of the way that we conceive of them intellectually. If human beings were constituted by multiple substantial forms—by distinct substantial forms of soul and body, for instance, or by distinct vegetative, sensory, and rational souls, or by the form of substance, the form of animal, and the form of human—Aquinas does not see how that multiplicity would be compatible with the unity evident in human life. He maintains instead that the very same substantial form, the form of human being, makes us rational, sentient, vegetative, and corporeal. We are essentially all of these, in the distinctively human way.

Aquinas therefore develops a hylomorphic account that provides the metaphysical foundation for the deep unity that he finds in the lives of organisms. While he offers multiple arguments for this view, there is one to which he returns from his early to his mature writings, an argument that made it clear to his contemporaries and successors just what the stakes are in accepting or rejecting the unicity of substantial form.[5] Aquinas begins by appealing to the principles of his theory of material substance. A thing's substantial form gives it its *esse*—that is, its existence or actuality of being. That substantial form therefore makes it both to be and to be one thing, absolutely speaking. For instance, Socrates's substantial form makes him to be both human and gives him the sort of unified life outlined above. Of course, Socrates has any number of additional forms, such as those making him short, dark, ironic, snub-nosed, and athletic. But those are his accidental forms, and describing him as athletic or ironic is to describe him as unified not absolutely speaking, but only in a certain respect. These are additional forms. They come to Socrates over and above his already constituted humanity. He can gain and lose them while remaining the same substance, precisely because they come to something already constituted in its essential unity.

Suppose, by contrast, that the form of human being is just one among other substantial forms in a thing. Perhaps something with the substantial form of body, or the substantial form of animal, gains the form of human being. In that case, something already constituted in its essential unity gains a further form, which must therefore come to it as a mere accident. The result will be not a substantial unity, but instead an accidental unity; and the form of human being will inhere in Socrates in the way in which his athleticism or height inheres in him. Socrates could lose his humanity and yet remain the same substance. Alternatively, he might consist in an aggregate of multiple substantial forms, such as the substantial form of body, of animal, and of human being. In that case there would be even less unity, since he would simply be a cluster of substances, none of which inheres in any other.[6] For Aquinas, the chief advantage available to Aristotelian hylomorphism over Platonic dualism is its capacity to explain the deep unity in the life of an organism. The pluralists, in Aquinas's view, have given away that advantage. By contrast, Aquinas proposes that a single substantial form of human being inheres in prime matter to constitute Socrates. Human nature is not simply rational; it is also animal, vegetative, and corporeal. Therefore, the form of human being organizes prime matter into the organic body that functions in the ways characteristic of human life. Socrates does not *have* a body. Socrates *is* his body (Kenny 2002: 15–16).

Once Aquinas had offered this clear and well-reasoned account, philosophers and theologians were finally in a position to grasp the importance of the topic and its connections to a wide range of issues in metaphysics, ethics, psychology, and theology. Defenders of the unicity thesis stressed the advantages to which Aquinas had called attention, while opponents pointed out the large price that defenders had to pay. Duns Scotus, for instance, argued for a moderate pluralism by appealing to the common view that a corpse is numerically the same body as the one that the animal had in life. When an animal dies, its soul no longer informs its matter. For Aquinas, who maintains that an organism's soul is itself the form of corporeity, when the animal dies its body is destroyed and something else—the corpse—is generated. Socrates's dead body is therefore not numerically the same item as his living body. However, despite his view's implications for traditional funerary rites and the veneration of relics, Aquinas can still argue that pluralists pay a larger price by having to provide a more cumbersome account of the unity of material substances.[7] We find a more problematic objection raised by Richard of Middleton and William Ockham. When Socrates dies, his body will be destroyed and a new substance, a corpse, will be generated. But that corpse appears to have the same accidents as Socrates's body: it will be short, dark, snub-nosed, and so on. Still, no matter how alike the corpse's accidents are to those that Socrates had, no matter if they are indistinguishable to the senses from Socrates, none of them can be numerically the same as the accidents that Socrates had. That is because Socrates's accidents inhered in *Socrates*, and accidents cannot simply migrate from one substance to another. However, there is no plausible explanation for how the new substance came to have properties just like those of the old substance: it can't be the hemlock (since there is nothing about hemlock that produces corpses that are short and dark and snub-nosed), or Socrates's accidents (since they perish before the new accidents come to be). After ruling out many more proposals, Ockham concludes that the only plausible explanation is that the accidents are in fact numerically the same, which requires them to inhere in a substance—Socrates's body—that persists after Socrates's death.[8]

While some philosophers, such as Radulphus Brito, were willing to uphold Aquinas's view despite these objections, other supporters of unicity revised Aquinas's thought to withstand Ockham's objections. Francisco Suarez, for instance, argues that unicity is compatible with the numerical persistence of accidents through substantial change because the accidents themselves inhere directly in prime matter.[9] However, accepting Suarez's view means abandoning Aquinas's two-tier schema of material being that so elegantly captures the distinction between substantial and accidental forms. Although the various permutations of Aquinas's views remained controversial, all parties to the debate were in Aquinas's debt for setting out the stakes so clearly, in particular for demonstrating the desirability for ontological economy. As a result, even pluralists, heeding Aquinas's warnings, tended to posit the smallest number of substantial forms needed to stave off the unwanted consequences attending unicity.[10]

3. Acquired and Infused Virtue

Aquinas's ethical writings, in particular his mature works, are impressive in both the number and the range of sources from which he draws. While the Bible and Aristotle serve as chief influences, Aquinas also summons stoics, neoplatonists, Greek and Latin Church Fathers, canonists, Jewish and Islamic philosophers, and an array of twelfth- and thirteenth-century Christian authors. What is striking is not the size and breadth of this list of thinkers. Aquinas does not simply note them, or use their ideas as foils to his own. Instead, he invites them to a dialogue, weaving together the disparate strands of their thought into an innovative and coherent moral theory.[11] Drawing on the likes of Aristotle, Nemesius, Augustine, Averroes, and Albert, he develops a moral psychology that underlies his account of human action and passion. He integrates his theory of virtue with that moral psychology with advice from Aristotle, Averroes, and Peraldus. Ulpian, Gratian, and Roland of Cremona help him explain the nature of law and its relationship to virtue and human action, while his arguments for the necessity of grace and distinctively Christian virtues and gifts benefit from contributions from Augustine and Hugh of Saint Cher. Finally, Aquinas shows how those Christian elements build on and complete the purely natural elements he discusses. In this chapter, I will sketch one small but representative aspect of Aquinas's ambitious ethical project: the grounding of his account of distinctively Christian—that is, infused—virtue in his more general Aristotelian account of virtue.

Readers can find Aquinas's basic explanation of moral virtue throughout his corpus, but he offers the greatest detail in his *Disputed Question on the Virtues in General* and in the Second Part of the *Summa theologiae*. In those works, he explains that virtue is not a capacity, like the will or sensory appetite. Our capacities are part of our human nature and we have them by natural necessity. Virtues, by contrast, are good *habitus*, that is, habits or dispositions that perfect our appetitive capacities and are acquired by a long process of habituation that trains them to be responsive to rational considerations. At the same time, that training of our appetites helps us to see more clearly what is really valuable and how to achieve it.[12]

These virtues carry out two basic functions, one at the outset of the decision-making process and one at the execution stage.[13] Drawing on Aristotle (NE 1144a7–9), Aquinas notes that virtue makes our ends right (DQCV 2c, ST II-II 47.6sc). By keeping our appetites from eliciting wayward desires before we have made a thoughtful decision, virtue prevents our appetites from distorting our moral vision and judgment. In addition, by calling attention to morally salient considerations, virtue helps us to keep the right ends in view as we deliberate (*DQE* 12.1c, DQVG 4, 5). Once we have deliberated and settled on a course of action, virtue makes that action prompt, unwavering, and pleasurable (DQVG 2c, ad 1, ad 2; a.5 ad 10; a.8 ad 6, ad 7). Acting in keeping with our natural tendencies is pleasurable; and, since habits are a 'second nature' (DQVG a.8 ad 16, a.9c), acting on our virtues will likewise be pleasurable. That pleasure and natural tendency will promote the prompt and unwavering action required by virtue.

Following Aristotle, Aquinas writes that virtuous activity is intrinsically connected to human happiness. Virtuous activity is the dominant component of the sort of natural happiness that Aristotle discussed. However, as a Christian, Aquinas believes in a completely fulfilling happiness that consists in the vision and love of God in the next life. According to Christian teaching, we cannot by our own natural powers merit that sort of happiness; we can achieve it only through God's grace. However, Aquinas does not think that we are purely passive recipients of this divine largesse. God's grace is just the first step toward meriting eternal happiness. We must take the second by acting out of love for God and neighbor for God's sake. Keeping those ends in mind, and acting for those ends promptly, unwaveringly, and with delight will require virtue. Since acquired virtue directs us only to the happiness of this world, God's grace must manifest itself through divinely infused virtues that enable us to work toward our supernatural end. Although infused virtues may sometimes direct us to act differently than their acquired counterparts, the two species of virtue function in the same way. By modeling this essential element of the Christian moral life on his well-established Aristotelian theory of virtue and its function, Aquinas respects the Christian doctrine that salvation is a gift of God while at the same time presenting a clear account of what role we must play as agents to respond to that gift and merit eternal happiness (ST I-II 51.4, 63.3, 4; DQVG 10, 13).

There is some reason to wonder whether the integrative account that I have just offered is entirely accurate.[14] After all, Aquinas draws his preferred definition of human virtue from Augustine rather than from Aristotle: 'Virtue is a good quality of the mind, by which one lives rightly, which no one uses badly, which God works in us without us' (DQVG 2, ST I-II 55.4). However, Aquinas explains that he prefers this definition for precisely Aristotelian reasons: it captures virtue's formal ('good quality'), final ('by which one lives rightly, which no one uses badly'), material ('of the mind'), and efficient causes ('which God works in us without us'). The content of the first three elements of the definition accords perfectly well with Aristotle's account of virtue. Aristotle argues that moral virtue is a good habit or disposition, and therefore belongs to the category of quality. In fact, to make the definition more precise, Aquinas suggests changing 'quality' to the more precise 'habit' (*habitus*), thereby making its definition more explicitly Aristotelian. Aquinas takes the clauses 'by which one lives rightly, which no one uses badly' to mean that each virtue directs us to its proper good. It is of course the final clause that is un-Aristotelian, and Aquinas acknowledges that, in this traditional form, the definition applies only to infused virtue. That is why he explicitly explains how to adjust the definition so as to account for acquired moral virtue.[15] In the DQVG, he then goes on for the next seven articles to discuss acquired and infused virtue indiscriminately (aa. 3–7) or to focus on acquired virtue in particular (8–9). After devoting two articles to infused virtue (10–11), he turns again to treating both sorts together.[16]

However, there are other and more compelling reasons for questioning the integrative account. Because infused virtue directs us to our supernatural happiness, it must be infused by God and not acquired by our actions over a long period of habituation. Likewise, it is lost not gradually, but all at once: we corrupt infused virtue not by habituating ourselves to performing bad actions, but by a single act of serious sin. How, then, can infused virtue be a relatively permanent and stable disposition, as Aristotle characterized virtue? Finally, acquired virtue gives us not only facility, but readiness, to perform good actions unwaveringly and with pleasure. Those with infused virtue may experience some hesitation and conflict, and so infused virtue appears to function differently.

While it is true that we gain and lose infused virtue all at once and not by a process of habituation, Aquinas nevertheless lends support to the view that even infused virtue is a stable and relatively permanent disposition, although its stability is explained differently. Aristotle had argued that the moral virtues are reciprocally connected, so that we cannot acquire any one of them without acquiring all of them. Aquinas accepts Aristotle's conclusion not just for the acquired, but for the infused virtues as well (I-II 65.1, 65.2, 65.3; DQCV 2). This complex of virtues strengthens us in all that we need to do to achieve eternal happiness, and so it defends us against temptation of any sort. As the result of divine grace, these virtues fix our hearts on God so firmly that we would not want to be separated from him by serious sin (I-II 109.8c). Therefore, infused virtue does lend to our lives a stability in the good, a stability characteristic of Aristotelian virtue.

Finally, if infused moral virtue did not under ordinary circumstances make our activity prompt, unwavering, and pleasurable, then the activity it elicited would be morally lacking (I-II 58.3 ad 2, DQVG 8 ad 6). We would not perform acts expressing love of God and neighbor wholeheartedly, thanks to persistent wants and passions at variance with the demands of morality. In short, on this view, infused moral virtue would fail to accomplish the task for which Aquinas says that we need virtue (DQVG 1c, ad 13, 4, 8 ad 6; I-II 107.4c), giving us no increased capacity to perform acts without moral flaws. Fortunately, this not at all what Aquinas maintains. Speaking of both acquired and infused virtue, he says that 'a habit in itself causes one to act readily and with pleasure' (DQVG 2 ad 2). This assertion does not in fact contradict his claim that those with infused virtue do not always act readily and with pleasure. Aquinas explains that sometimes factors external to a particular habit can interfere with the normal functioning of that habit. If a sleepy mathematician finds it hard to do proofs, the problem is in her drowsiness, not in the habit of mathematics. Likewise, when someone with bad acquired habits receives grace and an infusion of new virtues, those lingering but decaying old dispositions can interfere with the functioning of an infused virtue. However, the problem is not in the new virtues; it is in something external to them (DQVG 10 ad 16). This issue does not arise in the same way for acquired virtue, as Aquinas explicitly states, only because someone with acquired virtue cannot have lingering contrary dispositions to run this sort of interference. Therefore, habits of infused moral virtue function in our moral psychology precisely as habits of acquired moral virtue do. Although he remains faithful to the necessities of Christian dogma, Aquinas layers his account of Christian virtue on that of acquired virtue with an elegance and economy that allows him to discuss both species together for most of the *Disputed Question on the Virtues in General*.

4. The Pedagogy of the *Summa Theologiae*

Despite widespread concern to convey their doctrines, methods, and ways of life, philosophers have not always earned high marks for pedagogy. However, many philosophical greats are also master pedagogues. Socrates's various methods, in particular his elenchus and creative use of irony, inspired philosophers as diverse as Augustine, Boethius, Kierkegaard, and Nietzsche, themselves all renowned for pedagogy. Descartes, Spinoza, Adam Smith, and Wittgenstein can likewise claim titles as model pedagogues. That so many of the greats were also concerned with effective teaching is no coincidence. In some cases, the very vocation that put philosophy at the center of their lives was itself a vocation to teach others, to understand their needs and foibles more accurately, as we see with Socrates and Kierkegaard. Others, including Socrates, the stoics, and Wittgenstein, conceived of philosophy as a sort of therapy, curing us of our deep misconceptions and misdirected passions. Hence, the very practice of philosophy is in part a sort of pedagogy. Others still, such as Descartes and Augustine, gave attention to the order and process of discovery as part of the philosophical message that they were trying to convey.

Aquinas attends to pedagogy for all of these reasons, or for reasons very much like these. In his commentaries he is always attentive to organizing principles and to the flow of ideas, writing plainly, concisely, yet comprehensively about texts—such as Aristotle's *Metaphysics* or the Gospel of John—that are often dark and recalcitrant. We see his concern with pedagogy in his published disputations as well, which use objections and authoritative texts to uncover the complexities of philosophical and theological problems, thereby opening the way to innovative solutions. Most impressive, however, are the instructive ways in which Aquinas structures his long systematic works, the *Summa contra gentiles* and the *Summa theologiae*.[17]

In the Prologue to the *Summa theologiae*, Aquinas writes:

> Because a teacher of catholic truth ought to instruct not just the advanced but also has the task of educating beginners . . . our intention in this work is to relay what pertains to Christian religion in a way suitable for the education of beginners.

Just who these 'beginners' are is a matter of some controversy.[18] Aquinas might be referring generally to those without an elite education in theology at a major university; or he might be referring more narrowly to the sort of friars whom Aquinas had been teaching in the Dominican house of study in Orvieto, modestly gifted but far from brilliant Dominicans in need of sufficient training to preach, hear confessions, and give moral and spiritual guidance. Whatever the case, from among the many hindrances that these 'beginners' face, Aquinas cites 'the multiplication of pointless questions, articles, and arguments'—the fact that 'what these beginners need to know is not relayed as the order of the discipline requires, but as the exposition of books demands or as the right moment for a disputation presents itself.' The typical Dominican course of study was no exception to these problems: students generally covered Raymond of Pennafort's *Summa de casibus* and William Peraldus's *Summa de vitiis et virtutibus*, together with study of select canonists, the Bible, and perhaps parts of the fourth book of the *Sentences*. Such a syllabus would result in a course of study that was repetitive, disunified, and narrowly focused (Boyle 1982).

It is likely, therefore, that Aquinas meant the *Summa theologiae* to serve as a way of introducing these Dominicans to what he considered the essential topics of Christian religion (*religio*). However, when we realize what Aquinas means when he speaks of 'Christian religion', we will also see that the way in which he presents his topics will itself be part of the content of his teaching. The word *religio* in this context does not mean a set of doctrines or a membership in a denomination. Instead, it means the way of life characteristic of those who follow Christ: those who learn the truths, acquire the virtues, and lead the life directed to eternal happiness with God (Kerr 2002: 166).[19] The work will therefore not serve as a catechism; nor will it be a work whose purpose is to define Christian teaching for purely dogmatic or apologetic purposes. Aquinas means the *Summa* to be more practical than the standard Dominican texts, not in spite of its systematic presentation of a theology expounded by the aid of sophisticated metaphysics, epistemology, philosophy of language, and action theory, but precisely because of these characteristics. Its focus on Christian teaching is directed to the formation of those who wish to live this distinctive way of life and those who mean to instruct others on how to do so. While that way of life will involve much more than just philosophy (for example, worship, reception of sacraments, participation in a community of faith), we will see shortly just how much Aquinas relies on philosophy to pass on that way of life to his readers.

Once Aquinas realized that he needed to widen the scope of Dominican education, the problem he faced was that of how to organize thousands of complex arguments ranging over wide ranging topics in a way that would prove fruitful for his readers. One possibility would be to write a second commentary on the *Sentences* with these new goals in mind. After all, the *Sentences* had a certain order: it addressed the basic principles of Christianity as expressed by the Nicene Creed and overlaid that structure with a neoplatonic scheme that first treats God, then the emanation of creatures from God, and finally the return of creatures to God. While teaching in Rome, where he was most free to experiment with curriculum, Aquinas had in fact begun a new commentary on the *Sentences* in a spare and simple prose style, perhaps with the aim of using it to remedy the flaws in typical Dominican education (Boyle 1982; Davies 2014: 8–14; Jordan 2016: 36–7). However, the *Sentences* is weakest in just those areas that the Dominicans most needed: a rich theoretical account of virtue and sin that could be put to use by preacher-confessors. Moreover, Peter Lombard did not structure his work for the benefit of those not already well schooled in the discipline. Of course, in addition to the *Sentences*, there were shorter works that had their own logic, such as those structured according to the six days of creation or the seven capital vices. None of these would do for a work that aimed to cover the entirety of the discipline—and not just to cover it, but at the same time to master problems of enormous complexity, uncover their interrelations, and structure them according to a unified scheme that would be pedagogically fruitful and philosophically illuminating. In his second year of teaching in Rome, instead of continuing with the new *Sentences* commentary, Aquinas began the *Summa theologiae*. No one since Aristotle, and perhaps not again until Kant, would show the capacity for such breathtaking breadth and depth that Aquinas achieves in this work, and perhaps no one is his peer in the organization of such rich material into a coherent vision.

Aquinas divides the *Summa theologiae* into three large 'Parts'. In the First Part, after a brief argument that sacred teaching (which concerns God and the way of life that leads to him) is a science on the Aristotelian model, Aquinas discusses these:

> the existence and nature of God; the Trinity; creation in general; angels; material creation; human beings; divine governance.

In the First Part of the Second Part, Aquinas treats these:

> human happiness; action theory; passions; habits and virtues in general; sin; law; grace.

In the Second Part of the Second Part, we find the following:

> the theological virtues, their associated virtues, their opposed vices; the cardinal virtues, their associated virtues, their opposed vices; freely given graces and states of life.

In the Third Part, Aquinas was able to complete these discussions:

> the incarnation; the works and passion of Christ; the sacraments of baptism, penance, and the Eucharist.

Had he been able to finish the Third Part, he would have gone on to discuss the remaining sacraments as well as immortal life.

From this table of contents, the *Summa* might look like no more than so many separate treatises on a wide range of disparate issues relevant to philosophy and theology. That impression is likely to be particularly strong in the world of contemporary academia. To meet the needs of our academic terms, as well as those of our publishers, *we* divide the *Summa* into easily taught treatises. The result is that we have created separable units that contain Aquinas's supposed philosophy of religion, his metaethics, his philosophical anthropology, his theology, and so on. However, Aquinas himself meant the work to be studied as a whole and in order.[20] What appear to be separable units turn out to be integral parts of this larger whole, very carefully structured to convey, in its extraordinary diversity and complexity, the one architectonic lesson on the way of life that leads to eternal happiness.

There have been many suggestions for how we are to understand the structure of the *Summa*.[21] In this short discussion, I cannot do justice to this topic. I will therefore point out just one structuring feature of the work. Aquinas means this text to serve as a way of instructing students in the distinctively Christian way of life, and he selects and orders his topics for just that purpose. Because this volume concerns great philosophers in particular, I will concentrate on one essential aspect of the Christian way of life that had been central to the philosophical tradition since classical antiquity: the need to know oneself.

To understand the best way of life for human beings, we need to know ourselves—that is, know what our nature is, what our good consists in, and how in general we reach it. While it might look as if Aquinas does not get started in earnest on this project until the middle of the First Part, is not fully invested in addressing it until the Second Part, and abandons it entirely in the Third, in fact nearly every page of the *Summa* contributes to it. Even the treatment of angels in I qq. 50–64, which might appear to be a quaint bit of useless medieval speculative lore, instructs humans about themselves. Aquinas conceives of angels as intellectual creatures endowed with free choice, and in those respects much like humans. They are, however, incorporeal intelligences, and once we grasp how such beings learn, think, choose, and act, we are ready to understand why embodied creatures cannot operate in the same way. So, when Aquinas begins his explicit treatment of human beings at I 75, he contrasts our ways of learning, thinking, and knowing with those of the angels. We acquire intelligible species (likenesses or representations of what is intelligible) by abstracting them from imagination formed by sensory experience, while angels acquire exemplar species emanated from God (ST I 55.3 ad 1; cf. In II *Sent.* 3.3.2 ad 1). Unlike the 'thick' exemplar species that the angels have (ST I 84.5), our abstracted species are 'thin', and so to grasp the quiddity of a material being we need to appeal to a concrete individual presented by our imagination (ST I 84.7): angels grasp truths by instantaneous insight, while we reason discursively, deliberate before choosing, and often change our minds.[22]

Aquinas ends the First Part with a discussion of divine governance: God moves all things in keeping with their natures. Because rational creatures are capable of self-government, God does not move them by giving them natural or instinctual appetites, as he does for non-rational creatures. He allows them scope to determine their actions for themselves, helping them through such external means as precepts and prohibitions (I 103.5, 105.3–105.5). Aquinas begins the Second Part of the *Summa theologiae* by reminding us of our own self-governance, thereby linking the opening of the Second Part with the end of the First. But he also links it to the beginning of the First Part:

> As Damascene says, human beings are said to be made in God's image, insofar as 'image' signifies a being that is intellectual, free in its choice, and capable of exercising power in its own right. Therefore, after treating the exemplar—God—and all that proceeds from divine power according to his will, we must next investigate his image, human beings, insofar as they too are the source of what they do in that they have free choice and power over their doings.

We now see that the First Part's account of God is not simply Aquinas's course in philosophy of religion, to be followed by his course on angelology and that on anthropology. Humans cannot understand themselves until they grasp that they are like God in their capacities of thinking, planning, choosing, and acting. It is precisely these capacities that make them capable of perfect happiness—the activity of contemplating and loving God in the next life—and of acquiring the characteristics in this life needed to avoid moral pitfalls and to merit perfect happiness.[23] The remainder of the Second Part, therefore, explores precisely these issues.

The Third Part of the *Summa* might seem entirely too narrowly focused on Christ to bring us to further self-knowledge. Although Aquinas argues that Christ is truly human, he is unique among humans in that he is also divine, and a discussion of Christ might therefore seem to be an unlikely place for us to learn about ourselves. But Aquinas's purpose is not to write a treatise on the metaphysics of the hypostatic union. He discusses the consequences that union has for us (qq. 25–6), about the saving fruits of Christ's passion (qq. 48–9), about Christ as head of the Church and as a source of grace for us (q. 8). This latter discussion becomes more important as we read about the sacraments instituted by Christ: it is by membership in the Church that we become members of Christ's body and we avail ourselves of his reconciling us to God. Reception of the Eucharist in particular aids us: not only does it confer the grace that helps us to live well but, unlike other food that we assimilate to our own bodies, it assimilates us to the body of Christ (III 73.3). If the Second Part teaches us that to achieve the happiness that is our final end we must accept God's help in remedying our flaws, the Third Part tells us what precise role we play in God's plan to remedy those flaws.

Within the overarching structure of the *Summa* that leads to self-knowledge about ourselves as members of the human species, the Second Part—by far the largest—is structured to lead each individual to self-knowledge about his or her *particular* moral condition as well. The opening five questions ask us to consider whether we have set the right goal in life for ourselves, or whether our lives are so disordered that we are pursuing the sorts of goals that cannot make us happy. In what follows, we discover what makes us morally responsible, and what states, actions, passions, and omissions we are in fact responsible for (I-II 6–89). By attending to the nature and causes of sins, we learn not only how to be on our guard against them, but also to distinguish the degree to which we are agents of our own failures (I-II 71–89). In addition, by seeing which virtues a particular sin opposes, we can also determine just how serious a failure our own sins are (II-II 1–170). If we occasionally eat what the doctor has told us not to eat, but only when we are very hungry and tired, those are small offences compared to cool-headed acts of cheating others out of their paychecks. In the second case, we sin against justice and charity, virtues that concern our right relationship with our neighbors, and without any excusing factors. In the first, we sin only against temperance, and our agency is hampered by the hunger and fatigue that we feel. By carefully attending to both the seriousness of the offence and our particular psychological state, we can gain better insight into how seriously we have faltered in striving for happiness and what sort of remedies we need to secure and strengthen us. By our own natural powers, we can strive to acquire virtue, which makes us resolute in the good, ready to pursue what's good when we need to do so, and gives us a certain pleasure in acting well (I-II 49–67). In addition, by divine grace, we may attain virtues that make us friends of God and allow us to merit eternal life (I-II 62–67, II-II 1–46). Even the most theoretical discussions of the Second Part of the *Summa*, such as those on action theory and the moral psychology of sin, are important for those who want guidance in the Christian way of life for themselves or for those whom they advise.

5. Conclusion

Aquinas's work spans nearly every field that we recognize in twenty-first-century philosophy. In addition, he draws into his discussions thinkers from classical Greece, early Christianity, Judaism, and Islam, not to mention dozens of early medieval and scholastic thinkers. However, if we highlight this expanse of topics and thinkers, stressing the encyclopedic character of Aquinas's work, we will grasp what makes him learned but not what makes him brilliant. In particular, I want to call attention to the ways in which Aquinas creatively interweaves strands from his vast learning. His arguments for the unicity of substantial form link together his philosophical anthropology, physics, and metaphysics. His theory of virtue integrates his theological ideas about grace and salvation, a well-developed version of Aristotelian virtue theory, and an innovative account of human action. A lesser philosopher might have penned a *Summa theologiae* as a textbook in which important topics were treated in relative isolation. Aquinas, by contrast, authors a pedagogical masterpiece structured to cast new light on traditional topics. Assiduous and disciplined readers who work their way through the text question by question will be rewarded by the unexpected insights that earlier discussions allow them to form. Similarly, later discussions invite readers to return to earlier ones and see them in a new light. It is a shame that so few readers, whether medieval or contemporary, have found those rewards or accepted those invitations.

Notes

1 I use the following abbreviations for Aquinas's works: ST = *Summa theologiae*, ST I = First Part of the *Summa*; ST I-II = First Part of the Second Part; ST II-II = Second Part of the Second Part of the *Summa*, ST III = Third Part of the *Summa*, SCG = *Summa contra gentiles*, DQVG = *Disputed Question on the Virtues in General*, DQCV = *Disputed*

Question on the Cardinal Virtues, DQE = *Disputed Questions on Evil*, DQS = *Disputed Questions on the Soul*, DQSC = *Disputed Questions on Spiritual Creatures*. For articles of the ST or disputed questions, I use the following abbreviations: c = corpus or body of the article, ad = response to objection, sc = *sed contra* or 'on the contrary'.

2 It was in opposition to Aquinas's philosophically sophisticated arguments for unicity that increasingly plausible and well-defended arguments for pluralism emerged. On this history, see Michael (1992) and Pasnau (2013: ch. 25).

3 For helpful discussions, see Brown (2005) and Brower (2014).

4 The most famous pluralist text in Aquinas's time was the *Fons Vitae* of Ibn Gabirol (Avicebron), a twelfth-century philosopher who presents a Platonic version of this thesis. His work became influential on Latin Christian thinkers, most notably on Bonaventure. While Aquinas finds in Averroes another supporter of unicity, others, such as Richard of Middleton, found in Averroes a supporter of pluralism. See Richard's *De gradu formarum*, in Zavalloni (1951: 35–169).

5 See, for instance, SCG II c. 58, ST I 76.3, 76.4, DQS 9 and 11, DQSC 3.

6 See, in particular, SCG II c. 58.

7 Scotus's argument for pluralism is found in *Ordinatio* IV d. 11 q. 3. In q. 4 he offers that more cumbersome argument for unity. A single, ultimate, completive form makes the substance what it is. However, the potentiality for that completive actuality need not be prime matter. It can be prime matter actualized by prior forms, a composite that itself stands as potentiality for that final actuality.

8 For Ockham's views, see *Quodlibet* II, q. 11. See also Adams (1987: 648–50).

9 Suarez' view is found in *Disputationes metaphysicae* XV. See also Pasnau (2013: 587).

10 On this subsequent history, see the excellent discussions in Michael (1992) and Pasnau (2013: ch. 25).

11 For Aquinas, the Bible is not just another source, alongside Aristotle and Averroes. The sacred doctrine based in biblical revelation is definitive. However, Aquinas also relies on his own philosophical and theological interlocutors to help determine what the most plausible interpretation of the Bible is.

12 See, in particular, ST I-II 55.1, 55.2, 56.4, 56.6, 58.4, 58.5, 63.1, 63.2, 64.1, 64.2; DQVG 1, 4, 5, 8, 9, 13.

13 I explain these functions in greater detail in Hause (2007).

14 There has been considerable discussion on the extent to which Aquinas adopts, transforms, and/or subverts Aristotle. There is no doubt, for instance, that the role that Aquinas gives to gifts and fruits of the Holy Spirit has no counterpart in Aristotle (see, e.g., Pinsent [2012] and Stump [2012]). My thesis here is limited. I am arguing only that Aquinas offers accounts of both acquired and infused moral virtue, that he develops an Aristotelian account of acquired virtue as one basis of an ethical theory whose plausibility should be evident to anyone, that he models his account of infused moral virtue on that of acquired virtue, and that the explanatory power of the latter serves as basis for his presentation of the former. A thoughtful and measured alternative reading is found in Kent (2014), who rightly points to one further un-Aristotelian feature of Aquinas's ethics: habits such as virtues are under the control of our will. But I take that to be a function of Aquinas's innovative action theory rather than a new element in the account of virtue itself. For further discussion, see Hause (2010).

15 The responses to DQVG 2 objections 18–21, now missing or never written, would have further explained how to adjust the definition. No matter, since articles 8–9 constitute a detailed account of just how we acquire virtue through our own activity.

16 The argument that Aquinas's appeal to the Augustinian definition supports the view that Aquinas's account of virtue is un-Aristotelian is found in Stump (2012). Stump further asserts that acquired virtue is not 'true' virtue: It is not connected to prudence and reciprocally related to all the other virtues. However, she reaches this erroneous conclusion because she confuses the so-called natural virtues or natural inclinations with genuine acquired virtue. See DQVG 8c and ad 19 as well as DQCV 2, where Aquinas explicitly contrasts these natural virtues (which are not really virtues) with acquired virtues (which are really virtues, but imperfect ones).

17 Due to space limitations, I cannot do justice to both works, which (despite significant overlap in content) have very different structures and goals. I will therefore limit my remarks to the *Summa theologiae*. That decision might seem perverse for a volume on great *philosophers*, since the SCG is (despite its ultimate theological aims) the work that relies exclusively on philosophy for the first three of its four books. However, the ST is still deeply philosophical at every turn and does more to establish Aquinas as a *great* than the SCG does. For good discussions of the SCG's pedagogy and structure, see Hibbs (1995); Kretzmann (1997, 1999); Jordan (2006); and Michon (2014).

18 See, for instance, Boyle (1982) and Kerr (2002).

19 See also Jordan (2016: 36).

20 A point stressed by Jordan (2016).

21 I am not assuming that the work as a whole can be explained by just one set of structuring principles; there may be multiple overlapping structuring principles at work. The most influential discussions include Chenu (1939), which argues that the *Summa theologiae* is structured, as Aquinas thought the *Sentences* were, on the neoplatonic emanation-return model. That influential thesis finds support with Torrell (2005: 17–62, esp. 27–8), but faces serious questions from Te Velde (2006: 9–35), who instead develops Persson (1970) and Corbin (1974) in seeing in each part a move to increasingly concrete topics and a shift in perspective.

22 I am grateful to Therese Cory for this distinction between emanated and abstracted species.

23 Te Velde (2006) has argued clearly and compellingly for these links between these texts in the First Part and the opening of the Second Part.

References

Adams, Marilyn McCord 1987. *William Ockham*. Notre Dame, IN: University of Notre Dame Press.

Aquinas, Thomas 1852–73. *Opera Omnia*, Parma: Petrus Fiaccodorus.

Aquinas, Thomas 1882. *Opera Omnia*, Rome: Commissio Leonina.

Aquinas, Thomas 1947. *Summa Theologica*, trans. the Fathers of the English Dominican Province, New York: Benziger Brothers.

Boyle, Leonard E. 1982. *The Setting of the* Summa Theologiae *of Saint Thomas Aquinas*, The Etienne Gilson Series, 5, PIMS: Toronto.

Brower, Jeffrey E. 2014. *Aquinas's Ontology of the Material World: Change, Hylomorphism, and Material Objects*, Oxford: Oxford University Press.

Brown, Christopher 2005. *Aquinas and the Ship of Theseus: Solving Problems about Material Objects*, London: Continuum.

Chenu, M.-D. 1939. Le plan de la somme theologique de Saint Thomas, *Revue Thomiste* 47: 93–107.

Corbin, Michel 1974. *Le chemin de la théologie chez Thomas d'Aquin*, Paris: Editions Beauchesne.
Davies, Brian 2014. *Thomas Aquinas's* Summa Theologiae: *A Guide and Commentary*, New York: Oxford University Press.
Duns Scotus 1894. *Ordinatio* IV, d. 43–49, in *Opera Omnia* XX and XXI, Paris: L. Vivès.
Hause, Jeffrey 2007. Aquinas on the Function of Moral Virtue, *American Catholic Philosophical Quarterly* 81: 1–20.
Hause, Jeffrey 2010. Introduction, in *Thomas Aquinas, Disputed Questions on Virtue*, ed. and trans. Jeffrey Hause and Claudia Eisen Murphy, Indianapolis: Hackett: ix–xxiii.
Hibbs, Thomas 1995. *Dialectic and Narrative in Aquinas: A Reinterpretation of the* Summa Contra Gentiles, Notre Dame, IN: University of Notre Dame Press.
Jordan, Mark 2006. *Rewritten Theology: Aquinas after His Readers*, Oxford: Blackwell.
Jordan, Mark 2016. Structure, in *The Cambridge Companion to the* Summa Theologiae, ed. Philip McCosker and Denys Turner, New York: Cambridge University Press: 34–47.
Kenny, Anthony 2002. *Aquinas on Being*, Oxford: Clarendon Press.
Kent, Bonnie 2014. Aquinas's Ethics and Aristotelian Naturalism, in *Debates in Medieval Philosophy: Essential Readings and Contemporary Responses*, ed. Jeffrey Hause, New York: Routledge: 313–24.
Kerr, Fergus 2002. *After Aquinas: Versions of Thomism*, Oxford: Blackwell.
Kretzmann, Norman 1997. *The Metaphysics of Theism; Aquinas's Natural Theology in* Summa contra Gentiles I, Oxford: Clarendon Press.
Kretzmann, Norman 1999. *The Metaphysics of Creation: Aquinas's Natural Theology in* Summa contra Gentiles II, Oxford: Clarendon Press.
Michael, Emily 1992. Averroes and the Plurality of Forms, *Franciscan Studies* 52: 155–82.
Michon, Cyrille 2014. 'To Make the Truth Known': The Aim and Structure of the *Contra Gentiles*, in *Debates in Medieval Philosophy: Essential Readings and Contemporary Responses*, ed. Jeffrey Hause, New York: Routledge: 271–84.
Ockham, William 1980. *Quodlibeta*, in *Opera Theologica* IX, St. Bonaventure, NY: Franciscan Institute.
Pasnau, Robert 2013. *Metaphysical Themes 1274–1671*, Oxford: Clarendon Press.
Persson, Per Erik 1970. *Sacra Doctrina: Reason and Revelation in Aquinas*, trans. Ross MacKenzie, Minneapolis, MN: Fortress Press.
Pinsent, Andrew 2012. *The Second Person Perspective in Aquinas's Ethics: Virtues and Gifts*, Abingdon: Routledge.
Stump, Eleonore 2012. The Non-Aristotelian Character of Aquinas's Ethics: Aquinas on the Passions, *Faith and Philosophy* 28: 29–43.
Te Velde, Rudi 2006. *Aquinas on God: The 'Divine Science' of the* Summa Theologiae, Aldershot: Ashgate.
Torrell, Jean-Pierre 2005. *Aquinas's* Summa: *Background, Structure, and Reception*, trans. Benedict M. Guevin, Washington, DC: Catholic University of America Press.
Zavalloni, Roberto 1951. *Richard de Mediavilla et la controverse sur la pluralité des formes*, Louvain: Institut supérieur de philosophie.

7

DESCARTES AS A GREAT PHILOSOPHER

Comprehensive Physics, Methodological Systematicity, and Mechanistic Embodiment

Gary Hatfield

1. Introduction

There is no doubt that Descartes is a great philosopher. In many areas of philosophy, the most recent writings invoke his positions as benchmarks for orienting current thought (often through opposition to him). Thus, in the philosophy of mind and the philosophy of perception, one finds frequent reference to Descartes's mind-body dualism, his (actual or presumed) account of the place of sensory experience in the economy of human knowledge, or his (actual or presumed) model of deliberative action. With the clear vision of hindsight, we can see that he changed the way in which the mind-body relation was conceived and that he proposed a view of sensory qualities that promoted (in effect) a distinction between primary and secondary qualities. In the second half of the seventeenth century, his comprehensive natural philosophy, based on particulate matter in motion, was widely discussed and adopted in its fundamentals. It advanced the conception of a single, indefinitely large universe, constituted of a single type of matter, that set the stage for Newton's work. Any one of these achievements[1] would be enough to preserve Descartes's name among the great philosophers, on the grounds of his extensive influence on later thought. The fact that he changed the game in these ways (and several others) presumably is why he appears on virtually every top-five list of the greatest Western philosophers.

But what made his philosophy great? That is, leaving aside why we must acknowledge him as a great philosopher, what was it about his philosophy that made it great?[2]

From what has been said, we can see that Descartes had several new things to say. It is part of his greatness that he did not simply offer an array of new ideas; he worked them out and related them systematically. He did not merely offer hints, but he articulated in detail a new way of looking at mind, matter, the ordered world of nature, and the senses. His novel metaphysics was paired with an epistemology of the pure intellect, which held that the human mind has direct insights, through its innate ideas, into the essences of mind, matter, and God.

A less obvious, but equally consequential, aspect is that he spoke in ways that his contemporaries could understand and find compelling. He offered criticisms of previous philosophy, and especially of the dominant scholastic Aristotelian ontology of form and matter. Many others were criticizing these aspects of the extant theory of nature. Yet Descartes was heard.[3] Was his greatness in how he framed his criticisms, or in the fact that he backed them with an alternative ontology and epistemology, or both? It seems the latter. He initially made his case for preferring his natural philosophy over established or other newly proffered frameworks in terms of comparative advantage: he believed, and many accepted, that his vision of nature was clearer and more compelling than what was otherwise on offer—a judgment that might be made without considering his metaphysical arguments. Those arguments, which were exceedingly well crafted, were also heard, even if they did not always convince.

Another aspect of Descartes's greatness is the deep structure and texture to his thoughts, such that not only could his contemporaries hear new things in what he said, but we can do so as well. His mind-body dualism is often rued. Yet his description of a domain of conscious phenomenal experience that seems irreducible to matter has not been overcome, despite the great diversity of ongoing projects having that aim. For many years, the actual working details of his notion of mind-body union and interaction were ignored. But, with the new interest in embodiment in philosophy, new things can be heard in Descartes's extensive discussions of embodiment, whether as regards the teleology of the senses, the active role of brain processes in producing appropriate behavior, or the cognitive structure of the emotions.

Descartes is frequently targeted for (allegedly) purveying a hyper-intellectualized view of human action, as sense-plan-move (for example, Wheeler 2005: chs. 2–3). Yet a close examination of his works shows that he understood, nay, insisted, that many human actions (or behaviors) are not governed by reason, deliberative or habitual; that the whole human being must be considered as embodied; and that a major role must be assigned to non-mentally governed processes in explaining human behavior. His general approach to the body as automaton was highly influential in his own times and was recognized as a landmark achievement by physiologists of the nineteenth and early twentieth centuries, including Emil du Bois-Reymond (1912: 300–1), T. H. Huxley (1896: 167, 181), William James (1890: 1: 130), and Charles Sherrington (1963: 152–3). In this domain, a further greatness factor results from the fact that, long after he wrote, there is still more to be discovered in his works, genuinely, by new readers.

After sketching Descartes's intellectual biography, this chapter illustrates three aspects of his greatness: his comprehensive and systematic natural philosophy as elaborated in detail; his adaptation of various styles or genres of writing to his evolving conceptions of method, so that method and content are well integrated; and his fundamental contributions to how an embodied mind might perceive and feel. These are not the only elements of his achievement, but they do illustrate central aspects of his accomplishments. The chapter ends by considering some common criticisms of Descartes, concluding that they do not diminish his greatness.

2. Background and Context

Descartes was born in Touraine in 1596.[4] He received a good education at the Jesuit school, La Flèche, in nearby Anjou. After a stint in law school (at the behest of his family), he began his adult years in Breda (United Provinces, Netherlands), where in 1618–19 he served in the army of William of Nassau. While stationed there, he enjoyed conversations with Isaac Beeckman, a local schoolmaster, natural philosopher, and mathematician. Beeckman posed problems to Descartes in mathematics, music, hydrology, and what he called 'mathematical physics'.[5] Descartes responded by developing some mathematical results that informed his discovery of the basis for algebraic geometry (including Cartesian coordinate systems). He also composed a treatise on music, which was published shortly after his death.

At the beginning of his intellectual career, Descartes was interested in a variety of mathematical and physical problems, but he had no vision of a unified mechanistic physics, of the sort he described some years later. He was a (very successful) dabbler. Two things happened to change this. While living in Bavaria north of Munich, he had a series of dreams on November 19, 1619. These convinced him that he should seek to reform philosophy. He already had some preparation for this mission, from having recognized some generalized techniques in his solutions to mathematical problems based on relations among line segments. During the 1620s, he worked on his *Rules for the Direction of the Mind*, which was to be a treatise on method. It offered methodological advice on solving mathematical problems and promised application to intellectual problems more generally. It remained incomplete on the latter point, mainly suggesting a reduction of complex notions to 'simple natures' (Rules 6, 8, 12).[6] This work did not promulgate a general metaphysics of matter or the vision of a general science of nature.

Second, after abandoning the *Rules* and moving back to the Netherlands in 1628–9, he began to think more closely about the general foundations of natural philosophy. He soon arrived at the conclusion that all matter could be viewed as having only the properties of size, shape, position, and motion. This result was connected to insights into the existence of God, the nature of the soul, and the dependence of the eternal truths on God's will (to Mersenne, 1: 144–6).[7] As he subsequently recalled, upon arriving in the Netherlands he worked on a small treatise of metaphysics, which formed the basis for Part Four of the *Discourse on the Method* (published in 1637). As retrospectively described in 1637, this metaphysics included the conclusion that the mind is 'a substance whose whole essence or nature is only to think, and which does not require any location nor depend on any material thing in order to exist' (6: 33). It also included the contention that the idea of God, as a perfect being, must have been placed in his mind by an actually existing perfect being. Parts Five and Six of the *Discourse* sketch some aspects of Descartes's natural philosophy, and they call attention (6: 76) to his new description of the basic properties of matter in the *Meteorology*, published along with the *Discourse*. But nowhere does the work directly announce that the essence of matter is extension.

Descartes explicitly framed Part Four as but a sampling of his metaphysics. Accordingly, it does not reveal the full foundations of his natural philosophy (6: 31, 40–1). Indeed, he confided to his correspondents that the *Discourse* did not reveal his strongest arguments for his new metaphysics (including his conception of matter) because those arguments required introducing a radical form of skepticism (involving a deceiving demon or deceiving God) so as to induce his readers to 'withdraw their minds from their senses' (to Mersenne, 1: 350; also 1: 563). Instead, he offered an empirically based argument in support of his new natural science.

This argument appealed to the unity and simplicity of the explanatory basis for his accounts of natural things. Explanations would be framed in terms of particulate matter having the properties of size, shape, position, and motion. Descartes compared his unified explanatory framework with the variety of 'substantial forms' (an active principle that develops the properties and guides the behavior of each natural kind) and 'real qualities' (explained later) posited in scholastic Aristotelian accounts. He boasted of being able to fit a single type of cause (particulate matter in motion) into explanations for a variety of effects, including: 'vision, salt, winds, clouds, snow, thunder, the rainbow, and the like' (to Morin, 2: 200). These reflections on his empirical justificatory strategy also fit his *World, or Treatise on Light* and *Treatise on Man*, works originally composed in 1630–3. The *World* imagines the creation of a new world in 'imaginary space' (11: 31): that is, a merely imagined space that scholastic Aristotelians envisioned beyond the finite bubble of the known universe as bounded by the sphere of fixed stars. This new world is constituted of bare particulate matter 'in which there is absolutely nothing that everyone cannot know as perfectly as possible' (11: 33–4), which means, nothing but size, shape, position, and motion. Descartes's reconceived natural world is recommended by the clarity, unity, and simplicity of the causes that it posits to explain a wide variety of natural phenomena (see also *Discourse*, 6: 76).[8]

Neither of these works was published during Descartes's lifetime (the original French versions appeared first in 1664). Samples of his new natural philosophy appeared in the *Discourse* and the appended essays on *Meteorology* (earth and atmospheric science) and *Dioptrics* (on light, vision, and lenses). Accordingly, Descartes's correspondents pressed him to publish his metaphysics and his complete physics (2: 564, 662). He eventually obliged by publishing the *Meditations on First Philosophy* in 1641 and the *Principles of Philosophy* in 1644. The first work, as he explained to Mersenne, contained 'the foundations' of his physics (3: 233, 297–8), but not overtly described as such. With hindsight, we can see these foundations on display, especially in the conclusion that the essence of matter is extension (7: 63, 71); in the conclusion that God exists, is no deceiver, and conserves the universe from moment to moment (7: 49); in the separation of mind from matter (7: 78); and in the reconception of sensory qualities and the mechanization of sensory processes (7: 78–89). The *Principles* offered a precis of Descartes's metaphysics in Part One, set out in textbook style. It then first made public his 'complete' physics, at least for non-living things: his general physics of moving corpuscular matter in Part Two; the solar system and stars in Part Three; and the formation of the Earth and the properties of minerals and other natural kinds, along with a discussion of the senses, in Part Four. The remainder of this essay addresses some of the virtues displayed in the aforementioned works and others, including the *Passions of the Soul* (published in 1649).

3. A Comprehensive and Systematic Natural Philosophy

Descartes's physical writings are organized around the 'assumptions' announced in Discourse One of the *Meteorology* and earlier stated in the manuscript for the *World*. These assumptions concern the nature of matter. In the *Meteorology*, Descartes described the particulate matter that constitutes earthly bodies as all made of 'the same material', which is divisible 'in an infinity of ways' (6: 238–9). He described all earthly bodies as 'composed of many small particles of various shapes and sizes', which are not distributed within a void, but are surrounded 'by very fine material' that fills all space (6: 233). In the *World* (chs. 5–6), he proposed that the entire universe, including the sun, stars, and other planets, is constituted of this one type of matter, divided into particles that enter into patterns of motion. In the *Principles*, he introduces the formal apparatus that each type of (created) substance has an essence or chief attribute (extension for corporeal things, thought for minds), and that the further modifications of substances are called 'modes', which, for material things, are size, shape, position, and motion (pt. I, arts. 53, 65, 69). He further describes the parts of matter as following three laws of motion, which themselves result from God's conserving action (*World*, ch. 7; *Princ.*, II.36–44; also *Discourse*, 6: 42). As he observed in the *Meteorology* (6: 239), *World* (chs. 1–2, 5–6), in correspondence from the 1630s and 1640s (2: 200; 3: 500, 648–9), and in the *Principles* (II.4), he didn't posit any other qualities, such as heat and cold, or wet and dry, as fundamental to this matter. Rather, these qualities (as object-properties) are to be explained through bare particles in motion (*Princ.*, IV.198). Besides matter, the only other type of created being is mind, whose powers must be invoked to explain human sensation, human action, and human cognition.

After recapitulating his metaphysics in *Principles*, Part One, Descartes offered, in Parts Two to Four, a systematic physics that followed the order of scholastic Aristotelian textbooks, which he hoped his *Principles* would replace (Gaukroger 2002: ch. 2). Such textbooks began with 'general physics', a presentation of fundamental Aristotelian concepts, and then went on to the non-living world, divided into the heavens and Earth, and the living world of ensouled beings, including plants, animals, and human beings.[9] Part Two of Descartes's *Principles*, corresponding to 'general physics', describes the fundamental properties of matter as noted earlier, including the laws of motions and the (notoriously defective) rules of impact. It gives a definition of motion (arts. 24–9) as translation in relation to other bodies—as opposed to the Aristotelian conception of motion as alteration, which included qualitative change as a prime instance. Here he also reinterprets the notion of 'natures' (art. 23) to mean systems of corpuscles having characteristic patterns of motion (and rest) that explain the observable properties of various types of earthly body: one nature for the magnet (consisting of shaped particles in motion and other, static shaped structures), another for salt, another for water, and so forth.

In Part Three, Descartes describes the hypothesis that the sun, stars, and planets were not created by God as they now appear, populated by mature plants and full-grown animals, but instead that all of the things we see, including plants and animals, arose from the particles put into motion by God at the creation, through processes in which the initially chaotic soup of particles settled into patterns. Accordingly, the initial chaos produces particles of various sizes and shapes, which fall into three types: the ultrafine dust that fills all space not occupied by larger particles; spherical particles that constitute the medium of light; and larger (but still sub-visible) particles that differ in size and shape so as to form various bodies, including earthy matter, air, fire, and water, and indeed all the types of bodies that we observe. Out of the chaos of motion vortices arise, with stars at the center and planets embedded in a swirling stream of matter. In this way, Descartes seeks to account for observable astronomical phenomena, including sunspots, the moons of planets, and comets that traverse the vortices. Part Four then describes the evolution of the Earth from a burnt-out star, the formation of stratified layers, the rising up of mountains as a deformation in the outer layer of Earth's structure (a sinking, tilting, and raising of the crust), and the formation of rivers and seas. It offers an explanation of gravity that avoids attraction or action at a distance, instead invoking the pressure of the vortical matter that rotates about the Earth. It continues with explanations of a wide range of non-living things and their properties, including water, air, heat, fire, minerals and gemstones, metals, the Chemists' salt, sulphur, and mercury, the burning of a candle and the smoke flowing from the flame, gunpowder and its constituents, lime, glass, the magnet (including William Gilbert's descriptions of its properties), and the attractive forces (static electricity) observed in amber, glass, and other substances when rubbed (explained by particles in motion).

Toward the end of Part Four (art. 188), Descartes mentions the intended but unwritten fifth and sixth parts, respectively on plants and animals and on human beings. Part Four 'borrows' from the sixth part to give a brief account of the action of the sensory nerves and the nature of sensory qualities. This material, which provides an account of what came to be called primary and secondary qualities (by Robert Boyle and John Locke), provides a natural philosophical basis for his discussion of sensory qualities in Part One. The topic of living things was one to which Descartes devoted considerable effort over the years, from the early *Treatise on Man*—in fact, a treatise on the animal in general (to Mersenne, 2: 525–6)—to accounts of the senses in the *Dioptrics* and the Sixth Meditation, attempts to understand the generation of animals by mechanical processes (posthumously published), and a treatment of the human passions as resulting from brain processes that interact with mind (as detailed in the *Passions*). In support of his investigations into animal physiology, he studied many anatomical texts and performed dissections of animal parts obtained at local butchers (to Mersenne, 1: 263, 2: 525).[10]

As already mentioned, another aspect of the metaphysical foundations of Descartes's physics is the strict separation of mind and matter as distinct substances: his (in)famous dualism.[11] As a framework for natural philosophy, his dualism led him to reject soul-like entities from explanations of both non-living and living beings (3: 648–9; *Treatise* 11: 202)—save the human being, who has both body and mind. This meant a mechanical explanation of living things and a restriction of sentience and thought to humans. But his dualism also required that there be some form of mind-body union and interaction, as part of the explanation, in the human case, of sensation, voluntary motion, and felt passions. These elements of Descartes's physics (broadly construed) are addressed in section 5.

What can we learn from this detailed accounting of Descartes's comprehensive natural philosophy? As already indicated in section 2, he believed that the fact that he developed such a comprehensive natural philosophy by postulating patterns of motion (and rest) in particulate matter is a point in favor of his system. It shows the unity and simplicity of his vision of a total world. He reimagined the world with a thoroughness and clarity not found in the other major proponents of a new, mechanistic, and corpuscular universe. The unity, simplicity, and variety of this new world are expressions of great philosophical intelligence, at work to reveal the possibilities of a reconceived natural world.[12]

Two things are especially remarkable about the new universe that Descartes envisioned. First, the austerity of the properties he ascribed to matter. Many writers opposed the Aristotelian scheme and hoped to do away with substantial forms as active principles that direct the organization of various types of body (various natural kinds) and govern their characteristic operations. Most of them nonetheless posited some active quality or force to things, whether weight (driving bodies downward), hot and cold, or other active principles (Henry 1986). Descartes, by contrast, ascribed to matter only extension and its modes: size, shape, position, motion, and, he sometimes added, divisibility (*Princ.*, II.20). Within physics, the laws of motion are to be interpreted kinematically, as laws describing motion in a direction, with changes in speed and direction as the result of impact. Motion is not a power, and the matter possessing motion does not thereby manifest an active principle. Motion is nothing but 'the translation of one part of matter, or one body, from the vicinity of those bodies immediately contiguous to it and which are regarded as at rest, into the vicinity of other bodies' (*Princ.*, I.25). His concept of motion concerns not the activity of bodies but merely their transference in relation to other bodies (I.27). God is the cause or active principle behind motion (I.36), inasmuch as he conserves motion in matter according to the three laws. By treating motion in matter in a purely kinematic manner (as transference), Descartes was able to describe natural interactions in terms of the modes of size, shape, position, and motion alone (Hatfield 1979).[13]

Second, from his foundation of matter in motion, he reconstructed the observable universe in great detail. The partial listing of topics from the *Principles* given herein is already quite impressive. His imagination was very active in describing characteristics of particles that correlate with observable properties. The particles of oil have a branchy structure and stick together, like tumbleweeds, accounting for viscosity. Liquid water consists of eel-shaped particles that flow more easily than oil and that attach to salt so as to make it dissolve. Magnetism is explained by oppositely threaded particles: the threads differ according to the whether the magnetic effluvia flow out of the north pole or the south, and magnetic bodies contain oppositely threaded channels for receiving these effluvia, with some set to receive the northern-threaded effluvia, some the southern-threaded effluvia. Some of his ideas were more lasting than others, including his vision of the natural evolution of the solar system out of swirling matter (Jastrow and Cameron 1963) and the formation of the topology of the earth from natural processes (Oldroyd 1996; Şengör 2009: 65–7). He offered an influential conception of the world as evolving over time, from earlier states of organization.

Of course, Descartes's explanations were challenged. Leibniz, once a great admirer, came to speak of the 'fine novel of physics'[14] that Descartes had produced, which, he believed, would soon be forgotten. Still, many important figures of the latter seventeenth century were deeply influenced by Descartes's vision, including Leibniz, Spinoza, and Newton in their youths. His treatment of nature was more systematic and comprehensive than that of other corpuscularians such as Hobbes, Boyle, and Gassendi.

What led to the comprehensive systematicity of his natural philosophy? By his own account, Descartes discovered the foundations of his physics while thinking about metaphysics, including God and soul, during 1628–9. There is some plausibility in this, as he reported the breakthrough to Mersenne early in 1630 (1: 144, 182) and, some years later, he referred back to a metaphysical treatise (in Latin) that he had begun at this time (1: 350). It is plausible that his insight included the banishment, from purely material things, of soul-like active principles such as substantial forms, and also of 'real qualities', and the equation of matter with extension—positions that he advanced in the *World*, but without providing a metaphysical argument. The insight might also have included the consolidation of the conscious aspects of sensation, imagination, memory, understanding, and will in a mental substance, as the flip side of the coin of a non-animistic concept of matter.

Perhaps Descartes's account of how he achieved the vision of material nature expressed in the *World*, the *Treatise on Man*, *Dioptrics*, *Meteorology*, Parts Two to Four of the *Principles*, and the *Passions* is correct. If so, that would mean that his metaphysical thinking deeply informed his new vision of nature. At the same time, Descartes was able to present his systematic vision without its metaphysical support, by presenting his corpuscularian 'general physics' as an assumption, or as the fabular tale of a world constructed in imaginary space. In this respect, the systematicity of his physical vision, the use of a few properties of matter in motion to articulate a comprehensive physics, doesn't require a metaphysical foundation for its presentation, a mark of the coherence of that vision.

In the end, Descartes thought that it was better to reveal the metaphysical foundation. If that foundation was indeed supported as strongly as he believed (see section 4), he was right to reveal it. But he also acknowledged an interest in seeing whether the vision might itself suffice for persuasion. As he wrote to Antoine Vatier (perhaps) in 1638, he chose to make portions of his physics public without its metaphysical foundations, for two reasons. First, he believed himself actually to possess those foundations. But, second, he also 'wanted to see whether the simple exposition of truth would be sufficient to carry conviction without engaging in any disputes or refutations of contrary opinions' (1: 563).[15] Just as Descartes at first presented his systematic physics without also presenting its full metaphysical backing, so, too, we can evaluate his physics taken on its own. And in fact the witness of history suggests that the vision itself was compelling. For, leaving aside authors such as Arnauld, Spinoza, Malebranche, and Leibniz, who had their own metaphysical ambitions, in the second half of the seventeenth century Descartes's description of nature in the *Principles* and *Treatise* received as much attention as, or even more than, his metaphysical *Meditations*.[16]

4. Method and Style

Descartes is notorious for his claims to possess a special method for achieving knowledge. In Part Two of the *Discourse*, he describes four rules that constituted his new method, which he characterized as a distillation of what was valuable in logic, geometrical analysis, and algebra. These rules summarize central aspects of his *Rules*.

The first was 'never to accept anything as true that I did not evidently know to be so', and 'to include nothing more in my judgments than what presented itself to my mind so clearly and so distinctly that I could have no occasion to place it in doubt' (6: 18). It in effect states Descartes's criterion of clear and distinct perception, which can be found in the *Rules* (Rules 2 and 3). It also describes certain knowledge as indubitable (as in Rule 2).[17] The next two rules advise breaking problems down into parts and seeking knowledge of the complex from the simple. These simplest entities (or 'simple natures', as in Rule 6) include properties or activities such as 'thinking', 'existence', and 'perfection' (6: 33–4), which, in Part Four of the *Discourse*, are used in proofs for the existence of God and of the mind as a thinking thing distinct from the body.[18] The simple notions might also include Cartesian matter as possessing only size, shape, position, and motion, as described (in 1637) by the 'suppositions' mentioned earlier. The fourth rule advises checking everything thoroughly.

Descartes's notions of method are somewhat intricate, and his conception of the source of clear and distinct perceptions changed with his metaphysical insights of 1629. We can gain some appreciation of these intricacies by considering a passage from the Second Replies, in which Descartes responds to the request in the Second Objections that he set out his arguments 'in a geometrical fashion' (7: 155). He first remarks that two things should be distinguished in the geometrical 'manner of writing': the order of presentation and the method of demonstration. As to order, it consists in making sure that 'the things that are put forward first must be cognized entirely without the aid of what comes later,' and the later must be demonstrated only by the earlier (7: 155). He confirms that this was his practice in the Six Meditations. As it happens, however, the order followed in those Meditations can be further described using a distinction between methods of demonstration, into analytic and into synthetic. The analytic method, which Descartes believed to be the secret method of ancient mathematicians, follows the path of discovery, ascending from given thoughts to more basic notions from which they follow. Synthesis, by contrast, starts with definitions, postulates, and axioms, and descends to theorems and problems through small demonstrative steps that can be easily grasped. The Six Meditations follow the analytic method of demonstration.

The 'order of presentation' of the Six Meditations is an order of learning. The things known without relying on what comes later are the meditator's own thoughts, the move from those thoughts to a thinking thing, the awareness that clarity and distinctness sustain this move, the division of ideas into types, the distinction between the formal and objective reality of ideas, the discovery of the idea of God along with the proviso that he is perfect and so is no deceiver, and so on, to include the distinction between intellect and will, the claim that the essence of matter is extension, the distinction between thinking being (or substance) and extended being, the proof of an external world, and the reconception of the role of the senses in knowing that world.

This order of learning in metaphysics coincides with the analytic method as a method of discovery. Accordingly, Descartes holds that the synthetic method of demonstration, an instance of which he now constructs for the Second Objectors, is less suited to metaphysics than to mathematics (geometry). The metaphysical demonstrations of the Second Replies start from definitions, including the definition of 'idea', 'objective reality of an idea', and 'substance', all given at the beginning, in contrast to the order of discovery. The first proposition proved synthetically is the existence of God (as opposed to the *cogito* result achieved first in the order of learning and of discovery).

But, Descartes believes, the basic notions of metaphysics are not evident to the novice thinker in the same way as are the basic notions of geometry. Accordingly, in metaphysics, the order of learning should follow the analytic method of demonstration (in order to discover the basic notions). By contrast, since the primary notions in geometry (definitions, axioms, and postulates) are 'easily accepted by anyone at all' because they accord with sensory experience (7: 156), one could follow an order of learning in geometry that corresponded to the synthetic method of demonstration, starting with the most basic notions and constructing the rest.

Descartes believed that this difference in initial intelligibility arises because the primary notions of metaphysics are obscured by beliefs that we acquire in the normal course of cognitive development, so that these notions can be made clear and distinct only through concentrated effort and attention. As children and as practically functioning adults, he contended, we rely on the senses daily and, as a result, we uncritically accept that the properties of things 'resemble' the phenomenal qualities that we experience and that guide our interactions with things (7: 35; also, *Princ.*, I.66–72). He therefore held that a special procedure of thought, involving a radical doubt, was needed to fully reveal his metaphysics of matter as possessing only the modes of extension (size, shape, position, and motion), and also to reveal the cognitive functions by which God and the essences of mind and matter are perceived. The radical doubt is needed to 'withdraw the mind from the senses' so that it can function as a pure intellect, completely abstracted from sensory experiences (7: 9, 14, 31, 72–3, 172).[19] For these reasons, the analytic order of demonstrations is best suited to metaphysics, if the reader is to be guided to a clear understanding of fundamental notions.

For bringing the reader to an awareness of metaphysical first principles, Descartes chose to compose the Six Meditations as 'Meditations', rather than casting them as 'Disputations', as would be typical in philosophy, or 'Theorems and Problems', as in geometry (7: 157). In Descartes's context, the practice of meditation was related to spiritual exercises. He would have engaged in such exercises while at La Flèche. The usual Jesuit exercises, stemming from the *Spiritual Exercises* of Ignatius of Loyola (founder of the Jesuit order), were organized around three ways or stages of meditation: purging the senses and sensuality; experiencing the goodness of Christ through divine illumination; and seeking unity with the divine will. In the Ignatian tradition, these ways were carried out by three faculties: memory, understanding, and will. Memory is used to recall the suffering of Christ and the temptations of the flesh; the understanding, as illuminated, draws the implications to avoid sin; and the will then seeks union with the divine will so as to choose the good.

The parallel with Descartes's Six Meditations is striking: the First Mediation is purgative, the Second and Third illuminative, and the Fourth involves retraining the will. However, there is an important difference. Consonant with the doctrines of orthodox scholastic Aristotelianism, Ignatius accepted that God can only be cognized in analogy with created things. Ordinary scholastic doctrine held that all thought is based on images, and so involves the senses and imagination.[20] Descartes was seeking, in his Six Meditations, to uncover the pure intellect as a faculty of cognition that could operate independently of sensory images, by means of which he claimed to know not only God and the soul but also the attribute of extension in matter (7: 72–3). Accordingly, his metaphysical meditations could not follow the Ignatian mode, which remained connected to sense and imagination. He instead followed the tradition of Augustinian meditation, stemming from the *Confessions*, in which the seeker after God turns away from sensory memory and the experience of the world and perceives God directly with the fleshless eye of the mind. It is this fleshless eye that Descartes sought to cleanse of sense-based prejudices through his metaphysical meditations (Hatfield 1986).

The relation between Descartes's explicit theory of cognition and the content of his metaphysics is another manifestation of the systematicity that characterizes his philosophy. He left aside the image-based Aristotelian theory of cognition and affirmed the existence of a pure intellect that accesses its own content in the form of innate ideas. It is then a mark of Descartes's greatness that he adopted the literary genre of scripted meditations in order to lead the reader to an awareness of the pure intellect. Of course, if there is no pure intellect, then his efforts do not hold up in the end. But, given his theory of cognition, his choice of literary mode—Augustinian meditation—is admirable.

The *Meditations* is aptly described as a philosophical gem, in part because of the close fit between the manner of composition and content of its arguments. Nonetheless, some of its arguments, concerning the existence and nature of the thinking thing, the existence of God, the cognitive structure of judgments, and the proper conception of the functions of sense perception, are admired on their own. Whether or not his arguments are convincing in the end, Descartes's metaphysical writing has drawn the attention of generations of philosophers for the intricacy and power of his argumentation. And yet there are also criticisms that some conclusions, such as the *cogito* result (that 'I exist'), or the idea of God, or the perception that thought is the essence of mind (Sixth Meditation), arrive with too little argumentation. However, these results might now be seen to rely on the meditational structure of the text, in which Descartes brings readers to see these conclusions for themselves (or not) as the result of a process of intuitive intellection that must be experienced through the cognitive activity of each reader. The text becomes a guide, rather than serving as an independent formal structure.[21]

More generally, Descartes employed several different writing styles to convey his content for various audiences (and also wrote sometimes in French, for a wider audience, and sometimes in Latin, for a more learned audience). I've mentioned the *Principles* (Latin), structured as a textbook, as well as the *World* and *Treatise* (French), offered as a fable detailing the imaginary creation of a new world beyond the pale of this one. The fabular presentation of the latter works allowed Descartes to explore the possibilities of his radically new conception of the physical world under the pretense of a fictional story. The *Discourse* is written as an autobiographical portrayal, in the French literary style of the musings of an *honnête homme*.[22] As he said in the *Discourse*, 'Reading all the good books is like having a conversation with the most cultivated persons [*honnestes gens*] of past centuries, who were their authors—and indeed a studied conversation, in which they reveal only their best thoughts' (6: 5). Clearly, Descartes meant the *Discourse* to provide a sample of his best thoughts, in a recognizable seventeenth-century genre. He also composed, but didn't finish, a French dialogue entitled *The Search for Truth by Means of the Natural Light*, in which the discussants were a scholastic Aristotelian, an *honnête homme* (as person of good sense), and a stand-in for Descartes.

He also published several treatises on specific topics. These included the *Passions, Geometry, Meteorology*, and *Dioptrics* (all in French). The latter work was constructed, he maintained, so as to be 'intelligible for everyone' (6: 82–3), including the poorly educated craftsmen who would fashion lenses and build telescopes or other devices for improving vision. And indeed Descartes had hoped that a French instrument maker, Jean Ferrier, would join him in the United Provinces in order to build a lens-grinding machine of Descartes's design (1: 17, 32–69).

5. Mechanistic Embodiment

As part of his mechanistic account of nature, Descartes developed an intricate theory of the functioning of animal and human bodies. For (non-human) animals, this meant providing mechanistic explanations for all of their behaviors (*Treatise*, 11: 202), including those that his Aristotelian (and Galenic) predecessors explained through the sensitive soul. The sensitive soul (or sensitive power) was ascribed irreducibly cognitive abilities, including sense perception, imagination, and memory. Descartes, by contrast, sought to explain all animal behavior, including manifestations of animal cunning, through brain mechanisms, which included a mechanical associative memory (*Treatise*, 11: 177–9). On his view, animals have no minds (*Discourse*, 6: 58–9; Fourth Replies, 7: 229–31): accordingly, animal behavior that is appropriate to environmental circumstances occurs in the absence of mental guidance.

Even for human beings, Descartes believed that 'most of the motions that occur inside us in no way depend on the mind' (Fourth Replies, 7: 229). These include not only physiological processes such as digestion, respiration, and heartbeat—which he explained mechanistically, in contrast to the vegetative powers of the Aristotelians—but also waking actions such as walking and singing 'when they occur without the mind attending to them' (7: 230). In the *Treatise*, he explained walking through nervous processes that are, through a neural mechanism, reciprocally shunted first to the muscles of the left leg, then the right (11: 196–7). Additional examples of mechanistic action include extending the arms to break a fall (7: 230), blinking the eyelids when a hand is thrust toward the face (*Passions*, art. 13, 11: 338–9), and running from a frightening animal, which can happen 'without any contribution from the soul' (art. 38, 11: 358).

Descartes's position on the behavioral manifestations of purely mechanical bodily processes and his understanding of the active role of the nervous system and brain in producing sense perceptions and emotions (passions) have been widely misunderstood. This partly stems from Gilbert Ryle's portrayal of the Cartesian mind as a ghost in the machine, controlling the body as if it were an homunculus sitting in a control room pulling levers (1949: 52–4).[23] It is as if the mind were watching the external world on television screens and wittingly controlling the muscles to produce appropriate behavior. In fact, Descartes held that the mind is not aware of the specific brain mechanisms that it (sometimes) controls (for Arnauld, 5: 221–2). Rather, when a person wills to do something, the mind automatically influences the appropriate physiological mechanism through established psychophysiological regularities of which it is not immediately conscious. One example is the adjustment of the eyes for near and far distance. Descartes observes that 'if we want to dispose our eyes to look at a far-distant object, this volition causes the pupils to grow larger' (*Passions*, art. 44, 11: 361–2). But the mind does not wittingly manipulate the nerves that control the pupil. Rather, mind and body are so tethered 'by nature' (that is, by innate and instinctual psychophysiological rules) that the appropriate adjustment results from the desire to see the distant object. If, however, 'we think only of enlarging the pupil, we may indeed have such a volition, but we do not thereby enlarge it' (11: 362).

Recent philosophers of mind complain that Descartes treats the human mind as functioning wholly or largely independently of the brain. John Searle says Descartes held that 'the brain does not really matter to mind' (Searle 1992: 44). Jerry Fodor repeats an even more widely held interpretation: that, according to Descartes, 'how the world is makes no difference to one's mental states' (Fodor 1980: 64). Accordingly, they suggest that, in Descartes's considered opinion, we might have all our present sensory experiences and contemplate various imagined scenes without any need for a body.

This mistaken interpretation comes from confusing various moments in Descartes's search for metaphysical certainty in the *Meditations* for his final doctrines. In Meditations Two to Five, Descartes accepts the (epistemic) possibility that he (or the meditator) exists as a disembodied mind and yet has the same sense perceptions as usual (which would be caused by God or perhaps by an evil deceiver). This is, however, merely a stage in the meditative process. Meditation Six teaches Descartes's considered position, that the human being is naturally embodied so that, normally, sense perception occurs only through the mind's interaction with the body and, via the sense organs, with external objects (7: 78–81). A human being is a unit composed of mind and body:

> Nature also teaches me, by these sensations of pain, hunger, thirst, and so on, that I am not merely present in my body as a sailor is present in a ship, but that I am very closely joined and, as it were, intermingled with it, so that I and the body form a unit.
>
> *(7: 81)*

In his theory of mind-body union and interaction, there is no possibility that sense perceptions, imaginings, or even dreams could occur without brain activity. Only the perceiving of pure ideas by the pure intellect can occur without brain activity.

One of Descartes's aims in the *Meditations* and *Principles* was to introduce a new theory of sense perception and sensory qualities. He understood the orthodox Aristotelian theory of such qualities to be based on the notion of manifest resemblance: red things possess the quality red, and our experience of that quality resembles the quality in the object. In sense perception, a sample of that quality, called an 'intentional species' (*Dioptrics*, 6: 85), is transmitted through the medium of air to the sense organ, where it is received and transmitted into the brain, to the seat of the sensitive soul (or sensitive power). This species does not turn the brain red, but rather is expressed as an experience of the red quality as it exists in the object.

Descartes rejected manifest resemblance as a prejudice of youth (*Meditations*, 7: 35; *Princ.*, I.66–72). He sought to replace the transmission of intentional species through the medium of air with a purely mechanical account of the processes by which the sense organs are affected. In the case of color, he posited that red objects have a surface microstructure that induces a certain amount of spin (rotation about an axis) in particles of light; blue objects induce a spin of a different speed (*Dioptrics*, 6: 92). These particles affect the nerves though contact, setting up a certain vibration or tugging in the nerves, which is transmitted into the brain. Certain brain processes then cause the perceiver to experience phenomenal red, in accordance with psychophysiological regularities (6: 130).

Descartes changed the assessment of the value of the senses and their cognitive roles. In the Aristotelian account, manifest sensory qualities reveal the basic properties of natural things. The most basic qualities are hot, cold, wet, and dry, but there are also secondary forms such as color.[24] In Descartes's scheme, size, shape, position, and motion are the most basic properties of corporeal substance. Manifest color experience does not reveal the size, shape, and motion of the spinning particles. Descartes instead establishes the basic qualities through pure perceptions of the intellect (7: 82–3). The primary role of the senses is to inform the perceiver of beneficial, and of harmful, objects in the vicinity. The senses make bodies more easily discriminable by presenting them as having colors and other sensory qualities. When used properly (under good conditions of observation), the senses can indicate some of the basic properties of things. Thus, in calculating the size of the sun, the natural philosopher needs to measure the angular relation between the half moon and the position of the sun (*Princ.*, III.5–6). Further, the experience of pain warns us of damage to the body. In the Sixth Meditation (7: 85–9), Descartes provided a lengthy discussion of how pains are localized, describing in detail the nervous mechanisms in the 'machine' of the body. That Meditation also discusses both the limitations of the senses and their functional role in preserving the body (or the mind-body complex).

More generally, Descartes held that the brain plays an active role in the integrated mind-body unit that constitutes the human being. In the case of the frightening animal, brain processes alone may induce the person to turn and flee. These same brain processes also produce the felt passion of fear in the mind. The function of this felt passion is then to induce the person to want to continue to run. Because the passions are directly caused by brain processes, the person does not first have a conscious experience of the animal, before becoming frightened of it on the basis of the experience; rather, the fear of the animal and the mental experience of the form and location of the animal are both caused by brain processes, at the same time. The feeling of fear then (defeasibly) draws the will to want to continue the bodily response already in progress (in this case, running). Descartes notes that the mind can override the bodily response and, let us say, cause the person to go motionless in the presence of the frightening animal. He also makes the astute observation that the mind cannot simply will away the fear that it feels but must seek to remediate the fear indirectly, by thinking of the dishonor that exhibiting fear might produce in some circumstances, or by attending to aspects of the situation that do not engender fear (*Passions*, arts. 45–7).

Two especially remarkable instances of the functional integration of brain processes with mental states may be mentioned. One arises in Descartes's theory of vision, with respect to the perception of distance and the attendant physiological mechanisms for adjusting the eyes. The second occurs in his account of brain processes and attention.

In the *Dioptrics* (6: 137–40) and the Sixth Replies (7: 437–8), Descartes summarizes standard accounts of distance perception that involve tacit computation (or associative learning) to connect pictorial information in the retinal image with distance. He repeats the widely held view that, for objects of known size, distance can be perceived by taking into account (through inference or associative memory) the visual angle subtended by the object. A human being of a known size looks to be farther away if he or she takes up less of an angle at the eye (less of the total visual field).

But, in addition to this traditional account, Descartes posited, in the *Dioptrics* and *Treatise*, a physiological mechanism by which distance in the third dimension might be directly perceived, without mental calculation (or association). Descartes was aware, as had been Kepler (who discovered the retinal image), that the eye must adjust with distance so as to keep the image sharp. He in fact envisioned a steady-state physiological process by which the extra force that (he believed) results from a sharply focused image maintains an equilibrium state in the brain, which tends toward the accommodation of the eye for image clarity (*Treatise*, 11: 186–8). That, by itself, is a remarkable bit of physiological imagination. But Descartes also held that the adjustment of the eye for viewing things at different distances is controlled mechanically by a central brain state, which can be presumed to co-vary with the distance to seen objects. The eye adjusts the lens to be rounder for near vision, flatter for far vision (11: 155–6). The attendant central brain state might then affect the mind in accordance with a psychophysiological regularity, so that the brain state for maintaining focus for a nearby object causes a perception (a phenomenal experience) as of an object at a specific distance, and the various brain states for maintaining good focus for objects farther away cause perceptions of the objects as farther away (*Treatise*, 11: 183, 185–8; *Dioptrics*, 6: 137). He offered a physiological mechanism to explain the immediate perception of three-dimensional depth, at a time when most theorists held that depth or distance cannot be perceived directly (Hatfield 2015).

Descartes also developed an account involving a fine-grained integration of brain processes and phenomenal attention. In the *Passions* (arts. 70–2, 75), he explains that if we see something surprising, this focuses our sense organs on the object and captures our attention. Remarkably, he posits that the experience of novelty is caused by brain states that specially respond to things not seen before. These brain states then maintain the physical focus of the sense organs upon the object (just as physiological processes cause the body to turn and run from a frightening animal). These same physiological processes then cause a mental state of attention. Accordingly, the mind does not simply direct attention within the domain of phenomenal sensory experiences; there is dynamic give-and-take with brain processes. When a novel object comes into view, the physiological state is stronger because of the brain's response to novelty. The resultant passion of wonder then draws the will, which may subsequently choose to remain attentive to the novel object or seek to break attention. We have here causal loops of mind-body interaction functionally integrated over time.

Another example concerns competition for attention. Descartes was aware that objects may compete for attention and that it is difficult to attend to two things at once. Although he allows that mental limitations might also be involved, he invokes an interplay among physiological resources to explain limitations on the scope of attention (*Treatise*, 11: 185–6). The brain has finite resources for use in responding to objects. A stronger physiological response to one object limits the physiological response to another object. These physiological states then produce a stronger or weaker attentional focus on the objects in question. One can expect that this process involves dynamic interaction. Sensory focus on a musical performance (for example) might alter the brain processes in such a way that these processes themselves reduce the physiological effect of audience rustlings. The fact of sensory fixation results in a strengthened physiological state, which then helps to sustain mental attention by physically reducing the neural resources available for other objects (Hatfield 2017).

As these examples make clear, Searle's pronouncement that, for Descartes, 'the brain does not really matter to mind' does not hold up. The brain matters greatly, both for the control of behavior without a mental contribution and for the control of thought and behavior when the mind is involved. Descartes was an early pioneer in the field of physiological psychology (Hatfield 2016).

6. Conclusions

Descartes changed the problem-space of philosophy, and he contributed questions and answers about the unity of the mind, the operation of the senses, and the unity of the physical world that remain under discussion. He also wrote in a way that reached his audiences, then and now, including his brilliant adaptation of the meditative mode of writing to his metaphysical meditations, and the creation of a systematic textbook of the metaphysics, basic physics, and particular explanations of the natural world. Especially the *Meditations* contains arguments and proposals that continue to attract attention, including his *cogito* reasoning, his arguments for the existence of God, his analysis of judgmental error as occurring when the will affirms a proposition that the intellect does not fully understand, and his reconception of the function of the senses. This legacy shows that Descartes is a great philosopher both for his intricate metaphysical arguments and for his contribution to advancing a new scientific picture of the world. Moreover, it seems likely that his metaphysical results helped to engender this new picture.

As has been mentioned, the physiologists du Bois-Reymond, Huxley, and Sherrington praised Descartes as a great physiologist. Identifying him as a physiological hero aided their own programs for banishing vitalism from physiology in favor of mechanistic explanations grounded in physics and chemistry. They said very little about the details of his physiological explanations, by contrast with the more thorough examination offered by the physiological psychologist Franklin Fearing (1930, 18–28). But the earlier physiologists did highlight a tendency in modern thought on which Descartes left a strong imprint: the deanimation of nature.

The unity of Descartes's vision of the cosmos expresses itself in his mechanistic world constituted by particulate matter, devoid of active principles and 'real qualities'. He banished substantial forms, attractive forces, and even impact forces (on one reading) from his world. The clarity of this vision is one of Descartes's strengths, no doubt.

Still, one might contend that his de-animation overshot the mark. There is some question as to whether Descartes's mechanistic natural philosophy can accommodate the functional notions appropriate to describing living things. In particular, there are questions about whether his metaphysics of particulate matter would allow him to recognize functionally integrated physical systems, as opposed to retreating to a position that notions of life and functional integration depend on a relation to a soul. The issue can be argued both ways, and I hold that Descartes's natural philosophy can accommodate notions of function.[25] Nonetheless, the fact that the issue is controversial may suggest some unfriendliness (even if unintended) toward the concept of living systems in his fundamental outlook as received.

The exclusion of force from matter also has its drawbacks. Leibniz (1695) found the lack of a notion of force in matter to be a great defect in Descartes's conception. The prominence of forces in classical Newtonian physics (as developed) and in post-Newtonian quantum mechanics suggests that, in his kinematic view of matter, Descartes may have overextended his de-animizing project. Still, it is a testament to the staying power of his ideas that vortical explanations of gravity (Fontenelle 1752), as also the *vis-viva* controversy among Cartesians, Newtonians, and Leibnizians, could extend into the second half of the eighteenth century (Nollet 1771–84: 1: xx, and lesson 3; vol. 2, lesson 5).

Finally, the most frequent criticisms of Descartes concern his dualism. Those critics who charge that Descartes's dualism gives little or no role to the brain in behavior and thought are simply mistaken. A more appropriate criticism would be that Descartes opposes reduction of the mental (or the psychological) to the physical. But even this characterization is only partly correct. As we've seen, he assigned some functions for producing situationally appropriate behavior to his mechanistic physiology. This is a kind of reduction of psychological functions to material systems. Indeed, all of non-human animal psychology must, in Descartes's accounting, be ascribed to purely mechanical causes. Still, he held that human consciousness, reasoning, and choice cannot be reduced, a point that can be stated independently of his substance dualism. This claim, of the irreducibility of the mental to the physical, has by no means been proven wrong. At present, the mind-body problem remains a problem, with no definite solution. Mind-body dualism is not in favor, but other non-reductive positions, including emergence and property dualism, remain in play. For better or worse, even here there is, at present, no chance of escaping Descartes's presence. He is, and remains, a part of our philosophical landscape, for as far as we can see.[26]

Notes

1 This list leaves aside, as primarily mathematical and scientific, his achievements in analytic or algebraic geometry and in optics (the sine law of refraction as a contribution to physical optics). The list includes his work in natural philosophy, which can be called 'science' but which is philosophical in that he reconceived the world according to a new fundamental conception of matter.

2 In suggesting that Descartes was a great philosopher and asking what made (and makes) his philosophy great, I do not presuppose eternal standards of greatness that I then apply. Historically contextualized standards of greatness will do fine for my purposes, and I understand the factors mentioned herein as operating within their various historical contexts.

3 Others who advocated a new vision of nature were also heard, including Thomas Hobbes, Pierre Gassendi, and Robert Boyle. But, in the development of the new science, Descartes's systematic approach gained a wider audience across Europe than did they (although Boyle may have edged Descartes in Britain), or than did Galileo's works, which were not widely read or understood in the latter half of the seventeenth century (Segre 1998; Palmerino and Thijssen 2004). It is emblematic that, in Shapin (1996), only Boyle (on whose works Shapin has written extensively) was mentioned on more pages (38) than Descartes (35), who outpaced Bacon (28) and Galileo (26).

4 On Descartes's life and works, see Gaukroger (1995) and Rodis-Lewis (1998).

5 Rodis-Lewis (1998: 29–32); but see Descartes (1969–75: 1: 159), where, in a letter to Beeckman, he claims to have learned nothing from the latter's 'mathematical physics'.

6 Descartes's works are referred to, where possible, by English title (sometimes abbreviated) and section or part number. Where page numbers are needed, reference is made to Descartes (1969–75), the Adam and Tannery edition, cited by volume and page number (omitting the usual 'AT' as redundant in this context). The standard translation of Descartes's works into English is by Cottingham et al. (Descartes 1984–85, 1991), which gives the pagination in AT in the margins. All translations are mine.

7 Marin Mersenne, a Minim priest, was Descartes's chief correspondent from 1629 until his death (1648) and served as Descartes's literary agent in collecting the Objections to the *Meditations*. Information on Descartes's correspondents, including also Morin, Elisabeth of Bohemia, and Vatier (mentioned later), can be found in Gaukroger (1995).

8 Discussions of Descartes's empirically based justificatory strategy for his corpuscularian natural philosophy include Laudan (1966); Clarke (1982); and Hatfield (1985).

9 An example: Eustachius a Sancto Paulo, *Summa philosophiae quadripartita*, third part, 'Physica', as translated in Ariew, Cottingham, and Sorell (1998: 80–92; see table of contents: 70). The Aristotelian notion of soul extended to all living things, including plants; three types of soul (or powers of the soul) were distinguished: vegetative, sensitive, and rational.

10 Hall's edition of the *Treatise* (Descartes 1972: xxvi–xxxiii) discusses the historical context of Descartes's physiological thought.

11 Descartes's dualism faced objections immediately. Notable early challenges include those in various of the Objections to the *Meditations* (7: 100, 122–3, 173, 197–205, 261–5, 334–45, 413–14, 420, 485–7, 502–8) and in correspondence from Princess Elisabeth of Bohemia, who sought an account (which was never fully delivered) of how an immaterial, non-extended mind could interact with a material, extended body (3: 660–8, 683–5, 690–5; 4: 1–3).

12 Schuster (2013: ch. 12) plausibly argues that Descartes's bold new cosmogony and cosmography were intended to provide an empiricist justification (from explanatory power and systematicity) for his corpuscular mechanism. More broadly, he interprets Descartes as pursuing a justificatory rhetoric of 'system' in the *World* and *Principles*.

13 Not everyone accepts a purely kinematic interpretation of Descartes's laws of motion; for a recent overview of the discussion, see Platt (2011).

14 Leibniz (1679: 785). Descartes, Author's Letter, French translation of *Principles*, had suggested that one 'go through [the book] at first exactly like a novel', without straining one's attention or stopping at difficulties (9A: 11–12); but Leibniz is playing on the fictional character of novels. See also Leibniz (1692) for detailed critical examination of, among other things, Descartes's laws of motion and rules of impact.

15 His wording about 'refutations' suggests that his metaphysics was needed to refute the doctrines of substantial forms and real qualities (through a direct intellectual perception that the essence of matter is extension and that such forms and qualities are not modes of extension), because his empirical justification only showed that he could construct a physics without them. The metaphysical argument would, accordingly, be more decisive. Hatfield (2014: ch. 9) develops this interpretation; Menn (1995) offers a contrasting account, in which real qualities are excluded because accepting them would require treating them as separable substances, like minds.

16 Gaukroger (1995: 380–2; and in other publications) maintains that the immediate legacy of Descartes's work was his natural philosophy, detached from its metaphysical justification, a point that can, in part, be accepted. Descartes himself already complained (to Mersenne, 4: 510–11) that Regius, who published a physics inspired by Descartes, didn't properly convey his metaphysics. Still, many of Descartes's closest followers, while giving extensive coverage to his physics, also gave some attention to metaphysics (*pace* Gaukroger), including Antoine Le Grand, Pierre Regis, and Jacques Rohault (Hatfield 1996).

17 The *Rules* also mentions Socratic doubt (in Rule 12), using it to illustrate a *cogito*-like point: that, in saying he doubts, Socrates must be assumed to understand both that he is doubting and the notions of truth and falsity (10: 421). There is no 'method of doubt' in the *Rules*, if that means the use of skeptical arguments to challenge one's beliefs (see Broughton [2002: 4–10]).

18 The proof for mind-body distinctness is fallacious, as Descartes grudgingly (and perhaps only tacitly) allows in the Preface to the *Meditations* (7: 8). On the fallacy, see Hatfield (2014: 254).

19 At the beginning of Meditation Six (7: 72–3), Descartes explicitly contrasts 'imagining' a triangle or a pentagon with a purely intellectual grasp, which does not involve images of the imagination (which depend on the brain, and so are akin to sensory images) but relies only on the 'pure understanding' (or 'pure intellect').

20 The dependence of thought on an image and the need for analogy in knowing God was the prevalent view among the scholastics with whom Descartes was most familiar, including Thomas Aquinas, Franciscus Toletus, the Coimbran commentators, and Antonio Rubio. But some authors, including Albert the Great, ascribed to an orthodox Aristotelian view of sensory perception while allowing direct intellectual perception of God and the soul (Hatfield 1998: 959–61).

21 On this point in relation to the ontological argument, see Nolan (2005).

22 On the character of the *honnête homme* in seventeenth-century letters, though without much discussion of Descartes, see Lévêque (1957).

23 Ryle (1949: 52) says that believers in the ghost draw inferences from visible behavior to 'unwitnessable operations taking place on the [chess] player's private stage', which is analogous to inferring from observed movements of railway signals to 'unseen manipulations of the levers in the signal-box'. He allows that believers in the ghost don't literally talk about levers, because they don't claim to know exactly how mind influences matter; but he nonetheless offers the analogy as capturing their intent.
24 In the Aristotelian scheme, the intellect (in human beings) is required to extract the essence of color qualities (or other qualities) from sensory experience. But it remains that sensory experience, through intentional species, presents a sample of color as it is. This contrasts with Descartes's conception of color qualities as subjective effects.
25 Rodis-Lewis (1990: 29) makes organic unity depend on mind-body union; Des Chene (2001: 11), on human projection or else divine intention. Others find in Descartes a notion of functional integrity (teleological or systematic) independent of mind for both animal and human bodily machines: Hatfield (2008: 411–17); Brown (2012); and Hutchins (2015).
26 Devin Curry provided insightful comments on previous drafts.

References

Ariew, Roger, Cottingham, John, and Sorell, Tom (eds.) 1998. *Descartes' Meditations: Background Source Materials*, Cambridge: Cambridge University Press.

Broughton, Janet 2002. *Descartes's Method of Doubt*, Princeton: Princeton University Press.

Brown, Deborah J. 2012. Cartesian Functional Analysis, *Australasian Journal of Philosophy* 90: 75–92.

Clarke, Desmond M. 1982. *Descartes' Philosophy of Science*, Manchester: Manchester University Press.

Descartes, René 1969–75. *Oeuvres de Descartes*, ed. Charles Adam and Paul Tannery, new edn., eleven vols., Paris: Vrin.

Descartes, René 1972. *Treatise of Man*, trans. Thomas Steele Hall, Cambridge, MA: Harvard University Press. (Standardly referred to in English as the *Treatise on Man*.)

Descartes, René 1984–85. *Philosophical Writings of Descartes*, trans. John Cottingham, Robert Stoothoff, and Dugald Murdoch, two vols., Cambridge: Cambridge University Press.

Descartes, René 1991. *Philosophical Writings of Descartes: The Correspondence*, trans. John Cottingham, Robert Stoothoff, Dugald Murdoch, and Anthony Kenny, Cambridge: Cambridge University Press.

Des Chene, Dennis 2001. *Spirits and Clocks: Machine and Organism in Descartes*, Ithaca, NY: Cornell University Press.

du Bois-Reymond, Emil 1912. Gedächtnisrede auf Johannes Müller, Gehalten in der Leibniz-Sitzung der Akademie der Wissenschaften am 8. Juli 1858, in *Reden von Emil du Bois-Reymond*, vol. 1, ed. Estelle du Bois-Reymond, Leipzig: Veit: 135–317.

Fearing, Franklin 1930. *Reflex Action: A Study in the History of Physiological Psychology*, Baltimore: Williams and Wilkins.

Fodor, Jerry A. 1980. Methodological Solipsism Considered as a Research Strategy in Cognitive Psychology, *Behavioral and Brain Sciences* 3: 63–109.

Fontenelle, Bernard de 1752. *Théorie des tourbillons cartésiens: avec des réflexions sur l'attraction*, Paris: Hippolyte-Louis Guerin.

Gaukroger, Stephen 1995. *Descartes: An Intellectual Biography*, Oxford: Clarendon Press.
Gaukroger, Stephen 2002. *Descartes' System of Natural Philosophy*, Cambridge: Cambridge University Press.
Hatfield, Gary C. 1979. Force (God) in Descartes' Physics, *Studies in History and Philosophy of Science Part A* 10: 113–40.
Hatfield, Gary C. 1985. First Philosophy and Natural Philosophy in Descartes, in *Philosophy, Its History and Historiography*, ed. A. J. Holland, Dordrecht: Reidel: 149–64.
Hatfield, Gary C. 1986. The Senses and the Fleshless Eye: The *Meditations* as Cognitive Exercises, in *Essays on Descartes' Meditations*, ed. Amélie O. Rorty, Berkeley: University of California Press: 45–79.
Hatfield, Gary C. 1996. Was the Scientific Revolution Really a Revolution in Science?, in *Tradition, Transmission, Transformation*, ed. F. Jamil Ragep and Sally P. Ragep, Leiden: Brill: 489–525.
Hatfield, Gary C. 1998. The Cognitive Faculties, in *The Cambridge History of Seventeenth-Century Philosophy*, ed. Daniel Garber and Michael Ayers, Cambridge: Cambridge University Press: 953–1002.
Hatfield, Gary C. 2008. Animals, in *A Companion to Descartes*, ed. Janet Broughton and John Carriero, Oxford: Blackwell: 404–425.
Hatfield, Gary C. 2014. *The Routledge Guidebook to Descartes'* Meditations, Abingdon: Routledge.
Hatfield, Gary C. 2015. Natural Geometry in Descartes and Kepler, *Res Philosophica* 92: 117–48.
Hatfield, Gary C. 2016. *L'Homme* in Psychology and Neuroscience, in *Descartes'* Treatise on Man *and Its Reception*, ed. Delphine Antoine-Mahut and Stephen Gaukroger, New York: Springer: 269–85.
Hatfield, Gary C. 2017. L'Attention chez Descartes: aspect mental et aspect physiologique, *Les Ètudes philosophiques* 171: 7–26.
Henry, John 1986. Occult Qualities and the Experimental Philosophy: Active Principles in Pre-Newtonian Matter Theory, *History of Science* 24: 335–81.
Hutchins, Barnaby R. 2015. Descartes, Corpuscles and Reductionism: Mechanism and Systems in Descartes' Physiology, *Philosophical Quarterly* 65: 669–89.
Huxley, Thomas H. 1896. On Descartes' 'Discourse Touching the Method of Using One's Reason Rightly and of Seeking Scientific Truth', in *Methods and Results: Essays*, New York: D. Appleton: 166–198.
James, William 1890. *Principles of Psychology*, two vols., New York: Holt.
Jastrow, Robert and Cameron, A.G.W. 1963. Preface and Introduction, in *Origin of the Solar System*, ed. Robert Jastrow and A.G.W. Cameron, New York: Academic Press: vii–ix.
Laudan, Laurens 1966. The Clock Metaphor and Probabilism: The Impact of Descartes on English Methodological Thought, 1650–65, *Annals of Science* 22: 73–104.
Leibniz, Gottfried Wilhelm 1969 (1692). Critical Thoughts on the General Part of the *Principles* of Descartes, in *Philosophical Papers and Letters*, 2nd edn., ed. Leroy Loemker, Dordrecht: Reidel: 383–412.
Leibniz, Gottfried Wilhelm 1969 (1695). Specimen Dynamicum, in *Philosophical Papers and Letters*, 2nd edn., ed. Leroy Loemker, Dordrecht: Reidel: 435–52.
Leibniz, Gottfried Wilhelm 2006 (1679). Letter, in *Sämtliche Schriften und Briefe*, Series 2, *Philosophischer Briefwechsel*, 2nd edn., vol. 1, ed. Leibniz-Forschungsstelle der Universität Münster, Berlin: Akademie Verlag: 775–82.
Lévêque, André 1957. 'L'honnête homme' et 'l'homme de bien' au XVII siècle, *Publications of the Modern Language Association of America* 72: 620–32.

Menn, Stephen 1995. The Greatest Stumbling Block: Descartes' Denial of Real Qualities, in *Descartes and His Contemporaries: Meditations, Objections, and Replies*, ed. Roger Ariew and Marjorie Grene, Chicago: University of Chicago Press: 182–207.
Nolan, Lawrence 2005. The Ontological Argument as an Exercise in Cartesian Therapy, *Canadian Journal of Philosophy* 35: 521–62.
Nollet, Jean Antoine 1771–84. *Leçons de physique expérimentale*, 7th edn., six vols., Paris: Durand.
Oldroyd, David Roger 1996. *Thinking about the Earth: A History of Ideas in Geology*, Cambridge, MA: Harvard University Press.
Palmerino, Carla Rita and Thijssen, J.M.M.H. (eds.) 2004. *The Reception of the Galilean Science of Motion in Seventeenth-Century Europe*, Dordrecht: Kluwer.
Platt, Andrew R. 2011. Divine Activity and Motive Power in Descartes's Physics, *British Journal for the History of Philosophy* 19: 849–71.
Rodis-Lewis, Geneviève 1990. La Conception de *L'Homme* dans le cartésianisme, in *L'Anthropologie cartésienne*, ed. Rodis-Lewis, Paris: Presses Universitaires de France: 19–38.
Rodis-Lewis, Geneviève 1998. *Descartes: His Life and Thought*, trans. Jane Marie Todd, Ithaca, NY: Cornell University Press.
Ryle, Gilbert 1949. *The Concept of Mind*, London: Hutchinson.
Schuster, John 2013. *Descartes-Agonistes: Physico-Mathematics, Method & Corpuscular-Mechanism 1618–33*, Dordrecht: Springer.
Searle, John 1992. *The Rediscovery of the Mind*, Cambridge, MA: MIT Press.
Segre, Michael 1998. The Never-Ending Galileo Story, in *The Cambridge Companion to Galileo*, ed. Peter Machamer, Cambridge: Cambridge University Press 388–416.
Şengör, A.M.C. 2009. Chapter VI: The Dawn of Modern Geology: Descartes, Varenius, Steno, Hooke, and the Two Kinds of Deformation of the Earth's Rocky Rind, *Geological Society of America Memoirs* 196: 65–764.
Shapin, Steven 1996. *The Scientific Revolution*, Chicago: University of Chicago Press.
Sherrington, Charles 1963 (1940). *Man on His Nature: The Gifford Lectures Edinburgh 1937–8*, Cambridge: Cambridge University Press.
Wheeler, Michael 2005. *Reconstructing the Cognitive World: The Next Step*, Cambridge, MA: MIT Press.

8
ÉMILIE DU CHÂTELET ON WOMEN'S MINDS AND EDUCATION

Karen Detlefsen

1. Introduction

What makes a philosopher great?[1] More fundamentally, what makes someone a *philosopher*? I do not pretend to be able to answer fully these difficult metaphilosophical questions, but I shall make the argument for the narrower claim that the eighteenth-century thinker, Émilie Du Châtelet, was a great philosopher. Of course, to make *that* claim, I do have to set *some* criteria about what it means to be a great philosopher, against which Du Châtelet's accomplishments can be measured. I shall indeed propose such criteria, even while acknowledging that there are many other conceptions of philosophical greatness (just as I believe that there are many ways of being a philosopher). So I open this paper with an argument for specific criteria for greatness. I then turn to Du Châtelet's arguments about women, their minds, and education, which, I contend, allow her to meet the articulated criteria for greatness.

The case for Du Châtelet's greatness—and specifically the criteria I shall identify as those that qualify her for the accolade—starts, ironically, with a consideration of her exclusion from the canon of Western philosophy. One may take this exclusion as a worrying sign that she may not obviously be one of the greats. For, the argument goes, the canon just is a result of the sage judgment of philosophers throughout history having sorted philosophers into those who are great, and thus are represented in the canon, and those who are not great, and thus are not so represented. In particular, the early modern canon in philosophy as it stood for the better part of a century is well-known to almost every professional philosopher—indeed, to almost every student in the English-speaking world who has taken a course in seventeenth- and eighteenth-century European philosophers. For these centuries are captured by what has been termed the 'standard narrative'. According to this narrative, the seventeenth century was the century of the continental rationalists (Descartes, Spinoza, and Leibniz), and the eighteenth century was the century of the British empiricists (Locke, Berkeley, and Hume), and Kant synthesized the two traditions by taking the good from each, discarding the bad from each, and thus bringing the progression of the early modern period to its fruition. This story focused primarily on the epistemology of the listed thinkers, with investigation of metaphysical claims insofar as they emerge from the focus on epistemology. There was very little attention paid to value theory, with the exception of an interest in freedom as it follows from theoretical beliefs about the nature of the human and her interaction with the material world and with God.

One immediate answer to the argument that Du Châtelet isn't among the greats because she is not represented in this narrative is to point to the various sociological pressures that are quite distinct from the intrinsic philosophical value of any given person's body of work, and that contribute to the selection of some figures being ushered into the canon, while leaving others out. To imagine that philosophy is exempt from such pressures appears, at best, naïve.[2] As just one example of many possible ways of bringing extra-philosophical influences to a consideration of canon formation, Alberto Vanzo (2016) has recently argued that the standard narrative of the early modern period in Western philosophy (articulated earlier) solidified as a result of teaching pressures quite distinct from the unique excellence of those philosophers and their work on specific questions. Similarly, Lisa Shapiro has recently set out to think critically about the early modern philosophical canon that we do happen to have, with the aim 'to show how our canon might be different' (2016: 367).

Still—and here is how a consideration of Du Châtelet's exclusion from the canon starts to give us an entrance into her greatness, as I shall argue for it— perhaps one very pertinent sociological fact to bear in mind when considering the philosophical canon is the unjust and unequal access to education experienced by people in early modern Europe, with one very obvious way in which this played out being the differential access to education experienced by women and by men. Women, the argument goes, due to their gender, suffered the injustice of being undereducated and thus less able to philosophize in a way that would earn the badge of greatness *qua* philosophers. But this point, together with Shapiro's urging that we rethink the canon of early modern philosophy, is precisely the entrance I need for making my case in Du Châtelet's favor.

How so? Shapiro suggests that we, as researchers, might approach the seventeenth and eighteenth centuries in a range of ways that could shake us out of our dependence upon a rigid philosophical canon conceived of in terms of a small number of figures and their small number of texts and questions. Shapiro suggests instead that we focus on questions that animated philosophers of this period—and there are many, many such questions—thus opening up the canon to a large and diverse range of figures and texts, including a large and diverse range of genres. Indeed, this work started several decades ago when Gary Hatfield and Desmond Clarke, followed quickly by others, recognized that thinkers such as Descartes were motivated at least as much by their investigations into physics as by questions in epistemology and metaphysics.[3] Similar expansions of the canon have followed, with greater attention being paid to social-political and ethical philosophy in this period,[4] as well as to several other spheres of philosophical inquiry, including, for example, questions to do with human passions.[5] The example that Shapiro gives of a question that might animate an expanded history with a more inclusive and exciting canon than is found in more standard approaches to the period, is to trace ideas about the nature of the human mind, including ownership of one's own thoughts. She writes (2016: 373):

> If we consider how a view of the mind as intrinsically self-aware, or at least capable of self-awareness, gets taken up in the historical context, we will find ourselves presented with a set of possibilities both for reframing questions and for including a new heterogeneous set of figures. In the seventeenth century, accounts of mind were intertwined with debates about the rationality of women, with accounts of learning, and with models of education and a movement to educate women. The discussions highlight the significance of owning one's own thoughts—what consciousness affords—for rationality, the need for education to cultivate that ownership, and the tension between that end of education and the way the institution of education itself inculcates customs and habits in students, that is, the tension between our autonomy and the customs and habits required to become fully free autonomous agents.

Shapiro proceeds to give a sketch of what a history of the early modern period focused on mind in this way might look like, with discussion of René Descartes, Marie de Gournay, Anna Maria van Schurman, John Locke, François de Poulain de la Barre, and Mary Astell. What is crucial to remember about rethinking the canon by encouraging engagement with a range of questions such as those Shapiro suggests, is that, in paying attention to such questions, historians of philosophy are not distorting the past. For thinkers of the early modern period just were intensely interested in the individual human thinker, and in the freedom of the individual to exercise the powers of her own mind.

My goal in this chapter is to take up this story in order to see the original ways in which Du Châtelet engages with questions surrounding human minds, ownership of one's mind, and the role that education plays in such ownership. I will specifically examine the ways in which Du Châtelet addresses these issues with respect to women. With this in mind, the three criteria, which I believe can be used to measure greatness in Du Châtelet's case, are as follows.

First, she is engaged with a cluster of questions of central interest to philosophers in her period—the human mind, education, and the like—even if these questions have been subsequently underappreciated within philosophy. It should be noted at this juncture that Du Châtelet is, rightly, best known for her contributions to natural philosophy in mid-eighteenth-century France. More effectively than any other French thinker, she brought Newtonian physics to the French intelligentsia, with acute attention being paid to the subtle technical details of that physics.[6] Her own original system of natural philosophy, as captured in the *Institutions de physique*, is only now garnering the attention it deserves among historians and philosophers of science and historians of philosophy.[7] And her unpublished and newly discovered manuscript on optics is itself a treasure trove of philosophical riches.[8] In some sense, focusing on her natural philosophy would make it easier to establish her greatness. But there are very specific reasons why I choose the philosophical topics that I do, in order to discuss Du Châtelet's place in the history of philosophy, reasons that come partly to light in the second criterion of greatness, but that come to light much more fully in the third criterion.

So, second, in addressing issues surrounding human (and, specifically, women's) minds, education, and the like, Du Châtelet exhibits a combination of precision and creativity that is one mark of some of the best philosophy. Moreover—and here is one reason why I choose to look at the very specific topics that I do look at in Du Châtelet's *oeuvres*—she brings to bear on these topics an epistemically privileged point of view. As with other women of this period—as well as some admirably empathetic men such as Poulain and, somewhat later, J.S. Mill—Du Châtelet's lived experience allows her to engage more directly and viscerally with questions of minds, self-ownership of the mind, and education specifically as those questions pertain to women. She brings to these questions a kind of knowledge more readily (though not exclusively) accessed by having lived through the effects of being a member of a socially disadvantaged group.[9]

Third, I take it that Du Châtelet joins a long line of philosophers of the early modern period, including many other women, whose aim in addressing the cluster of questions under investigation is to bring philosophy to bear on human lives. Specifically, the moral prescriptions she urges are intended to improve the quality of the lives of women living at her time. Philosophy can have many aims or purposes, but using philosophy as a tool to improve human life is surely among them, and that Du Châtelet wields this tool to improve the lives of a sizable number of people is among the very compelling reasons why I take her to be a great philosopher. So I turn now to Du Chatelet's thinking on minds, education, and women to make good on this claim.

2. Women's Minds, Education, and Seventeenth-Century Context

Alongside her prowess in theoretical philosophy, Du Châtelet also thought and wrote about topics more naturally thought of as belonging at least in part to practical philosophy—theories about biblical texts and theology (1792), ideas about human freedom (1947a), and philosophies about happiness and other topics in ethics (1779). It is this latter area of her thought with which I shall be concerned in this chapter. Specifically, I aim to examine her position in a history of thinking about women's natures, women's minds, women's social roles, and how education interacts with these features of women's lives.

Du Châtelet opens her treatise on natural philosophy, in the preface to the *Institutions*, with a direct concern about education. Indicating that the work is intended as a textbook for her son, and writing to him, she begins (2009, preface I and VII: 116, 119–20):

> I have always thought that the most sacred duty of men was to give their children an education that prevented them at a more advanced age from regretting their youth, the only time when one can truly gain instruction. You are, my dear son, in this happy age when the mind begins to think, and when the heart has passions not yet lively enough to disturb it . . .
>
> You must early on accustom your mind to think, and to be self-sufficient. You will perceive at all times in your life what resources and what consolations one finds in study, and you will see that it can even furnish pleasure and delight . . .
>
> Guard yourself, my son, whatever side you take in this dispute among philosophers [Newton and Descartes], against the inevitable obstinacy to which the spirit of [national] partisanship carries one; this frame of mind is dangerous on all occasions in life; but it is ridiculous in physics [and] the search for truth.

A number of points in this passage are worthy of note. First, Du Châtelet implies that one's own mind and one's own thoughts can and ought to belong to oneself, in the sense that they can and ought to be within one's self-control and free from inappropriate external influence. This is implied by her urging her son to accustom his mind early on to be 'self-sufficient', and her later cautioning that he avoid falling prey to believing something due to a nationalist sentiment. Second, Du Châtelet is explicit that education in one's youth is crucial for developing a mind that can own itself in the sense of being under one's own control rather than too easily swayed by the influence of others. Third, Du Châtelet indicates that there are ethical duties associated with the cultivation of such minds. It is a parent's duty to develop such a mind in her child. But also implicit in this passage is the idea that individual thinkers have an ethical duty to make use of their well-educated minds both to cultivate their own happiness and more importantly, perhaps, to avoid falling prey to factors—such as nationalist sentiments—that negatively influence the pursuit of truth.

Similar ideas about the nature of the human mind, its powers, and moral questions about the mind and its powers had been floating around in Europe for at least 100 years prior to Du Châtelet's discussion of them, as Shapiro argues in her paper (including the quotation in section 1). Considered in this context,

Du Châtelet on Women's Minds and Education **133**

the ideas captured by Du Châtelet at the outset of the *Institutions* belong to a tradition dating back at least to Gournay in the early modern period.[10] Du Châtelet, then, belongs in the intertwined early modern histories of ownership of one's own thoughts and mind, education, and women's special relationship to these themes. She has much company in this history, including a number of other women similarly interested in this nexus of themes.

In order to underscore Du Châtelet's innovations in her treatment of these issues, I offer a brief account of Mary Astell's views on women's minds and education. Astell represents the theologically grounded account typical of those pushing for women's equality in the century before Du Châtelet, a grounding significantly muted in Du Châtelet's own work. It is this move *away* from theology that is central to Du Châtelet's innovations on these questions. Astell is perhaps best known for her two-part plea for women to educate themselves, *A Serious Proposal to the Ladies* ([1694] 1996; [1697] 1996). Astell spends the first part of her *Serious Proposal* diagnosing the ills that women face by living in the world of customs that pervert women's true natures, and by living in a world of men who enforce those customs. She does so extremely effectively, with a clear understanding of the psychological burdens women face by internalizing these perverted natures encouraged by custom. In her masterful book on Astell, Jacqueline Broad identifies in Astell's writings 'two types of woman or female characters—the one weak and dissatisfied, the other strong and at peace with the world'. The description that Broad gives of Astell's 'weak and dissatisfied'— that is, non-virtuous—woman is striking to the extent that it captures the quality of the psychological burdens born by women in her time. Here is part of Broad's description (2015: 1; Broad cites SP I: 92):

> Her happiness depends upon other people, material things, and circumstances beyond her control. She is especially concerned with the opinions of men: she likes to hear herself complimented, she enjoys one man's attention, and she welcomes the gaze of others. Because her pleasures arise from 'the constant flattery of external Objects', she is 'perpetually uneasy', and she is anxious about 'the great uncertainty and swift vicissitudes of worldly things'.

By focusing on their bodily beauty, their ability to use sexual allure to manipulate men, and by spending too much time on frivolous pursuits and on succumbing to their passions, women have participated in their own *mis*education by following the customs of their society (for example, SP I: 55, 67–8, 77, 94, 101; SP II: 126, 130, 133, 139–40, 170). They have neglected to cultivate their true, God-given nature: namely, their souls or minds. She encourages women to correct course when she writes, 'I suppose then that you're fill'd with a laudable Ambition to brighten and enlarge your Souls, that the Beauty of your Bodies is but a secondary care' (SP II: 122; cf. I: 54). In doing this, women not only will cultivate their true, God-given natures, but they also will be better able to fulfill their human purpose or *telos*: namely, to serve God.

The second part of the *Serious Proposal* sets out exactly how women can correct course, and Astell thus offers a solution to the ills noted earlier. Her proposed solution is the institution of a religious retreat where women will gain superior education focused on fulfilling their duties to God so as to strengthen their true natures: namely, their natures as rational mind or souls (Astell 1705: 171). Within this religious retreat, women will be able cultivate their rational minds by following an essentially Cartesian method for gaining knowledge, with elements of the Cartesian-inspired Port Royal logic of Arnauld and Nicole (SP II: 166) also playing a key role in Astell's method. She sums up her account with six rules, with the sixth capturing the idea of relying upon one's own mental resources to exercise control over one's own mind, and thus own one's own thoughts. She writes, in that rule, that we ought 'to judge no further than we Perceive, and not to take anything for Truth, which we do not evidently Know to be so' (SP II: 178). Astell also alerts us to various sources of error that normally derail us from the path to true knowledge, and crucial sources of error are the senses and related aspects of our embodied nature such as the passions (ibid.). She thus encourages us to 'withdraw ourselves as much as may be from Corporeal things, that pure Reason may be heard the better' (SP II: 164).

A crucial element of Astell's philosophy is the role that faith plays in her epistemology and method. According to Astell, all humans have different 'Modes of Understanding'—faith, science and opinion (SP II: 149), but '[k]nowledge in a proper and restricted sense' (ibid.) belongs to the scientific mode of understanding because it starts from premises clearly and distinctly known and reaches conclusions through deduction (SP II: 149–53).[11] Science is differently contrasted with opinion and faith. 'Now tho there's a great difference between Opinion and Science, true Science being immutable but Opinion variable and uncertain, yet there is not such a difference between Faith and Science as is usually supposed. The difference consists not in the Certainty but in the way of Proof' (SP II: 150). Truths understood through faith are no less certain than those understood through science. Beliefs from faith depend not upon knowledge that we find within our rational minds, but upon testimony of a person whom we believe (SP II: 151). Indeed, Astell turns to biblical evidence in order to shore up many beliefs, thus indicating that faith is the source of many beliefs in her estimation.

This reliance upon faith and the testimony of others in a position of epistemic authority as an important source of how we come to know truths somewhat undermines the claim that Astell represents, in an uncomplicated way, an example of one committed to the ideal of women having full (or at least robust) control over their own minds and thoughts, even while, in general, she does tend in the direction of self-ownership and self-control of one's thoughts. But Astell's commitment to turning to biblical authority for many of the truths that she claims human can know does put a wedge between her and Du Châtelet, as we shall see. But, moreover, even while Astell's reliance on faith does mean that she relies upon testimony and the epistemic authority of others, her focus on interpreting *for herself* the biblical texts shifts at least some of the epistemic authority back to the individual, and in this case, to an individual woman. Indeed, Astell's sometime creative interpretation of the Pauline texts, which she calls upon to insist upon women's *natural* equality with men, does indeed indicate that Astell is quite content to co-opt significant epistemic authority in her treatment of the biblical passages.

Closely related to themes about the mind's self-awareness and the individual's ownership of her own thoughts are themes clustered around the idea of self-knowledge. One obvious way in which these two themes—the mind's self-awareness and the ownership of one's thoughts, on the one hand, and self-knowledge, on the other—are closely tied together acknowledges the fact that many in the early modern period associated the *self* with one's *mind*, such that coming to better understand features of one's mind just does amount to coming to have better self-knowledge. This is certainly true of Astell.

Ursula Renz offers helpful thoughts about different forms of self-knowledge found throughout the history of philosophy, as well as a cluster of different kinds of problems and questions associated with the topic of self-knowledge (2016: 1–18). Particularly important for my concerns in what follows is a form of self-knowledge that Renz calls 'self-knowledge of one's being subject to the human condition'. Also particularly important for my concerns are two specific kinds of question associated with self-knowledge, both identified by Renz: namely, the moral impact of self-knowledge, and the role that different forms of second- and third-person perspectives on the self can play in one's self knowledge. Let me now elaborate on these aspects of Renz' schema, while tying them into Astell.

First, self-knowledge of one's being subject to the human condition is a form of self-knowledge that allows one to learn about oneself by applying one's general understanding about human kinds to oneself—recognizing, that is, that what is true about being human in general applies to the self in particular. For Astell, understanding that there is a basic, God-given, universal human nature that captures the essence of all humans and not just, for example, of all men, is crucial to her educational prescriptions for women. Only by coming to know themselves clearly as rational creatures can women embark on the journey to recover that self within the religious retreat Astell recommends. That this conception of the woman/human is, for her, anchored in religious beliefs about what God made when he made a woman/human gives her the most powerfully sanctioned account of women's equality with men possible in an age when theological commitments similar to Astell's were commonplace.

Second, turning to *questions* or *problems* that Renz takes to be important to the issue of self-knowledge, those associated with the moral impact of self-knowledge focus on how, precisely, self-knowledge might ennoble the self or have a positive impact on moral conduct and actions. In Astell's case, the moral upshot of women knowing themselves to be members of the human community in the way just described is clear. Only by having knowledge of the self as rational minds created by God can a woman/person pursue the moral imperative of cultivating that mind through excellent education in order to serve God.

Third, questions associated with the role that different forms of second- and third-person perspectives on the self can play in one's self-knowledge focus on the role of one's historical understanding of the cultural values shaping one's commitments, or on how one's relationship with God contributes to self-knowledge. Astell is acutely aware of the role of cultural values of her historical time in *perverting* women's true natures such that they cease to understand, or to know, clearly what their essence is, and what is morally required of them because of that essence. Astell is also acutely aware of the importance of exposing, through education, those historically contingent, and indeed dangerous, cultural values so that women can start down the path of self-knowledge. And ultimately it is the woman's/human's relationship with God that provides the anchor for Astell's claims to women's natural equality with men, and their consequent duty to avail themselves of superior education to realize their equal natures.

3. Du Châtelet's Innovations on Women's Minds and Education

On the woman question, there are clear points of agreement between Astell and Du Châtelet writing a century later. The following passage from Du Châtelet's preface to her translation of Bernard Mandeville's *Fable of the Bees* underscores the later philosopher's affinity with Astell when it comes to thinking about women's minds and education (2009: 48–9):

> Let us reflect briefly on why for so many centuries, not one good tragedy, one good poem, one esteemed history, one beautiful painting, one good book of physics, has come from the hands of women. Why do these creatures, whose understanding appears in all things equal to that of men, seem for all that, to be stopped by an invincible force on this side of a barrier; let someone give me some explanation, if there is one. I leave it to naturalists to find a physical explanation, but until that happens, women will be entitled to protest against their education. As for me, I confess that if I were king . . . I would allow women to share in all the rights of humanity, and most of all those of the mind. Women seem to have been born to deceive, and their soul is scarcely allowed any other exercise . . .
>
> I am convinced that many women are either ignorant of their talents, because of flaws in their education, or bury them out of prejudice and for lack of a bold spirit. What I have experienced myself confirms me in this opinion . . .

I hold myself to be quite fortunate to have renounced in mid-course frivolous things that occupy most women all their lives, and I want to use what time remains to cultivate my soul.

The points of overlap with Astell are notable. Women have rational minds; women have suffered through a lack of good education—education to which they ought to have access—and women's knowledge of themselves and their natures as rational creatures has been perverted due to prejudicial (and seemingly wrong) ideas about what kinds of creatures they actually are.

Du Châtelet also shares Astell's belief that study of worthwhile subjects (for example, natural philosophy)—that is, true education—can provide a balm for women living in a time and culture that grossly misconstrues their natures, to the psychological detriment of women. Astell, for example, underscores the importance of women being able to continue to develop their rational minds once having left the religious retreat so as to marry a man; this continued cultivation of their mental capacities is one important way of gaining relief from a marriage should it be terrible (SP I: 56).[12] In a similar vein, Du Châtelet also underscores the value of education for all, but most especially for women. For example, she writes thus in her *Discourse on Happiness* (2009: 357):

> Undeniably, the love of study is much less necessary to the happiness of men than it is to that of women. Men have infinite resources for their happiness that women lack. They have many means to attain glory . . . but women are excluded, by definition, from every kind of glory, and when, by chance, one is born with a rather superior soul, only study remains to console her for all the exclusions and all the dependencies to which she finds herself condemned by her place in society.

These points of resonance notwithstanding, there are significant points of departure between Du Châtelet and Astell, points that explain why Du Châtelet's thoughts on women's minds, ownership of their minds and thoughts, education, and self-knowledge develop in a significantly divergent direction. Two of these points of departure are, first, their treatment of customs, which may well pervert women's nature or derail women from pursuing education for the sake of their minds and their selves; and second (and relatedly), their different approaches to the role that God plays in their philosophies. I'll treat each in turn.

For Astell, her views on the nature of custom are fairly straightforward. Customs that go against the nature of things as prescribed by God are wrong and ought to be worked against, and customs that are in accordance with the nature of things as prescribed by God are laudatory and ought to be followed. On the topic at hand—women's minds and their education—Astell is clear on what she takes to be the nature and purpose of all humans, women included, as made by God, and so it is relatively easy for her to identify bad and laudatory customs. Women's focus on frivolous behavior, beauty, their sexuality, what others think of them, and the like are all behaviors cultivated by customs that pervert women's true nature, thus going against God's will.[13]

Du Châtelet's views on custom are much harder to discern, and they seem to pull in different directions. In one of the few comments on matters to do with moral philosophy that the reader finds in the *Institutions*, Du Châtelet is writing about the importance of the principle of sufficient reason (for short, the PSR), and the importance of it to human thought. Specifically, she is trying to impress upon her reader that, far from physics being the only sphere of human inquiry that requires humans to reason in accordance with the PSR (along with the principle of contradiction), there is *no* sphere of human inquiry in which these two great principles of human reasoning, and especially the PSR, is irrelevant. Her example is custom. She writes (IP 1: 11: 132):

> The principle of sufficient reason is also the foundation of the rules and customs founded only on what is called *propriety*. For the same men may follow different customs, they may determine their actions in many ways; and when one chooses to prefer those that are most reasonable over others, the action becomes good and could not be condemned; but the action is said to be unreasonable as soon as there are sufficient reasons for not committing it, and it is certainly on these same principles that one custom may be judged better than another, that is to say, when it has more reason on its side.

Unlike for Astell, who is relentless and decisive in denouncing various customs, Du Châtelet's approach to how we think about customary actions here in the *Institutions* is considerably more open to deliberation and a potential open-ended back and forth on how we might think about any given custom. Granted, Astell has a sharp focus on very specific customary actions—namely, those that women engage in that result in those women demeaning themselves as humans. The scope in Du Châtelet's claim is much broader, and there is no specificity given to the customs that might be subject to our evaluation in terms of the PSR. So, despite the less critical response in the *Institutions*, one might imagine Du Châtelet taking the kind of decisive and negative stance toward specific customs that we see in Astell. Indeed, her account of human happiness in the *Discourse* does suggest a fairly skeptical and critically minded approach to a close cousin of custom—namely, prejudice. Du Châtelet claims in the *Discourse* that there are five elements that most contribute to human happiness, and one that has prominent place is freeing oneself from prejudice (2009: 349). Understanding prejudice to be action-guiding attitudes that are inculcated by customary ways of thinking (Lascano 2017),[14] one can take this claim to be an example of Du Châtelet taking a much stronger stance *against* custom than one finds in the *Institutions* discussion of it. Yet elsewhere in the *Discourse* we find a departure from this more negative view of custom, when Du Châtelet acknowledges the power of custom and social censure to enforce certain forms of human behavior. In this context, Du Châtelet is trying to capture what motivates people to be virtuous, and her conclusion is not that virtue itself is motivating. Rather, she notes, public disdain has a kind of power through shunning that a formal law never could (2009: 353; Lascano 2017). One could well imagine that public disdain is associated with customary social norms, and Du Châtelet's position on such disdain underscores the power of custom to enforce virtuous behavior, thus casting custom in a positive light. Her uncritical acceptance of this power problematizes how we think about her approach to custom.

The quotation from the *Institutions* does, however, alert us to features of Du Châtelet's *method* for reaching truths, which in this case helps to illuminate her account of custom. Recall that the context of that passage is to show the role of the PSR in our reasoning through many different kinds of problems, including figuring out which customs are the best to follow. The PSR is one of two of Du Châtelet's great principles of human reasoning, the other being the principle of contradiction (PC). A brief crash course on the role of these two principles in Du Châtelet's thought is helpful. Early in the *Institutions*, she writes (IP 1: sec.8, in [2009: 128]):

> The principle on which all contingent truths depend, and which is neither less fundamental nor less universal than that is contradiction, is *the principle of sufficient reason.*

The PSR is that which picks out contingent truths, or truths the negation of which are not contradictory. So it is contingent that I am sitting, because were it to be the case that I am not sitting, there would be no contradiction. The PC is that which picks out necessary truths, such as truths of mathematics, for the denial of those truths are contradictory. Contingent truths have their metaphysical grounding in God, for they could be different (without embodying a contradiction) had God chosen to create a different world. God himself is guided by the PSR to choose to actualize the best world (IP 2: secs 25, 26, 28, in [2009: 143–4]):

> [God] chose the succession of things that constitute this universe to make it actual because this succession pleased him most . . . But the choice he made of this world he did not make for no reason, for supreme intelligence would not behave without intelligence . . . So this world is the best of the possible worlds

I'll return in a bit to what Du Châtelet takes to be relevant in our (human) way of thinking about the perfections of the created world; but, from an abstract perspective, precisely because God chose to create this, the best possible world, we can assume that, no matter what we might or might not know about it, there are perfections that apply to both non-human and human nature, ones that guided God in his choice during creation.

So, as with Astell, for Du Châtelet, there are right courses of moral action—there are good customs—and they are right insofar as they align with the natures of things that God has created in bringing about this best possible world. But there is an important point of departure between Astell and Du Châtelet that is relevant here. For Astell, at least when it comes to customs proper in the realm of human behavior, we can know with certainty what many of those are. She believes that we can know the essence of all humans, men and women alike, as being rational minds, and she grounds that knowledge claim primarily in a Cartesian-like argument for the real distinction between mind and body, but also in a belief that God created *all* humans in his likeness, a belief grounded in biblical authority. That is, she draws upon two of her modes of understanding—science and faith—both of which she believes deliver certain truths, to come to the conclusion of women's and men's equality, which is the basis of her being able to reject decisively customs that demean women's human nature. Unlike Astell, Du Châtelet does not believe we can know, with certainty, many contingent truths. Our lack of certainty with respect to contingent truths is due to the complexity of the created world. She writes (IP 1: sec. 9, in [2009: 131]):

> any man who makes use of his reason must not be content with knowing that a thing is possible and that it exists, but he must also know the reason why it exists. If he does not see this reason, as often happens when things are too complicated, he must at least be certain that one could not demonstrate that the thing in question cannot have a sufficient reason for its existence.

So, returning to the quotation about the PSR being used to deliver information about, for example, proper customs, the reason why Du Châtelet indicates that we might well return to such contingent truths and change our minds about them is that the complexity of the world makes their actual truth value hard for humans to find. Indeed, I believe she harbors such uncertainty about whether women and are naturally equal to men—an uncertainty not found in Astell. The passage from the *Fable of the Bees* cited earlier is equivocal on women's true nature, and on whether historical examples of women not having contributed as many great products of the mind as have men is the result of their natures or a lack of education, even while Du Châtelet herself will side with the latter. Here, again, is the relevant section (2009: 48–9, my emphases):

> Let us reflect briefly on why for so many centuries, not one good tragedy, one good poem, one esteemed history, one beautiful painting, one good book of physics, has come from the hands of women. Why do these

creatures, whose understanding *appears* in all things equal to that of men, seem for all that, to be stopped by an invincible force on this side of a barrier; let someone give me some explanation, if there is one. *I leave it to naturalists to find a physical explanation*, but until that happens, women will be entitled to protest against their education. As for me, I confess that if I were king . . . I would allow women to share in all the rights of humanity, and most of all those of the mind. *Women seem to have been born to deceive, and their soul is scarcely allowed any other exercise.*

So, while both Astell and Du Châtelet are concerned about customs and what they do to humans and their lives, Astell is much more decisive in certain very specific customs being *wrong* because following them perverts women's true God-given nature, and her decisiveness is grounded in her modes of knowledge that, she believes, deliver certain truths. Du Châtelet relies upon the PSR to provide understanding about human customs, but that principle cannot deliver certain truth.

This brings me to the second significant point of departure between Astell and Du Châtelet: their different approaches to the role that God plays in their philosophies. Already we have seen these different approaches in how they understand God's role in human knowledge and thus in method. But their differences run deeper yet. In the second chapter of her *Institutions*, Du Châtelet starts out with the claim that (IP 2: sec. 18, in [2009: 138]):

The study of nature raises us to the knowledge of a Supreme Being; this great truth is, if possible, even more necessary for good physics than for ethics; and it must be the foundation and the conclusion of all research we make in this science.

Her reasons for the positive claim about the value of knowing God for physics has to do with the architectonic principle of a thoroughly orderly and intelligible world, organized in accordance with the fewest numbers of laws leading to the greatest variety of effects (IP 3: sec. 28, in [2009: 144]). What I am interested in is the more muted response here to God's role in our moral lives, for this serves as a contrast with Astell. This muted reaction is underscored in Du Châtelet's later *Examination of the Bible*, an extended discussion of several books of both the Old and the New Testaments, in which she systematically undermines the authority of the Bible as a whole by showing repeated examples of claims therein that cannot withstand scrutiny once we call upon the knowledge we have of the natural world. There is not enough water on the earth to create Noah's flood; snakes do not eat dirt.[15] What we know about God through our study as physicists of his natural creation makes it clear that human understanding of God on the display in the Bible is woefully off-track, and so we can reject that book as offering any authority with respect to the truth at all.

This contrast with Astell shows up elsewhere in Du Châtelet's corpus as well. Like Astell, she is keen on rooting out unhelpful customs and prejudices. A prejudice, for Du Châtelet, is roughly equivalent to a bad custom for Astell, or a custom that goes against what is true. Du Châtelet writes (2009: 352):

> a source of happiness is to be free from prejudices . . . Prejudice is an opinion that one has accepted without examination, because it would be indefensible otherwise. Error can never be a good thing, and it is surely a great evil in the things on which the conduct of life depends.

But, unlike Astell, Du Châtelet takes aim at religion as a paramount source of prejudice, thus further underscoring her departure from Astell on the role of certain aspects of theology in our practical lives (ibid.):

> I know there are other prejudices than those of religion, and I believe that it is good to shake them off, though no prejudices influence our happiness and unhappiness so much as those of religion.

So while, for Du Châtelet, God himself is the ultimate source of all truths, including moral truths, we are not to find those in the Bible or in religious authority, and these moral truths that ground proper human behaviors and customs are (as contingent) extremely difficult for us to discern.

Du Châtelet, like Astell, links education of women, and the consequent improvement of their minds, with increased self-knowledge, and, again like Astell, Du Châtelet certainly favors an expansion of an individual's self-knowledge. In the preface to her translation of Mandeville's *Fable of the Bees* (cited at the outset of this section), we get an account of self-knowledge similar to Astell, albeit with some important caveats. Like Astell, Du Châtelet seems to take self-knowledge to amount to the recognition of being subject to the human experience (again, drawing on Renz' taxonomy). She writes: 'if I were king . . . I would allow women to share in all the rights of humanity, and most of all those of the mind'. Also, like Astell, Du Châtelet grapples with the question of the roles that different forms of second- and third-person knowledge play in one's knowledge of oneself, most specifically what Renz identifies as the role of the historical understanding of culture in the formation of one's self. And again, like Astell, Du Châtelet clearly recognizes the impediments of her current culture upon women's development and knowledge of themselves as creatures of intellectual ability. She underscores women's lack of education as well as their engaging in frivolous pursuits, largely due to prejudice (or what Astell would think of as detrimental custom). But Astell also calls upon the human's relation to God and what Astell believes that we can know of our God-given nature as a form of third-person knowledge, and Du Châtelet does not share this belief. As a result (and we have seen this already), Du Châtelet cannot make especially robust claims about self-knowledge ennobling oneself or having a positive impact upon our moral conduct and actions.

In her rejection of biblical and other religious authority, Du Châtelet is left with a challenge and a promise. The challenge arises because, unlike Astell, who anchors her claim to women's natural equality with men at least in part in her reliance upon biblical authority, Du Châtelet has no recourse to such an anchor. As a result, she is at a possible disadvantage when thinking about women and education, just as, in keeping with the argument I just made, Du Châtelet's claims regarding self-knowledge and a possible link with ennobling the self are less robust and certain than the claims we find in Astell.

I should note that Du Châtelet still has open to her an avenue by which she could argue for the importance of education, for women and men alike, and this is the promise of her work. To my knowledge, she does not explicitly avail herself of this argument, even though she lays the groundwork for it in her discussion of education at the outset of the *Institutions*; this is the quotation with which I opened section 2. Recall from there that she is explicit about the parental duty to educate their children; and parts of that passage imply that individuals also have an ethical duty to cultivate their own minds so as to retain self-control over them in the face of pressures to succumb to external authority. One may argue, on the basis of these two ethical requirements, that pursuing education so as to increase one's understanding of the natures of things—including of human beings and our capacities—is desirable or even required in order to become better acquainted with reasons for how things are in the world. This ties in with the discussion of contingent truths and the role of the PSR in human knowledge of such truths. For while we cannot know with certainty the natures of things, including whether men and women have essentially different kinds of minds, increasing our understanding of things in the world can bring us increasingly better understanding of such facts. So, while Astell grounds her belief that humanity has an obligation to ensure high-quality education for women in an understanding of the human's God-given nature, Du Châtelet could ground a claim to humanity's obligation to ensure high-quality education for all people in a claim about our need to amass ever-increasing knowledge in order to increase the probability that we will latch upon the correct reasons for why God made things in the world in the way that he did. While Du Châtelet urges this attitude when it comes to knowledge about the natural world, she does not, as far as I know, argue along these lines when it come to the moral world, including whether or not women are ethically due an education.

Still, in decoupling herself from religious and biblical authority, Du Châtelet stands to gain over Astell something of great significance to women. Astell's reliance on the Pauline texts of the Bible may allow her to establish the natural equality of men and women, but it famously saddles her with a commitment to the subordination of wives to husbands within marriage ([1700] 1996: 48–9, 52) and there is little room for women to actively work toward social and political change on this, and indeed on many other matters. Du Châtelet is free from that formal constrain on women, and so she is, in principle, at liberty to argue for social activism against certain social customs, which Astell secures safely beyond the purview of custom, placing them instead into the category of the God-ordained nature of things. But again, to my knowledge, she does not *actually* argue for such activism in any of her writings, although, in fairness, many aspects of how she lived her life exhibit precisely the kind of activism that I believe her philosophy allows. But in her late text, *Discourse on Happiness*, where she addresses human happiness, including the kinds of virtues that we should pursue in order to secure happiness, we are left with repeated examples of quietism, where Du Châtelet encourages acquiescence to the status quo, and just trying to make the best of it for the purposes of being as happy as possible in generally unhappy circumstances. For example, to cite a passage already quoted, she writes (2009: 357):

> Men have infinite resources for their happiness that women lack. They have many means to attain glory, and it is quite certain that the ambition to make their talents useful to their country and to serve their fellow citizens . . . But women are excluded, by definition, from every kind of glory, and when, by chance, one is born with a rather superior soul, only study remains to console her for all the exclusions and all the dependencies to which she finds herself condemned by her place in society.

Here women's education can serve as a balm to their demeaned place in society. But I see no reason why, given Du Châtelet's own broader commitments, such education might not have been used for the more satisfying goal of producing powerful minds working toward changing the status quo, to whatever degree possible, for the betterment of women in general. That Du Châtelet helped to open up *this* possibility, in an age when women's unjust and unequal treatment was standard, allows us to see her as making great contributions to the history of philosophy.

Notes

1 I ask this question without considering the more basic question of whether it even makes sense to pose the idea of philosophical greatness. Lisa Shapiro is explicit in questioning 'the very idea of a "great philosopher"' (2016: 366). I take it as given, and provide some arguments for that in this opening section, that it is meaningful to speak of philosophical greatness even while acknowledging that there are many forms that such greatness might take.
2 For one sweeping account of the sociology of the history of Western philosophy, see Collins (1998).
3 For early examples of that work, see Hatfield (1979) and Clarke (1979). Others who laid early groundwork in Descartes's natural philosophy include Stephen Gaukroger (1980) and Daniel Garber (1992).

4 For example, see the collected lectures in the history of value theory that John Rawls taught (2000).
5 For an early example, see Susan James's (1999) work.
6 Du Châtelet's contributions to Newtonianism in France include, probably most notably, her translation with commentary of his *Principia*, first published posthumously in 1756, and her original text on natural philosophy, which includes some Newtonian elements, *Institutions de physiques*, first published in 1940.
7 For some early trailblazing work on Du Châtelet's natural philosophy, see Barber (1967); Janik (1982); and Kawashima (1993). More recent contributions include those by Sarah Hutton (2004a, 2004b). In the past decade, there has been a cascade of research on Du Châtelet's work in general, but most notably on her natural philosophy.
8 Bryce Gessell and Andrew Janiak of Duke University are currently working on diplomatic and normalized transcriptions along with a complete English translation, and annotations and notes of this text. These final works will be published on the *Project Vox* website.
9 This is a case of what would later be theorized in philosophy as standpoint epistemology. One huge benefit to our discipline of recovering lost philosophers is that we discover many early examples of philosophical material that only later became part of mainstream philosophy, and that Du Châtelet and others are examples of what is theoretically represented by standpoint epistemology is a case in point.
10 See Gournay (1622). For a small handful of the many other thinkers engaged with this issue, see Descartes (1637); van Schurman (1638); and Poulain (1676).
11 As this description of the scientific mode of understanding makes clear, Astell's use of 'science' is, of course, different from our own. For Astell, as for others writing in the seventeenth century, 'science' derives from *scientia* and refers to certain knowledge such as the sort we might derive from indubitable first principles together with deductive reasoning.
12 On this, see Duran (2006).
13 Commentators who have dealt with aspects of this aspect of Astell's work include Broad (2007) and Detlefsen (2016).
14 I have benefited greatly from Lascano's work in this chapter and other presentations in my understanding of Du Châtelet's value theory, including her complex views on custom.
15 See Zinsser's introduction to *Examinations of the Bible*, in Du Châtelet (2009: 202).

References

Astell, Mary 1705. *The Christian Religion, as Profess'd By a Daughter of the Church of England: In a Letter to the Right Honourable, T.L. C.I*, London: R. Wilkin.
Astell, Mary 1996 (1694). *A Serious Proposal to the Ladies*, part I in *Political Writings*, ed. Patricia Springborg, Peterborough, ON: Broadview Press. Cited in text as SP I: page number.
Astell, Mary 1996 (1697). *A Serious Proposal to the Ladies*, part II in *Political Writings*, ed. Patricia Springborg, Peterborough, ON: Broadview Press. Cited in text as SP II: page number.
Astell, Mary 1996 (1700). *Some Reflections upon Marriage*, in *Political Writings*, ed. Patricia Springborg, Cambridge: Cambridge University Press: 1–80.
Barber, William H. 1967. Mme du Châtelet and Leibnizianism: The Genesis of the *Institutions de physique*', in *The Age of Enlightenment: Studies Presented to Theodore*

Besterman, ed. W. H. Barber, J. H. Brumfitt, R. A. Leigh, R. Shackelton, and S.S.B. Taylor, Edinburgh: University Court of the University of St. Andrews: 200–22.

Broad, Jacqueline 2007. Astell, Cartesian Ethics, and the Critique of Custom, in *Mary Astell: Reason, Gender, Faith*, ed. William Kolbrener and Michal Michelson, Aldershot: Ashgate: 165–79.

Broad, Jacqueline 2015. *The Philosophy of Mary Astell: An Early Modern Theory of Virtue*, Oxford: Oxford University Press.

Clarke, Desmond 1979. Physics and Metaphysics in Descartes' Principles, *Studies on the History and Philosophy of Science* 10: 89–112.

Collins, Randall 1998. *The Sociology of Philosophies: A Global Theory of Intellectual Change*, Cambridge, MA: Harvard University Press.

Descartes, René 1637. *Discours de la méthode pour bien conduire sa raison, et chercher la vérité dans les sciences*. Leiden.

Detlefsen, Karen 2016. Custom, Freedom and Equality: Mary Astell on Marriage and Women's Education, in *Feminist Interpretations of Mary Astell: Re-Reading the Canon*, ed. Alice Sowaal and Penny A. Weiss, University Park: Pennsylvania State University Press: 74–92.

Du Châtelet, Émilie 1740. *Institutions de Physique*, Paris: Prault. Cited in the text as IP: section number: page number (as found in du Châtelet 2009).

Du Châtelet, Émilie 1779. Discours sur le Bonheur, in *Huitième Recueil philosophique et littéraire de la Société Typographique de Bouillon, Tome 8*, Bouillon: Société Typographique de Bouillon: 1–78.

Du Châtelet, Émilie 1792. *Doutes sur les Religions Révélées Adressées à Voltaire*, Paris: Ouvrage Posthume.

Du Châtelet, Émilie 1941. Examen de la Genèse, in *Voltaire and Madame du Châtelet: An Essay on the Intellectual Activity at Cirey*, ed. Ira O. Wade, Princeton: Princeton University Press: 48–107.

Du Châtelet, Émilie 1947a. De la liberté, in *Studies on Voltaire: With Some Unpublished Papers of Mme. du Châtelet*, ed. Ira O. Wade, Princeton: Princeton University Press: 92–108.

Du Châtelet, Émilie 1947b. Grammaire Raisonnée, in *Studies on Voltaire: With Some Unpublished Papers of Mme. du Châtelet*, ed. Ira O. Wade, Princeton: Princeton University Press: 209–41.

Du Châtelet, Émilie 1947c. Mme. du Châtelet's Translation of the Fable of the Bees, in *Studies on Voltaire: With Some Unpublished Papers of Mme. du Châtelet*, ed. Ira O. Wade, Princeton: Princeton University Press: 131–87.

Du Châtelet, Émilie 2009. *Selected Philosophical and Scientific Writings*, ed. Judith P. Zinsser and trans. Isabelle Bour and Judith P. Zinsser, Chicago: University of Chicago Press.

Du Châtelet, Émilie (trans.) and Newton, Isaac. 1756. *Principes Mathématiques de la Philosophie Naturelle: par Feue Madame la Marquise Du Chastellet*, 2 vols., Paris: Desaint & Saillant.

Duran, Jane 2006. Mary Astell, in *Eight Women Philosophers: Theory, Politics, and Feminism*, Urbana: University of Illinois Press: 77–105.

Garber, Daniel 1992. *Descartes' Metaphysical Physics*, Chicago: University of Chicago Press.

Gaukroger, Stephen 1980, *Descartes: Philosophy, Mathematics and Physics*, Brighton: Harvester Press.

Gournay, Marie de. 1622. *Égalité des Hommes et des Femmes*.

Hatfield, Gary 1979. Force (God) in Descartes' Physics, *Studies in History and Philosophy of Science* 10: 113–140.

Hutton, Sarah 2004a. Emilie du Châtelet's *Institutions de physique* as a Document in the History of French Newtonianism, *Studies in History and Philosophy of Science* 35: 515–31.

Hutton, Sarah 2004b. Women, Science, and Newtonianism: Emilie du Châtelet versus Francesco Algarotti, in *Newton and Newtonianism*, ed. J. E. Force and S. Hutton, Dordrecht: Kluwer: 183–203.

James, Susan 1999. *Passion and Action: The Emotions in Seventeenth-Century Philosophy*, Oxford: Clarendon Press.

Janik, Linda Gardiner 1982. Searching for the Metaphysics of Science: The Structure and Composition of Madame du Châtelet's *Institutions de physique*, 1737–1740, *Studies on Voltaire and the Eighteenth Century* 201: 85–113.

Kawashima, Keiko. 1993. Les idées scientifiques de Madame du Châtelet dans ses *Institutions de physique*: un rêve de femme de la haute société dans la culture scientifique au Siècle des Lumières, 1ère partie, *Historia Scientiarum* 3: 63–82.

Lascano, Marcy 2017. *Emilie du Châtelet: God, Freedom, and Happiness*, manuscript.

Poulain de la Barre, François 1676. *De l' Égalité des deux sexes, discours physique et moral où l' on voit l' importance de se défaire des préjugez*. Paris.

Rawls, John. 2000. *Lectures on the History of Moral Philosophy*, ed. Barbara Herman, Cambridge, MA: Harvard University Press.

Renz, Ursula 2016. Introduction, in *Self-Knowledge: A History*, New York: Oxford University Press.

Shapiro, Lisa 2016. Revisiting the Early Modern Philosophical Canon, *Journal of the American Philosophical Association* 2: 365–83.

Van Schurman, Anna Maria 1638. *Dissertatio De Ingenii Muliebris ad Doctrinam, & meliores Litteras aptitudine*. Paris.

Vanzo, Alberto 2016. Empiricism and Rationalism in Nineteenth-Century Histories of Philosophy, *Journal of the History of Ideas* 77: 253–82.

9
WHAT'S SO GREAT ABOUT HUME?

Don Garrett

1. Introduction

A 'philosopher', as I will use the term, is anyone who investigates the answers to fundamental questions—that is, questions on which many other important questions depend in some crucial way. In this sense, there are and have been many philosophers—some devoted and some only occasional, some good, some bad, and some middling—in many different times and places, concerned with many different questions. To be 'great', as I will use the term, is to achieve extraordinary things—that is, to have exceptional successes (judged in accordance with some valid standard of assessment) that are produced by effort and skill. In this sense, there are and have been great scientists, great artists, great political leaders, great humanitarians, and great individuals in many other fields of endeavor, even though (despite the famous line from Shakespeare) none of them was 'born great'. While some individuals may have been gifted with greater capacities for philosophy than others have, I will not try to adjudicate whether there is such a thing as 'genius' in philosophy or whether, if there is, it is necessary for greatness. A 'great philosopher', then, is simply someone who has produced, through skill and effort, exceptional successes in investigating the answers to fundamental questions. By this standard, David Hume was a great philosopher—indeed, one of the greatest. Before trying to explain why, however, some preliminary observations are in order, both to forestall confusions and to organize the discussion to follow.

2. Preliminary Observations

As I have defined the term, one can be great without being influential, and one can be influential without being great. Although it is usually desirable that extraordinary achievements should have at least some large-scale effects, such achievements can and all too often do occur in circumstances that prevent them from having any significant effects at all, either immediately or subsequently. At the same time, people who happen to be better placed often have enormous influence without any extraordinary achievements, and indeed many people have enormous influence of one kind or another through what are, by any valid standard of assessment, thoroughgoing failures. Moreover, even when individuals are both great *and* influential, they are not always influential through the extraordinary achievements that make them great.

It is worth observing that it is possible to have achievements as a philosopher that are both extraordinary and influential without leaving any writings of one's own at all—consider, for example, both Socrates and Confucius. Nevertheless, for philosophers, as for literary artists and some others, one notable kind of influence lies in having some or all of one's writings accepted as 'canonical'—that is, accepted into a group of works widely agreed, in some time and place, to be of particularly high quality and importance. Especially when these judgments are correct, a canon—whether of 'great books' generally, of 'classics of philosophy' more specifically, or of some other kind—can play a very positive role in preserving works of great value, in facilitating education and training, and in providing common points of reference and even of self-understanding for a community. At the same time, of course, canons can also be dangerous in many ways. Excellent works that are not included in the canon will often be undervalued and underutilized. Moreover, when the exclusion of important work of high quality is directly or indirectly the consequence of implicit or explicit biases, the result is typically to exclude valuable perspectives while at the same time reinforcing the very biases that contributed to the exclusion. Conversely, works that are included in the canon can easily be overvalued and overutilized simply as a consequence of their inclusion. In addition, the very fact that these works are so often read, while so many excluded works of the same and earlier periods are not, can naturally lead both to misunderstandings of their meanings and overestimations of their originality. Finally, the relatively sharp distinction between canonical and non-canonical works can lead to an exaggerated sense of the sharpness of the distinction between being great and being very good. The topic of canonicity deserves—and has received—considerable critical attention; the point to emphasize about it for present purposes is simply that a philosopher may be great without being canonized and canonized without being great.

A philosopher may arrive at the right answers to fundamental questions without this outcome being an extraordinary achievement. For example, those answers might be accepted by accident, or through common errors, or as the result of being convinced by the good arguments of others. To be sure, a philosopher's achievement may still be extraordinary even if someone else has in fact produced it or something like it before; but if so, it must have some element or aspect of originality, at least in its context, to justify the claim to success that is exceptional. Conversely, and even more importantly for present purposes, a philosopher may produce an extraordinary achievement in philosophy without actually arriving at the right answer to a fundamental question. This is because it can be an extraordinary achievement (that is, an exceptional success in accordance with a valid standard of assessment) to produce through effort and skill something that serious attempts to investigate fundamental questions *should employ* or at least *take seriously into account*, at some stage of inquiry. Philosophical achievements—and scientific achievements, too—are often of this sort. For this reason, extraordinary achievements in philosophy may be of many different kinds, and at many levels of generality. For example, they may be original concepts or clarifications of concepts, original questions or problems, original theses or principles, or original arguments. They may also be original methodological approaches—whether these are approaches to a few, to many, or even to all philosophical questions.

Hume's philosophy has been influential for 250 years, and his philosophical writings have been largely accepted into the European canon, at least, for the last 200 years. Moreover, his influence has grown even greater in recent decades: a recent large-scale survey (Bourget and Chalmers 2014) found that more contemporary philosophers identified themselves and their work as 'Humean' than identified themselves and their work with any other historical philosopher (Aristotle was second, and Kant was third). This is certainly strong evidence that Hume is a great philosopher; but it is not by itself conclusive and in any case does not by itself explain wherein his greatness lies. Accordingly, I will argue for his greatness more directly and specifically by detailing some of his extraordinary achievements. In doing so, I will not be arguing simply that the answers he offered to fundamental questions are correct—even though I believe that a good many answers he offered *are* largely correct. Rather, in the next three sections I will argue that Hume can claim extraordinary achievements of each of the particular kinds just mentioned. One further and particularly important kind of achievement that is often not fully appreciated, however, is what I will call a 'field framework'. This is, at a minimum, a conception of a subject of inquiry and of one or more sources of information about it plus a structure of logically related concepts, distinctions, principles, and methods that together provide a guiding framework for formulating and addressing a broad range of questions within an entire field or domain of philosophy. Such a framework may itself be original even if many of its individual elements are not. In the final section, I will argue that among Hume's most extraordinary achievements are his original and positive field frameworks for both ethics and epistemology, which provide a basis for investigating in new ways fundamental questions about how to act and what to believe.

3. Philosophical Concepts and Questions

Philosophical questions and answers to them must all be framed with concepts, and partly for this reason it can be a major achievement simply to originate or clarify a concept that can play an important role in the attempt to formulate, investigate, and answer such questions. Of the many significant philosophical concepts that Hume helped to develop or clarify, I will mention five: those of 'constant conjunction', (inferential) 'reason', 'convention', 'standard of judgment', and 'taking in a good sense'. Each concept permits the formulation and examination of new philosophical questions.

Hume was by no means the first philosopher to observe that nature is in many respects *uniform* in its operations across times and places; nor was he the first to formulate the concept of 'laws of nature' as the general features of the world in accordance with which events occur or are produced in uniform and predictable ways. Nor was he the first to ask about the relation between laws of nature and causal powers: for example, so-called occasionalists such as Nicolas Malebranche located all causal power in God rather than in the law-governed objects in nature themselves. Hume did, however, develop and popularize the specific concept of 'constant conjunction'—that is, the concept of a relationship between two classes of resembling events in which all or most events of one class are followed immediately by an event of the other class in such a way that the human mind is stimulated to make an inference from the occurrence of an event of one kind to the occurrence of an event of the other kind. He develops this concept in part because he denies both that we have pre-experiential insight into causal powers and that we have immediate experience of causal powers or their operations either in nature or in the mind. Instead, he proposes, we are simply predisposed to respond to observed regularities by associating the two kinds of things that are regularly conjoined with each other and by making inferences from the occurrence of something of one kind to the occurrence of something of the other. His development of this concept allows the formulation of the question of the *relation between* constant conjunction itself and the causal connections that structure the natural world and our experience of it. While some have sought to *reduce* the relation of causation to mere constant conjunction—thereby defending a so-called regularity theory of causation that identifies one with the other—others have proposed that genuine causation requires that something further either be added to constant conjunction or be allowed to supplant it.

The interpretation of Hume's own answer to this question remains controversial. As I read him, he holds firmly that the origin and nature of the concept of causation itself dictates that a particular kind of constant conjunction is *necessary and sufficient* for the existence of a causal relation, and also that this fact has many important philosophical consequences. At the same time, however, I read him as a skeptic on the further question of whether all causal relations in fact have something significant in common *in addition* to being instances of constant conjunction (Garrett 2015: 200–6)—even though he recognizes that we almost irresistibly tend to suppose that they do, as a result of psychological confusions that he seeks to explain. David Lewis's (1986: Intro.) well-known concept of a 'Humean Mosaic' as a spatiotemporal distribution of local fundamental properties is, as the very term implies, a direct descendant of Hume's concept of constant conjunction, and the same is true of his related concept of 'Humean Supervenience' as that through which such a distribution of properties determines what the causal relations and counterfactual truths of a possible world are. These two concepts have, in turn, been at the center of much important recent work in metaphysics.

Hume was also not the first philosopher to use the term 'reason' to designate a faculty of making inferences. For example, John Locke does so in *An Essay Concerning Human Understanding*, even as he notes that the term can have other meanings as well, such as 'true, and clear Principles' (1975: 668–669). But whereas many other philosophers tended to use the term 'reason' as a term of approval, and often broadly enough to include many or all cognitive faculties indiscriminately, Hume strictly delimits the concept of 'reason' to the faculty of making inferences, *and* he treats that faculty as subject to natural psychological causal laws and susceptible to sustained empirical investigation in its elements and operations. He follows Locke and others in recognizing just two broad species of inference, 'demonstrative' and 'probable', but he elaborates on their character in a distinctive way. Specifically, he holds, *demonstrative reasoning* establishes 'relations of ideas' (such as mathematical truths) whose denials always imply an ultimately unthinkable contradiction of some kind, while *probable reasoning* concerns 'matters of fact' whose denials are always at least conceivable and are able to be established only by extrapolation from experience in a way that implicates causal relations.

This sharpening of the scope of 'reason' allows Hume to formulate and then address several highly focused questions: (i) whether the mind's 'presumption' of the uniformity of nature that makes all probable reasoning possible is *itself* the result of an exercise of reason; (ii) whether reason alone can produce voluntary action; and (iii) whether moral distinctions can be made by reason alone. His negative answers to these three questions, in turn, allow Hume to recognize and describe important roles for specific mental faculties and operations *in addition* to inference. These further faculties and operations include 'imagination' and 'habit' in the case of probable reasoning; 'passion' in the case of voluntary action; and 'sympathy' and 'moral sense' in the case of morality. In this way, narrowing the scope of reason brings with it an enhanced capacity for a finer and potentially more accurate delineation of causal roles that is essential to a scientific cognitive, conative, and affective psychology and, in turn, to a philosophy grounded in a scientific understanding of humanity.

Again, Hume was certainly not the first philosopher to think about how human beings manage to cooperate; but he was the first to formulate clearly the concept of a 'convention' as something that is simpler and more fundamental than a promise or a contract. A convention, as he defines it, is the 'suitable resolution and behaviour' that very often naturally results from a 'common sense of interest[,] mutually express'd . . . and . . . known to all' that lies in performing one's part in a coordinated set of actions *on condition that the others do so as well*. His own example is deservedly classic: 'Two men, who pull the oars of a boat, do it by an agreement or convention, tho' they have never given promises to each other' (2007: 3.2.2.10), for each sees that both are better off if each rows on his own side, each sees that the other sees this fact as well, and each is therefore willing to row as long as the other does so, too. Armed with this concept, Hume is able to formulate the question of whether some or all virtues are 'artificial' in the specific sense of depending for their existence on a convention. He answers, persuasively, that many virtues (such as benevolence, prudence, and courage) are natural, but that such virtues as respect for property, fidelity to promises, and allegiance to government are artificial because they consist in the desire and disposition to act in accordance with the specific rules of one or another convention. David Lewis's (1969) own influential concept of 'convention', as a special case of the so-called Nash equilibrium that is central to modern game theory, is explicitly derived from Hume's concept. So, too, is Lewis's related concept of 'common knowledge' as what is known to all members of a given group, known by them all to be known by them all, known by all to be known by all to be known by all, and so on. This latter concept is widely useful in game theory, epistemology, philosophy of language, and even computer science.

Nor was Hume the first philosopher to think of moral and aesthetic judgment as each derived from its own kind of internal 'sense'—that is, a capacity for sentiments or feelings of distinctive kinds—in a way that makes them analogous to judgments derived from the external senses about such so-called secondary qualities as color, sound, taste, and smell; in this, he was influenced by the third Earl of Shaftesbury and especially by Francis Hutcheson. He was, however, the first to formulate clearly the general concept of a 'standard of judgment' associated with a particular concept or predicate derived from such a sense. This concept allows him to investigate the question of how sense-based judgments of virtue or vice (in the moral case), and of beauty or deformity (in the aesthetic case), can be correct or incorrect—that is, true or false—despite the diversity of individual felt reactions that result from the same stimulus among different persons and occasions. Specifically, he proposes that in the course of developing concepts (which he calls 'abstract ideas') of such qualities as colors, virtue or vice, and beauty or deformity from the raw materials of distinctive color sensations or moral or aesthetic sentiments, respectively, human beings converge through a natural social process on a standard of judgment that they come to accept as authoritative in principle for resolving classificatory disagreements.

In each of the cases under consideration, Hume suggests, this standard consists of a favored perspective (which might not be one's own) *from which* to sense or feel and a favored set of endowments (which again might not be one's own) *with which* to sense or feel. For example, in 'Of the Standard of Taste', he declares that the basic standard of judgment for colors is 'daylight, to a man in health'

(1987: 234). The standard of judgment for virtue and vice, he holds, is constituted by the 'general points of view' of those closest to and most affected by the individual whose character is judged, combined with a discriminating 'delicacy' of moral sentiment, accurate knowledge of the causal tendencies of character traits, and a susceptibility to 'general rules' about them (2007: 3.3.1). The standard of judgment for beauty and deformity, he declares, is 'strong sense, united to delicate sentiment, improved by practice, perfected by comparison, and cleared of all prejudice' (1987: 241). The concept of a standard of judgment allows for the combination of what is often called 'sentimentalism' about the origins of a kind of judgment with the possibility of objective truth or falsehood about its subject matter. The possibility of such combinations is important in morals, in aesthetics, and—I will later suggest—in epistemology as well.

Finally, Hume observes that the terms for certain concepts, including those of specific virtues (such as benevolence and fidelity to promises) and of virtue itself, are universally 'taken in a good sense'—that is, have a recognized commendatory role—and that this constitutes part of the very meaning of such terms. Thus he writes:

> [A]s every tongue possesses one set of words which are taken in a good sense, and another in the opposite, the least acquaintance with the idiom suffices, without any reasoning, to direct us in collecting and arranging the estimable or blameable qualities of men.
> *(1999: 1.10)*

> The word virtue, with its equivalent in every tongue, implies praise; as that of vice does blame: And no one, without the most obvious and grossest impropriety, could affix reproach to a term, which in general acceptation is understood in a good sense; or bestow applause, where the idiom requires disapprobation.
> *(1987: 228)*

This concept of a term's 'being taken in a good sense' as an element of its meaning may be regarded as an extension or broadening of the concept of 'attributed relations' that he proposes and invokes in connection with his account of concepts ('abstract ideas') generally:

> In talking of *government, church, negotiations, conquest*, we seldom spread out in our minds all the simple ideas of which these are compos'd. 'Tis however observable, that notwithstanding this imperfection we may avoid talking nonsense on these subjects, and may perceive any repugnance among the ideas, as well as if we had a full comprehension of them. Thus if instead of saying, *that in war the weaker have always recourse to negotiation*, we should say, *that they have always recourse to conquest*, the custom, which we have

acquir'd of attributing certain relations to ideas, still follows the words, and makes us immediately perceive the absurdity of that proposition.
(2007: 1.1.7.14)

Such 'attributed relations', understood as a set of licensed and approved inferences involving a concept and providing part of the meaning of the term expressing it, are what would now be called a concept's *inferential role*. The concept of a term's 'being taken in a good sense' seemingly entails not merely licensed and approved inferences but also licensed and approved mental transitions to sentiments, passions, and volitions as well—what might be called a broader *conceptual role*.

With the concepts of a 'standard of judgment' and of 'being taken in a good sense', Hume can distinguish what would now be called the *descriptive content* of moral statements from what would now be called their *expressive content*. With this distinction in hand, in turn, he is in a position to investigate not only how moral terms come to pick out the particular qualities or things that they do, but also how and why they come to have a *normative character*—that is, how they come to portray things as *good* or *bad, right* or *wrong, prescribed* or *proscribed*. (For contemporary uses of a similar distinction, see Fletcher and Ridge 2014.)

4. Philosophical Theses and Arguments

In some cases, Hume proposes important and original philosophical theses as basic principles without offering substantial argumentation for them. In other cases, he proposes important philosophical theses and provides original arguments for them. In yet other cases, he provides original arguments for important philosophical theses that had already been under discussion. Among his original theses and principles, some are so distinctive and influential that they have come to carry his name.

One such principle for which Hume provides no substantial argumentation is that his fundamental distinction between two kinds of propositions, mentioned previously, is exhaustive and mutually exclusive. This principle has subsequently come to be called 'Hume's Fork':

> All the objects of human reason or enquiry may naturally be divided into two kinds, to wit, *Relations of Ideas*, and *Matters of Fact*. Of the first kind are . . . every affirmation, which is either intuitively or demonstratively certain . . . . Propositions of this kind are discoverable by the mere operation of thought, without dependence on what is any where existent in the universe. Matters of fact, which are the second objects of human reason, are not ascertained in the same manner; nor is our evidence of their truth, however great, of a like nature with the foregoing. The contrary of every matter of fact is still possible; because it can never imply a

contradiction, and is conceived by the mind with the same facility and
distinctness, as if ever so conformable to reality.

(2000: 4.1)

Hume's Fork is a forerunner of the central distinction between *a priori* and *a posteriori* truths employed by Immanuel Kant. The principle implies that there will be different kinds of processes for investigating and explaining the truth of the two kinds of propositions: ascertaining *matters of fact*, which carry information about what does or does not have 'real existence', will depend on experience in a way that *relations of ideas*, discernible in principle from reflection on representations, will not.

Although it has predecessors in distinctions provided by G. W. Leibniz (between 'necessary' and 'contingent' truths), John Locke (between objects of 'knowledge' and 'opinion'), and others, Hume's distinction is not equivalent to any of them, even though he does treat all and only relations of ideas as having an 'absolute' or 'metaphysical' (as opposed to 'causal') necessity. It is also not equivalent, despite a common misconception to the contrary, to Kant's separate distinction between 'analytic' and 'synthetic' truths, a distinction that depends on a notion of *one concept containing another* that is considerably narrower than the defining feature of Hume's relations of ideas.

A second important principle that Hume offers without argumentation is what Gottlob Frege later dubbed 'Hume's Principle':

We are possessed of a precise standard, by which we can judge of the equality and proportion of numbers; and according as they correspond or not to that standard, we determine their relations, without any possibility of error. When two numbers are so combined, as that the one has always a unit answering to every unit of the other, we pronounce them equal; and it is for want of such a standard of equality in [spatial] extension, that geometry can scarce be esteemed a perfect and infallible science.

(Hume 2007: 1.3.1.5)

Although in this passage Hume was not specifically considering the case of infinite quantities, his proposed general standard of equality has proven invaluable in that context: the cardinality of the real numbers is greater than that of the natural numbers precisely because—as Georg Cantor later proved—the former cannot be placed in one-to-one correspondence with the latter. The final clause of the passage also announces the subsequently fruitful proposal that space is not perfectly Euclidean (that is, in strict conformity with the axioms of Euclid's geometry) but is instead only approximately so—even though Hume's reasons for the proposal have to do specifically with his somewhat idiosyncratic denial of the infinite divisibility, even in principle, of finite spatial extensions.

Hume suggests, without direct argumentation, a third important principle, in a passage added to a section of *A Treatise of Human Nature* about moral distinctions just prior to its publication:

> For as this *ought*, or *ought not*, expresses some new relation or affirmation, 'tis necessary that it shou'd be observ'd and explain'd; and at the same time that a reason shou'd be given, for what seems altogether inconceivable, how this new relation can be a deduction from others, which are entirely different from it.
>
> *(2007: 3.1.1.27)*

Under the name 'Hume's Is/Ought Principle', 'Hume's Law', or 'Hume's Guillotine', this passage is often interpreted as claiming that one can never properly infer a proposition about what *ought* to be the case from propositions that concern only what *is* the case. So interpreted, the principle in question has often been taken to state a fundamental truth about the relation between normative propositions and merely factual propositions, and many attempts have been made to refine its formulation and to defend its truth against apparent counterexamples. More modestly, however—and arguably more in keeping with Hume's own language and intentions (Garrett 2015: ch. 8)—the passage may be interpreted as stating only that a legitimate transition from non-normative premises to a normative conclusion always requires, at a minimum, special explanation and justification. This requirement might be explained as a consequence of the expressive function of normative language, the terms of which are 'taken in a good sense'. In any case, however, the principle has usefully informed much subsequent thinking about normativity and normative qualities.

Of the original theses for which Hume also provides an important original argument, several involve his limited concept of reason, his concept of constant conjunction, or both. For example, after first arguing that all beliefs about matters of fact that go beyond present perception or memory depend on probable reasoning, Hume argues that all probable reasoning treats kinds of events or objects that have been frequently or constantly conjoined in observed instances as also being conjoined in unobserved circumstances (often, but not exclusively, future circumstances). All probable reasoning thus depends on what he calls a 'presumption' of the uniformity of nature, and he asks about the *source* of this presupposition (2000: 4.14–23; 2007: 1.3.6.1–12). He rightly takes his question about the source of the presumption of the uniformity of nature that underlies probable reasoning to be an original one, and his answer that this source is *not* itself an exercise of reason is an original one as well. His argument for that conclusion is one of the best known and most influential in the history of philosophy. It takes the form of a dilemma. No demonstrative reasoning can produce the presumption of the uniformity of nature because the denial of that uniformity is conceivable and implies no contradiction; and no probable reasoning can produce the presumption because all probable reasoning *already* presupposes it. Since all reasoning is either demonstrative or probable, the presumption of the uniformity of nature on which all probable reasoning depends is not itself a product of reason. He goes on to argue that the presumption is effected instead by a different mental operation—'custom or habit'—that does not require formulating the presumption as a proposition or belief at all.

Historically, many interpreters have taken Hume to intend also the stronger conclusion that beliefs about the future or other unobserved matters of fact are never *epistemically justified* in any degree. This conclusion has therefore come to be called (using a common term for inferences that project from observation to unobserved cases) 'Hume's Inductive Skepticism' and the problem of rebutting it 'Hume's Problem of Induction'. In fact, this is a more radical conclusion than Hume ever endorses or would accept (Garrett 2015: 172–237), but his initial question of cognitive psychology does have an important epistemic consequence nonetheless: namely, that there can be no sound non-question-begging *argument for* the truth of the presumption of the uniformity of nature on which probable reasoning depends. It is central to Hume's epistemology, as I understand it, that a belief can have epistemic merit, as being probably true on the basis of one's experience, without there being a sound non-question-begging *argument* for the truth-conduciveness of the process that produced it.

A second example of an original thesis defended by an original argument concerns Hume's question of whether reason alone can motivate voluntary action. He argues that motivation requires having some 'concern' that only a desire or other passion, not produced simply by an inference to a conclusion, can provide (2007: 2.3.3). (He also offers a second original but less influential argument, based on his distinctive view of passions as themselves non-representational but associated with ideas that are representational.) If it is assumed that some belief about the means to satisfy one's 'concern' is *also* needed in order to yield voluntary action, the consequence is what has come to be known as the 'Humean Theory of Motivation': that voluntary action requires the presence of both a desire or similar passion and a belief about the means to the object of the desire or other passion. For his part, Hume does not foreclose the possibility that one's concern might be for something that one can produce or do *immediately*—say, raising one's hand or imagining the color red—*without* any belief about a means to producing it, and also without its being regarded as a means to anything else. However, he would presumably grant at least that such belief-less action is a comparatively rare occurrence.

Hume combines this conclusion *that reason alone cannot motivate* with his further observation that *morality is by its nature motivating* in order to construct an original argument for his conclusion that the source of moral distinctions does not lie in reason alone and must instead lie at least in part in something more intimately involved in the passions—namely, the pleasures and pains of moral sentiment (2007: 3.1.1.10; he offers other arguments as well). Although the general question of the respective roles of 'reason' and 'sentiment' in morality was not original to Hume, to the extent that his operative concept of reason is distinctive, his version of the conclusion itself may also be considered original.

Subsequent reflection on Hume's moral theory has led to the formulation of what is now called 'Hume's Problem' (Smith 1994). This much-discussed problem consists in the plausibility and yet joint incompatibility of the following three propositions:

- *Moral Cognitivism*: Moral judgments express beliefs that are true or false.
- *Moral Internalism*: Moral judgments are intrinsically motivating (to at least some extent).
- *Belief/Desire Motivation*: No belief is intrinsically motivating; motivation always requires a corresponding desire or passion.

Some commentators have supposed that Hume's moral sentimentalism precludes his accepting Moral Cognitivism, but such an interpretation fails to appreciate the role of the standard of judgment for morals in making truth and falsehood in moral judgment possible. Instead, Hume himself would resolve the problem by a careful interpretation of Moral Internalism. Much as the human ability to make color distinctions is grounded in the human ability to have different color sensations, so too for Hume the human ability to make moral distinctions is grounded in the human ability to have sentiments of moral approbation and disapprobation. Morality as a whole is naturally motivating, on his view, because these moral sentiments are pleasures or pains, respectively, and because pleasure and pain naturally incite passions. This does not require, however, that any individual moral judgment must be intrinsically motivating, any more than every belief about the color of an object must be accompanied by color sensations or other feelings (Garrett 2015: 277–9). Whenever an individual moral judgment does motivate, it does so by engaging with passions that have arisen ultimately through the pleasure or pain of moral sentiments.

The status of religious beliefs is a topic of particular interest to Hume, and he offers important original arguments for important original theses in response to fundamental questions about a number of them. One example concerns the epistemic standing of reports of miracles. In *An Enquiry concerning Human Understanding*, he provides an original argument for the original conclusion that testimony for the occurrence of a miracle must meet a very high standard—namely, that the falsehood of the testimony must be more 'miraculous' than the occurrence of the miracle testified to would be (2000: 10.1–13). His argument appeals to (1) his correlation of probability with constancy of conjunction; (2) his doctrine that a kind of testimony provides evidence only in so far as we have experience of its being regularly conjoined with the truth of what is testified;

and (3) his conceptions of miracles as violations of laws of nature, and of laws of nature as the most pervasive and constant regularities.

Another example, from *Dialogues Concerning Natural Religion* (Hume 1947), concerns the epistemic standing of what is now often called 'the argument from design' (or 'the teleological argument') for the existence of a divine intelligent cause of the universe. According to the argument from design, just as human artifacts evince an orderliness and 'adaptation of means to ends'—whereby the parts of things interact in such a way as to provide some benefit—that indicates their origin in intelligent design, so too the orderliness and adaptation of means to ends apparent in nature are strong evidence that there is a divine intelligent cause of the universe. Hume concludes that this theistic argument does not meet the standards for a strong argument from analogy. He does so in part on the grounds that orderliness and adaptation of means to ends are very often *not* observed to be preceded by intelligent design but *are* very often observed to result from—because constantly conjoined with—many immediate causes *other* than intelligent design, including animal and vegetable generation. To the objection that these immediate causes must *themselves* ultimately result from design by an unperceived intelligent cause, Hume argues that such an appeal is both unnecessary and fruitless, for the orderliness and adaptation of means to ends required within a postulated divine mind would require just as much explanation as would the orderliness and adaptation of means to ends in nature.

Finally, several of Hume's most important original arguments are offered in support of conclusions that are not themselves original. For example, he appeals to his original principle that constant conjunction is necessary and sufficient for a causal relation in order to argue that human voluntary actions are causally determined in the same sense that other events in nature are. He also appeals to his sentiment-based account of moral judgment to argue that the ordinary freedom to do that which we will—and not any supposed metaphysical freedom from the causal determination of our wills—is sufficient for moral responsibility for voluntary actions. This is because the former kind of freedom suffices to make an action an expression of a character trait and hence to stimulate a felt moral response. The result is to render human voluntary action and its moral assessment a fitting object of scientific investigation and understanding.

5. Philosophical Methodology

Hume describes what is perhaps his own most significant contribution to philosophical methodology as the project of providing 'foundations for all of the sciences' in a 'science of human nature' that is itself to be founded on 'the experimental method' (2007: Intro.; for more extensive discussion, see Garrett forthcoming). In present-day terms, this is the promising methodology of employing the findings of empirical cognitive, conative, and affective psychology in the endeavor to answer fundamental questions about the conduct and content of various other fields of inquiry. Hume did not foresee controlled laboratory experiments in psychology, instead proposing that we 'glean up our experiments'—including what Francis Bacon called 'crucial experiments'—from the careful observation of human life. (He did, however, treat animal psychology as an important resource for the science of human nature in virtue of our psychological kinship with animals.) To be sure, many philosophers before Hume supposed that a better understanding of human cognition would provide benefits to other sciences. In *An Essay Concerning Human Understanding*, for example, Locke presented himself as studying 'human understanding' with the aim of being an 'Underlabourer' for such natural philosophers as Isaac Newton, Christiaan Huygens, and Robert Boyle, 'clearing Ground a little, and removing some of the Rubbish, that lies in the way to Knowledge' (Locke 1975: 10). Hume, however, treats the science of human nature—encompassing not only the understanding but also the passions, the will, and sentiments of taste—as itself the most valuable branch of knowledge and one that is essential to fully grounding the sciences of 'logic, morals, criticism [aesthetics], and politics' as well as 'mathematics, natural philosophy [natural science], and natural theology'. While its intended contributions to mathematics and natural philosophy concern such topics as infinite divisibility and the nature of spatial relations, its contributions to natural theology evidently consist primarily in showing the epistemic poverty of such theology, its psychological origins, and its lack of essential connection to morality and natural science.

By 'logic', Hume understands the science that explains 'the nature of our ideas' and 'the principles and operations of our reasoning faculty' (2007: Intro. 5). His explanation of 'the nature of our ideas' involves a distinctive conception of thought. He agrees with many of his predecessors that thought is conducted with representations—which he calls 'ideas'—derived from experience. Somewhat more distinctively, he holds that all ideas or their parts are ultimately derived from 'livelier' mental entities encountered in sensory or felt experience—which he calls 'impressions'—that they otherwise exactly resemble in qualitative character. In a crucial break from many of his predecessors, however, Hume does not hold that mental representations are *intrinsically* representational. Instead, because of their qualitative similarity to impressions, ideas are well-suited to serving as representations by modeling or otherwise standing in for impressions and things related to them. What exactly ideas represent, and how they do so, is determined by the causal role they play on particular occasions (Garrett 2006) and this therefore is itself subject to empirical investigation.

The doctrine that all ideas or their parts are copied from impressions leads Hume to reject the view of many of his predecessors that there is a separate faculty of 'intellect' with its own, higher, kind of representations that might serve as a more powerful source of non-experiential knowledge. This, in turn, supports a general *methodological empiricism*—on the whole congenial to modern science—that emphasizes the importance of allowing observations to drive theory, rather than allowing theorizing that is largely independent of experience to determine the interpretation of observations. It also leads Hume to his well-known, influential, and often beneficial methodological recommendation that the meaning of concepts be clarified by attention to the kinds of experiences that generate them.

Hume's subsequent empirical investigation of 'the principles and operations of our reasoning faculty', focused primarily on probable reasoning, is intended to help provide methodological foundations for all of the sciences that seek or depend on causal explanations—that is, all of the sciences previously mentioned, except for mathematics. His most fundamental thesis in this area is that the human mind is so structured as to discern causal relations on the basis of constant conjunctions without any pre-experiential insight into causal relations or immediate experience of 'causal power'. In consequence, he concludes, experience of constant conjunction must serve as the ultimate guide to causal relations and, in turn, the ultimate source of knowledge or belief about matters of fact that go beyond personal experience. In this way, he cleverly proposes that the empirical investigation of human cognition provides support for the importance of empirical investigation itself.

One further natural result of Hume's approach to 'logic' is what would now be called *methodological naturalism*: the program of giving explanations without appeal to entities or phenomena that are in some way 'outside of nature'. Among the purported phenomena to be excluded are kinds of causes—such as miracles or metaphysical 'free will'—that would be outside the ordinary laws of nature that are accessible to empirical investigation. Other phenomena to be excluded from explanatory use include the divine, or the supernatural more generally; representational powers that are not themselves subject to further explanation; and normativity that is not itself subject to further explanation. In Hume's view, normativity is a natural phenomenon involving shared appreciation or deprecation, together with their motivating interpersonal consequences, whereby the terms for certain concepts—such as those of particular virtues or vices, and of virtue or vice in general—take on a distinctive commendatory or censuring function as part of their meanings: they come to be 'taken in a good sense' or a bad sense. Hume's accounts of how virtue and vice inspire the passions of pride and humility, love and hatred, together with his account of how the latter passions spur benevolence and anger (understood as desires to benefit or harm, respectively) are essential elements in his 'foundations' for morals. Hume's methodological naturalism is a striking historical inspiration for the methodological naturalism that is prominent—perhaps even predominant—in contemporary philosophy.

Finally, Hume's science of human nature also leads him to a methodological use of skepticism that is significantly different from that of any of his predecessors. The ancient Pyrrhonian skeptics, as Sextus Empiricus explains, sought to find equally balanced considerations on either side of any given question so as to produce suspension of judgment and a resulting tranquility. René Descartes employed skeptical scenarios—envisioned situations in which one would have one's present experience or evidence and yet one's beliefs would be false—as challenges to be overcome: knowledge would be secure only when one could vindicate the use of one's cognitive faculties by eliminating the prospect of such scenarios. In contrast, Hume rejects the Pyrrhonian pursuit of total suspension of judgment as he understands it, partly on the ground that it is incompatible with human nature, and he rejects Descartes's initial challenge to vindicate one's faculties against scenarios of error on the ground that it constitutes a demand that is both insurmountable and arbitrary. Instead, he practices a distinctive version of what he calls 'consequent skepticism' in which skeptical doubts arise only after empirical inquiry into mental operations produces surprising and disturbing discoveries about them (2000: 12.3–5). These discoveries may all be interpreted as providing probable arguments for the conclusion that our cognitive faculties do not generally deliver probable truths.

Because this species of skepticism arises after inquiry has been allowed to proceed and definite results in cognitive psychology have been obtained, it is potentially more pressing and compelling than the others. Confronting this kind of skepticism, Hume holds, properly has two results, both of them salutary: (1) an overall lowering, but not a complete destruction, of one's degree of confidence in the truth of one's beliefs, resulting in a 'due modesty' and lack of zealotry; and (2) restraint from pronouncing at all on topics—such as 'the origin of worlds' or the possibility of hidden and unintelligible causal powers in nature—that we find to be beyond the capacity of our limited faculties. The combination of these two outcomes is what he calls 'mitigated skepticism'.

6. Philosophical Frameworks

Endeavoring to answer questions and solve problems systematically within a field of philosophy typically requires operating within a broad framework that involves, at a minimum: a conception of a broad subject matter to which the questions or problems belong; a conception of one or more sources of information about that subject matter; a structure of logically related concepts, distinctions, and principles to be applied in bringing that source of information to bear; and methods for bringing that structure to bear on the question at hand. Although a field of philosophy may have more than one viable framework at a given time, the number of coherent and relatively comprehensive frameworks available is almost always small. A coherent and appealing field framework that can be deployed and compared against others can therefore often be an especially valuable resource. The best such frameworks are flexible, capable of being revised as conditions warrant.

To take one well-known example, Aristotle provided a framework for the field of metaphysics. Within this framework, metaphysics is the study of 'being qua being', and its theses are established through demonstrations whose premises are grasped by the intellect. It distinguishes between ten kinds of beings or 'categories'—including substances, qualities, quantities, and relations—but substance is the most important, in as much as it is the kind of being on which the others depend. A substance has an essence by which it is what it is, and its species can be defined through a specification of its essence. The framework draws a fundamental distinction between actuality and potentiality, and another between form and matter, with individual substances understood as compounds of form and matter, and their essences understood as substantial forms. One fundamental principle of Aristotelian metaphysics is the Principle of Non-contradiction: 'the same attribute cannot at the same time belong and not belong to the same subject and in the same respect.' Metaphysics, so understood, is meant to provide a basis for 'natural philosophy', the study of nature as an internal principle of motion (or change) and rest. Explanation within natural philosophy appeals to Aristotle's well-known four kinds of 'causes', which appeal, respectively, to matter, to form, to the initiator of change, and to the *telos*—that is, purpose or end—toward which things of a given kind strive or tend. This general framework endured into the early modern period and proved itself strikingly adaptable to new questions and concerns, including those raised by the requirements of Christian theology.

Similarly, Immanuel Kant provided a distinctive field framework for ethics. In this well-known framework, ethics is concerned in the first instance with the character of actions and motivations of rational agents in relation to duty, conceived of as the requirements of a moral law—a subject matter that is to be sharply distinguished from (even if it is also closely related to) other aspects of human life and action. This normative moral law may be expressed in 'categorical imperatives' that are—unlike 'hypothetical' imperatives—binding regardless of the preferences or inclinations of the agent. The fundamental source of ethical information and direction, in this framework, is 'practical reason'. Practical reason requires, at a minimum, a certain kind of consistency on the part of rational agents: for example, that they act only on maxims for action that they could consistently will for everyone to act on. It also requires (what Kant intended to be equivalent) that each person treat all rational agents not merely as means but as ends in themselves, possessing an intrinsic and inalienable 'dignity' that makes them non-interchangeable and 'without price'. These requirements can be used as tests for the conformity of actions to duty. Duties can be either to others or to oneself, but in either case that which is of fundamental value is not the actual consequences of one's actions but is, rather, the quality of the will that produces action in accordance with duty from respect for the moral law. Happiness itself is good only if it is deserved, by accompanying a will that is motivated by duty. Moral agency and responsibility require 'autonomy', understood as the capacity to prescribe a law to oneself. Indeed, morality has categorical normative force, in this framework, precisely because it reflects a law that rational agents impose on themselves through their own authoritative rationality. Genuine autonomy makes rational agents more than merely parts of nature that are ultimately determined by causes that lead outside oneself. This general Kantian framework, often adapted in one way or another, has informed a great deal of subsequent moral theorizing. In particular, work in applied ethics often proceeds by seeking to answer a moral question in terms of this framework and comparing the answer with answers obtained by other methods.

Nevertheless, there is a viable and largely contrasting Humean framework for ethics. In this framework, the primary subject matter of ethics is not duty or moral law but is, rather, the virtues and vices of human character. Unlike Aristotle's earlier virtue-centered ethics, however, Hume's does not presuppose the metaphysical thesis that human beings or other things have an essential *telos* or purpose. It also treats ethics as being less sharply demarcated from other aspects of human life than the Kantian framework does, since any mental characteristic—even such natural abilities as wit, eloquence, or good sense—can be evaluated as a virtue or vice. While reasoning, as Hume conceives it, has several important roles to play in ascertaining the consequences of character traits and in applying the standard of judgment, the original source of ethical information is a moral sense, understood as a capacity for feelings of a distinctive character. These feelings are most typically stimulated by the sympathetic consideration of the effects of mental traits on their possessors and others, with traits that are either useful or agreeable eliciting feelings of approbation, and those that are harmful or disagreeable eliciting feelings of disapprobation. Crucially, the primary objects of these feelings are the traits themselves; particular actions are assessed *morally* only or chiefly in so far as they are indicative of virtues or vices. The originally diverse sentiments produced by the moral sense are subject to 'correction' by means of a preferred perspective and a set of endowments constituting a standard of judgment. Moral agency and responsibility do not require freedom from ordinary causal determination as long as the agent's actions are in fact expressions of their characters. The normativity of morality does not result, in this framework, from the autonomy of self-command through reason outside nature; rather, it is a natural phenomenon of human life resulting from the shared appreciation or deprecation of mental qualities and from the social consequences of those responses.

Adjudicating the relative merits of these two ethical frameworks is a complex and controversial matter. In support of Hume's claim to greatness, however, I will note just four advantages of the framework that he developed. First, because it does not require that human beings be conceived as standing in any sense outside nature, it is immediately and without revision compatible with the methodological naturalism that has become prevalent in many other fields of philosophy. Second, because its most fundamental source of information is feeling about character traits rather than reason about moral law, it can more easily accommodate and explain cases in which it is indeterminate what the morally best action would be, on the grounds that different actions would manifest different virtues and that the standard of judgment allows for some degree of variation in response. Third, precisely because it provides an important role to feeling as well as to reasoning, it also provides additional resources with which to make and justify moral decisions that cannot plausibly be made and justified on narrow grounds of consistency or the conditions of rational agency alone. Fourth, because it makes sympathy an essential element in moral discrimination and motivation, it offers a more plausible and empirically well-supported explanation of the moral failure of psychopathy, as rooted in a failure of sympathy or empathy rather than in a failure of reason. For these reasons and others, most contemporary empirical research in moral psychology tends to operate with a framework closer to Hume's than to Kant's. (For discussion of moral psychology in a Humean framework, see Gill 2014.)

Although philosophers have come to recognize that there is a distinctive and positive Humean framework for ethics, it is less well-recognized that there is an equally distinctive and positive Humean framework for epistemology, as opposed to a merely negative set of skeptical arguments. In this positive Humean framework, the primary subject matter of epistemology is beliefs and their probable truth or falsity relative to a specified body of experience; this is in contrast to frameworks that make the concepts of knowledge or justification primary. Beliefs, in the primary sense, are understood to be mental representations having a degree of confidence or conviction that is sometimes or always felt and available to consciousness; the truth of a belief consists in its accurately representing what is in fact the case. The immediate source of information about probability is felt confidence, which may arise from sense perception, reasoning, or memory. Crucially, the capacity for felt degrees of confidence functions as a kind of original 'sense of probability' in much the same way that the capacity for felt moral sentiments functions as a kind of moral sense in Hume's ethical framework. Degrees of confidence are, in general, responsive to what Locke and Hume call 'conformity to past experience': accordingly, the more in conformity to past experience a belief is, the greater the probability that it is true. Divergent degrees of confidence, like divergent moral sentiments in the ethical case, are properly adjusted by appeal to a standard of judgment involving a preferred perspective of maximal experience and a preferred set of psychological endowments that include some cognitive operations (such as sensitivity to analogy) and exclude others (such as wishful thinking and reliance on prejudices). Within this framework, mathematical rules of probability—including the probability calculus and Bayes's Theorem—may be understood not as purely *a priori* normative constraints on probability but rather as rules adopted either as predictive of the judgments of probability that would result from employing the standard of judgment or as elements incorporated into the preferred set of cognitive endowments themselves. The normativity of epistemology in this framework, much like the normativity of ethics in the Humean ethical framework, is a natural phenomenon of human life resulting from the felt and shared appreciation or deprecation of the relevant qualities and from the social consequences of those responses. (For a more detailed account of this framework as it is found in Hume's writings, see Garrett 2015: 137–68ff.)

Adjudicating the relative merits of epistemological frameworks, like adjudicating the relative merits of ethical frameworks, is a complex and controversial matter. In support of Hume's claim to greatness, however, I will note just five advantages of the epistemological framework that he developed. First, because it does not require that human beings or their recognition of epistemic normativity be in any sense outside nature, it is immediately compatible with the methodological naturalism that has become prevalent in many other fields of philosophy. Second, because its fundamental source of information is felt degrees of confidence, it can easily accommodate and explain cases in which the precise probability of a state of affairs is indeterminate relative to present information, on the ground that the standard of judgment allows for some degree of variation in the degree of confidence of a response. Third, because it regards mathematical rules of probability only as attempted implementations and refinements of a concept of probability derived ultimately from degrees of confidence, it can easily accommodate and explain cases in which mathematical treatments of probability yield problematic or unsatisfactory results. Fourth, because it allows that a felt conviction by itself provides some (defeasible) evidence that the object of that conviction is probably true, it provides resources with which to make and justify judgments of probable truth, even when these result immediately from sense perception or memory, without any process of reasoning.

Finally, because it appeals to a *sense* of probability as the source of the concept of probability, the framework explains both why we should be entitled to begin inquiry by provisionally trusting our faculties to deliver probable truths and why its seeming that something is probably true is itself defeasible evidence that it is probably true. In doing so, it provides the resources for a distinctive diagnosis of and response to radical or total skepticism. Thus, for example, Hume's own consequent skepticism, discussed previously, invokes a series of probable arguments—employing reasoning from empirical findings—for the conclusion that reason or other human cognitive faculties generally yield beliefs that are not probably true. At the same time, however, those very faculties, in providing the beliefs in question, also provide some information that those beliefs *are* probably true—information that the proponent of total skepticism ignores. The final outcome of this conflict, in which evidence that our beliefs are generally not probably true is weighed and balanced against the continuing evidence that they are probably true, may be the kind of diminution without annihilation of degree of confidence that Hume describes and endorses as one element in mitigated—as contrasted with 'excessive'—skepticism.

7. Concluding Observation

Although he was deeply influenced by many predecessors, David Hume was nonetheless the author of many extraordinary achievements in philosophy. These include original concepts, questions, theses, arguments, methodological approaches, and frameworks—only some of which have been described here—across a wide range of areas. Many of these achievements have been influential, even while a number of them have been misunderstood. Others, and especially his positive overall framework for epistemology, have not yet had the influence that they deserve. Taken together, however, they leave no doubt that Hume merits a prominent place among the great philosophers.[1]

Note

1 I gratefully acknowledge Jonathan Cottrell for helpful comments on an earlier version of this chapter.

References

Bourget, David and Chalmers, David J. 2014. What Do Philosophers Believe? *Philosophical Studies* 170: 465–500.
Fletcher, Guy and Ridge, Michael (eds.) 2014. *Having It Both Ways: Hybrid Theories and Modern Metaethics*, New York: Oxford University Press.
Garrett, Don 2006. Hume's Naturalistic Theory of Representation, *Synthese* 152: 301–19.
Garrett, Don 2015. *Hume*, London: Routledge.
Garrett, Don forthcoming. Hume's System of the Sciences, in *A Treatise of Human Nature in the Human Mind*, ed. Angela Coventry and Alex Sager, London: Routledge.
Gill, Michael B. 2014. *Humean Moral Pluralism*, Oxford: Oxford University Press.
Hume, David 1947. *Dialogues concerning Natural Religion*, ed. Norman Kemp Smith, Indianapolis: Bobbs-Merrill.
Hume, David 1987. Of the Standard of Taste, in *Essays Moral, Political, and Literary*, ed. Eugene F. Miller, Indianapolis: Liberty Fund: 226–249.
Hume, David 1999. *An Enquiry concerning the Principles of Morals*, ed. Tom L. Beauchamp, Oxford: Clarendon Press; references are by section and paragraph number.
Hume, David 2000. *An Enquiry concerning Human Understanding*, ed. Tom L. Beauchamp, Oxford: Clarendon Press; references are by section and paragraph number.
Hume, David 2007. *A Treatise of Human Nature*, ed. David Fate Norton and Mary Norton, Oxford: Clarendon Press; references are by book, part, section, and paragraph number.
Lewis, David 1969. *Convention: A Philosophical Study*, Cambridge, MA: Harvard University Press.
Lewis, David 1986. *Philosophical Papers*, vol. 2, New York: Oxford University Press.
Locke, John 1975. *An Essay Concerning Human Understanding*, ed P. H. Nidditch, Oxford: Clarendon Press.
Smith, Michael 1994. *The Moral Problem*, Malden, MA: Wiley-Blackwell.

10
IS KANT A *GREAT* MORAL PHILOSOPHER?

Allen Wood

1. What Is a 'Great Philosopher'?

The question posed by the title of this chapter—and by the title of this book—needs first to be itself put in question. So I must request the patience of those readers who began this chapter thinking they were going to read mainly about Kant. A book advertised to be about 'great philosophers' must of necessity be about the concept 'great philosopher' as well as about particular philosophers. That concept needs to be discussed before we can say how it might apply to Kant.

'Greatness' = Actual Influence

An affirmative answer to the question may seem obvious, since there is no doubt in most people's minds that, for the past two centuries, Kant has been among the most studied and most influential philosophers in the history of ethics. If that is all that qualifies some figure as a 'great moral philosopher', then the question would answer itself.

Even when understood in this superficial way, the issue may be more complicated than we might have realized. It is a fact, well-documented recently by Michelle Kosch (2015), that, for much of the nineteenth century, the chief source of 'Kant's' moral philosophy was taken not from Kant's writings at all, but from the *System of Ethics* (1798) of J.G. Fichte. It would not today be uncontroversial to claim that Fichte is among the greatest or most influential of modern moral philosophers. Fichte does not even appear, for instance, in Terence Irwin's *The Development of Ethics: A Historical and Critical Study* (Oxford: Oxford University Press, 2011), a massive three-volume history of Western moral philosophy that many would regard as comprehensive, or even all-inclusive, in scope. As I will be arguing later in this chapter, much of what passes today as 'Kantian ethics' is not really there in Kant's writings, but has been added by misreadings. Philosophers conventionally regarded as 'great' in the sense of *influential* may not actually be the ones whose influence is associated with their names.

'Greatness' as Merited Influence

Kant has no doubt had some influence or his name would not even be used in referring to the views of Fichte, or Rawls, or others who truly authored the ideas associated at a given time with 'Kantian' ethics. When we ask whether Kant is a 'great' philosopher, we mean to ask about more than influence. Greatness would have to consist in the *reasons why* the philosopher's thought *deserves* to be as widely studied as it is.

The concept of 'greatness' as 'merited influence' is roughly the right concept we are looking for. But it is easily misunderstood in fairly disastrous ways. It needs to be questioned, as Kant would put it, *quid iuris* (KrV A84/B116). That is, the concept's entire legitimacy must be put in question.

Sometimes, the concept 'great philosopher' assumes that the history of philosophy contains, in the form of a canon of hallowed texts, a repository of perennial wisdom to which our thinking ought to defer, and we are, at least figuratively, to sit in awe at the feet of 'great philosophers'. We are to treat the texts of 'great moral philosophers' as we might treat the advice of wise counselors to whom we would go for advice in times of trouble or moral confusion.

Kant, who insisted that affirming our human dignity consists above all in thinking for ourselves, would be the first to condemn this entire way of thinking (WA 8:41–2). That concept of 'great philosopher' also sets us up for disillusionment—or worse. Philosophy, as Hegel said, is always a child of its own time. Philosophers are also fallible human beings, adding to the prejudices of their age idiosyncratic errors of their own. Kant, for instance, articulated the principle that all human beings are equal in dignity. But he nevertheless thought that women were generally intellectually inferior to men, and he accepted the patriarchal family and political system of his day. Kant was notably ahead of his time in attacking the multi-faceted injustice of European colonialism,[1] but he also inherited from Linnaeus, and then further developed, the theory that the human species is divided into four races, within which the white European race occupies a superior place. There is a sizable literature whose aim is to alert people to the shocking facts of Kant's sexism and racism.[2] We certainly should be aware of these aspects of Kant's philosophy, and we should reflect on their significance. But sometimes there seems to be the implicit inference that Kantian moral principles—for instance, the equal dignity of all human beings—are really sexist or racist in content wherever these principles might be found or taken up: for instance, in the thinking of the many Kantians today who are feminists, or in the post-apartheid constitution of South Africa. The inference usually is left implicit because it is obviously invalid, and its conclusion is absurd on its face.

I think the real point of this literature is to address itself to people who might be tempted to regard Kant's authority as supporting sexist or racist thinking today. Someone might then think,

> If a great philosopher such as Kant could hold the view that women should be under the authority of men, and that white Europeans are intellectually superior to Asians, Africans, and native Americans, then when we take offense at the expression of the same views by our contemporaries, this is no more than narrow-minded "political correctness" on our part.

That thought would be preposterous and offensive—even worse than the absurd view that Kantian principles are sexist or racist wherever they are found. But to focus on Kant would mislocate the problem. The problem is the worldview associated with the assumed concept 'great philosopher' as 'wise man to be admired and deferred to'.

2. Why Should We Study Past Philosophers?

Let me then make a new start. Why should we study past philosophers? Here we must deal right away with the fact that not all philosophers think there is any *philosophical* value at all in studying them.[3] The views of past philosophers are infamously the object of endless dispute. This led Descartes, and has led many since, to think that what is needed is an entirely new and 'scientific' way of approaching intellectual inquiry, one that has been freed from any dependency on, or connection with, what past philosophers have thought or written. During the nineteenth century, there was a powerful movement that rejected 'philosophy' entirely. Stephen Hawking and Steven Pinker now think that philosophy is wholly outdated and should not continue to exist at all but should be replaced by science. A fashionable movement even within philosophy itself holds that philosophy can remain viable only by turning to the findings of empirical science. Some think that moral philosophy in particular should base itself on empirical psychology, social science, and even neuroscience.[4] They argue that, since past philosophers did not have our modern findings at their disposal, we should forget about the history of philosophy.

The Nature of Philosophical Questions

My own view is pretty much the opposite of that one. Philosophy is the study of a set of questions that are fundamental to our thinking, but there will never be a free and honest consensus on how they should be answered. In moral philosophy, the inquiry begins with questions about how we ought to live and what kinds of people we ought to try to be. Such inquiries inevitably lead to conceptual questions about what we mean by notions such as 'good' and 'right', and to questions about the objects, if any, to which these notions apply. They also ask about the principles, if any, which ought to determine our conduct, and what reasons, if any, we have for following those principles.

Philosophical questions may seem just as natural to children as they do to adults.[5] But once we begin to get into these questions—especially once we begin to examine what we are already taking for granted when we ask them—we soon discover that we could not possibly have been the first ones to ask them. We inherit them from the past. When we ask them, we cannot even understand what we are asking unless we begin to understand this past—in other words, the history of philosophy. It is therefore naïve—not in a childlike or innocent sense of that term—when philosophers or others think that they can afford to ignore the history of philosophy. We can't ask philosophical questions at all, except insofar as we are open to understanding the past that the questions bring with them. For one thing we learn from the study of philosophy is that, although we cannot answer philosophical questions, we can come to understand them better. We need to study the history of philosophy because it helps us to acquire this understanding.

Universities might cease to support academic departments that make it their business to ask such questions. The result would be only that the same conversations would appear in other venues, and their quality would probably also decline markedly.[6] How big a loss it would be if there were no academic departments of philosophy takes us right back to the original question with which I said that moral philosophy begins: what sort of life should we live and what kind of people should we be? Even rejecting philosophy is just another way of engaging in it. However pointless philosophical inquiry may be, it is also unavoidable.

3. 'Great Philosopher': A More Useful and Realistic Concept

Philosophical questions themselves have a history. This creates a certain collective need for there to be some historical texts shared among philosophers so that the interpretation and critical discussion of the texts can be part of the philosophers' informed philosophical conversations. So let's base our concept of 'great philosopher' on this collective need. A 'great philosopher' is the author of whatever texts (or other means of communication) philosophical inquirers use at a given time as the objects of the historical side of their activity. More precisely, since our interest in a philosopher's 'greatness' is always an interest in the *reasons why* the thought of the philosopher is studied, a 'great philosopher' is one whose thought we would *do well* to treat in this way.

If this is how we understand 'great philosopher', then we should not expect the list of 'great philosophers' to remain constant over time. As our philosophical conversations change, the historical products on which they have most reason to focus is likely to change, too. Although it may sound morbid to say so, there is a certain competition for 'greatness' among the dead.[7] But the combatants aren't corpses. They are the living interpreters of the writings of past philosophers. This is inevitable because even philosophers whose focus is primarily historical have only a limited amount of collective time, attention, and capacity for appropriative understanding. A philosopher who is 'great' at one time may cease to be 'great' at a later time, not because of any change in the thought of that philosopher but merely because of the direction in which the later philosophical conversation has gone.

In place of veneration, deference, and trust toward 'great philosophers', I suggest the basic attitude of intellectual sympathy and patience combined with constant critical mistrust. We learn from past philosophers only by questioning and raising objections to what they say. We learn from them equally by attaining to their insights and gaining insight into their errors. This could not exist without something like an attitude of trust. The *authority* of a great philosopher is never the authority of the philosopher's person, but only that of the intellectual strength of certain theories and arguments.

Some philosophical texts count as 'great' in part because they seem to have been designed, either by their original author or by others, to have this quality. The clearest example is Aristotle. We do not know much about the original sources from which the Aristotelian corpus came, but what we have are sources upon which the Peripatetic school, led by Andronicus of Rhodes, active in Rome about 60 BCE, based the Aristotelian corpus that we now have. Clearly, these redactions have been immensely successful. They became not only the objects of critical reflection and commentary by the Peripatetics, but also later by great Islamic philosophers and then by great Western scholastics. They are still being interpreted and commented on today by the best scholars of ancient Greek philosophy. We are still learning from them.

The greatness of a philosopher always has a certain 'ants to the picnic' quality about it. Some philosophers have in fact attracted the attention of more, and of better, minds than others. Once the greater number of better minds have been drawn to a certain philosopher, that fact all by itself gives still more good minds a new reason to study the philosopher. Greatness is more a property of the ongoing study of the philosopher than of any qualities or virtues of what the philosopher originally thought or wrote. Aristotle would not be as great were it not for Avicenna, Averroes, Aquinas, and Scotus. Kant's greatness depends on the work of Maimon, Fichte, Hegel, Lotze, Cohen, Cassirer, Rawls, and many others, including those of us who still study him.

4. How Kant Is a Great Moral Philosopher Because He Has Been *Misunderstood*

A possibly counterintuitive consequence of this concept of 'greatness' is that a philosopher can become 'great' by being misread and misunderstood. I believe that a very significant part of Kant's greatness as a moral philosopher has this source. My own work on Kant has consisted in no small part in the attempt to correct the common misunderstandings of Kant's ethics. But if creative misreadings of a philosopher can be part of what makes the philosopher's thought worth thinking about, then those misreadings, too, as well as attempts to correct them, constitute the philosopher's greatness.

Kant the Moralistic Monster

Part of what might make it philosophically rewarding to discuss a moral philosopher is the way in which the philosopher is seen (whether correctly or incorrectly) to exhibit certain errors or vices, intellectual or moral. Kant's greatness conspicuously exhibits this phenomenon.

In the past two centuries, our culture has tended to become more morally permissive about many matters—sexuality is probably the most conspicuous of these. We have also come to doubt whether the folkways associated with our moral practices are any better than those associated with the practices of other cultures or subcultures. We have come to see traditional morality as too cold, too tyrannical and inhuman, too strict, absolutist, and inflexible. Decent people regard these changes in perception as changes for the better. But traditional morality and its attitudes still have defenders, especially among social conservatives, and many philosophers would like to argue the case for a more humane set of attitudes against an ugly adversary formidable enough that their victories over traditional morality will be meaningful and significant.

To many philosophers, Kant seems well-suited to play the repulsive role required by this little drama. The very term 'categorical imperative' raises the hair on the back of their necks. Kant understands morality as a set of commands for the *rational* part of you, apparently standing as superior over your natural inclinations: the 'emotional' part of you. Kant says that beneficence from duty has moral worth, while beneficence from sympathy does not. What has moral worth is the rational suppression of your human nature. My late lamented friend Jerry Cohen interpreted it this way (2014: 150): 'Kant believes that he is most morally admirable who has a rotten soul, but acts against its natural dictates.'

Kant seems to be (again in Jerry's immortal words) 'the deontologist supreme'. Kant rejects an ethics based on happiness or concern for good consequences in favor of an ethics based on required or forbidden actions. The whole ugly *Gestalt* seems confirmed when Kant appears to hold extremely strict views on a number of moral and political topics, especially on lying and on sexuality. He harshly condemns both masturbation and 'paederasty'. He defends the death penalty for murder, and denies the right of revolution even against unjust governments. Another friend of mine was once trying to impress upon me the philosopher's commitment to a certain strict moral principle, with which I strongly disagreed. (This is another very well-known philosopher, whom I will not name, but if

I did you would recognize it.) This philosopher said, 'I am a real Kantian about this issue!' My reply was, 'Oh, I see. When you say you are a "Kantian", what you mean is that you are irrationally inflexible and irresponsibly heedless of the harmful consequences of your actions.'

For many, that's what it means to be a 'Kantian'. This nasty image accounts in no small part for his greatness as a moral philosopher, because it is why many think it worthwhile to discuss Kant's views. I am tempted to say that the long practice among moral philosophers of casting Kant in this villainous role makes him rather like Voltaire's God: if he did not exist, it would be necessary to invent him. Those who study Kant carefully know it to be an invention.[8] As John Rawls put it, Kant's is 'not a morality of austere command but an ethic of mutual respect and self-esteem' (1971: 265). Kantian ethics is an ethics of individual self-government, free interaction with others, and consequent openness to moral reflection and moral change. Some of Kant's personal moral opinions seem overly strict to us because they reflected either the morality of his time and place or his own personal idiosyncrasies. But his fundamental moral orientation was to support independence of mind, thinking for oneself, and a humane and non-judgmental attitude toward others. The basic spirit of Kant's ethics is therefore on the very opposite side of the cultural divide from the one where these critics would place it.

Kant began as a partisan of Hutcheson's morality of natural sentiment, but quickly turned toward a more rationalist approach, when he perceived that sentiments lacked both the stability and the objectivity needed to ground moral judgments. The remnants of his conversion are what people often detect in his writings, although in their misreading it takes on an exaggerated and distorted form.[9] In fact, Kant does not oppose reason to feeling or emotion. He always retained a place for moral feelings in the psychology of the virtuous agent. Without them, he thinks, we could not be rational agents at all. Aesthetic feelings relating to beauty and sublimity are essential to our being either free agents or moral beings.[10] Kant's description of virtues and vices associated with our duties includes ways that we ought to feel and ought not to feel. Kant understands some feelings as direct responses to reason and as natural expressions of rational valuation.[11]

Kant the Formalist 'Universalizer of Maxims'

Moral philosophers usually think that the first task of moral theory is to provide us with some criterion of right and wrong, which tells us what we should, and what we should not, do. This is the function of 'intuitions' in British rationalist ethics and of the greatest happiness principle in hedonistic utilitarianism. Kant's *Groundwork* is an attempt to find and justify a 'supreme principle of morality', so readers have naturally thought that the discovery of a moral criterion was its main aim. Kant formulates the moral principle in three different ways, as follows:

First Formula

> FUL *Formula of Universal Law:* '*Act only in accordance with that maxim through which you at the same time can will that it become a universal law*'
> (Kant, Groundwork 4:421; cf. 4:402);

with its variant,

> FLN *Formula of the Law of Nature:* 'So act, as if the maxim of your action were to become through your will a **universal law of nature**'
> (Groundwork 4:421).

Second Formula

> FH *Formula of Humanity as End in Itself:* '*So act that you use humanity, as much in your own person as in the person of every other, always at the same time as an end and never merely as a means*'
> (Groundwork 4:429).

Third Formula

> FA *Formula of Autonomy:* '. . . the idea *of the will of every rational being as a will giving universal law*' (*Groundwork* 4:431; cf. 4:432), or

> 'Not to choose otherwise than so that the maxims of one's choice are at the same time comprehended with it in the same volition as universal law'
> (Groundwork 4:440; cf. 4:432, 434, 438)

with its variant,

> FRE *Formula of the Realm of Ends:* 'Act in accordance with maxims of a universally legislative member for a merely possible realm of ends'
> (Groundwork 4:439; cf. 4:433, 437–9)

The first formulation that we encounter in both the First and Second Sections of the *Groundwork* is FUL. And in the First Section it is applied immediately to an example, in which an agent considers making a promise that he does not intend to keep, in order to gain money that he urgently needs. In the Second Section, FUL is supplemented by FLN, and then applied to four examples, in each of which the agent is tempted to violate a duty by making an exception to it based on his particular situation, needs, or desires. In these cases, the agent formulates a 'maxim' (a subjective principle) on which he proposes to act. FUL and then FLN are used to show that the maxim is impermissible because it cannot be willed to be a universal law (or law of nature).

It has been generally assumed that these two formulas (between which readers often see no significant difference) are intended to supply us with a general criterion of right action. It is generally thought that Kantian moral deliberation begins with an agent's proposing to act on some maxim, and then the function of FUL/FLN is to provide a principle that will show some maxims to be permissible and others not. Following John Rawls, FUL/FLN has come to be identified with 'The Categorical Imperative', and its 'universalizability' test for maxims has come to be called by many the 'CI-Procedure'.

A large part of the 'greatness' of Kant's moral philosophy—its deserved importance as an object of philosophical interpretation, discussion, and controversy—has been the claims commonly understood (that is, *mis*understood) to be associated with these formulas. From early on in the reception of Kant's moral philosophy, critics have questioned whether his arguments based on FUL/FLN can succeed in showing all immoral courses of conduct to be immoral. There has been endless debate about what counts as a 'maxim', what counts as 'universalizability' of a maxim, and which maxims do, and which don't, in fact pass the 'universalization' test proposed by FUL/FLN. It is generally supposed that Kant's entire theory stands or falls with the capacity of the 'universalizability' test to give the 'right' results. By the 'right' results are meant those agreeing our 'intuitions'—not only about Kant's own examples but also about all creatively concocted maxims designed to serve as counterexamples to Kant's imagined claims.

Those who think that Kant's universalizability test can be so interpreted that it succeeds are generally thought of as on the Kantian side of these debates, while those who think that the test necessarily fails are thought to be on the 'anti-Kantian' side. This puts me in an embarrassing position: I think that the test does not work as a general test of maxims but that this boring fact does matter at all for Kant's actual theory. There are also attempts to mediate the dispute by offering some variation or revision of Kant's principle that captures its essential spirit and succeeds in agreeing with our considered judgments, even if his version does not.[12] Using the concept of philosophical 'greatness' I have developed, it contributes substantially to Kant's *greatness* as a moral philosopher, even if the controversy is not really about Kant at all. I will now devote a short space to stating, briefly and a bit dogmatically, why I think that the whole controversy is wrongheaded.

As we have seen, the principle of morality presented in the *Groundwork* is formulated in three different ways. If you look carefully at what Kant says, I think you can see that there is a fairly clear division of labor between these formulas. They have different tasks to perform. And none of them is supposed to provide the general criterion of right and wrong that philosophers assume is the task of a philosophical principle of morality. Kant tells us that we do not need philosophy to tell us what to do (G 4:405). The most urgent thing that we need philosophy to do is to enable us to unmask and correct our tendency to deceive ourselves about moral demands, arguing that they are less burdensome on us than they seem to be. That is the task assigned to FUL/FLN. These formulas are not defended by showing how their results harmonize with our intuitions or considered judgments. They are argued to follow from the concept of the moral worth of actions, consisting in acting from duty, as the law by which duty necessitates or constrains the will (G 4:400–2), and then from the formal side of the concept of a categorical imperative (G 4:421).

For Kant, the moral deliberation they address begins not with a maxim but with a duty—of which Kant offers us four, taxonomically arranged (G 4:421–4). These duties are not derived from FUL or FLN, but, for the moment, are simply given to us. In each case, the agent is tempted to make an exception to the duty in question. The 'maxim' to be tested is a principle on which an agent imagines acting that would propose to rationalize the exception. The test proposed by FUL/FLN is supposed to show the agent, who despite this temptation is still basically honest and committed to morality, that the exception is not warranted. At the conclusion of the four examples, Kant summarizes the limited purpose for which FLN has been used (G 4:424). This confirms what earlier he described as the most urgent reason why we need moral philosophy (G 4:405).

Where do these four duties come from? Kant proceeds to derive a new formula of the moral law, FH, from the matter of the concept of a categorical imperative (G 4:427–9). He then applies FH to the same four examples, and this time he derives the four duties assumed in using FLN (G 4:429–30). So it is the function of FH, not of FUL or FLN, to be the formula from which duties are derived. Kant then combines FUL/FLN with FH to get FA (and later its variant, FRE) (G 4:431–3). The function of this most encompassing formula, as we learn in the Third Section, is in the deduction or justification of the moral principle, through its connection with freedom of the will, which cannot be demonstrated but must be presupposed as a property of every rational will (G 4:446–8).

Thus, it is a basic error to employ FUL/FLN as a general test of maxims or a general criterion of right and wrong. Its use by Kant is restricted to unmasking sophistical attempts to make unwarranted exceptions to already recognized duties. For Kant, there is no general criterion of right and wrong. There is a set of duties, moral rules, and concepts, which often appear as virtues and vices in Kant's Doctrine of Virtue (MS 6:417–74). These duties are to be applied to particular cases through moral *judgment* or *appraisal*, which Kant regularly distinguishes from moral reasoning or deliberation. The application of duties to particular cases by judgment cannot be reduced to reasoning from principles (MS 6:411, TP 8:275; cf. KrV A132–4/B171–4; Anth 7:199). FUL/FLN are instead described as rules, norms, or 'canons' aiding judgment (*Urteil*) or appraisal (*Beurteilung*)—specifically, by unmasking sophistical attempts to make unwarranted exceptions to already recognized duties in particular cases (G 4:403–4, 424, 426, cf. KpV 5:67–71).

For Kant, there never could be any principle or procedure that serves as a general criterion for right and wrong or that tells us what to do. Kant's greatness as a moral philosopher, to the extent that it consists in disputes about whether FUL/FLN can serve as such a principle or procedure, is based entirely on a fundamental error, a basic misreading of the entire theory present in the *Groundwork* and later texts. Once Kant has been systematically misread in this way, however, the controversies over FUL/FLN (as so misunderstood) acquire a life of their own. Nothing I say here could hope—or is intended—to put an end to them. This is all the truer since, as I have admitted, this basic misreading is (and always has been) the dominant interpretation of Kant. Nor is anything like that my intention. My only hope is to rescue Kant's actual thoughts from the dismal wreckage. But even this attempt to correct the misreading belongs to the broad field of philosophical activity associated with controversies about FUL/FLN.

Kant the Constructivist

Beginning in 1980, the greatest moral philosopher of the twentieth century, John Rawls, offered an interpretation of Kantian ethics (and metaethics) that he called 'Kantian constructivism' (Rawls 1980). Rawls claimed that Kant did not view moral truth as the correspondence of moral judgments to some independently existing moral reality (what Rawls liked to call an 'order of values'). Instead, Rawls argued, moral truth is for the Kantian to be 'constructed' using a deliberative procedure: namely, the 'CI-Procedure' identified with the universalizability test proposed in FUL/FLN. From this reading of Kant, Rawls proposed that he was committed to an anti-realist metaethics—that there is no objective moral truth independently of our judgments. Morality is merely a projection of those judgments. If there were a moral truth, Rawls argued, that would contradict Kantian autonomy. We would not be legislators of the moral law. Acceptance of an independent moral reality or order of values commits us to a principle of heteronomy, basing morality on 'material determining grounds' (G 4:440–5, KpV 5:40–1). These thoughts were pursued by many of Rawls's students and followers, perhaps most definitively, and also most radically, by Christine Korsgaard (1996). It remains controversial whether Kant is a constructivist. (For my own part, I am sure he is not.) It is even controversial what moral constructivism is. The attempts to develop and defend 'Kantian constructivism', as well as the criticisms directed at it, both as philosophy and as Kant-interpretation, undeniably constitute part of Kant's 'greatness' as a moral philosopher. This greatness, too, is based entirely on *misunderstandings* of Kant.

Part of the error is simply the use of FUL/FLN as a 'CI-Procedure'—a general criterion of permissibility or a general criterion of right and wrong. But there are serious errors also in the interpretation of Kant's conception of autonomy. The constructivist interpretation depends on claiming that for Kant we actually do legislate the moral law and are its authors. Kant never says this, however, and in fact clearly commits himself to its denial. The principle of autonomy (FA) for him consists in claiming we may view 'the *idea* of the will of every rational being as a will giving universal law' (G 4:431). An idea for Kant is an *a priori* concept to which no empirical instance can ever be adequate. He does not claim that you or I or any other rational being legislates the law. The legislator of a law is someone who attaches sanctions to it; its author is someone whose will determines its content. Kant says that we may *consider* ourselves its legislator and *regard* ourselves as its author (G 4:431). This is because, when we obey the law, we align our will with it and it is therefore as if we gave the law to ourselves (G 4:436–7). Among laws given to our will, Kant distinguishes *positive* laws from *natural* laws. The former are those given by an external authority, such as the ruler or legislator of a state, who may determine the law's content (as its author) and attach rewards or punishments to it (as its legislator). The moral law, however, is a natural law, which obligates us solely through our own reason. Natural laws, he says, have neither a legislator nor an author (MS 6: 227). God may be *regarded* as the legislator (not the author) of the moral law, insofar as he apportions happiness according to worthiness among his creatures. The bindingness of the moral law does not depend on this: the moral law has no legislator. What is right and wrong, good and bad, Kant says, does not depend on God's will, or on yours or mine either (G 4:439). The moral law has no author, but our will may be *regarded* as its author when we will according to it. Rather, it is 'good or bad in itself', goodness and badness, right and wrong, lie 'in the nature of things . . . the essence of things' (VE 27: 261–2, 282–3, 29:633–4). Kant's position thus invokes precisely that 'moral reality' that Rawls thinks that Kant rejects. A material principle of heteronomy is one based on some value or end *distinct* from the objective rightness or wrongness of actions required or prohibited by categorical imperatives. The objective validity of the moral law is no threat to it.

Rawls's 'constructivist' reading of Kant on this point gets Kant *exactly wrong*. Again, the part of Kant's greatness that is due to moral constructivism is based on a misreading.

5. Why Kant Is a Great Moral Philosopher Even When He Is *Not* Misunderstood

Not all of Kant's greatness as a moral philosopher depends on errors. In fact, there is far too much in his texts on moral philosophy, and in the philosophical scholarship on them, that is worthy of discussion and *not* based on error for me even to begin to document that part of Kant's greatness. Although a few of his moral opinions are conspicuously backward, and now rightly considered ridiculous or offensive, the fact remains that his treatments of nearly all moral topics contains thinking from which we greatly benefit by reflecting on them. Many of the writings that repay study deal with the empirical side of Kant's view of human nature, history, politics, and religion (MS, Anth, I, KU, MA, R, SF, EF, TP, VE, VpR, VP). What I have just said is often true even of his thinking on topics that, for the most part, he gets grossly wrong (see Herman 1993; Wood 2008). Instead of taking on that hopeless task of even beginning to expound what we can learn from studying Kant's moral philosophy, I will end with a brief exposition of the one central idea really present in his ethics (not the result of misunderstanding) that is basic to what is both most distinctive in his ethical thought and still valuable for us to think about.

Humanity as End in Itself and Human Dignity

Kant's second formula of the moral law (FH) says that we should treat humanity or rational nature in our own person and the person of others always as an *end in itself*, never as a means only. He also makes the claim, not equivalent to this one, that humanity or rational nature has *dignity*. It is controversial how Kant proposes to defend these claims, or whether his defence succeeds. But the claims themselves represent, in my view, what is most to be treasured about the moral outlook of our modern world. They are very far from having been fully understood, and their truth is even farther from having been incorporated into our social institutions and way of life. But that is all the more reason why we benefit from reflecting on them, and therefore why Kant is to be considered a great moral philosopher on account of them.

Kant thinks that an action is anything within the power of the agent that is chosen as a means to some end to be brought about that the agent has set (G 4:427). Such ends have only subjective validity, since their rational authority over the agent depends on the contingent fact that the agent has set them. But there is one end to be produced having an objective rational validity because all finite rational agents must set it: their own happiness. Further, there are also ends whose rational authority is independent of being set by an agent and ends that are not to be produced but are existent or self-sufficient. The concept of such an end is that of an *end in itself*. This is the only kind of end that could ground a categorical imperative, or motivate obedience to one.

How is it possible for something to be an end without being an object or state of affairs to be produced? This question all by itself displays a pitiful poverty of philosophical imagination. An end is anything for the sake of which we act. This includes objects to be produced, but it might also include existing beings for whose sake we act because we value them and express our valuation of them in our actions. Human beings, and the rational nature in them, are *ends in themselves* in just this sense. They have a value that reason commands us to respect and to care about independently of our subjective wishes or desires. This value, and these attitudes of respect and caring, are for Kant the foundation of morality. The objective moral property of being an end in itself belongs universally and equally to all human beings simply in virtue of their rational nature, by which Kant means their capacities to set and pursue ends, to aim at their own happiness, and to obey moral laws.

Rational nature in persons also has *dignity*. Originally, the concept of dignity was the concept of a high social status attaching to certain people. Kant still continues to use it in this way when he speaks of offices within the state as 'dignities' (MS 6:328–30). But, absolutely speaking, 'dignity' for Kant refers to a kind of value distinct from 'price' (G 4:434–5). A valuable thing has a *price* if its value may be rationally sacrificed or traded away in exchange for something with an equal or greater price. It has *dignity* if it could never be rational to trade away its value for anything else, even for something else having dignity. According to Kant, human persons, and the rational nature in them, have dignity.

This does not mean that human life could never be sacrificed. A person, or their humanity, is not to be identified with any state of affairs with which they are associated—for instance, the state of affairs of their existing or continuing to exist. This would be to treat them as ends to be produced (or preserved), not as self-sufficient ends in themselves. Each person, and the humanity or rational nature in each person, is, for Kant's ethics, a value that makes a claim on us entirely independently of our contingent wishes or desires (a person is an end in itself). This value is also a dignity—it may not be sacrificed or traded away for anything else.

Rational nature in persons must not be treated only as a means, but it certainly may be treated as a means. Another formulation of Kant's moral principle is FRE—namely, that all rational beings should be thought of as an ideal community (a 'realm of ends') and their ends should be thought of as shared, mutually agreeing, and mutually supporting. As members of the realm of ends, we should both be ends and the means to the ends of others insofar as they and their ends belong to the realm of ends.

We ought to hear something socially and historically radical—even downright impudent—in the now often used Kantian term 'human dignity'. This is a term that we should never take for granted as a pious platitude. For what it says is that no social status that anyone can claim—on the basis of birth, or qualities, or their accomplishments, and no status based on their power, wealth, or honor—could ever amount to something higher than the status they can claim simply as human beings, as rational and moral persons. The lowliest starving third world peasant has dignity as much as the richest American, and Adolf Hitler had dignity as much as Mahatma Ghandi or Nelson Mandela. In this sense, Kant's ethics is radically egalitarian—not directly about the distribution to people of any benefits or entitlements, but about the inherent personal worth of human individuals.

The concept of the innate human right to freedom (independence of constraint by the choice of another) that grounds Kant's philosophy of right and political philosophy is independent of the ethical value of persons as having dignity and being ends in themselves (Wood 2014a, 2014b). But clearly these ideas are closely allied: they express the same philosophical vision. Another allied idea is Kant's conception of *enlightenment*: each person should think for himself or herself, and not be subjected to the intellect of any other (WA). But this also means that we should think universally, from the standpoint of all others, and think consequently (KU 5:294–5, Anth 7:220, 228). Kant thinks that no one can follow these principles perfectly, but that we all must try.

Every human being has equal dignity and is an end in itself. This means that rational adults, in their personal, familial, economic, and political lives must be treated as equals. None may be subjected to the arbitrary authority of others—as, for example, workers are to their capitalist employers. All persons are morally entitled to the respect and concern of others. We may not ignore the needs of others for food, housing, or medical care. Human beings are all one family, one community. The future of our entire species, and every member of it, is the proper concern of all of us, and we cannot exempt ourselves from caring about it.

The implications of Kant's principle are radical and far-reaching. Kant himself obviously did not fully or consistently think through the conclusions that follow from his most basic moral principle. He did not follow his own rule to think from the standpoint of all others and to think consequently. We should therefore read Kant critically, never deferring to his errors. But we should also never condescend to him or criticize him for failing to think consequently from his principles, since neither have we. We have not even begun, in our attitudes and social practices, to follow these consequences of Kant's basic principle where they lead. If a *great philosopher* is one whose thoughts deserve our intense, serious and critical reflections, then the thought that humanity in every person is an end in itself possessed of dignity is the thought that most makes Kant a great moral philosopher.

Notes

1 See Ripstein (2014), and also essays in Flikschuh and Ypi (2014).
2 Regarding Kant on women, see Schott (1993), and most of the essays in Schott (1997). Regarding Kant on race, see Eze (1997), Bernasconi (2002), and Mills (2005).
3 At least until recently, the philosophers conventionally regarded as 'great' were all, as the phrase has it, *dead white men*. Those who declaim against negative stereotypes everywhere else are strangely susceptible to this one, and regard it as a ground for dismissing the traditional 'canon' of great philosophers. I think that it is properly philosophical always to question the canon, along with everything else, but not on the ground of racial, gender, or any other stereotype.
4 A compendium can be found in Doris and the Moral Psychology Research Group (2012); and a thoughtful review and critique of this movement in moral philosophy is Appiah (2010).
5 My colleague David Hills says, 'Philosophy is the ungainly attempt to tackle questions that come natural to children using methods that come natural to lawyers.'
6 There is considerable empirical evidence that academic philosophy now attracts more talented minds than are attracted to most other academic disciplines, whether humanistic or scientific. See www.physicscentral.com/buzz/blog/index.cfm?postid=5112019841346388353 and www.statisticbrain.com/iq-estimates-by-intended-college-major.
7 Those same 'dead white men'. But it looks as if dead women and dead people of color will increasingly become welcome additions to the contest as time passes.

8 When you point out to these critics that some of Kant's extreme and morally traditionalist conclusions do not follow from his principles, their reply is sometimes to chide you for not having 'respected the unity of his thought'. But the unity of any philosopher's thought consists in how its parts do or don't fit together; if they do not, then it would be the very reverse of respecting its unity to ignore this fact and treat it as a dogmatic mindless monolith. For these critics, however, the unity of Kant's thought consists precisely in its being a dogmatic mindless monolith, and the point for them is not to understand it but only to reject it.

9 To see Kant as an enemy of human emotion because he does not ground ethics on emotion is like seeing Obamacare as fascism, complete with death panels and gulags, simply because it uses law to reform the US private health insurance system, enabling millions to afford health care who could not do so before.

10 See Guyer (1993). Again, a long list of insightful discussions of this topic could be given. As with much good Kant scholarship these days, one hardly knows where to start. The smartest ants now living have swarmed over the picnic. Notice how many of them, contrary to Kant's opinion, are women. When I was there, I did not detect his turning over this grave in Kaliningrad, but maybe he is.

11 There is a large and still growing literature on this very rich topic. For a recent approachable introduction, see Cohen (2014) and Williamson (2015). More generally, a corrective to the common misreadings can be found in much recent literature on Kantian ethics.

12 The most ambitious recent version of such an attempt is to be found in Parfit (2011).

References

(Ak) *Immanuel Kants Schriften*. Ausgabe der königlich preussischen Akademie der Wissenschaften (Berlin: W. de Gruyter, 1902–). Unless otherwise footnoted, writings of Immanuel Kant will be cited by volume: page number in this edition.

(Ca) *Cambridge Edition of the Writings of Immanuel Kant* (New York: Cambridge University Press, 1992–) This edition provides marginal Ak volume: page citations. Specific works will be cited using the following system of abbreviations (works not abbreviated below will be cited simply as Ak volume: page).

(Anth) *Anthropologie in pragmatischer Hinsicht* (1798), Ak 7
Anthropology from a pragmatic point of view, Ca Anthropology, History and Education

(EF) *Zum ewigen Frieden: Ein philosophischer Entwurf* (1795), Ak 8
Toward perpetual peace: A philosophical project, Ca Practical Philosophy

(G) *Grundlegung zur Metaphysik der Sitten* (1785), Ak 4
Groundwork of the metaphysics of morals, Ca Practical Philosophy

(I) *Idee zu einer allgemeinen Geschichte in weltbürgerlicher Absicht* (1784), Ak 8
Idea toward a universal history with a cosmopolitan aim, Ca Anthropology History and Education

(KrV) *Kritik der reinen Vernunft* (1781, 1787). Cited by A/B pagination.
Critique of pure reason, Ca Critique of Pure Reason

(KpV) *Kritik der praktischen Vernunft* (1788), Ak 5
Critique of practical reason, Ca Practical Philosophy

(KU) *Kritik der Urteilskraft* (1790), Ak 5
Critique of the power of judgment, Ca Critique of the Power of Judgment

(MA) *Mutmaßlicher Anfang der Menschengeschichte* (1786), Ak 8
Conjectural beginning of human history, Ca Anthropology History and Education
(MS) *Metaphysik der Sitten* (1797–8), Ak 6
Metaphysics of morals, Ca Practical Philosophy
(R) *Religion innerhalb der Grenzen der bloßen Vernunft* (1793–4), Ak 6
Religion within the boundaries of mere reason, Ca Religion and Rational Theology
(SF) *Streit der Fakultäten* (1798), Ak 7
Conflict of the faculties, Ca Religion and Rational Theology
(TP) *Über den Gemeinspruch: Das mag in der Theorie richtig sein, taugt aber nicht für die Praxis* (1793), Ak 8
On the common saying: That may be correct in theory but it is of no use in practice, Ca Practical philosophy
(VE) *Vorlesungen über Ethik*, Ak 27, 29
Lectures on Ethics, Ca Lectures on Ethics
(VP) *[Vorlesungen über] Pädagogik*, Ak 9
Lectures on Pedagogy, Ca Anthropology, History and Education
(WA) *Beantwortung der Frage: Was ist Aufklärung?* (1784), Ak 8
An answer to the question: What is enlightenment? Ca Practical Philosophy Philosophy

Secondary Sources

Appiah, Kwame Anthony 2010. *Experiments in Ethics*, Cambridge, MA: Harvard University Press.
Bernasconi, Robert 2002. Kant as an Unfamiliar Source of Racism, in *Philosophers on Race: Critical Essays*, ed. Julie K. Ward and Tommy L. Lott, Oxford: Blackwell: 145–66.
Cohen, Alix (ed.) 2014. *Kant on Emotions and Value*, Houndmills: Palgrave Macmillan.
Cohen, G. A. 2014. *Lectures on the History of Moral and Political Philosophy*, ed. Jonathan Wolf, Princeton: Princeton University Press.
Doris, John M. and the Moral Psychology Research Group (eds.) 2012. *The Moral Psychology Handbook*, Oxford: Oxford University Press.
Eze, Emmanuel Chukwudi 1997. The Color of Reason: The Idea of 'Race' in Kant's Anthropology, in *Post-Colonial African Philosophy: A Critical Reader*, ed. Emmanuel Chukwudi Eze, Oxford: Blackwell: 103–40.
Flikschuh, Katrin and Ypi, Lea (eds.) 2014. *Kant and Colonialism: Historical and Critical Perspectives*, Oxford: Oxford University Press.
Guyer, Paul 1993. *Kant and the Experience of Freedom*, Cambridge: Cambridge University Press.
Herman, Barbara 1993. Could It Be Worth Thinking about Kant on Sex and Marriage? in *A Mind of One's Own: Feminist Essays on Reason and Objectivity*, ed. Louise M. Antony and Charlotte Witt, Boulder, CO: Westview Press: 49–67.
Johann Gottlieb Fichte, System of Ethics (1798), translated by Daniel Breazeale and Guenter Zoeller. Cambridge: Cambridge University Press, 2005.
Korsgaard, Christine M. 1996. *The Sources of Normativity*, ed. Onora O'Neill, Cambridge: Cambridge University Press.
Kosch, Michelle 2015. Fichtean Kantianism in Nineteenth Century Ethics, *Journal of the History of Philosophy* 53: 111–32.
Mills, Charles 2005. Kant's *Untermenschen*, in *Race and Racism in Modern Philosophy*, ed. Andrew Valls, Ithaca, NY: Cornell University Press: 169–93.

Parfit, Derek 2011. *On What Matters*, vol. 1, Oxford: Oxford University Press.
Rawls, John 1971. *A Theory of Justice*, Cambridge, MA: Harvard University Press.
Rawls, John 1980. Kantian Constructivism in Moral Theory, *Journal of Philosophy* 77: 515–72.
Rawls, John 2000. *Lectures on the History of Moral Philosophy*, ed. Barbara Herman, Cambridge, MA: Harvard University Press.
Ripstein, Arthur 2014. Kant's Juridical Theory of Colonialism, in *Kant and Colonialism: Historical and Critical Perspectives*, ed. Katrin Flikschuh and Lea Ypi, Oxford: Oxford University Press: 145–69.
Schott, Robin May 1993. *Cognition and Eros: A Critique of the Kantian Paradigm*, University Park: Pennsylvania State University Press.
Schott, Robin May (ed.) 1997. *Feminist Interpretations of Immanuel Kant*, University Park: Pennsylvania State University Press.
Williamson, Diane 2015. *Kant's Theory of Emotion: Emotional Universalism*, New York: Palgrave Macmillan.
Wood, Allen W. 2008. Sex, in *Kantian Ethics*, ed. Allen W. Wood, New York: Cambridge University Press: 224–39.
Wood, Allen W. 2014a. The Independence of Right from Ethics, in *The Free Development of Each: Studies on Freedom, Right and Ethics in Classical German Philosophy*, ed. Allen W. Wood, Oxford: Oxford University Press: 70–89.
Wood, Allen W. 2014b. Kant's Political Philosophy, in *The Palgrave Handbook of German Idealism*, ed. Matthew C. Altman, Basingstoke: Palgrave Macmillan: 165–85.

11
'HOW IS METAPHYSICS POSSIBLE?'

Kant's Great Question and His Great Answer

Nicholas F. Stang

1. Introduction

There are at least two ways to be a 'great' philosopher. The first is to ask a *question*, either a question that has never been asked before, or one that has never been asked in precisely that way, or perhaps even to revive an old question that has been forgotten. The second is to give an *answer* to a question, one that is more correct, more interesting, or more plausible—or whatever other virtues that answers to philosophical questions can have—than previous answers to that question. Of course, it is possible to do one without the other. Heidegger asked a question ('What is being?') that had been asked many times before in the history of philosophy, but which had, according to him, been forgotten. One can think that, in doing so, Heidegger was doing something 'great' in philosophy even if one thinks that the various answers he gave to that question over his lifetime were incorrect. Conversely, Frege gave a new answer to a question ('What are numbers?') that is almost as old as philosophy, an answer that is, arguably, better than any answer that had been given before.

Kant has the rare distinction of both asking new questions and offering systematic, plausible, and well-motivated answers to them. Rare, but not unique: Plato and Aristotle spring immediately to mind as philosophers who did both. Kant has the further distinction (also shared by Plato and Aristotle) of having done so in virtually every one of (what we now think of as) the main areas of philosophy: logic, metaphysics, epistemology, philosophy of mind, philosophy of science, ethics, political philosophy, and aesthetics. While I think there is a way of seeing those questions, and those answers, as specifications of a single question and a single answer ('To what does reason answer?' 'Itself.'), I will focus, for the sake of space and because another chapter in this volume addresses Kant's moral philosophy, on Kant's achievement in metaphysics.

While some of his early works from the 1750s and 1760s are outstanding works of philosophy and repay close attention, his claim to greatness rests on the *Critique of Pure Reason* (*CPR*: 1st edition 1781; 2nd edition 1787), and the 'Critical' system of philosophy he constructed on its basis. This is a verdict shared by Kant himself, who wrote that 'prior to the development of critical philosophy there had been no philosophy at all' (Ak. 6:206).[1]

Kant asks, and answers, many questions about metaphysics in the *CPR* but they are all downstream of a single guiding question, a question he famously formulates in the Introduction to the second edition as 'How is metaphysics possible as a science?' (B22). The 'possibility of metaphysics', however, can refer to several different things and, consequently, Kant's main question contains at least three separate questions about the possibility of metaphysics:

1. How is metaphysics possible *epistemically*? How is it possible for us to attain *knowledge* (or whatever epistemic state we are aiming for) in metaphysics?
2. How is metaphysics possible *scientifically*? How is it possible for us to attain in metaphysics not only knowledge, but the systematically organized knowledge Kant calls 'science' (*Wissenschaft*)?
3. How is metaphysics possible *semantically*? How is it possible for our claims to have the content, reference, and other semantic properties that they must have in metaphysics?

Each of these questions corresponds to a distinct way in which metaphysics might be defective: it might be epistemically defective because we can never acquire knowledge in metaphysics; it might be defective as a science because whatever knowledge we have of metaphysics can never rise to the level of a science; and it might be semantically defective because our claims can never have a properly metaphysical content or our concepts can never refer to properly metaphysical topics, and so forth.

Kant gives systematic answers to all three questions in the *CPR*, but in a single chapter I cannot hope to address all of them. Much contemporary Kant scholarship has focused on Kant's answer to (1) and the related problem of synthetic *a priori* knowledge. Instead, I will focus on Kant's answer to (3) and his account of the semantic possibility of metaphysics.

I do so for two reasons. First, I think that his semantic critique of pre-Kantian metaphysics is more fundamental to his overall argument than his epistemic critique is. Second, I think that Kant's question about the semantic possibility of metaphysics is philosophically deeper than the other two and poses a powerful challenge even to contemporary metaphysics in the analytic tradition.

In addition to the distinction with which I began, one can also make another distinction in the ways that philosophers can be great. A philosopher can be great in virtue of making an important intervention in a specific historical context, or in virtue of some contribution (for example, a question, or an answer) whose importance transcends its specific historical context and can continue to be significant long after that historical moment has passed. These are by no means mutually exclusive, and I will be arguing that Kant's question about the semantic possibility of metaphysics is one such instance.

In section 2 I will argue that the core of Kant's semantic critique of metaphysics is a question about the *reference* of metaphysical concepts: assuming that concepts in metaphysics refer, what explains this putative fact? In unpacking what this question means, I try to formulate it in terms more general than Kant's specific cognitive semantics, in order to facilitate the project of the rest of the chapter, in which I argue that neither pre- nor post-Kantian philosophers have adequately addressed it.[2] In section 3 I explain how Kant came to this question by generalizing a question that Hume raised about the concept of cause and effect; I then show why Kant's predecessors (for example, Locke, Leibniz, Wolff, and Baumgarten) lacked the resources to explain satisfactorily the reference of metaphysical concepts. In section 4 I examine contemporary metaphysics and theories of reference, and argue that it is at least questionable whether contemporary metaphysicians are better able to answer Kant's question than pre-Kantian ones are. I argue that this 'explanatory gap' is a serious problem for such metaphysicians, for it entails that they cannot explain why metaphysics is (semantically) possible. Kant's question, then, is not only of historical interest; it also poses a deep challenge to the possibility of both pre-Kantian and contemporary metaphysics, and thus constitutes a problem that any metaphysician should grapple with. In section 5 I explain Kant's own answer to this question, while omitting (for reasons of space) his argument that this is the *only possible* such answer.

The target audience for this chapter is not Kant specialists—their conviction that Kant was at least a very good philosopher can be taken for granted—but rather philosophers, especially metaphysicians, who remain unconvinced that Kant was really all that 'great' when it comes to metaphysics. Consequently, I will focus less on defending my interpretations of Kant's texts than on motivating Kant's question and his answer.

2. Kant's Question

In a famous letter from 1772 to his former student Marcus Herz, Kant writes (Ak. 10:129):[3]

> I noticed that I still lacked something essential, something which, in my long metaphysical studies, I, as well as others, had failed to consider, and which in fact constitutes the key to the whole secret of metaphysics, hitherto hidden even from itself. I asked myself this question: What is the ground of the relation [*Beziehung*] of that in us which we call 'representation' to the object?

Later in this letter Kant announces the aim of systematically answering this question in a work that he anticipates will be done within three months. In fact he did not finish it for another nine years, and it appeared under the title *Critique of Pure Reason*. Many streams in Kant's thinking fed into the writing of the *CPR* and its famous question, 'How is metaphysics possible?'; but the aspect of that question on which I want to focus—'How is metaphysics possible semantically?'—begins with this passage in the letter to Herz.

Before we can understand why Kant's question is important and innovative, we must first understand what it means. 'What is the ground of the relation (*Beziehung*) of that in us which we call "representation" to the object?' First, 'representation' (*Vorstellung*) is Kant's general term for mental states (roughly equivalent to 'idea' in Locke or 'perception' in Hume). It becomes clear in the rest of the Herz letter, and in other texts, that Kant is particularly concerned with the relation of a specific kind of representation to their objects: namely, concepts. At this point in his philosophical trajectory, he finds the 'relation' of the other main class of representations (intuitions) to their objects relatively unproblematic.[4] Concepts are general representations: a concept does not represent an individual object; it represents a general class of objects (Ak. 9:91). Thus, my representation of all red objects is a concept (the concept <red>) while my representation of a particular fire truck is not.[5] While Kant's question is originally raised at the level of representations *überhaupt*, in this chapter I will be concerned with it only as a question about specifically conceptual representation. Unpacking Kant's syntax slightly, the conceptual version of the question becomes this: what is the ground of the relation of our concepts to their objects?

However, it is harder to determine precisely what 'relation' between concepts and objects Kant has in mind in this passage. For the sake of brevity, I will simply state my own view: the relation in question is what is now called *reference*. Kant is interested in the relation between general concepts and the entities and structures in the world they are 'about': for example, the relation between the concept <*substance*> and substantiality.[6] But some of our concepts are not like <*substance*>; they do not refer to anything at all. Kant's examples of such 'usurped concepts' (A84/B116) are <*fate*> and <*fortune*>, but to this list we might add <*witch*>, <*phlogiston*>, and so forth. What explains the difference between the concepts that do refer and concepts that are merely 'usurped'? Why do <*water*> and <*substance*> refer but <*fortune*> does not? Kant's question is thus closely related to questions about linguistic reference that were discussed in mid-twentieth-century analytic philosophy (for example, 'Why does 'water' refer to water?').[7] Kant's question differs from those questions about reference, though, in at least one crucial respect: he raises the question at the level of thought (concepts) rather than of language (words). However, as we will see, the Kantian question about the reference of metaphysical concepts (for example, <*substance*>) can also be raised in a linguistic register about the reference of terms (for example, 'substance') in metaphysical theories.

In order to make Kant's question dialectically relevant to as wide a range of views in metaphysics as possible, I want to remain as neutral as possible among different theories of what reference is, so I will opt for a very minimal characterization: reference is contribution to truth value. Our thoughts are true or false, and in some cases their truth conditions involve things in the world. (There may also be analytic truths whose truth conditions do not involve anything in the world.[8]) I will say that some items in the world are referred to by a thought if those items figure in the truth conditions of the thought.[9] For instance, the thought *water is wet* is true if and only if water is wet: since water figures in the truth conditions of *water is wet*, that thought refers to water. Intuitively, that thought refers to water because <*water*> refers to water, but this requires building more complexity into our toy semantics. For instance, if we say that in general *Fa* is true if and only if the referent of 'a' is F, then *water is wet* is true just in case whatever <*water*> refers to is wet. This only extends the notion of reference to singular terms; to extend it to terms in the predicate position, we need to add this: *Fa* is true if and only if the referent of *a* is in the extension of the referent of F. We can then ask, of some such pair of concept and referent, why that concept refers to that referent. This detour through some rather un-Kantian semantics underlines an important point: Kant's question can be raised independently of any particular theory of reference and, most importantly, independently of his own highly controversial semantic doctrines (for example, his subject-predicate theory of judgment).[10]

Given the centrality of the notion of reference to the rest of this chapter, it will be helpful to be as precise as possible at the outset. We must distinguish between three semantic features of a concept (or a word in our language): (1) its meaning, (2) its reference, and (3) its extension. For instance, the meaning of <*substance*> might be given by 'that of which other things are predicated and is not predicated of anything else'. But this is separate from its reference. If there are no things that are ultimate subjects of predication (it is predicates 'all the way down'), then <*substance*> fails to refer; assuming this is not the case, <*substance*> refers to *substance*, which, for ease of exposition, we can think of either as the property of being a substance or as the *kind* to which all substances as such belong (for my purposes, it will not matter greatly which we choose). The extension of <*substance*> is all individual substances. This is not to be identified with its referent. If some substances are generated or corrupted, the referent of <*substance*> does not change (it refers to substance) but its extension does. Separating reference from extension is crucial for understanding Kant's question in the Herz letter. Kant's question is not a purely metaphysical question at the level of objects (extensions of concepts), such as 'Why are there substances at all?' or 'What makes substances substances?'; it is the semantic question about why <*substance*> refers. It thus corresponds not to a purely physical question, such as 'Why is there water?' or 'What makes a sample of water water?', but instead to a semantic question about why <*water*> refers.

The Kantian question, 'Why do our concepts refer to the objects they do?', has its contemporary counterpart in the question, 'Why do the words of our language refer to the objects they do?' Answering that question in general (*überhaupt*) is no easier, but also no more difficult, than giving a general theory of linguistic reference. To the contemporary philosopher, as for the eighteenth-century philosopher, there are many candidates for such a theory (descriptive theories, causal theories, direct reference theories, etc.) and the challenge is to find a model that extends to all of the cases for which one wants to account.[11] The challenge, of course, is that some theories (for example, causal theories) are better suited to explaining some kinds of cases (for example, names for ordinary objects) than others (for example, names of numbers). Kant's point in the letter to Herz is that none of the theories of conceptual reference given by his predecessors (theories of how our concepts are 'related' to objects) is much help at all in explaining why metaphysical concepts refer. And Kant's point holds even today, with our much more sophisticated theories of reference, as I will argue in section 4.

Recall from above the two ways in which the possibility of metaphysics might be questionable: (i) we might question the epistemic possibility of achieving knowledge of our metaphysical theories, and (ii) we might question the semantic possibility of referring to anything using our metaphysical concepts. Kant does have an argument that calls into question the *epistemic* possibility of acquiring knowledge in metaphysics: knowledge in metaphysics (he argues) must be both synthetic and *a priori*, and so we require an explanation of how we could know something *a priori* if it is not an analytic truth. However, I do not focus here on the problem of synthetic *a priori* knowledge, for three reasons. First, I am making the case for the continuing relevance of Kant in metaphysics, and it is harder to show that the problem of synthetic *a priori* knowledge remains one with which contemporary metaphysicians should be concerned, since many of them have jettisoned the analytic-synthetic distinction and few are committed to the strictly *a priori* status of metaphysics. Second, I want to make a case for the (relative) *originality* of Kant's question, and there are good reasons to think that the problem of synthetic *a priori* knowledge was known to Kant's rationalist predecessors (though not under that name).[12]

Third, and most important, the reference question is more fundamental than the problem of synthetic *a priori* knowledge. Even if this problem were solved, or dissolved, the reference problem would remain. For instance, even if metaphysics were thoroughly analytic (as many of Kant's contemporaries held), we would still ask why these concepts that we are analyzing are about anything, rather than being empty concepts like <*witch*> or <*phlogiston*> or <*fate*>. Even if we abandoned the assumption that metaphysics must be strictly *a priori*, and held that metaphysics is continuous with the natural sciences, and that its epistemology is broadly abductive (resting on inference to the best explanation), we could still ask why the concepts that figure in these theories refer to anything. And even if we took a Kantian direction and held that metaphysical knowledge must be synthetic and *a priori* and had an explanation of how such knowledge is possible, we would still need a *separate* explanation of why the concepts that figure in such synthetic *a priori* knowledge refer. The reference question is thus separate from, and more fundamental than, the knowledge question.

This raises two questions. What is so hard about explaining the reference of metaphysical concepts? And (why) must the metaphysician offer such an explanation? I address these questions in the next section.

3. Kant's Question Before Kant

While none of the pre-Kantian philosophers with whose writings I am familiar devotes the focused attention to the reference of metaphysical concepts that Kant does, it is not hard to find in their writings implicit or explicit answers to Kant's question. In this section I discuss several of the more prominent such answers and argue that none of them succeeds. But first I want to discuss the relation of Kant's question about metaphysical concepts to a similar question raised by Hume.

(i) Hume

In the Preface to the *Prolegomena* Kant writes, 'I freely admit that it was the remembrance of David Hume that awoke me from my dogmatic slumber' (Ak. 4:260). It is likely that Kant's 'remembrance' was of Hume's discussion of causation in the first *Enquiry*, specifically §VII ('Of the Idea of Necessary Connection').[13] In that section Hume begins by formulating a more precise version of his famous 'copy' principle: every simple idea (an idea not composed out of further ideas) is a copy of some impression, its 'original'. Hume then inquires into what the 'original' of our idea of necessary connection could be and rejects various candidates. In Part II of §VII he argues that the only suitable impression is 'a customary transition of the imagination from one object to its usual attendant'. Having observed one kind of object (for example, fire) constantly followed by another kind of object (for example, smoke), when we encounter the first object we immediately imagine the second object, and that feeling of imaginative transition is the 'original' of our idea of a necessary connection between the objects.

In the *Prolegomena* Kant writes (Ak. 4:257):

> Hume started mainly from a single but important concept in metaphysics, namely, that of the *connection of cause and effect* (and of course, also its derivative concepts, of force and action, etc.), and called upon reason, which pretends to have generated this concept in her womb, to give him an account of by what right she thinks that something could be so constituted that, if it is posited, something else necessarily must thereby be posited as well; for that is what the concept of cause says.

Kant is here translating Hume's question, formulated in terms of impressions, ideas, and copies, into the terms of his own cognitive semantics. An idea, for

Hume, represents (is an idea 'of') more than just the individual impression from which it was copied (or the set of simple impressions from which it is copied, if the idea is complex) when it is imaginatively associated with other individual ideas that resemble the original impression in some determinate respect.[14] Ideas 'used abstractly' in this way constitute Hume's explanation of how we represent generality. They thus correspond to Kantian concepts. Hume's copy principle, in Kantian terms, is his theory of how concepts (ideas) 'relate to' (refer to) their objects (impressions). In the *Prolegomena*, and in the 1772 letter to Herz, Kant presents himself as raising Hume's question about the idea of necessary connection, but detaches it from the copy principle and the rest of Hume's specific cognitive semantic theory: why do concepts (general representations) refer to their objects? But Kant also generalizes Hume's question to all of the *a priori* concepts of metaphysics (Ak. 4:260):

> So I tried first whether Hume's objection might not be presented in a general manner, and I soon found that the concept of the connection of cause and effect is far from being the only concept through which the understanding thinks connections of things *a priori*; rather, metaphysics consists wholly of such concepts.

But if Kant had read the *Treatise*,[15] he would have known that Hume raises this problem not only about <cause-effect> but also about many of (what Kant would consider) the other *a priori* concepts of metaphysics: possibility, existence, substance, personal identity, and so forth. Does this compromise the originality of Kant's question? Yes, somewhat, but it does not eliminate it. For what Kant saw was that a version of 'Hume's problem' arises even if one is not as radical an empiricist as Hume, and that contemporary non-Humean metaphysicians lacked an answer to this problem (see below). What is more, he not only saw that Hume's problem generalizes (even on non-Humean premises); he saw 'how' to generalize it: it applies to all the *a priori* concepts of metaphysics. Rather than treating this as a piece of Kantian technical terminology to be explicated in terms of other technical terminology, I will instead consider the role that the notion of '*a priori* concept' plays in the problem for metaphysics that Kant is trying to motivate. This will be easiest to see by looking at his reasons for thinking that another of his predecessors, Locke, failed to explain why metaphysical concepts refer.

(ii) Locke

Kant writes in the *CPR* (A85/B117):

> I therefore call the explanation of the way in which concepts can relate to objects *a priori* their transcendental deduction, and distinguish this from the empirical deduction, which shows how a concept is acquired through experience and reflection on it.

If the 'relation' of a concept to its object is the reference of that concept to that object (*those* object*s*) then a 'deduction' of a concept is an explanation of why it refers to objects.[16] Kant here distinguishes a 'transcendental deduction', which is said to be the only possible explanation of why *a priori* concepts (like those in metaphysics) refer, from an 'empirical deduction', which explains why a concept refers by tracing it back to the experience from which it was abstracted. Kant explains a few pages later why such an 'empirical deduction' of metaphysical concepts like <*cause-effect*> is impossible (A91/B123):

> If one were to think of escaping from the toils of these investigations by saying that experience constantly offers examples of a regularity of appearances that give sufficient occasion for abstracting the concept of cause from them, and thereby at the same time thought to confirm the objective validity of such a concept, then one has not noticed that the concept of cause cannot arise in this way at all. [. . .] For this concept always requires that something A be of such a kind that something else B follows from it necessarily and in accordance with an absolutely universal rule.

An empirical deduction of a concept explains why it refers, by tracing the concept back to an experience from which the concept was originally abstracted. We can think of this explanation as having roughly the following form: one experiences an object (for example, a cause-effect pair), one forms the concept of all other objects that resemble this object in relevant respects, and this concept refers to all other such objects that resemble the object in the relevant respect. One page earlier, Kant names Locke as a thinker who attempted to give such an 'empirical deduction' of the concept of causation.[17]

It is worth taking the effort to understand Kant's rejection of empirical deductions of metaphysical concepts because this remains a potentially attractive strategy for contemporary metaphysicians, many of whom are not wedded to the *a priori* status of metaphysics.[18] Metaphysical concepts, according to this line of thought, are broadly 'empirical' concepts and their reference is explained in a fashion similar to that of other empirical concepts: one experiences an object with a certain property, one abstracts a concept of that property, and that concept then refers to any object with the relevant property. Kant rejects such an empirical deduction of <*cause-effect*> because, he claims, this is a concept of a necessary connection (the cause necessitates the effect) and experience never presents us with necessary connections. If correct, this undermines the possibility of an empirical deduction because, although we might experience events that stand in necessary connections, we do not experience them *as* necessarily connected, and so nothing about our experience explains why our concept would have this modal content. This objection brings out a key feature of a Lockean empirical deduction: my experience of an object that is F only explains why my concept refers to all objects that are F if the property F can figure in the content of my experience. On the Lockean picture, concepts get their content from the content of experience. In Locke's own terms, the ideas that I abstract can only represent qualities that resemble sensory ideas that I perceive.

But the Lockean has at least two responses to this Kantian argument. First, one might simply *deny* that the content of experience is as modally impoverished as Kant here claims it is,[19] and insist (though Locke himself would not) that we simply *do* experience the necessity of the relation of cause and effect. Second, one might point out that not all concepts in metaphysics are concepts of necessary connections. Indeed, even in Kant's own theory, it is far from clear that the categories of quantity and quality (for example, <unity>, <totality>, <reality>, <limitation>) have a modal content that cannot be present in experience. So the Lockean might hold that, regardless of whether or not <cause-effect> admits of an empirical deduction, many (most) other metaphysical concepts do.

However, Kant has the resources to respond to this defense of empirical deductions, for this modified Lockean story is ultimately no explanation at all. Translating Locke's theory into Kant's terminology, the Lockean explains the content of concepts (what properties they refer to) by means of the content of experience. But if our concepts are going to refer to a certain class of properties, we need an explanation of why properties of that class are represented in experience.

Simplifying slightly Locke's complex distinction between primary and secondary qualities and focusing on the primary qualities of objects (for example, shape, size, volume), what explains the match between the properties (qualities) of the object and the content of the experience is a causal connection: some primary qualities in the object cause me to experience it as having those qualities (to perceive ideas that resemble those primary qualities).[20] This causal constraint allows the Lockean to explain why we are not massively mistaken in our formation of empirical concepts (Locke's abstract ideas): we do not systematically form concepts of properties that objects lack, because the presence of those properties is among the causes of the experience whose content grounds the content of the concepts. What plays the corresponding role, in the Lockean picture, in the case of metaphysical concepts? It is not enough for the Lockean to say that various metaphysical properties (causation, substantiality, unity, etc.) are represented in experience; in order to explain why concepts abstracted from such experiences refer to the properties (qualities) in objects, the Lockean must explain why those experiences, in representing such properties, do not suffer massive reference failure.

Ironically, the Lockean may be in the best position to explain this in the case on which Kant focuses: cause and effect. Arguably, the very causal powers of objects cause us to experience them as causally related. But this is not a promising strategy to pursue with other metaphysical concepts, which seem to refer to properties that are causally inert. Without substantial additional argumentation, the Lockean has given no explanation of why, for instance, the relation of inherence by which an accident is *in* a substance (Kant's first category of relation) or the totality of a set of parts (Kant's third category of quantity) plays a corresponding causal role. There are thus good reasons, both in the eighteenth and in the twenty-first century, not to look to a Lockean 'empirical deduction' for the explanation of why metaphysical concepts refer.

Finally, we can give a provisional account of what '*a priori*' concepts are: concepts whose putative reference cannot be explained by an empirical deduction. It is because the concepts of metaphysics cannot be 'deduced' empirically that Kant seeks a different origin for them than experience, though his theory of the origin of *a priori* concepts will not be our topic here. This also shows that there are *a priori* concepts that are not specifically metaphysical concepts (e.g., mathematical concepts).

(iii) Logicism

As I argue extensively in Stang (2016), Kant's predecessors in the German rationalist tradition—Leibniz, Wolff, and Baumgarten—hold what I call a 'logicist' account of possibility: it is possible that *p* if and only if *p* does not entail a contradiction. In particular, this entails that a concept is possibly instantiated if and only if the proposition that it is instantiated does not entail a contradiction. Assuming that the *a priori* concepts of metaphysics are logically consistent (an assumption Kant grants) it follows that they are possibly instantiated, and hence, in this sense, refer at least to possible objects: they refer to the possible objects that instantiate them.[21] For convenience, I will refer to Leibniz, Wolff, and Baumgarten as *logicists*.

Note, however, that from the fact that it is possible that there is an F it does not follow that F refers; it follows merely that *possibly* F refers. This point—that the possibility that F refers does not entail that *there is* an object (even a logically possible one) to which F refers—is closely related to Kant's famous claim that existence is not a 'real predicate', a doctrine from which (on my reading) the logicists dissented. But even if we grant them the assumption that for every logically consistent concept there are logically possible objects that fall under it (and thus that *there are* objects that may or may not exist), this shows merely that the logical possibility (consistency) of a concept establishes that it refers to logically possible objects. This answers Kant's question about the reference of metaphysical concepts only at the cost of 'lowering the bar' for what counts as reference. On this view, a 'usurped concept' such as <*fortune*> (or <*witch*>) refers just as much as <*substance*>: since both are logically consistent, they refer to logically possible objects. But even the logicists would want to distinguish between usurped concepts and genuinely referring concepts, for without such a distinction, metaphysics is on a par with astrology and witchcraft.

To return to a point from the previous section, this is not a request for an explanation of why there are substances; that would be an explanation of why <*substance*> has a non-empty extension, not why <*substance*> refers. In fact, by parity of reasoning the logicist explanation in the previous paragraph of why, for example, <*substance*> is a concept of logically possible objects is merely an explanation of why it has a non-empty extension: there are logically possible substances. It does not explain why <substance> refers to substance, which for our purposes we can think of as the property possessed by all substances.[22] One way of appreciating this point is that logically atomic concepts are, trivially, logically consistent, but this by itself does not explain why they refer, for it does not distinguish between referential logically atomic concepts (which compose all other meaningful concepts) and logically atomic concepts that do not refer.

In his 1763 work *The Only Possible Ground for a Demonstration of the Existence of God*, Kant puts the point this way (Ak. 2:80–1; Kant 1992: 125):

> Suppose that you can now no longer break up the concept of extension into simpler data in order to show that there is nothing self-contradictory in it—and you must eventually arrive at something whose possibility cannot be analyzed—then the question will be whether space and extension are empty words, or whether they signify [*bezeichnen*] something. The lack of contradiction does not decide the present issue; an empty word never signifies anything self-contradictory. If space did not exist, or if space was not at least given as a consequence through something existent, the word 'space' would signify [*bedeutet*] nothing at all.

Kant's point is that the mere logical consistency of a concept does not explain why (in my terminology) it 'refers to' (*bezeichnet, bedeutet*) anything, because there can be logically consistent concepts that refer to nothing, as <space> would if space were impossible. Kant's way of making this point is to distinguish between logical possibility and 'real' possibility (which we would now call 'metaphysical' possibility), which Kant repeatedly equates with the 'thinkable'. In his pre-Critical metaphysical works of the 1760s, Kant argues that not all logical possibilities are really (metaphysically) possible: not all logically consistent concepts refer to really possible properties. The question then becomes that of why metaphysical concepts refer to really possible properties, and not merely to logically possible properties.

But this might seem to beg the question against the logicists, who think that logical possibility entails real (metaphysical) possibility. However, while the logicists maintain, *contra* Kant, that logical and 'real' (metaphysical) possibility are coextensive, they acknowledge that these are separate notions, for these have distinct definitions. A logically possible concept is one that contains no mutually contradictory marks (sub-concepts). What Kant calls 'real' possibility, however, they ground in the unlimited perfections of God. A logically atomic concept refers to some infinite perfection possessed by God (for example, understanding, power, will) and a logically consistent complex concept refers to some really (metaphysically) possible property composed of unlimited divine perfections. It follows that C is logically consistent if and only if it refers to some really possible property. The logicists thus seem to have a well-thought-out answer to Kant's question about concept reference: a concept refers to really possible (not merely logically possible) property just in case it is a logically consistent combination of atomic concepts of unlimited divine perfections.

Kant's pre-Critical works contain several complex and controversial arguments that real and logical possibility are not coextensive,[23] which have been extensively critically discussed by scholars.[24] However, I think that, in addition to the arguments that Kant gives explicitly, it is relatively clear, from a Kantian point of view, that the logicists have simply assumed precisely what stands in need of explanation: why do my concepts refer to the really possible properties to which they refer? Since the reference of complex concepts is explained by the reference of their atomic constituents, we can formulate this at the level of atomic concepts: why do my atomic concepts refer to unlimited divine perfections? The principal logicist answer to this question, shared by Leibniz and Baumgarten, is that God created me with a concept (or at least the capacity to come to reflective awareness of this concept) referring to that property. But then the Kantian question becomes this: In virtue of what did God do this? It is not enough, when pressed for an explanation, to simply say 'God did it'; one must say what God did, and why, in virtue of doing that, he made it the case that the semantic relation of reference obtains. If we assume that semantic facts about what concepts refer to are not brute facts (a premise accepted by all of the logicists), then there must be some fact *p* in virtue of which my concept <*substance*> refers to substantiality, and God created me with a concept that refers to substantiality in virtue of making it the case that *p*; what, then, is *p*? Nor will it help for the logicist to claim that concepts are individuated by their referents: if it is essential to my concept <*substance*> to refer to really possible substances, in virtue of what did God create me with this very concept with this content, <*substance*>, rather than another one (e.g., a usurped one, like <*fortune*>)?[25] It is not clear that logicists can answer this question.

Further pursuing this question within rationalist metaphysics would take us too far afield. In this section I hope to have established that Kant's question about the explanation of metaphysical concept reference poses a deep challenge to the metaphysics of his forebears. In the next section I will argue that it is by no means clear that contemporary metaphysicians are in a better position to answer it.

4. Kant's Question Today

Since the question of metaphysical concept reference is, to my knowledge, even less discussed in contemporary metaphysics than it was in early modern philosophy before Kant, most of the 'answers' to Kant's question that I will consider are my own reconstructions from the contemporary literature, as are the 'Kantian' responses that I will discuss. Most contemporary theories of reference are theories about linguistic rather than conceptual reference, so in this section I will formulate Kant's question, and potential responses, in terms of the reference of linguistic terms in metaphysical theories.

Description

One might think that the reference of a term like 'substance' can easily be explained by thinking of it as a disguised descriptive term: 'substance' just means 'individual with properties, which is not itself a property of some further individual'. 'Substance' refers just in case the description refers. But this merely pushes the explanatory burden back one step; we need an explanation of why 'individual' and 'property' refer. This is why Kant raises his question about the categories, the basic metaphysical concepts in terms of which other metaphysical concepts are defined.[26]

Elimination and Deflation

Some contemporary metaphysicians deny, in Kant's terms, that metaphysical terms refer. Hofweber (2009), for instance, argues that syntactically singular terms for numbers, properties, and propositions do not have the semantic function of referring. Philosophers like Hofweber might thus be said to *eliminate* reference from metaphysics.[27] Other philosophers might be said to *deflate* the reference of metaphysical terms. According to the 'easy' approach to ontology defended by Thomasson (2015), sortal terms like 'number' or 'property' or 'proposition' are associated with application conditions, where it is analytic that, if the application conditions are satisfied, an object of the relevant sort exists and thus that the term refers. For instance, it is analytic (on Thomasson's view) that if Beyoncé's dress is red, then her dress has the property of being red and thus that 'property' refers. On Thomasson's view, there is nothing more to the reference of these sortal terms than the satisfaction of their application conditions. Neither the eliminativist nor the deflationist need be bothered by Kant's question about metaphysical reference. The eliminativist denies the explanandum while the deflationist can explain it (or explain it away) all too easily: she can simply point to the fact that the application conditions are fulfilled. Consequently, Kant's question poses no problem for the contemporary metaphysical eliminativist or deflationist. Kant's question poses a problem for the theorist who holds that reference is a substantive relation that partly explains why our metaphysical theories are true. As we will see below, there are several such theorists on the contemporary scene. I will refer to them as *non-deflationary realists*.[28]

Explanation by Division

Some readers versed in contemporary philosophy may be unimpressed with Kant's question in the first place, for they will think that it is all too easy to answer. Its appearance of difficulty, they will say, depends on a conflation of a psychological with a 'Platonic' (or Fregean) notion of a concept. If we distinguish between concepts as psychological entities or capacities and the meanings of those concepts—'Concepts' in the Fregean sense—then we can see that the reference of a given term divides without remainder into three factors: (i) the fact that our term expresses a Concept, (ii) the fact that that Concept has the meaning it does, and (iii) the fact that that Concept refers to what it does.[29] The first fact is a semantic one and admits of a semantic explanation, if any. The second fact is partly constitutive of what it is to be that Concept: Concepts are individuated by meanings, so it is part of what it is to be a given Concept to have the meaning that it does—for example, part of what it is to be the Concept <substance> is to be a Concept of individuals with properties. Finally, there is some fact about what the Concept refers to. In the case of ordinary empirical terms, whether the Concept refers and what it refers to will depend upon contingent facts about the world. For instance, the Concept expressed by the definite description 'the sixth Chairman of the State Council of the German Democratic Republic' does not refer, and the fact that the Concept expressed by 'water' in the mouths of English-speakers on Earth refers to water depends on the contingent fact that water, rather than XYZ, is in our environment.[30]

But the terms of metaphysical theories are presumably not like this; they refer necessarily, so there is a purely metaphysical explanation, if there is any explanation at all, of why a Concept with a given meaning refers.[31] Even if we reject the assumption that metaphysical concepts refer necessarily if they refer at all, and allow that it might be contingent that, for instance, <substance> refers, the important point still stands: the explanation of (iii) will be at the level of pure metaphysics, for it will be an explanation of why a Concept with some given meaning refers. For instance, it might be that the meaning of our term 'substance' is the Concept <substance>, whose meaning is given by: x is a substance if and only if x is an individual with properties. This Concept with this meaning refers because, for purely metaphysical reasons, there must be individuals with properties.

The problem with this explanation by division is that, by giving distinct explanations of these three factors, it leaves unexplained why the very same Concepts expressed by terms in our language refer. It remains, on this 'multifactor' view, a mystery why, in forming metaphysical theories, we do not massively misfire and use terms that express Concepts that fail to refer.

Compare the three-factor explanation of metaphysical concept reference to a 'three-factor' explanation of why we have true beliefs: (i) we form beliefs (understood as psychological states) that (ii) express certain propositions that essentially have certain truth conditions, and (iii) those propositions have their truth conditions satisfied by the concrete realm. The first fact admits of a purely psychological explanation, the second fact is explained by the essence of these propositions (they are individuated partly by their truth conditions, let us suppose), and the third fact has a purely physical explanation (why the concrete realm satisfies the truth conditions constitutive of the relevant propositions). But this story by itself leaves unexplained why we have *true* beliefs: the facts that make the propositions true play no role, within this story, in explaining why we form beliefs that express those propositions. Likewise, in the three-factor explanation of metaphysical concept reference, the fact that these metaphysical Concepts refer plays no role in explaining why there are terms in our theories that express them. Notice that this is not the case with concepts and beliefs about objects in our sensible environment: a given sensible fact (for example, the fact that there is coffee in my cup) or the fact that a given Concept refers (for example, the fact that <*coffee*> refers to that coffee) partly explains why we form a psychological belief that expresses a true proposition (the belief that there is coffee in the cup) or a term ('coffee') that expresses a referring Concept. But this explanation depends upon our sensory awareness of our environment, and in section 3 we saw some anti-Lockean reasons to be skeptical that perceptual experience can explain the reference of metaphysical concepts or the terms in metaphysical theories.

No Special Problem

Another dismissive response that a contemporary metaphysician might give to Kant's answer is that there is no special problem about metaphysics. We can raise explanatory questions about the reference of terms in any domain: natural scientific, mathematical, and so forth. If metaphysics is, in this respect, on a par with other sciences, then it would seem that Kant has failed to show that metaphysics is especially problematic. It would be nice to have an explanation of reference in metaphysics, but it would also be nice to have such an explanation in physics, mathematics, and so forth. There is no more reason, in the absence of such an explanation, to be skeptical of metaphysics than there is to be skeptical of physics or mathematics.

Recall that Kant's question is not the skeptical epistemic question: how do we know that metaphysical terms refer? It is an explanatory question: what explains the fact (assuming it is a fact) that metaphysical terms refer ('relate to their object')?[32] Once we recognize that Kant's question is fundamentally a demand for explanation, however, the 'no special problem for metaphysics' response is, to a great extent, dissolved. For there are explanations available of why the terms in physical theories refer. The most plausible of them rest, I take it, on notions like 'natural kind' (or on the more general notion of 'joint carving'—see below) and have something like the following form: the terms in our best scientific theories refer to the natural kinds that make them (approximately) true, if they are approximately true.[33] Kant's question is about the very terms used to explain why terms in natural science refer: why, for instance, does 'natural kind' refer to natural kinds? If we lack an answer to Kant's question, this does not undermine our claim to knowledge in physics. It shows, at most, that physics rests on an assumption—that its terms refer—an assumption that is explained only in the distinct science of metaphysics. So, in a certain sense, physics depends on metaphysics. But the nature of the dependence is explanatory, not justificatory. The lack of an explanation of metaphysical reference does not ramify into skepticism about our knowledge of physical theories, nor does it undermine the 'metaphysical' explanation of why physical terms refer; it shows merely that this explanation relies on an assumption (that 'natural kind' refers) that is not itself explained, a feature shared by (presumably) all explanations. It shows, at most, that metaphysics cannot 'look after itself'—it cannot explain one of its basic assumptions (that its terms refer) and it cannot appeal to some more fundamental science, because it is, allegedly, the most (explanatorily) fundamental science.[34]

Reference Magnetism

Finally, one might look to the idea of 'reference magnetism' for an explanation. The core idea of reference magnetism views is that certain entities (properties, concept extensions, etc.) are intrinsically more natural or 'suitable to be referred to' than others, and this is what breaks the tie among candidate referents that equally satisfy the descriptive contents of our theories. One might exploit a similar idea in explaining the reference of metaphysical terms: the world has a privileged metaphysical structure, and *ceteris paribus* our terms 'carve' the world at the joints of that structure.[35] However, for reasons of length, and because I criticize reference magnetism at length elsewhere, I will forgo any further discussion of this kind of explanation.

5. Kant's Answer

Having explained the meaning of Kant's question, and why various pre-Kantian and contemporary answers to it are less than fully successful, I will now explore Kant's own answer, his own explanation of why metaphysical concepts refer. As in the rest of this chapter, I will not be following Kant's text especially closely, both for reasons of brevity (fully grounding my interpretation in the texts would require much more space than I have here) and because my primary aim remains making the salience of Kant's question and his own answer to it clear to contemporary audiences.

The key idea in Kant's own explanation of why metaphysical concepts refer is a deceptively simple one: something may have a different structure in itself than it has in relation to something else. For instance, a cow in itself has a certain anatomical structure: these and those organs related in such and such a way. But in relation to our practice of butchery, a cow has a quite different structure. A butcher (quite literally) carves a cow at different joints than an anatomist does: in relation to butchery, a cow divides into the edible and inedible (bone, skin, certain organs) parts, and edible parts divide into various 'cuts' (top round, sirloin, etc.) that are in no sense the natural 'joints' of the cow.[36] This is an especially literal (and perhaps gruesome) example, but other examples abound. The physical elements have a certain structure, which is given by the periodic table of elements. The 'natural joints' among the physical elements are, for instance, the inert gases, the metals, the halogens, and so forth. But in relation to human biology the physical elements have a different structure with different joints. In relation to human biology the physical elements divide into (perhaps overlapping) classes such as those that are poisonous to humans, those that are essential constituents of our bodies, and so forth. The intuition behind the Lewis-Sider idea of naturalness and joint carving is that some ways of dividing things up are objectively more correct than others. But even when we consider some entity (cow) or system of entities (the elements) in relation to something else (butchery, human biology), we can still distinguish ways of dividing them up that are more 'correct' than others. For instance, in relation to butchery, dividing a cow into the front and back half is objectively incorrect; you would be doing butchery wrong if you divided the cow that way. Likewise, in relation to human biology, dividing the elements into those with odd and those with even atomic numbers is objectively incorrect; that is not a natural joint in the physical elements, even in relation to human biology.

Let us concentrate on one particular example of the difference between the structure of something in itself and its structure in relation to something else: the structure of the world in its own right (the topic of metaphysics, according to Wolff, Baumgarten, and Sider) and the structure that the world has in cognitive relation to us. Now, this distinction can be many different distinctions, depending on what cognitive relation is specified. For instance, the world might have a different structure 'in itself' than in relation to our beliefs about that structure, if our beliefs are mistaken about that structure. Likewise, the world might have a different structure 'in itself' than it has insofar as it is perceived by us. The world as perceived by us has a certain structure (spatiotemporal objects in motion with various perceptible properties) but, if current physics is accurate, the structure that it has in itself is quite different.

Kant holds that the subject matter of metaphysics should be understood, not as the nature of the world in itself and its structure, but as the structure of the world in cognitive relation to us. The relevant cognition relation is not *belief* or *perception*; it is what Kant calls *Erkenntnis*. This, however, is a technical term in his philosophy, so it provides little independent purchase on what relation he has in mind. This is reflected in the now standard translation of *Erkenntnis* as 'cognition', which is itself a technical philosophical term without a very precise meaning independent of the uses to which particular philosophers put it.

Because this is not primarily an exegetical chapter, I will simply cut to the chase and state what I take to be the closest analogue in contemporary philosophy to Kantian *Erkenntnis*, namely, understanding.[37] Applying this back to the idea with which we started, we can distinguish between the structure that the world has in itself and its structure as *understood* by us. It is important to understand that this is not the distinction between the structure that the world has in itself and the structure that we merely *believe* it to have. The difference arises from the difference between the state of understanding and the state of belief. These cognitive states are individuated by an internal standard. The individuating standard of belief is truth: one's belief that *p* is a successful belief (it satisfies the standard that makes belief what it is) when it is the case that *p*. What is the internal standard of successful understanding, the standard that (partly) individuates this achievement as the achievement that it is? One answer would be this: one understands X successfully when one carves X at its joints, when one understands the structure of X in itself. But this is not Kant's view about understanding. His view is that understanding has its own internal standard and structure that may be distinct from the structure of the object of understanding. Our understanding has, so to speak, its own terms, which may not be the 'terms' (joints) in the world itself. We successfully understand something when we understand it on our terms. The 'terms' of our understanding are the structure of anything understandable by us, and this is dictated, according to Kant, by the nature of our minds, *not* by the structure of the thing itself.

An example might be helpful. Consider teaching the definition of a derivative to a student. You first try to get the student to understand the notion of a converging sequence of real numbers, then you define the first derivative of a real-valued function at a point as the limit of a converging sequence of slopes. But your student cannot understand it in these terms; he can only understand it in visual-geometric terms: the derivative is a line orthogonal to a curve at a given point, and so forth. Your student has understood something, and that understanding has its own internal standard by which the student can succeed or fail in a given instance. For instance, if the student, given the curve for the function $f(x) = x^2$, thinks that the tangent of the curve at the origin points in the direction of the positive x-axis, he has failed to understand even according to the internal standard of his own visual-geometric understanding of what a tangent is. Likewise, the student has understood by his own standard if he realizes that the tangent is null at that point. The student has understood something about what you have taught him (the notion of a tangent) but has not understood it in its own terms: he has not understood the rigorous definition of a derivative as the limit of a converging sequence of slopes. Kant's point is that we are always in the position of this student: our minds are equipped with a set of concepts in terms of which we understand anything at all. Anything we can understand, we understand in these terms. These concepts describe the structure of any understanding we can possess, and thus they describe the structure of anything *as understood by us*.

It is not hard to see how to turn this into an explanation of why our concepts in metaphysics refer. First, we must distinguish two kinds of metaphysics—what Kant would call, in turn, 'immanent' metaphysics and 'transcendent' metaphysics (see A296/B352). The object of immanent metaphysics is the world *as understandable by us*. Its object is not the world *as actually understood by us*, for that is far more determinate and partly depends upon empirical discoveries in the natural sciences. One of the things we actually understand about the world is that the earth is billions of years old, but this does not mean that a world in which the earth is much younger is not understandable by us. The subject of immanent metaphysics is, so to speak, the complete space of how the world can be understood (not what actually happens to be understood). It is not about that space 'piecemeal'; it is about its structure, its joints: the topic of immanent metaphysics is the structure of the world as understandable by us. Kant's view, as we have seen, is that the structure of the world as understandable by us is determined by the structure of our own intellects. So there is a direct translation between the structure of our understanding of the world and the structure of the world as understood by us. The basic concepts of metaphysics are the most basic structures of our understanding: any understanding of anything is structured by those concepts. So the world as understood by us is structured by those concepts, which means that those concepts refer: they refer to joints, not in the world as it is in itself, but in the world as it is understood by us.

The topic of transcendent metaphysics, by contrast, is the world as it is in itself, the structure that it has in its own right, not in relation to anything else. We have seen that both the pre-Kantian rationalists and some contemporary philosophers take this to be the appropriate topic of metaphysics. The point of Kant's question—why do the basic metaphysical concepts refer?—is that the transcendent metaphysician cannot explain why her metaphysical concepts refer. Since the aim of metaphysics, on this view, is to correctly map the structure of the world in itself, and since that requires having concepts or terms that refer to that metaphysical structure, the transcendent metaphysician, if Kant is correct, cannot explain why transcendent metaphysics is possible. The practitioner of immanent metaphysics, on the other hand, can: since the structure of our understanding is the structure of the world as understood by us, then, if some set of concepts provides the structure of any possible understanding for any topic, those concepts refer to the joints in the world as understandable by us. To some, this may seem like it simply changes the topic: 'immanent' metaphysics is not really metaphysics at all. But if metaphysics is identified with transcendent metaphysics, then Kant's conclusion is simply that the possibility of reference in metaphysics is inexplicable. Only in immanent metaphysics, the heir to traditional metaphysics, is the reference of our concepts explicable.

Kant raised a question—how is metaphysics possible?—that has multiple dimensions: he inquires into the epistemic, the scientific, the metaphysical, and the semantic possibility of metaphysics. I have focused on the semantic aspect of this question, which I take to mean: why do the basic concepts of metaphysics 'relate to their objects'—that is, refer to them? I have argued that no one in the pre-Kantian or the post-Kantian tradition has a particularly successful answer to this question. Kant's proposal is to reconceive metaphysics as the immanent science of the structure of the framework in which we understand the world, and I have argued that we can explain how the basic concepts of that science refer. Kantian immanent metaphysics can answer the question about its own possibility that traditional transcendent metaphysics could not. If this does not constitute a great achievement in philosophy, I don't know what does.

Notes

1. See Förster (2012) for a discussion of what Kant meant by this astonishing claim. 'Ak' refers to the *Akademie* edition of Kant's writings (Kant 1902), which I cite by volume and page number. The *CPR* I cite in the standard A/B format. Translations of the *CPR* are from Guyer and Wood (Kant 1998).
2. I borrow the term 'cognitive semantics' as a description of Kant's theory from Hanna (2001).
3. Translation, with slight modifications, from Kant (1999: 133).
4. Kant alludes to the relation of empirical intuitions to their objects in the Herz letter itself (Ak. 10:130–1). He had outlined his theory of *a priori* intuitions and their relation to their objects (space, time) two years before in his 'Inaugural dissertation', *De mundi sensibilis atque intelligibilis forma et principiis* (Ak. 2:385–419; translation in Kant 1992).
5. I use angle brackets to denote the concepts that would normally be expressed by the italicized expression within: for example, <*substance*> is the concept of substance.
6. This is not the relation between <*substance*> and its extension, the set of substances. <*Substance*> would still have 'its object', even if it had a different extension (if one fewer or one more substance were to exist), so the 'object' of a concept (for Kant) is not its extension. I argue for this at length in Stang (forthcoming *b*).
7. Much of those debates were concerned with the reference of singular terms (names, definite descriptions) and indexical expressions; Putnam (1975) expands these issues to the case of natural-kind terms like 'water'.
8. In the course of criticizing the ontological argument for the existence of God, Kant points out that there can be true analytic judgments involving concepts that are not instantiated by any objects (e.g., 'God is omnipotent' is true, even if there is no God). See A595–6/B622–3.
9. Obviously, there are complicated issues here about tense and context-sensitive expressions like indexicals and demonstratives, which, for reasons of space, I cannot discuss here.
10. This also allows us to extend the notion of reference beyond the reference of singular terms to objects and predicates to properties. For instance, if we adopt a primitivist modal metaphysics on which modal facts do not obtain in virtue of anything non-modal we can give the truth conditions of modal sentences as follows: '$\Diamond p$' is true if and only if possibly *p*. In this case we could say that the modal operator $\Diamond$ 'refers' to possibility, since possibility facts contribute to truth conditions of sentences that involve it. Henceforth, to indicate that 'referents' can in principle be a broader category than objects I will speak of reference to 'entities and structures'.
11. See Devitt and Sterelny (1999) and Davidson (2007) for an overview of the issues and the present state of the debate.
12. For instance, by Crusius's theory of the highest material principles of thought; for discussion, see Heimsoeth (1956) and Hogan (2013).

13 Which of Hume's writings Kant had read, and, in particular, whether he had read the *Treatise*, is a matter of controversy among scholars. See Kuehn (1983); Kreimendahl (1990); and Beiser (2002: 43–7).
14 These are what Garrett (1997) calls 'revival sets' for ideas used abstractly.
15 Beiser (2002) offers this as further evidence that Hume had not read the *Treatise*.
16 In Stang (forthcoming *b*) I argue that Kant's locution '*the* object of a concept' never refers to the extension of a concept, much less to an individual object in that extension, but instead to what we might now call the 'content' of a concept.
17 See Locke (1975: bk. II, ch. XXI, §§1–4).
18 For example, Sider (2011: 162) and Williamson (2013: 423). Neither Sider nor Williamson would be attracted, though, to a Lockean 'empirical' deduction of the key terms in their metaphysical theories.
19 See Stang (forthcoming *a*) for extensive discussion of the modal content of Kantian experience (*Erfahrung*).
20 More precisely, the primary qualities of the body ground the object's power to produce in me ideas that resemble these qualities. In actual sense perception, these powers are activated and I come to perceive ideas that resemble qualities in bodies. Cf. Locke's *Essay* (1975: bk. II, ch. 8).
21 Careful readers will notice that this involves a transition from a claim of the form $\lozenge \exists Fx$ to a claim of the form $\exists (Fx \ \& \ \text{Possible}(x))$, where Possible($x$) is a predicate of objects rather than an operator on propositions. While many would reject the validity of this inference, I argue in Stang (2016) that Leibniz, Wolff, and Baumgarten are committed to the validity of this transition where F is an 'essential concept' (it picks out an object by its essential properties).
22 For ease of exposition I am going to be a bit cavalier about the exact ontological status of the referent here.
23 I reconstruct these arguments in detail in Stang (2016: ch. 3).
24 For critical discussion, see Chignell (2009); Stang (2010, 2016); Abaci (2014); and Yong (2014).
25 Note that this is not the question, 'Why (for what reason) did God create me with this concept?'
26 The derivative concepts are what Kant calls 'predicables of pure reason': see A82/B108.
27 Fictionalism about a problematic class of entities might also be thought of as eliminating reference to those entities: see, for instance, Rosen (1990) for a fictionalist account that *eliminates* reference to (Lewisian) possible worlds.
28 In forthcoming work, I explore the relation of metaphysical deflationism to Kant's own 'transcendental method' in metaphysics and I raise some Kantian (and post-Kantian) problems for the deflationist.
29 Fourth, there is the extension of the Concept, the set of things to which it correctly applies, but I will pass over that here.
30 I am assuming that 'water' expresses the same Concept in Earth English and in Twin-Earth English but refers to different things. But little in my argument hangs on this assumption; it is merely an illustration.
31 One could consider a view on which there are 'externalist' effects in the reference of metaphysical concepts (e.g., 'substance' refers to different things, depending on what world it is tokened in), but I will forgo discussion of that here.
32 This means that Kant is not committed to the implausible skeptical claim that, without a satisfactory explanation of the reference of, for instance, the terms of physics, our

putative knowledge of physics is jeopardized. We might have knowledge in physics even if we lack second-order knowledge of how this knowledge is possible (among other things, why physical terms refer in the first place).

33 Nor do I think that these considerations are foreign to Kant. See his account of why we must assume that the 'system' of our empirical concepts must track the 'system' of nature in the Appendix to the 'Transcendental Dialectic' section of CPR A642/B670–A668/B696.

34 At this point I anticipate yet another buck-passing move in the assertion that explaining the reference of metaphysical terms is the job of semantics. But a semantic theory that explains the reference of terms in metaphysics is going to have to include quite a lot of metaphysics; whether this is called 'semantics' or 'metaphysical semantics' or the 'semantics of metaphysics' is a matter of indifference to me.

35 For the original idea of naturalness as an explanation of reference see Lewis (1984) in response to Putnam (1977, 1980, 1981). Sider (2011) is the most developed contemporary version of the idea that the world has a privileged metaphysical structure.

36 I owe this example to an unpublished paper by Laura Franklin-Hall.

37 There is now a small—but growing!—literature on *Erkenntnis* and how (and whether) it differs from knowledge, *Wissen*. See Smit (2000); Hanna (2006); Watkins and Willaschek (2017); and Schafer (forthcoming).

References

Abaci, Uygar 2014. Kant's Only Possible Argument and Chignell's Real Harmony, *Kantian Review* 19: 1–25.

Beiser, Frederick C. 2002. *German Idealism: The Struggle against Subjectivism, 1781–1801*, Cambridge, MA: Harvard University Press.

Chalmers, David, Manley, David, and Wasserman, Ryan (eds.) 2009. *Metametaphysics: New Essays on the Foundations of Ontology*, Oxford: Clarendon Press.

Chignell, Andrew 2009. Kant, Modality, and the Most Real Being, *Archiv für Geschichte der Philosophie* 91: 157–92.

Davidson, Matthew (ed.) 2007. *On Sense and Direct Reference: Readings in the Philosophy of Language*, Boston: McGraw-Hill.

Devitt, Michael and Sterelny, Kim 1999. *Language and Reality: An Introduction to the Philosophy of Language*, Cambridge, MA: MIT Press.

Förster, Eckart 2012. *The Twenty-Five Years of Philosophy: A Systematic Reconstruction*, trans. Brady Bowman, Cambridge, MA: Harvard University Press.

Garrett, Don 1997. *Cognition and Commitment in Hume's Philosophy*, New York: Oxford University Press.

Hanna, Robert 2001. *Kant and the Foundations of Analytic Philosophy*, Oxford: Clarendon Press.

Hanna, Robert 2006. *Kant, Science, and Human Nature*, Oxford: Clarendon Press.

Heimsoeth, Heinz 1956. *Metaphysik und Kritik bei Chr. A. Crusius*, Kant-Studien, Ergänzungsheft 71, Köln: Kölner Universitats-Verlag.

Hofweber, Thomas 2009. Ambitious, yet Modest, Metaphysics, in David Chalmers, David Manley, and Ryan Wasserman (eds.), *Metametaphysics: New Essays on the Foundations of Ontology*. Oxford: Clarendon Press: 260–89.

Hogan, Desmond 2013. Metaphysical Motives of Kant's Analytic–Synthetic Distinction. *Journal of the History of Philosophy* 51: 267–307.

Kant, Immanuel 1902–. *Kants Gesammelte Schriften*, 29 vols., Berlin-Brandenburg (formerly: Royal Prussian) Academy of Sciences, ed., Berlin: Walter de Gruyter.
Kant, Immanuel 1992. *Theoretical Philosophy, 1755–1770*, ed. David Walford and Ralf Meerbote, Cambridge: Cambridge University Press.
Kant, Immanuel 1998. *Critique of Pure Reason*, trans. and ed. Paul Guyer and Allen W. Wood, Cambridge: Cambridge University Press.
Kant, Immanuel 1999. *Correspondence*, trans. and ed. Arnulf Zweig, Cambridge: Cambridge University Press.
Kreimendahl, Lothar 1990. *Kant—der Durchbruch von 1769*, Köln: Dinter.
Kuehn, Manfred 1983. Kant's Conception of 'Hume's Problem', *Journal of the History of Philosophy* 21: 175–93.
Lewis, David 1984. Putnam's Paradox, *Australasian Journal of Philosophy* 62: 221–36.
Locke, John. 1975 [1690], *An Essay Concerning Human Understanding*, ed. Paul Nidditch, Oxford: Clarendon Press.
Putnam, Hilary 1975. The Meaning of 'Meaning', *Minnesota Studies in the Philosophy of Science* 7: 131–93.
Putnam, Hilary 1977. Realism and Reason, *Proceedings and Addresses of the American Philosophical Association* 50: 483–98.
Putnam, Hilary 1980. Models and Reality, *Journal of Symbolic Logic*, 45: 464–82.
Putnam, Hilary 1981. *Reason, Truth and History*, Cambridge: Cambridge University Press.
Rosen, Gideon 1990. Modal Fictionalism, *Mind*, 99: 327–54.
Schafer, Karl forthcoming. Kant's Conception of Cognition and Our Knowledge of Things in Themselves, in *The Sensible and Intelligible Worlds: New Essays on Kant's Metaphysics and Epistemology*, ed. N. F. Stang and K. Schafer, Oxford: Oxford University Press.
Sider, Theodore 2011. *Writing the Book of the World*, Oxford: Clarendon Press.
Smit, Houston 2000. Kant on Marks and the Immediacy of Intuition, *Philosophical Review* 109: 235–66.
Stang, Nicholas F. 2010. Kant's Possibility Proof, *History of Philosophy Quarterly* 27: 275–99.
Stang, Nicholas F. 2016. *Kant's Modal Metaphysics*, Oxford: Oxford University Press.
Stang, Nicholas F. forthcoming a. Hermann Cohen and Kant's Concept of Experience, in *Philosophie und Wissenschaft bei Hermann Cohen*, ed. Christian Damböck, Dordrecht: Springer.
Stang, Nicholas F. forthcoming b. Kant and the Concept of an Object.
Thomasson, Amie L. 2015. *Ontology Made Easy*, New York: Oxford University Press.
Watkins, Eric and Willaschek, Marcus 2017. Kant's Account of Cognition, *Journal of the History of Philosophy* 55: 83–112.
Williamson, Timothy 2013. *Modal Logic as Metaphysics*, Oxford: Oxford University Press.
Yong, Peter 2014. God, Totality and Possibility in Kant's Only Possible Argument, *Kantian Review* 19: 27–51.

12
NIETZSCHE, THIS TIME IT'S PERSONAL

Ken Gemes

> Gradually it has become clear to me what every great philosophy so far has been: namely, the personal confession of its author and a kind of involuntary and unconscious memoir.
>
> (*BGE*: 6)

1. 'Why I Am a Destiny': Nietzsche's Challenge to Philosophy

Nietzsche makes philosophy personal, paramount, and profound. To do philosophy in his way takes both courage and insight.[1] Traditionally, philosophy often takes intuitions as basic, functioning as a justificatory grounding, as science takes the evidences of the senses.[2] Nietzsche questions our intuitions; moreover, he does so in a motivated rather than merely skeptical manner. He questions not just the justificatory status of what are taken to be some of our most fundamental mental representations, but our very access to those representations. Where a Cartesian philosophy says that what I know first and foremost are the contents of my mind, Nietzsche demurs on at least two grounds. First, following Schopenhauer and prefiguring Freud, he believes that a lot of one's thinking, and even feeling, is not consciously accessible. Second, like Hegel before him, Nietzsche believes that even the content of one's conscious thoughts are not self-transparent. It is for such reasons that he says, 'We are strangers to ourselves' (*GM* Preface: 1).

Nietzsche is fascinating because he treats philosophy as something more than an academic discipline; for him, it often seems to be a kind of life and death struggle. As Nietzsche's character Zarathustra dramatically puts it, 'Of all that is written I love only what a person hath written with his own blood' (*Z*, 'Reading and Writing'). Nietzsche demands that what we do in way of philosophy should somehow inform our whole life, and, conversely, he demands that our whole lives inform our philosophy. For many philosophers and scholars, much of their life is divorced from their professional work. This is one reason why Nietzsche says of the scholar that 'he is an instrument . . . but he is no goal' (*BGE*: 207). One senses that, for Nietzsche, ideally, philosophy would inform both our life and our death.[3] It is for such reasons that he says of Christianity that it is '[n]ot a belief but a doing . . . a being different' and that 'in reality there has only ever been one Christian and he died on the cross' (*A*: 39). In modern man, in particular, he bemoans what he takes to be a thorough disconnection between their theoretical knowledge and their lived life (cf. *UM* II passim).

A corollary of this demand for a deep link between philosophies and lived life shows another major point of divergence from the tradition of modern Western academic philosophy. If our lives are to inform our philosophy, and lives differ sufficiently, then different philosophies will be appropriate for different lives. Philosophers generally seek universal positions, whether about metaphysics, epistemology, or values—positions and propositions that aim to be true, or at least justified, for all humans. Against this one-size-fits-all mentality, Nietzsche allows, for instance, that values and moralities that are appropriate to some lives may be inappropriate for others.[4]

Beyond generally questioning the implicit philosophical egalitarianism of the tradition, he challenges some of our most explicitly cherished values—values on which we often pride ourselves, if not actually living by them, at least attempting to live up to them. These are values that we think of as part of the core of our identity. Embedded in Nietzsche's questioning of our values is a novel conception of what makes us human. For Nietzsche, we are not creatures with immortal souls, nor are we rational animals. Rather, we are animals with stories, animals that care to have and strive for meaning. For Nietzsche, we might say, man is the narrative animal.[5] Our meanings are reflected in our values. For someone who takes themselves to be a warrior, part of what is essential to their life story might be the narrative of their various martial victories and defeats. This warrior's narrative might explicitly or implicitly give emphasis to values such as honor and courage, rather than, say, Christian values of humility and compassion. The philosopher's tendency to discuss values in absolute terms apart from any narrative context is something that Nietzsche resists. He will discuss what is good for this or that individual, or, perhaps more broadly, what is good for this or that type of individual. But he generally eschews talk of what is good for all, or what is the good in itself.[6] That is part of his motivation for giving narrative genealogies of moralities. Those genealogies help to identify the values of at work in a given context, and, more controversially, what values are appropriate given that context.

Part of our particular modern context is what Nietzsche calls the death of God. As we shall see, for Nietzsche the problem for modernity—with its rejection of Christian narratives of divine creation and heavenly redemption—is that our need for meaning-conferring narratives is subverted by our will to truth. The latter tends to produce skepticism toward all of those grand narratives that would provide meaning. Nietzsche himself is adept at providing deflating counter-narratives that make us question established popular master narratives, and hence values, that we tend to identify as being central to our own identities. Most notably, he questions the value of compassion and the value of truth. These are values, especially the latter, that typically remain unquestioned. He does this by showing that those values come from a particular contingent perspective, a perspective, reinforced by various narratives, that was forged to serve certain interests, a perspective with which we need not, perhaps should not, identify. What is more, he provides other perspectives that emphasize alternative values. He argues that some of the civilizations that we most admire, civilizations from which we trace the beginnings of philosophy itself, were based on these alternative perspectives. Nietzsche aims with his counter-narratives to make us question both our values and our identity. In those counter-narratives, he includes both psychological and genealogical speculations. His use of both psychology and genealogical enquiries both disturbs and threatens our normal modes of philosophizing. Especially when it comes to the question of values, we are strangely caught—recognizing Nietzsche's apparent and indeed self-conscious committing of the genetic fallacy, and nevertheless in some way, even justifiably, succumbing to that fallacy! Recognizing that Nietzsche is working on us, arousing our affects and emotions, rather than only employing the more standard philosophical approach of detached argument and reasoning, can come to seem somehow legitimate.

Added to these worries about Nietzsche's rhetorical methods is the further suspicion that, when the dust has settled over Nietzsche's seemingly confusing amalgam of doctrines, what one is left with is a kind of philosophical autobiography—as suggested by the quotation prefacing this chapter. That worry is exacerbated when one reads in his mock autobiographical work, modestly entitled *Ecce Homo*, that when he had been writing of other philosophers and thinkers—for instance, Schopenhauer and Wagner—he had in fact been largely referring to himself (*EH* 'Birth of Tragedy': 4; *EH* 'The Untimely Ones': 2, 4).[7] Scholarly debates about his alleged master metaphysical doctrine of the will to power or his even more recondite doctrine of eternal return often seem to leave us with even less to go on than the philosophy-as-personal-confession line. Yet, for all that, there is something deeply challenging about Nietzsche, so that after a genuine encounter with him, we might, paraphrasing him, 'ask, utterly surprised and disconcerted, "What really was that which we have just experienced?" and moreover: "Who are we really?"' (*GM* Preface: 1). But, as Philippa Foot deftly put it, 'a confrontation with Nietzsche is a difficult thing to arrange' (2001: 210–11).

One thing that makes Nietzsche seem to talk past us is that, in contrast to what we take to be a philosophical mode, he adopts a decidedly psychological mode of enquiry. Where traditional philosophers ask a metaphysical/semantic question, 'What is the nature of truth?', Nietzsche presses the frankly psychological question, 'What is it in us that values truth?' That Nietzsche often characterizes himself as a psychologist (cf. *EH* 'Why I Am a Destiny': 4; *EH* 'Why I Write Such Good Books': 5) might give us additional grounds for wondering how, or even if it is appropriate, to assess him as a philosopher. But, against this, we should remember that many canonical philosophers, such as Hume and, more recently, Quine, seem to adopt a distinctly psychological mode, or at least one that is as much focused on questions about the etiology of beliefs as on more standard philosophical questions of metaphysics or epistemology, or, more specifically, normative questions of justifications. Indeed, while Nietzsche professes to be addressing psychological or genealogical/etiological questions about the genesis of belief, his eyes seem even more firmly fixed on frankly normative ends than, for instance, either Hume's or Quine's were.[8]

In the *Genealogy of Morality*, a work whose emphasis on etiological questions is emphasized in its very title, a work in which, it seems, Nietzsche's primary aim is to set out his 'ideas on the origins of our moral prejudices—for this is the subject of this polemic' (*GM* Preface: 2), he reminds us that in his earlier work, ostensibly on the same subject, 'my real concern was something much more important than hypothesis mongering . . . on the origins of morality . . . What was at stake is the value of morality' (*GM* Preface: 5). One suspects that the same concern is at the heart of his *Genealogy of Morality*. But even if here we see that Nietzsche is on the more recognizably philosophical ground of the normative, our heads are sent into a spin by his focus on the disconcerting question of the value of our values. Many philosophers will immediately be struck by the difficulties piled up in this notion. From what evaluative perspective are we to evaluate morality? It hardly helps that Nietzsche tells us that the question of 'what is the value of this or that value table or "morality"?' demands to be raised from the most diverse perspectives (*GM* I: 17). Are we also to raise questions about the relative value of those various perspectives?

Here it helps to tease apart an ambiguity in the use of the term 'value'. The term can be used in both a descriptive and an evaluative sense. We see both senses at work in such typically Nietzschean claims as 'The herd value happiness, contentedness, but I see no value in that' (for Nietzsche's way of expressing this claim, see *BGE*: 225). Here the first use of 'value' is descriptive; it marks the descriptive fact that the so-called herd take happiness and contentedness to be valuable. The second use is evaluative: it expresses a negative assessment of the value of happiness and contentedness. The same ambiguity attaches to the term 'morality'. It can be used in a normative fashion to refer to what is in some sense good, and it can be used in a descriptive sense to talk of what is taken by some relevant individual or social group as being good. When Nietzsche asks about the value of morality he is seeking to make an evaluative assessment of what we in the West as a matter of fact take to be moral. More particularly, he is making an evaluative assessment of what we commonly call Judeo-Christian morality and what he takes to be its more recent refinements, including Kantian deontology and utilitarianism.[9] In making such assessments we might wonder whether he is making a kind of immanent internal critique—judging some part, or perhaps even all, of Judeo-Christian morality using and tacitly endorsing some of the very standards of Judeo-Christian morality.[10] Or is he merely judging by his own possibly idiosyncratic standards, so that we might think that all of his vitriol that he displays to Judeo-Christian morality is merely another of those autobiographical expressions of his peculiar tastes? Or is he appealing to some non-Judeo-Christian evaluative norms that he both endorses and believes that his audience endorses at least tacitly to some degree or other (or are rightly sympathetic to, at some level or other)?

2. 'Have I Been Understood?—Dionysus versus the Crucified': Nietzsche's Challenge to Morality

What is the purpose of Nietzsche's critique of Judeo-Christian morality? To expose the truth about that morality? To lessen its hold on us? When Nietzsche tells us that 'the whole absurd residue of Christian fable, conceptual web-spinning and theology . . . could be a thousand times more absurd and we would not lift a finger against it', that certainly sounds like the matter of truth is not foremost. That he continues with 'What is it we combat in Christianity? That it wants to break the strong' (*KSA* 13: 27–8; see also *A*: 56, 58) might suggest that his critique is wholly instrumental, predicated on Christianity's alleged bad effects. But that would miss the point that, besides bemoaning what he takes to be Christianity's bad effects, he also takes it to be defective in its own right. It is defective and ugly in that it is, he argues, an expression of resentment. It is a central claim of his *Genealogy of Morality* that the Judeo-Christian world view, with its talk of an afterlife as reward for the dispossessed of this world, and its repudiation of the natural drives—for instance, drives of sexuality and aggression—is fundamentally an expression of resentment. This is not just resentment of the world in which one finds oneself dispossessed, but also to those very drives themselves. It is the demands of the drives, as much so as of the world that defies these demands, that is the cause of one's suffering. And in as much as social morality forbids outward aggression, it facilitates—if not explicitly encourages—expression of aggression against one's own drives.

Freud, possibly following Nietzsche, would later call this mechanism—whereby aggression that would, if not checked by social restraints, find an external object is redirected against the self—'repression' and 'internalization'. For Nietzsche, in learning to denigrate our natural drives, usually with accompaniment of an aggrandizing of our faculties of reason, we are in a sense repudiating ourselves. Here again we see a fault line between Nietzsche and much of the philosophical tradition. Philosophers have tended to identify the core of humanity with reason;

treating drives and instincts as something that only have their place under the dominion of reason. While Plato makes use of the metaphor of the chariot with the brutes of the appetites and the spirit that rightly are to be controlled by the charioteer of reason, Kant goes to the extreme of claiming that the drives, passions, feelings, and desires can have no part in genuinely moral reasoning. Nietzsche here stands with the Romantics, and with Schopenhauer and Freud, who locate our identity with will, instincts, or drives; elements to which we typically have little conscious access.

Nietzsche does not simply question some of our core values; he questions a story that is commonly told of the genesis of those values. That is part of the point of perhaps the most famous passage from Nietzsche, the one in which a madman announces the death of God.[11] In that passage, the audience who mocks the alleged madman asks, facetiously, 'Has he got lost . . . Has he gone on a holiday, emigrated?' (GS: 125). They take themselves to be thorough atheists, equivalents of our modern day secular humanists. The madman, through his use of a cavalcade of arresting metaphorical questions—'Who gave us the sponge to wipe away the entire horizon? What were we doing when we unchained this earth from its sun?' (BGE: 125)—intimates that they do not really understand what it means to live without God. Here the madman is presenting Nietzsche's claim that modern atheists mistakenly take themselves to have already made the decisive break with Christianity by rejecting belief in God. But, for Nietzsche, the core of Christianity is not its metaphysics but instead its values or normative commitments. Principal among those values is the value of truth and the value of compassion.[12] Nietzsche rejects the self-congratulatory narrative of the enlightenment that claims that—in throwing off the religious metaphysical baggage of God, divine creation, immortals souls, and the like—we have entered a new age far removed from that where tradition, authority, and superstition prevailed. Rather, the secular humanist, whether he espouses a Kantian deontology or instead some form of utilitarianism, still carries a fundamentally unquestioning regard for the core values of Christianity. For Nietzsche, it is the propaganda trick of the enlightenment apologists and secular humanists to make us focus on questions of metaphysics so as to elide the deep continuity of values with the Judeo-Christian tradition.[13] Because we do not even raise the question of the value of truth, or the value of compassion, Nietzsche says that we, contra the Enlightenment propaganda, have yet to make a decisive break with the past. Indeed, he claims, our rejection of the existence of God is not contra our Christian values but is in fact one of the more sublime manifestations of those very values. It is our religiously inspired commitment to truth as an ultimate value that leads us to believe that there is no God.[14] It is only when that same will to truth comes to question the value of truth and the value of compassion that the true overcoming of Christianity will be possible. Much of this is succinctly expressed in the following wonderful passage (GM III: 27):

Christianity as *dogma* [that is, the metaphysics of God, immortal soul, etc.] perished of its own morality [the morality which claims that everything ought to be sacrificed in pursuit of the truth]; in this manner Christianity as *morality* [a morality that elevates truth and compassion as ultimate values] must now also perish. We stand at the threshold of this great event. Now that the Christian truthfulness has drawn one conclusion after the other, in the end it draws its *strongest conclusion*, its conclusion *against* itself.

But then suppose that we do come to question these core Christian/enlightenment values. Are we to do so merely as part of a further internal critique? For instance, are we to question these values simply because, with the absence of their previous metaphysical ground (namely, God with his injunctions that sanction the elevation of truth and compassion), they lack the kind of justification that we have come to demand of all beliefs? While, no doubt, Nietzsche hopes that the notion of an internal critique will have rhetorical purchase, in fact he also motivates his interrogation of those values by pointing to other cultures that enshrined other norms and yet are both within our historical recollection and capable of providing some degree of resonance and identification. The ancient Greeks, who are often held as the paradigm of the heights of civilization (admittedly more so in Nietzsche's day than in ours), according to Nietzsche placed much less value on truth, at least the kind of theoretic truth that is in play here, and even less value in compassion, at least that type of compassion that assumes some fundamental equality of all humans. Societies that freely sanctioned slavery on a massive scale can hardly be held as enacting a morality of equality and compassion. In the Christian religious view, compassion is grounded in the egalitarian view that each of us has a God-given soul, a soul that gives each of us infinite value. For the secularist, it is grounded in the view that each of us has a capacity for reason, or perhaps for happiness, that confers inalienable value upon each of us. In a society that values honor above all else, one that takes slavery to be natural, such egalitarian values have little purchase. To the extent that we can resonate with the grandeur, if not the cruelty, of the ancient Greeks and their civilization, Nietzsche hopes that at least some of us might see some of the attraction of an alternative evaluative framework.[15]

Sometimes it seems as if Nietzsche is dangling a Faustian bargain before our eyes: would you be willing, indeed maybe even happy, to endorse suffering and cruelty, in order to achieve great heights? Or would you prefer a peaceable world of general contentedness bought at the price of general mediocrity? But why must these be our choices? Nietzsche's argument is that, to achieve great heights, one needs to take on great challenges and that such challenges inevitably involve both self-sacrifice and, typically, a good deal of failure, and hence suffering. Here the cruelty and suffering that Nietzsche has primarily in mind is self-cruelty and the would-be creative one's largely self-inflicted suffering. With that said, it is pretty clear that he is in certain cases not averse to the suffering of others if that is also part of the price to be paid for greatness. Nor is greatness to be predicated only of individuals. Societies themselves may have a certain grandeur, or conversely may themselves be worthy of contempt. Here Nietzsche's assessment often seems primarily driven by aesthetic criteria. Still, those who talk of the greatness of ancient Greece, Rome, or Renaissance Italy will not find his preferences to be totally idiosyncratic. Such greatness is not presumably to be measured in terms of general observance of universal moral laws or of promotion of maximal utility, or of democratic governance and norms of equality. It has been argued that, for Nietzsche, even the most downtrodden in such great societies may enjoy the best life possible for them in that through their hardships they are contributing to a great society, even if they care not one whit to make any such contribution, or even if they take no pleasure in the society's alleged greatness and beauty.[16] This level of condescension is, for many, staggering and itself morally repugnant. Of course, in Nietzsche's eyes that judgment is itself an expression of the continuing hold of Judeo-Christian values. Even conceding this, we might register that this wholesale disrespect of individuals' self-definitions of the good, when taken up by, for instance, state authorities, has a significant chance of leading to horrific consequences, indeed consequences that would be horrific by Nietzsche's own lights.[17] We might suppose that this is one more reason why he claims that few have the right to his thoughts, and that the values he holds are not suitable for all others.

Is, then, Nietzsche so far removed from us? Is he, as suggested earlier, merely using our values—for instance, our allegiance to the value of truthfulness—to subvert our very values, without himself having any allegiance to those values? In fact, it is pretty clear that he himself admires the ability to take on truths, especially painful truths (*EH* Preface: 3; *A*: 50). What, then, he seems to object to is the turning of truth into an ultimate value to which all other values can be sacrificed. Partly, he is against this because it is unbalanced: 'everything unconditional belongs in pathology' (*BGE*: 154).[18] Truth is, for Nietzsche, a very important value, but nevertheless one of many other important values, ones that are sometimes in competition.[19] Another value that Nietzsche seems to embrace is that of meaning, or what might better be called existential meaning. We shall soon see that he believes that the value of truth and that of meaning can be at loggerheads.

3. 'I Describe What's Coming: The Advent of Nihilism'[20]

When Nietzsche says that man will endure suffering, even seeking it out, so long as one provides a meaning to that suffering (e.g., *GM* III: 28), it appears as if Nietzsche is making some bold essentialist claim about human nature—namely, that man is the animal that seeks meaning. But if we take that meaning to be somehow global—so that all existence has a meaning—that is hard to square with his express fear of the character that Nietzsche labels as being the last human (*letzte Mensch*; strangely, since Nietzsche has sufficient misogyny in his own voice, translated as 'last man' in most English translations). Whether this refers to actual humans or instead to envisaged possible future humans is difficult to say. But what seems to characterize the last human is a total rejection of the demand that existence as a whole be seen as somehow meaningful. Rather, last humans find personal meaning in their career, their family; but existence as such is for them devoid of meaning, or more likely the question simply does not arise for them. For Nietzsche, it is not that it is an essential part of human nature to seek existential meaning. Rather, for him it is a kind of moral imperative that one seeks such meaning. Indeed, those interpreters who insist that Nietzsche is somehow a basically religious thinker might care to see here his essential religiosity. In as much as religion is fueled by the need to find existential meaning, we can see Nietzsche as a religious thinker, or, at least, as sharing the basic motivation of religious thinkers. But why this demand that we seek existential meaning? Because without it we become small, self-concerned, and pathetic, our horizons defined by the struggle for the corner office, a larger house, the next good meal. Where I have been talking of narrative, the early Nietzsche was prone to talk of myth, belying his already basically skeptical attitude to such narratives. In that voice, he says this: 'without myth every culture loses the healthy natural power of its creativity: only a horizon defined by myths completes and unifies a whole cultural movement' (*BT*: 24).

But how, then, do we find existential meaning? Typically, we do this though endorsing some meaning-giving grand narrative such as Christianity, Communism, Utilitarianism (admittedly the last is barely deserving of the title 'narrative'; this is said here as both concession and criticism!), or the like. Previously, it was stated that we might read Nietzsche as implicitly claiming that what separates us from the animals is the fact that we have narratives: that is to say, we care to have narratives. But were we to care only for a narrative of self-concern, then for Nietzsche we are little better than herd animals. It is at the point where we moderns look for a grand narrative, one that can confer existential meaning, that Nietzsche thinks there is an inevitable clash between the value of truth and the value of meaning. For where our will to truth is too strong, we refuse all of those grand narratives capable of giving the world meaning. The will to truth, pressed to the extreme, leaves us with a disenchanted world. For Nietzsche, this is the fundamental problem of modernity; our will to truth deprives us of those myths or illusions that serve to enchant existence. It is because he values those values that make us see beyond our own narrowly defined interests (careers, family, etc.) that he sees the need for some curb on our truth drive. Nietzsche prophesies a sad trajectory, from an overly strong will to truth disenchanting the world (the problem of modernity), to the time of the last humans, who have truly experienced the death of God and have given up on all grand narratives. The nihilistic last humans lack those types of ultimate values (including that of truth itself) that are capable of conferring existential meaning (the situation of post-modernity).[21]

One could perhaps embrace here some strong form of, for instance, moral realism, so that one believed that as a matter of fact existence as a whole is valuable and has meaning. But, for Nietzsche, this is as probable as embracing the benevolent father figure from traditional religion. Some would argue that Nietzsche is in fact an anti-realist about values. This may be true about the early Nietzsche, but the important point for him is not, for instance, whether existence does or does not have any meaning, but rather the historical-psychological fact that we moderns (note that this need not, for Nietzsche, include the actual majority of people alive in his or our time) no longer see the world as having meaning. Again, Nietzsche sees the problem from a psychological point of view.

In addition to seeing himself as a psychologist, Nietzsche sometimes saw himself as an untimely philosopher—one of his early works is entitled *Untimely Meditations*. He took himself to be saying things that his contemporaries could not—or perhaps positively did not want to—hear or understand. In a poignant moment of both hope and no little hubris, he reflects this untimeliness with the observation, 'Only the day after tomorrow belongs to me. Some are born posthumously' (*A* Foreword). Writing not in the usual philosophical stance of *sub specie aeterni* reflection, he was prescient in diagnosing a malady of our time. He called it nihilism and prophesied it to be the history of Europe for the next 200 years. He saw this nihilism, characterized by the absence of existential meaning, as the inevitable product of our relentless will to truth.[22] We have seen that he prophesied, in particular, that the will to truth will eventually undermine itself—recall his claim that 'Christianity as morality must now also perish.' After all, what is the basis of the claim that truth is to be valued as an ultimate end, rather than to be valued merely instrumentally? Today, seeing what appears to be the dying light of both the valuing of compassion and the valuing of truth as ultimate values, we might hanker after a little more devotion to those values. Strangely, this is not a hankering to which Nietzsche would be totally unsympathetic. True, he often rails against Christian values. He does so because he thinks that they tend to promote otherworldliness, a turning away from our natural drives and a general slandering of this, the one and only, world. But at least Christian values are capable of giving the world meaning. And that, for Nietzsche, is preferable to the last human who has abandoned the quest for existential meaning. It is worth noting that both Nietzsche and his creation Zarathustra reserve their deepest contempt—indeed (to use their own term), nausea—not for the Christian but for the last human. Better life denying existential meaning than no existential meaning at all. Nietzsche says, 'The individual must be consecrated to something higher than himself' (*UM* IV: 4). And, condescendingly enough, Nietzsche seems to think that, for many of us, life denying existential meaning is all of the existential meaning to which we can aspire: 'the ideas of the herd should rule in the herd—but not reach out beyond it' (*KSA* 12: 280). Meanwhile, he hopes to inspire some to find more life-affirming meaning: that is, values that glorify rather than denigrate our natural drives and this world. For Nietzsche, his true readers, his ideal readers, are not those academics who will glean this or that doctrine from his pages. That is not to say that no such doctrines are to be gleaned. But, for Nietzsche, that is the serious work of scholars, who, as we observed earlier, although worthy in their own right, are no ends in themselves.

But who are Nietzsche's ideal readers? Presumably they are what he calls 'higher men' or those who are capable, upon being liberated from self-denying Christian values, possibly through the influence of his own works, of becoming higher men. They are, despite Nietzsche's general glorification of drives and his attendant denigration of reason as a suppressor of the drives, not necessarily beings who simply give free reign to their natural drives.[23] What seems to characterize great men, for Nietzsche, is that they have a certain kind of unity in their drives. More commonly, this might be glossed under the notion of having a singular purpose that focuses all of one's energies. In Nietzsche's drive psychology, this is glossed in terms of having a master drive that harnesses other drives to its purpose instead of seeking to suppress them. Presumably, not just any purpose will do here. What Nietzsche seems to value most is artistic and, more generally, intellectual creativity. In his earlier works where he often has in focus those who are capable of providing existential meaning, he singles out 'philosophers, artists, and saints' (UM 'Schopenhauer as Educator': 5). Nietzsche, again prefiguring Freud, constructs an ideal of sublimation to contrast with the more usual occurrence of repression.[24]

For Nietzsche we moderns, having a 'heritage of multiple origins', are a jumble of drives that fight each other in attempts to find expression: 'Such human beings of late cultures and refracted lights will on the average be weaker human beings' (BGE: 200). We might ask why unity is needed for creativity. In the abstract, the idea of all of the drives being directed to a single purpose might seem like the best way for achieving a given purpose. But in fact some of the most creative individuals often seem to harbor huge internal conflicts that are not suggestive of a deep underlying unity. As Nietzsche often seems to be a proponent of agonal struggle, one wonders why the self that is composed of the drives could not, when functioning at its best, also be in the throes of deep agonal struggles that preclude any unity of the self. Here is another of those confounding points where one wonders if there is not an autobiographical point in play. Perhaps Nietzsche feels that what would be best for him in terms of reaching his creative potential, or some other goal, would be a unifying of the drives. Alternatively, this might be one of those points where he is implicitly invoking aesthetic criteria. Lack of unity can be inimical to beauty. Indeed, for Nietzsche, since repression is closely associated with resentment (which, for him, is clearly something inherently ugly and disfiguring), one could see that, for him, there may be strong aesthetic grounds for preferring unity. There is a famous passage where Nietzsche talks of giving style to one's character in terms of taking the different elements and unifying them into a whole. Interestingly, the passage ends with the observation that where such unity is lacking one may be dissatisfied with oneself and that this makes one an 'ugly sight' (*GS*: 290).

Many of the truly great philosophers do not simply give us particular doctrines. They also give us narrative visions of what it is to be human—human in the best, normatively loaded, sense of that term. Plato, Aristotle, Augustine, and even arguably Descartes and Kant, through their works exemplify or, more accurately, create certain characters: they construct narratives of development (typically of both their and our development). Possibly, we know more of these characters Plato, Aristotle, Augustine, Descartes, and Kant than we know of the flesh-and-blood humans Plato, Aristotle, Augustine, Descartes, and Kant. To sum up those characters, those narratives, by a few sentences or a handful of doctrines is no more possible then it is to sum up a literary work in the same way. Nietzsche, more than most philosophers, was conscious of this element of self-construction and of the importance of narratives for our sense of identity. Philosophy at its best does not simply tell us who we are; it is constitutive in making us who we are. This sheds some light on Nietzsche's understanding of how philosophy can help to fulfill the strange and enigmatic injunction, 'Become who you are' (*Z* IV, 'The Honey Offering'; see also GS: 270).[25] In characterizing philosophy, he saw it as neither exclusively science nor art. Philosophy, for Nietzsche, when done properly, is like art in that it creates narratives, but like science in that it generally aims for literal truth. For a writer of prose, a novelist, it is hardly a criticism that what they have written is not literally true; whereas the judgment that their work provides no interesting narrative would be damning.[26] For a scientist, the criticism that what they have written is devoid of literal truth counts as much more of an indictment than the criticism that they have provided little or nothing in the way of narrative. Nietzsche, as much as those named in the preceding list, brilliantly traversed this difficult-to-characterize philosophical terrain that encompasses both grand narrative and the search for truth. Best, then, to end with Nietzsche's own words on this difficult subject (*KSA* 7: 439):

> Great uncertainty as to whether philosophy is an art or a science. It is an art in its purpose and its production. But the means, representation in concepts, it has in common with science. It is a form of poetry.—It cannot be accommodated in any existing category: therefore we must invent and characterise a species for it.[27]

Notes

1 With that said, like certain adherents of psychoanalysis, Nietzscheans may fall into a complacent self-satisfaction under the assumption that they, with their various diagnoses of their own and others' hidden motivations, have reached insight and understanding unavailable to others. Such Nietzscheans are presumably not doing philosophy in Nietzsche's way.

2 This applies also to theories that aim at a reflective equilibrium between theory and intuitions. Such theories do not take intuitions as foundational certainties, but they nonetheless treat them as at least having what Nelson Goodman (1952: 163) characterized as initial credibility.
3 In his *Zarathustra* we read, 'Many die too late, and some die too early' (Z 'Voluntary Death'). This adds poignancy and irony to the fact that Nietzsche's body lived on a good ten years after his mind had largely departed. Still, even in the early days of his largely departed state he wrote some beautiful, although admittedly megalomaniacal, things—for instance, 'The unpleasant thing, and one that nags my modesty is that basically I am every name in history' (*SB* 8: 578).
4 Note that this need not slip into some comfortable relativism that makes each human the author of their own right values. Indeed, it is central to Nietzsche's philosophy that one may actually have values that are inappropriate to one's (appropriate) form of life.
5 This is not to say that the narratives that we give to our own lives have some privileged truth status. According to Nietzsche, any of us can be very wrong about who we are. What is essential is that we care about our narratives: we care about who we are. Non-human animals—at least the ones that we have so far encountered—have no such concerns.
6 Some would argue that he does in fact have some universal good—for instance, increase in power, or feelings of power. They, I suppose, would argue that all of those many places where Nietzsche says that what is good of one may be bad of another are to be read instrumentally and elliptically. For instance, they might claim that what he is saying is that while, for so and so, X may be good for attaining an increase in power, for such and such it is Y and not X that serves that same purpose. More difficult for such a reading are those passages where Nietzsche denies the existence of good in itself (e.g., *EH* Why I Write such Good Books: 4; *A*: 11).
7 That mockery of the self-serving genre of autobiography is part of the aim of *Ecce Homo* is suggested by his chapter titles, which include 'Why I Am So Clever', 'Why I Write Such Good Books'. However, *Ecce Homo*'s last words, 'Have I been understood?—Dionysus versus the Crucified', do suggest genuine megalomania.
8 When Quine lets on in *Roots of Reference* that '[m]ostly in this book I have speculated on causes, not justifications . . . not on values' (1974: 136), and that one could as easily have speculated about the etiology of 'our talk of witchcraft' (ibid.), it gives ammunition for claiming that his so-called epistemology naturalized, which 'falls into place as a chapter of psychology' (1969: 82), has nothing to do with standard philosophical questions of justification, but is only concerned with the psychology of belief acquisition. Similarly, while lay philosophers have taken Hume to be making some strongly normative skeptical point to the effect that our inductive practices are unjustified, in the sense that they are somehow illegitimate, there are Hume scholars who take him to be making a largely descriptive causal claim about the etiology of those practices—namely, that those practices are based on habit and not reason, or, at least, not reason as Cartesian philosophers conceive of it.
9 Of course, for Kantians the core of morality is to be defined by duty, whereas utilitarians typically take it to be defined by happiness maximization. But, from Nietzsche's perspective, in as much as both moralities naturally, if not inevitably, lead to an endorsement of concern for the weakest and an endorsement of something like the golden rule, and given the facts of their actual historical pedigrees, they are secular expressions of Judeo-Christian morality. It is worth keeping in mind here Nelson Goodman's very Nietzschean point that similarity is itself perspectival. For instance, from the perspective of the Anglican

the difference between themselves and the Catholic is substantial; from the perspective of the atheist, the Catholic and Anglican are essentially similar (cf. Goodman 1970).
10 Alternatively, the internal critique may be one involving values that Nietzsche does not himself endorse, but that he is willing to use as a means of lessening the hold of certain values on those who explicitly subscribe to those values.
11 It is worth repeating here Robert Pippin's observation that one should not identify Nietzsche with the madman (despite the sad and, in this context, ironic fact of Nietzsche's eventual insanity). The madman is one who feels totally bereft at, unhinged by, the absence of anchoring values (Pippin 2010: 47–51). In *GS* 343, Nietzsche describes the contrasting position of those 'free spirits', presumably like himself, who feel liberation, a new freedom, with the demise of the old values—a, perhaps frightening freedom to create their own values.
12 More recently, Larry Siedentop (2015) also argues that the core of enlightenment humanism is actually drawn from, and is a continuation of, the Christian tradition; although, unlike Nietzsche, he sees this continuity in a wholly positive manner and as the basis for allowing us to preserve what is good in the Judeo-Christian tradition. This is not unlike the line of arguments developed by nineteenth-century thinkers such as David Strauss, himself one of Nietzsche's *bêtes noires* (see *UM* Essay I).
13 Some would argue that what characterized the modern turn of the enlightenment is not a rejection of Christian metaphysics but instead the adoption of certain rationalist and/or empiricist methodologies. The elevation of testability by experience and/or rational derivation is, they argue, the sea change that heralds modernity. But note that the ground for accepting these methodologies ultimately rests on the claim that these methodologies, rather than previous methods that prioritized reference to alleged authoritative sources, are more likely to yield truth. Yet if, as Nietzsche argues, the valorization of truth as an ultimate value is itself a Christian value, then his point still stands. Alternatively, one might claim, *à la* Richard Rorty (e.g., 1979: 333), that the enlightenment's self-understanding as having its core in a rejection of traditional metaphysics and/or the adaption of new scientific methodologies is another self-misunderstanding. Further, one might follow Rorty (1989—see the opening quotation from Milan Kundera) in arguing that its real core is in its elevation of tolerance as the preeminent value. But again this validates Nietzsche's point if we follow him in taking the genesis of the value of tolerance to come from Christian values of compassion. What, after all, is tolerance other than an expression of such Christian values as that of turning the other cheek?
14 It is helpful here to distinguish between hypothetical or instrumental values (things that are valuable toward some or other end), final values (things that are valuable in themselves), and ultimate values (final values that trump other final values). Note that this allows that there may be more than one ultimate value in a given moral system.
15 In fact Nietzsche, like Freud after him, suspects that there is an element of suppressed aggressivity in us that allows us, perhaps only unconsciously, to take delight in cruelty. Those who endorse Judeo-Christian values may well acknowledge this claim but would press the point that, regardless of whether or not we do take pleasure in cruelty, we should not do so—that there is nothing praiseworthy in taking such pleasure even if it be in some sense natural to do so.
16 See Huddleston (2014) for more on this.
17 This is not unrelated to that consequentialist argument that claims that it would be better for many of us to be Kantian deontologists rather than consequentialists, since

followers of consequentialism can be led to horrendous actions under the mistaken belief that their actions are maximizing some good. The idea is that subscription to a Kantian ethics that involves an inviolable respect for individuals often yields better consequences than subscription to actual consequentialist ethics. Nietzsche himself would press the point that we should not all be Nietzscheans.

18 A not wholly unrelated point is made by those philosophers of science who claim that truth, although valuable, needs to be weighed against other desiderata—for instance, computable tractability.

19 Also he is against the overvaluing of truth because he thinks that it is somehow self-defeating. Consider the very claim that truth is more valuable than anything else. Is that claim itself true? Barring some implausible realism about such values, it is hard to answer affirmatively. Evolutionary theory might give us an account of why we do in fact value truth. It may even give an instrumental account of why truth is instrumentally valuable: namely, that it is valuable in that it facilitates the end of survival. But what it cannot do is fund the categorical claim that truth is an end in itself and indeed is more valuable than any other end in itself.

20 From *KSA* (13: 56).

21 For more on Nietzsche on modernity and post-modernity, see Gemes (2001).

22 It is tempting to gloss nihilism simply as the absence of values. But without further context that would be misleading. Nietzsche believes that as a matter of fact as long as we are alive we are valuing. For Nietzsche, where there is life there are drives, and where there are drives there is valuing. Your hunger drive does not incline you to value this chapter, although perhaps your intellectual drive does. One might argue that this talk of drives valuing is misleading and that at best drives incline or dispose one to value. Nietzsche, in his desire to belittle the role of active reflection, is perhaps deliberately crude on this point. In his notebooks he says, 'The aim is lacking; "why?" finds no answer. What does nihilism mean? *That the highest values devaluate themselves*' (*KSA* 12: 350). The reference to the absence of an answer to the question 'Why?' suggests that what he means by 'highest' are values capable of bestowing existential meaning.

23 It is worth noting that, where the drives are suppressed in the name of reason, Nietzsche simply takes this as in fact being the suppressing of one drive working through the medium of reason of another drive; 'While "we" believe we are complaining about the vehemence of a drive, at bottom it is one drive *which is complaining about the other*' (*D*: 109). This echoes both Schopenhauer's claim that it is always the will that is the active element in us and the intellect is merely a tool of the will, and to a certain extent Hume's famous dictum in his *Treatise of Human Nature* (1978: 2.3.3): 'Reason is, and ought only to be the slave of the passions, and can never pretend to any other office than to serve and obey them.'

24 For more on Nietzsche on sublimation and repression, see Gemes (2009).

25 Nehamas (1985) argues that a principal aim of Nietzsche's texts is to create the exemplary figure of Nietzsche the philosopher—not as an example to be imitated but, partly, as a figure to inspire others to acts of self-creation.

26 This is not to deny that within the novelist's fictions there may be intimations of greater truths, or perhaps the exhibition of novel and illuminating perspectives. For instance, some credit Turgenev's *Sketches from a Hunter's Notebook* with first showing a generation of Russians, including Tsar Alexander II who freed the serfs, that serfs are also people.

27 Thanks are due to Stephen Hetherington, Gudrun von Tevenar, Simon May, and especially, Andrew Huddleston for comments on earlier drafts.

References

Primary Works (by Friedrich Nietzsche)

(*A*) *The Antichrist* 1968. *Twilight of the Idols and the Antichrist*, trans. R.J. Hollingdale, London: Penguin.
(*BGE*) *Beyond Good and Evil* 1966, trans. W. Kaufmann, New York: Vintage.
(*BT*) *The Birth of Tragedy out of the Spirit of Music* 1993, ed. M. Tanner, trans. S. Whiteside, London: Penguin.
(*EC*) *Ecce Homo* 1969. *On the Genealogy of Morals and Ecce Homo*, trans. W. Kaufmann and R. J. Hollingdale, New York: Vintage.
(*GM*) *On the Genealogy of Morals* 1969. *On the Genealogy of Morals and Ecce Homo*, trans. W. Kaufmann and R. J. Hollingdale, New York: Vintage.
(*GS*) *The Gay Science* 1974, trans. W. Kaufmann, New York: Vintage.
(*KSA*) *Sämtliche Werke: Kritische Studienausgabe in 15 Einzelbänden* 1988, ed. G. Colli and M. Montinari, Berlin: de Gruyter.
(*TI*) *Twilight of the Idols* 1968. *Twilight of the Idols and the Antichrist*, trans. R.J. Hollingdale, London: Penguin.
(*UM*) *Untimely Meditations* 1983, trans. R.J. Hollingdale, Cambridge: Cambridge University Press.
(*Z*) *Thus Spoke Zarathustra* 1975, trans. R. J. Hollingdale, Middlesex: Penguin.

Secondary Sources

Foot, Philippa 2001. Nietzsche: The Revaluation of Values, in *Nietzsche*, ed. John Richardson and Brian Leiter, Oxford: Oxford University Press: 210–20.
Gemes, Ken 2001. Postmodernism's Use and Abuse of Nietzsche, *Philosophy and Phenomenological Research* 62: 337–60.
Gemes, Ken 2009. Freud and Nietzsche on Sublimation, *Journal of Nietzsche Studies* 38: 38–59.
Goodman, Nelson 1952. Sense and Certainty, *Philosophical Review* 61: 160–7.
Goodman, Nelson 1970. Seven Strictures on Similarity, in *Experience and Theory*, ed. Lawrence Foster and J. W. Swanson, Boston: University of Massachusetts Press: 19–29.
Huddleston, Andrew 2014. 'Consecration to Culture': Nietzsche on Slavery and Human Dignity, *Journal of the History of Philosophy* 52: 135–60.
Hume, David 1978 [1739–40]. *A Treatise on Human Nature*, 2nd edn., ed. P. H. Nidditch, Oxford: Clarendon Press.
Nehamas, Alexander 1985. *Nietzsche: Life as Literature*, Cambridge, MA: Harvard University Press.
Pippin, Robert 2010. *Nietzsche, Psychology, and First Philosophy*, Chicago: University of Chicago Press.
Quine, Willard van Orman 1969. *Ontological Relativity and Other Essays*, New York: Columbia University Press.
Quine, Willard van Orman 1974. *The Roots of Reference*, La Salle, IL: Open Court Press.
Richardson, John and Leiter, Brian (eds.) 2001. *Nietzsche*, Oxford: Oxford University Press.
Rorty, Richard 1979. *Philosophy and the Mirror of Nature*, Princeton: Princeton University Press.
Rorty, Richard 1989. *Contingency, Irony, Solidarity*, Cambridge: Cambridge University Press.
Siedentop, Larry 2015. *Inventing the Individual: The Origins of Western Liberalism*, London: Penguin.

13
WHAT MAKES PEIRCE A GREAT PHILOSOPHER?[1]

Cheryl Misak

1. Marks of Greatness

The question of what makes a philosopher one of the *great* philosophers will no doubt itself be a matter of contention. Perhaps one uncontentious thing we might say is that greatness must involve the ability to leap beyond what one's contemporaries are thinking and to launch the state of knowledge into new and unforeseen territory. We might also require the development of a new and original position or tradition, and that the position founded must be *right* or at least profound, not a defective idea that steers us in the wrong direction. We might also require of greatness that it manifest itself in breadth of scope or a contribution to a wide variety of problems. All of this is by way of distinguishing greatness or, to use a similarly amorphous term, 'genius' from mere cleverness, problem-solving ability, impressive facility with numbers, ability to synthesize a large variety of facts, or some such thing.

I shall suggest in the pages that follow that Charles Sanders Peirce (1839–1914), one of the founders of the philosophical tradition of pragmatism, meets this standard. I shall show how Peirce developed a new and promising account of meaning or understanding, as involving the practical effects and the conceptual role of our concepts. I shall also show how this account of meaning issued in new and promising theories of our core philosophical concepts of truth, knowledge, reality, probability, and so on. Those concepts, Peirce argued, must be connected to human belief and inquiry, with all that such a linkage involves.

A final mark of greatness, though, is less obviously met by Peirce. We might think that a philosopher who is truly great must have had a significant influence on the course of the history of philosophy. If no one of note takes up a thinker's ideas, does that not dim the light of even a philosopher of astonishing depth and breadth? It is here that Peirce might seem to have failed to make the bar. While he wanted badly to be considered a great philosopher, he went about it in a self-destructive way. For one thing, he was a difficult man personally. Paul Carus wrote to Lady Victoria Welby in England in 1898, igniting what would become a long and fruitful correspondence between Welby and Peirce:

> Charles S. Peirce . . . is a man of unusual ability, and one of the greatest logicians in the world . . . The sole drawback with him is that he is unmanageable in his private relations, and has thus been frustrated in his career; instead of holding a chair at the university, which would have been the place for him he is sitting on a little farm in Pennsylvania, dissatisfied with all the world, and sometimes even in straightened circumstances . . .
> *(York University: Clara Thomas Archives 1970–003/6)*

The upshot of being unmanageable in his personal relations was that Peirce was almost entirely locked out of academia. After a brief stint at Johns Hopkins, he was dismissed, never again to find work in a university. He published little, and his name was frequently misspelled—even on proofs of his own essays and in the American Philosophical Association's minutes recording his death.

To make matters worse, he had a technical mind and could not, or would not, make many of his ideas accessible to a non-technical audience. Save for a very small handful of friends in America—most notably, William James and Josiah Royce—he was almost completely disregarded in his own country during his lifetime. The international community of logicians knew about his work, but he had a minor impact upon the consciousness of philosophers in other countries. As far as the world of philosophy was concerned, the founder and spokesperson of pragmatism was William James, whose pragmatism was taken to be the doctrine that truth is what works, for this or that person, or this or that community. This version of pragmatism was scorned, and many historians of pragmatism describe the trajectory of the tradition as one always fighting against the philosophical establishment, always on the losing end.

I shall suggest, however, that this understanding of pragmatism is mistaken. Peirce's pragmatism, which is human-centered yet more objective than James's, had a posthumous and profound influence on two (also great) philosophers, C. I. Lewis and Frank Ramsey, who would then go on to shape the course of Western philosophy on both sides of the Atlantic. While these facts are not as well-known as they ought to be, I hope that they seal the question of whether Peirce was one of the great philosophers.

2. The Birth and Essence of Pragmatism

In 1907, Peirce reminisced about the birth of pragmatism:

> It was in the earliest seventies that a knot of us young men in Old Cambridge, calling ourselves, half ironically, half-defiantly, 'The Metaphysical Club',—for agnosticism was then riding its high horse, and was frowning

superbly upon all metaphysics—used to meet, sometimes in my study, sometimes in that of William James. It may be that some of our old-time confederates would today not care to have such wild-oats-sowings made public . . . Mr. Justice Holmes, however, will not, I believe, take it ill that we are proud to remember his membership . . . Chauncey Wright, something of a philosophical celebrity in those days, was never absent from our meetings . . . Wright, James, and I were men of science, rather scrutinizing the doctrines of the metaphysicians on their scientific side than regarding them as very momentous spiritually. The type of our thought was decidedly British. I, alone of our number, had come upon the threshing-floor of philosophy through the doorway of Kant, and even my ideas were acquiring the English accent.

(CP 5.12, 1907)[2]

Peirce always described pragmatism as a team effort, as he does here. Wright died young and even more unpublished than Peirce, but with Darwin as his fan. Peirce worked as a scientist for the U.S. Coast Survey, writing philosophy into the night, until he was fired from that job as well. Holmes's pragmatism has to be excavated from his legal theory, as it does not lie on the surface. It was James who became the face of pragmatism—indeed, he was America's most famous academic, in both philosophy and psychology.

The British accent came from the empiricists and their insistence that our concepts be linked to experience. Alexander Bain was especially important. He had argued that belief is that upon which one is prepared to act—belief must manifest itself in action. From this idea, Peirce said, 'pragmatism is scarce more than a corollary' (CP 5.12, 1907). Peirce made that connection clear in the few papers he published. Six were in, of all things, *Popular Science Monthly*, under the general title 'Illustrations of the Logic of Science'. There were also a few papers published in Paul Carus's *The Monist*. These were all that the philosophical public had access to when it came to understanding Peirce. They treated topics that would stay with Peirce for the rest of his life: belief, doubt, meaning, truth, logic, and probability.

It is the pragmatist theory of truth for which Peirce is best known, and, indeed, it is the essence of pragmatism. One route to it, as Peirce signaled, is via the dispositional account of belief. He argued that our background beliefs are not subject to Cartesian, 'paper', or 'tin' doubts. Such doubts are not genuine and cannot motivate action. An inquirer has a body of settled belief that is not in fact in doubt, against which to assess new evidence and hypotheses, and on which to act. The mere possibility of being mistaken about what one believes is not sufficient to give rise to a living doubt. He put it thus in 'What Pragmatism Is', one of those *Monist* papers:

> there is but one state of mind from which you can 'set out', namely, the very state of mind in which you actually find yourself at the time you do 'set out'—a state in which you are laden with an immense mass of

cognition already formed, of which you cannot divest yourself if you would . . . Do you call it doubting to write down on a piece of paper that you doubt? If so, doubt has nothing to do with any serious business.
(CP 5.416, 1905)

Belief is in part a disposition to act. Once that central idea is accepted, the pragmatist account of truth does indeed come along, almost as a corollary. The way that we evaluate or assess beliefs, or 'habits of action', is by seeing whether they are successful. Setting himself apart from James, Peirce argues that part of what it is to be successful is to not to be 'determined by accidental causes'. If an inquirer sees that a belief of theirs 'is determined by any circumstance extraneous to the facts', they will 'from that moment not merely admit in words that that belief is doubtful, but will experience a real doubt of it, so that it ceases to be a belief' (W 3.253, 1877). Were it to be successful in a robust way, and were that success to be connected to the way things are, then that is all we could mean when we say a belief is true. Truth is that which would be believed, or would stand up to all experience, were inquiry to be pursued as far as it could fruitfully go.

A second route to Peirce's account of truth is via his theory of meaning. Peirce articulated that theory of meaning as a theory of understanding: we 'must look to the upshot of our concepts in order to rightly apprehend them' (CP 5.3, 1902). In addition to the ability to define a concept and to pick out its objects, we need to say what would be different if beliefs about them were true. In order to get a complete grasp of a concept, we must connect it to that with which we have 'dealings' (CP 5.416, 1906). There is a lesson for philosophy here: 'we must not begin by talking of pure ideas—vagabond thoughts that tramp the public roads without any human habitation—but must begin with men and their conversation' (CP 8.112, 1900). Peirce's central idea about meaning is nicely summed up by David Wiggins (2002: 316): When a concept is 'already fundamental to human thought and long since possessed of an autonomous interest', it is pointless to take our task to be one of definition. Rather, we ought to attempt to get leverage on the concept, or a fix on it, by exploring its connections with experience and practice.

When Peirce applies this method to the concept of truth, he sees that the pragmatist must be set against 'transcendental' accounts of truth, such as the correspondence theory, in which a true belief is one that corresponds to, or gets right, or mirrors a believer-independent world (CP 5.572, 1901). Truth must be explained by the role that it plays in our practices of belief and inquiry, and transcendental accounts of truth build into their explanation an unbridgeable gap between truth and what we can know. It is a mark of pragmatism to reject such theories of truth and to replace them with something more human.

While James shared with Peirce these thoughts in their most general outline, the two pragmatists disagreed on some important particulars. James, in 'The

Will to Believe' and in his 1907 book *Pragmatism*, seemed to suggest that, if a belief in God worked for me, then I could take the belief to be true. Peirce thought that James's view amounted to 'Oh, I could not believe so-and-so, because I should be wretched if I did' (CP 5.377, 1877). Peirce was so disconcerted by how some versions of pragmatism were evolving that, in 1905, he tried to rename his position. The term 'pragmatism'

> gets abused in the merciless way that words have to expect when they fall into literary clutches . . . So then, the writer, finding his bantling 'pragmatism' so promoted, feels that it is time to kiss his child good-by and relinquish it to its higher destiny; while to serve the precise purpose of expressing the original definition, he begs to announce the birth of the word 'pragmaticism', which is ugly enough to be safe from kidnappers.
> *(CP 5.414, 1905)*

'Pragmaticism' should be used in a narrow sense—for his position only—and '"pragmatism" should hereafter be used somewhat loosely to signify affiliation with Schiller, James, Dewey, Royce, and the rest of us' (CP 8.205, 1905). But Peirce's new label was indeed ugly, and it never caught on.

Peirce thought that the major difference between his position and that of the other pragmatists was that his version required a belief's working to be connected to the facts. In 'The Fixation of Belief', one of those 'Illustrations of the Logic of Science' papers, he states that a 'fundamental hypothesis' is taken for granted in inquiry: 'There are real things, whose characters are entirely independent of our beliefs about them' and yet these real things can be discovered through empirical investigation (W 3:254, 1877). While this may make him sound like one of those transcendentalists, we shall see later that he means to say the minimum about facts and to escape the charge. And while James also at times asserted that a belief needs to be connected to the facts, he seems, as Tom Donaldson (forthcoming) argues, to have taken this to be a requirement only for what we would call straightforward scientific beliefs and beliefs about middle-sized objects. We shall see below that this goes against the grain of an important and original pillar of classical pragmatism—denying a hard and fast distinction between fact and value, or, to put it another way, having the pragmatist theory of truth range over all of our beliefs.

We already have a hint as to where Kant comes into Peirce's distinctive brand of pragmatism. Peirce argued that is a regulative assumption of belief and inquiry that there is something we are trying to get right. This, however, is all that we can say about the independent world from our human perspective. We cannot somehow step out of our system of belief and inquiry to speak to how the believer-independent world is. This idea might seem entirely due to Kant, but one way in which Peirce's position is groundbreaking is that he wanted to *naturalize* Kant. With respect to the principle of bivalence, which for Peirce is a related regulative assumption of inquiry, he says that

> when we discuss a vexed question, we hope that there is some ascertainable truth about it, and that the discussion is not to go on forever and to no purpose. A transcendentalist would claim that it is an indispensable 'presupposition' that there is an ascertainable true answer to every intelligible question. I used to talk like that, myself; for when I was a babe in philosophy my bottle was filled from the udders of Kant. But by this time I have come to want something more substantial.
> *(CP 2.113, 1902)*

For Peirce, a regulative assumption is a mere 'hope': 'we are obliged to suppose, but we need not assert' it (CP 7.219, 1901). Not only should the fact that an assumption is indispensable to our practices and abilities not convince us that it is a necessary truth; it should not even convince us that it is true. He says this:

> I do not admit that indispensability is any ground of belief. It may be indispensable that I should have $500 in the bank—because I have given checks to that amount. But I have never found that the indispensability directly affected my balance, in the least.
> *(CP 2.113, 1902)*

We must make these assumptions 'for the same reason that a general who has to capture a position or see his country ruined, must go on the hypothesis that there is some way in which he can and shall capture it' (CP 7.219, 1901).

It should be clear that Peirce was a resolute fallibilist. While maintaining that real doubt does not arise from the mere possibility of being mistaken about what one believes, he also held that no belief is, in principle, immune to real doubt. We cannot start with doubting everything, but neither can we start with indubitable propositions. We must start where we find ourselves, with a body of beliefs or expectations already settled and where one (or some relatively small subset) of them is thrown into doubt by a surprising or recalcitrant experience that upsets our expectation. Nor is our aim to arrive at indubitable propositions; it is simply to resettle belief so that this stays perfectly in line with experience and the other aims of inquiry. Nothing can be known with absolute certainty, even though many of our beliefs are practically certain in that they stand up to all experience and inquiry to which they have been exposed. Thus human inquiry 'is not standing upon the bedrock of fact. It is walking upon a bog, and can only say, this ground seems to hold for the present. Here I will stay till it begins to give way' (CP 5.589, 1898).

So, while drawing on British empiricism and on Kant, Peirce carved out a distinctive account of truth and knowledge, based on his pragmatist principle that we must look to how our philosophical concepts are intertwined with our practices. We might as well join everyone else in abandoning Peirce's ugly term for it and call that distinctive position 'pragmatism', remaining alert to the need to distinguish it from the pragmatism of James, Dewey, and those others.

One of its strengths is that it presents a unified account of belief and truth on which all of our legitimate beliefs—in ordinary matters, science, ethics, and so on—are truth-apt. Peirce offers us a broad account of experience and of the kinds of belief that can be evaluated as working or not. Sometimes he gives voice to this insight by distinguishing between two kinds of experience, correlating with two 'worlds' that we inhabit—the inner (or the ideal) and the outer (or the real). We interact with the outer world through a clash between it and our senses. We interact with the inner world by performing thought experiments. Inquiry, he says, has

> two branches; one is inquiry into Outward Fact by experimentation and observation, and is called Inductive Investigation; the other is inquiry into Inner Truth by inward experimentation and observation and is called Mathematical or Deductive Reasoning'.
> *(MS 408.150, 1893–5)*

In another of those *Monist* papers, he puts it thus:

> one can make exact experiments upon uniform diagrams; and when one does so, one must keep a bright outlook for unintended and unexpected changes thereby brought about in the relations of different significant parts of the diagram to one another. Such operations upon diagrams, whether external or imaginary, take the place of the experiments upon real things that one performs in chemical and physical research.
> *(CP 4.530, 1906)*

We have beliefs or expectations or habits of action in mathematics, and they too can be upset or surprised by experience. External facts are simply those that are 'ordinarily regarded as external, while others are regarded as internal' (W 2.205, 1868). The inner world may exert a comparatively slight compulsion upon us, whereas the outer world is full of irresistible compulsions. Nonetheless, the inner world can also be 'unreasonably compulsory' and have 'its surprises for us' (CP 7.659, 1903; CP 7.438, 1893). Peirce intended to leave the difference between these two kinds of experience vague: 'We naturally make all our distinctions too absolute. We are accustomed to speak of an external universe and an inner world of thought. But they are merely vicinities, with no real boundary between them' (CP 7.438, 1893).

He did not consider ethical beliefs in such detail, but here, too, there is room in principle for our ethical beliefs to be truth-apt. True beliefs, on Peirce's view, are habits of action that would be 'indefeasible' (CP 6.485, 1908), and some of our ethical beliefs might well be so. This is a powerful and unified account of truth and knowledge.

3. Logic

While the pragmatist theory of meaning, belief, and truth might be Peirce's most important contribution, it was by no means his only major one. When asked to describe himself, he said he was a 'logician'. W. K. Clifford reportedly thought him to be the greatest living logician, and the only one 'since Aristotle who has added to the subject something material'.[3] John Venn said that

> Mr. C. S. Peirce's name is so well known to those who take an interest in the development of Boolean or symbolic treatment of Logic that the knowledge that he was engaged in lecturing upon the subject to advanced classes at the Johns Hopkins University will have been an assurance that some interesting contributions to the subject might soon be looked for.
> *(1883: 594)*

There were indeed some interesting contributions on Peirce's horizon, even if, by the time he made some of them, he had trouble getting the community of logicians to take proper notice.

Peirce identified three kinds of reasoning, and made significant advances in the study of each of them. The three are deduction, induction, and his own contribution, abduction. Induction and abduction are fundamentally creative or 'ampliative'. They go beyond what is in the premises, unlike deduction, which explicates what is in the premises. They are thus capable of importing new ideas into our body of knowledge.

Abduction, or what we would now call inference to the best explanation, takes this form:

> The surprising fact, C, is observed.
> But if A were true, C would be a matter of course.
> Hence, there is reason to suspect that A is true.
> *(CP 5.189, 1903)*

This mode of inference is 'the operation of adopting an explanatory hypothesis' (CP 5.189, 1903). But, unlike many contemporary philosophers interested in inference to the best explanation, Peirce would not have been happy with the idea that explanatory power is an argument for the belief's corresponding to reality. A hypothesis's being a good or the best explanation of some phenomenon gives us a reason only to suspect that it is true. Once we have a hypothesis on the table as the best explanation, we test it by induction and see whether it holds up. In the meantime, the conclusions of abductive inferences are mere conjectures—we must 'hold ourselves ready to throw them overboard at a moment's notice from experience' (CP 1.634, 1898). For 'abduction commits us to nothing. It merely causes a hypothesis to be set down upon our docket of cases to be tried' (CP 5.602, 1903). It will be clear how consistent this approach is with Peirce's epistemology, outlined in the preceding section. Indeed, Peirce takes the three kinds of inference to lie at the heart of inquiry aimed at the truth.

Peirce takes the first step in inquiry to be an abductive inference. A hypothesis or a conjecture is identified that explains some surprising experience—some exception to what was expected or to what we believe. Consequences are then deduced from this hypothesis and are tested by induction. If the hypothesis passes the test of induction, then it is accepted—it is stable and believed, until upset by a new and surprising experience. Inquiry thus proceeds as follows: from abduction, to deduction, to induction.

Peirce thinks that, because abduction and induction both add to our knowledge, 'some logicians have confounded them.' I have argued that, once we disentangle them, we have a solution to the problem that Hume posed for induction.[4] Hume had delivered a devastating argument to show that the move from 'all observed A's are B's' to 'all A's are B's' is not justifiable. Peirce thought that his pragmatist view bypassed Hume's argument: its conclusion should worry only those who will be satisfied with nothing less than certainty. He argues that the kind of inductive inference with which Hume was concerned—what Peirce calls a 'crude induction'—is a weak form of inference that can be overturned by a single experience. We do, and should, believe that the sun will rise tomorrow; yet it might not. Whether fair or not to Hume, Peirce thinks that Hume's mistake is that he is a deductivist trying to get too much out of induction: 'all the old metaphysicians such as Hume support their scepticism by virtually assuming . . . that the only kind of valid inference is deductive' (Hardwick 1977: 142).

Peirce's deeper solution to Hume's problem anticipates that which was given much later by Nelson Goodman in *Fact, Fiction and Forecast* (1955). In a move well ahead of his time, Peirce thinks that we can see our way through Hume's problem by reframing it as a matter not for induction, but instead for abduction or hypothesis formation. The seemingly unsolvable problem of induction starts to disintegrate once we acknowledge that regularities abound, but that only some of them want explanations. Only unexpected or surprising regularities make a demand on us to make an inference to the best explanation. Once that demand is met by abductive inference, the job of induction is to test those abductive hypotheses. The problem of induction is turned into the problem of which abductively arrived-at hypotheses should be the ones selected for inductive testing.

Peirce also made creative advances in the logic of statistical reasoning. His pragmatist theory of meaning leads him to a hybrid theory of probability. 'To get a clear idea of what we mean by probability, we have to consider what real and sensible difference there is between one degree of probability and another' (W 3.279, 1878). An occurrence is more or less probable because, were an agent to perform indefinitely many inferences concluding that relatively similar events would obtain on the basis of relevantly similar evidence, he would ultimately discover that this sort of inference tended definitively to a certain degree of success. In the long run, the 'fluctuations become less and less; and if we continue long enough, the ratio will approximate toward a fixed limit' (W 3.281, 1878). This might today be called an agency theory of probability, in which probability is a matter of what inferences are good for the agent who is intervening in the world. But, in a signature move, Peirce wants to ensure that probability is grounded in fact. He adopts a kind of frequency theory of probability, applied to the success of inferences. The frequency theory has it that probability is the limit of the relative frequency with which an event occurs. What we mean when we say that 'the probability that this coin will land heads is .5' is that, were we to toss the coin very many times, independently and under conditions as identical as is possible, the percentage of times that the coin lands heads would converge upon 50.

A major problem for the frequency theory is how to make sense of the single case, and Peirce offers a novel solution to it in 'The Doctrine of Chances', another of those 'Illustrations' papers. On the frequency theory,

> in reference to a single case considered in itself, probability can have no meaning. Yet if a man had to choose between drawing a card from a pack containing twenty-five red cards and a black one, or from a pack containing twenty-five black cards and a red one, and if the drawing of a red card were destined to transport him to eternal felicity, and that of a black one to consign him to everlasting woe, it would be folly to deny that he ought to prefer the pack containing the larger proportion of red cards, although, from the nature of the risk, it could not be repeated.
> *(W 3.282–3, 1878)*

Peirce's solution coheres perfectly with his view that truth is what we would eventually come to, were we able to experiment into the indefinite future. He says that

> logicality inexorably requires that our interests shall not be limited. They must not stop at our own fate, but must embrace the whole community. This community, again, must not be limited, but must extend to all races of beings with whom we can come into immediate or mediate intellectual relation. It must reach, however vaguely, beyond this geological epoch, beyond all bounds. He who would not sacrifice his own soul to save the whole world, is, as it seems to me, illogical in all his inferences, collectively. Logic is rooted in the social principle.
> *(W 3.284, 1878)*

We need not actually engage in 'the heroism of self-sacrifice' in order to make sense of single-case probabilities. The requirement is merely that each of us should 'perceive that only that man's inferences who has it are really logical, and should consequently regard his own as being only so far valid as they would be accepted by the hero' (W 3.284, 1878). Inquiry and rationality involve getting our beliefs in line with experience, evidence, and reasons in an ongoing project. Logic or rational inquiry is rooted in a 'social principle', for investigation into what is true is not a private interest but is rather an interest 'as wide as the community can turn out to be' (W 2.271–2, 1868). Rationality is social in nature because it requires more evidence than what is before an individual or even before a community. In our efforts to understand reality, 'each of us is an insurance company' (W 2.270, 1869). We make bets that will pay out (or not) later. If 'the whole utility of probability is to insure us in the long run', then, to be fully insured, we need to collect, evaluate, and scrutinize as much evidence as we can. The more evidence that one takes in, the more likely one is to have successful actions. Peirce's pragmatist account of truth extends over all communities and times. What this or that community takes to be true is only a small part of the story.

Finally, what Peirce was most proud of was his formal logic or 'Existential Graphs'. In 1896, when he was 57, he developed a quantified, sound, and complete first-order diagrammatic logic.[5] The Alpha graphs cover propositional logic, the Beta extension covers first-order predicate logic with identity, and the Gamma extension covers modal notions, abstractions, and a meta-language for talking about the graphs themselves. This was done entirely independently of, and at the same time as, Frege developing his own system. The two great logicians seemed to be only dimly aware of each other. But once Frege's algebraic approach became dominant, Peirce's diagrammatic system appeared unfamiliar and cumbersome.[6] It thus remained buried, except to a few select logicians, during and after Peirce's lifetime. Don Roberts published his book on the graphs in 1973, but it is only now that Peirce's logic has stepped into (a rarified) light, with the artificial intelligence community seeing real value in the diagrammatic nature of his system. Peirce's logical graphs can represent abstract logical form, and they have been used to represent, for instance, the conceptual schemas in database systems.[7]

4. Perception, Categories, Signs

The third major contribution that I will discuss here is Peirce's intertwined account of perception, categories, and signs. James put forward a similar account of perception, and of course Kant and Aristotle attempted to set out a complete categorization of what is in the world. But the theory of signs is a novel contribution entirely of Peirce's. Indeed, he is thought of as the founder of semiotics or the theory of signs. Certain of his ideas in this realm, such as the type-token distinction, permeate contemporary philosophy. In Peirce's own words, not frequently reproduced in contemporary literature, that distinction is as follows:

> A common mode of estimating the amount of matter in a . . . printed book is to count the number of words. There will ordinarily be about twenty the's on a page, and of course they count as twenty words. In another sense of the word 'word', however, there is but one word 'the' in the English language; and it is impossible that this word should lie visibly on a page, or be heard in any voice . . . Such a . . . Form, I propose to term a Type. A . . . single object . . . such as this or that word on a single line of a single page of a single copy of a book, I will venture to call a Token.
> *(CP 5.537, 1906)*

Peirce's theory of signs is triadic, in a number of ways, and we shall see this triadicity appear also in his theory of perception and categories. First, the structure of representation itself is triadic, always involving a sign, an object, and an interpreter. Second, the relation between a sign and its object can take three forms, corresponding to icons, indices, and symbols.

Icons are signs that represent their objects by virtue of a similarity or resemblance—a portrait is an icon of the person it portrays, a map is an icon of a certain geographic area and, in exact logic, a diagram is an icon of validity's key forms. An icon represents structure. *Indices* are signs that point to their object by 'being really connected with it' (W 2.56, 1867)—a pointing finger, a demonstrative pronoun such as 'this' draws the interpreter's attention to the object. Smoke, for instance, is an index of fire. A *symbol* is a word, proposition, or argument that depends on conventional or habitual rules; a symbol is a sign 'because it is used and understood as such' (CP 2.307, 1901). This set of sign-types plays an important role in structuring thought. Symbols in their role as habits established by convention pick out general concepts. Indices in their role as unmediated pointers pick out specific individuals (and locate us in the real world at a particular place and time). Icons, in their role of conveying structure, might be said to represent logical form.

Peirce's categories also structure thought. He called them *Firstness, Secondness,* and *Thirdness.* Each of these categories, he argued, is present in everything that comes before the mind or everything that is experienced. In his early career he derived them—in the spirit of Kant—from the structure of the proposition, whereby a predicate (First) and its subject (Second) are united by a copula (Third). The key paper here is 'On a New List of Categories', in which Peirce was proud that he had reduced Kant's table of 12 to 3. Later in life he kept the same categories but pushed the derivation of them deeper, into phenomenology and mathematics, the latter being, for Peirce, the most fundamental science of all.

It is important to note that Peirce's categories are not properties but are *modes of being* that cannot actually be pulled apart. They are distinguished from one

What Makes Peirce a Great Philosopher? 239

another by the Aristotelian and then Scholastic method of abstraction or 'prescission', in which we may distinguish different elements of a concept by attending to particular elements and neglecting others. A First is something simple, monadic—a quality of feeling, image, or mere possibility. It is indescribable: 'It cannot be articulately thought: assert it, and it has already lost its characteristic innocence . . . Stop to think of it, and it has flown!' (CP 1.357, 1890). The difficulty of pinning down a category that is 'a special suchness' is not lost on Peirce (CP 1.303, 1894). It is perhaps helpful to focus on the idea that Firstness comes first: it is 'predominant' in being, in feeling, and in the ideas of life and freedom (CP 1.302, 1894). Even more importantly, given the continuity of Peirce's metaphysics with his logic of relations, a First is singular: 'a pure nature . . . in itself without parts or features, and without embodiment' (CP 1.303, 1894). The First is a relatum prior to any relation, that which makes relations possible.

A Second is a dyadic element—the duality of action and reaction. It is the category that 'the rough and tumble of life renders most familiarly prominent. We are continually bumping up against hard fact' (CP 1.324, 1903), and hence having revealed to us 'something within and another something without' (CP 2.84, 1902). But, as with the first category, this is all that we can say of our encounters with hard fact. Any articulation or thought of what we experience takes us into the third category—the triadic realm of experience proper, which involves interpretation, signification, intention, and purpose realized across time. As soon as we try to describe our encounters with the world, thought and symbols are involved.

While Peirce's theory of signs and categories is too complex to adequately explain here, that last sentence should make it clear enough how they are connected. His account of perception is also of a piece with his theory of signs and categories. Any perception that we can think of ourselves as having is a perceptual *judgment*, something that requires, in Peirce's terms, 'mediation' by some general concept. For instance, when I see a yellow chair, I see it *as* yellow, *as* a chair (CP 7.619–30, 1903). Peirce describes what he sees in his study:

> But hold: what I have written down is only an imperfect description of the percept that is forced upon me. I have endeavored to state it in words. In this there has been an endeavor, purpose—something not forced upon me but rather the product of reflection . . . I recognize that there is a percept or flow of percepts very different from anything I can describe or think. What precisely that is, I cannot even tell myself . . . I am forced to content myself not with the fleeting percepts, but with the crude and possibly erroneous thoughts, or self-informations, of what the percepts were.
> *(CP 2.141, 1902)*

As soon as we try to describe our encounters with the world, thought and language are involved. Any perception that we can think of ourselves as having is a perceptual judgment, something that requires a 'theory of interpretation' (CP 5.183, 1903) and all three categories.

Here we can see how Peirce's position is distinguished from another of the dominant and competing accounts of truth and knowledge of Peirce's time—the Hegelian idealism that was so popular on both sides of the Atlantic. Peirce thought that Hegel had things right, but for the fact that he whitewashed out the category of immediacy or Secondness:

> The truth is that pragmaticism is closely allied to the Hegelian absolute idealism, from which, however, it is sundered by its vigorous denial that the third category . . . suffices to make the world, or is even so much as self-sufficient. Had Hegel, instead of regarding the first two stages with his smile of contempt, held on to them as independent or distinct elements of the triune Reality, pragmatists might have looked up to him as the great vindicator of their truth.
>
> *(CP 5.436, 1904)*

The categories also present a new angle from which to view Peirce's argument against the correspondence theory. We have no unmediated access to the objects to which our beliefs are supposed to correspond. Everything we experience, in other words, is a mix of mind and the world. Our beliefs about what we experience are thus fallible. '[G]oing back to the first impressions of sense . . . would be the most chimerical of undertakings' (CP 2.141, 1902), and thus

> the knowledge with which I have to content myself, and have to call 'the evidence of my senses', instead of being in truth the evidence of the senses, is only a sort of stenographic report of that evidence, possibly erroneous.
>
> *(CP 2.141, 1902)*

Peirce is clear about this as early as 1868, in another of those rare published papers, 'Questions Concerning Certain Faculties Claimed for Man'. His key claim in this essay is that we cannot have an infallible intuition or a 'cognition not determined by a previous cognition . . . and therefore so determined by something outside of consciousness' (W 2.193, 1868). He says the following about the purported special faculty of intuition:

> There is no evidence that we have this faculty, except that we seem to feel that we have it. But the weight of that testimony depends entirely on our being supposed to have the power of distinguishing in this feeling whether the feeling be the result of education, old associations, etc., or whether it is an intuitive cognition; or, in other words, it depends on presupposing the very matter testified to. Is this feeling infallible? And is this judgment concerning it infallible, and so on, ad infinitum? Supposing

that a man really could shut himself up in such a faith, he would be, of course, impervious to the truth, 'evidence-proof'.

(W 2.194, 1868)

Being evidence-proof, for Peirce, would be a terrible thing. He thought that the following rule 'ought to be inscribed upon every wall in the city of philosophy: Do not block the way of inquiry' (CP 1.135, 1899). That slogan is a good summary of the insight beating at the heart of Peirce's pragmatism. It was a novel idea in 1868, and might well be thought of as the start of the new discipline that we call modern philosophy of science.

5. Influence

We have plenty with which to justify Peirce's greatness in terms of depth and breath. His pragmatism was a novel and important new position in the philosophical landscape. He argued that our philosophical concepts be linked to experience and practice, and he followed through on this idea by developing sophisticated accounts of our central philosophical concepts so that they are not vagabond thoughts tramping the public roads without any human habitation. He gave us a theory of belief on which belief is a disposition to act and hence is evaluable in human terms. He gave us a theory of truth on which what it is for a belief—any kind of belief—to be true is for it to be 'indefeasible' or for it to be the best that it could be as a belief. He gave us accounts of perception, signs, and reality that cohere with this human-centered account of truth.

But it would be a fly in the ointment of Peirce's alleged greatness if no one ever saw these ideas as important. Richard Rorty, one of the best-known pragmatists of the twentieth century, was of that view. He said that Peirce's 'contribution to pragmatism was merely to have given it a name, and to have stimulated James's' (1982: 61). Rorty didn't like Peirce's idea that there were right answers to our questions, and said that Peirce was engaged in 'just one more attempt to escape from time into eternity' (2010: 3). He compared the pragmatist Wilfrid Sellars with Peirce:

> That mixture of logic-worship, erudition, and romance was reminiscent of Peirce, with whose writings I had spent a lot of time, hoping to discover the nonexistent secret of his nonexistent 'System' . . . . Sellars and Peirce are alike in the diversity and richness of their talents, as well as in the cryptic style in which they wrote. But Sellars, unlike Peirce, preached a coherent set of doctrines.
>
> *(2010: 8)*

Peirce, said Rorty, was a 'system builder' and Sellars 'the debunking sort' (2010: 11). Rorty preferred those pragmatists who did away with the idea of truth and he took Dewey, James, and Wittgenstein to be the inspiration of his own debunking brand of pragmatism.

If Peirce's ideas didn't even get traction amongst pragmatists, then does that not dim the claim to his greatness? Fortunately, we do not have to try to answer the difficult and contentious questions about the relationship between lack of influence and lack of greatness. For not only is Rorty wrong in his assessment of Peirce's ideas; he is also wrong in saying that Peirce's major contribution was to stimulate James. Peirce in fact had a major influence on the course of philosophy, even if that influence is subterranean[8] or in need of excavation. For he had a profound impact on two of the greatest philosophers of the twentieth century, C.I. Lewis and Frank Ramsey, and their Peircean pragmatist ideas in turn have transformed philosophy. Lewis went on to teach and impart his ideas to a generation of famous Harvard pragmatists: Sellars, Quine, Goodman, and Putnam, to name the most prominent. Ramsey went on to influence Wittgenstein. That is, even two of Rorty's heroes, Sellars[9] and Wittgenstein, owe a tremendous debt to Peirce. The reasons for Peirce's influence being so subterranean are fascinating. I can only gesture at them here.

When Lewis returned to Harvard as a faculty member in 1920, he 'practically lived with [the] manuscript remains' of Peirce for two years. This massive bulk of papers had been left to Harvard in a state of disarray by Peirce's widow, and there was some hope that Lewis would start to put them into order (1968: 16). He was already on a Peircean path, guided there by Royce. Lewis dipped in and out of the Peirce papers for those two years, coming to the opinion that the 'originality and wealth [of this] legendary figure' was not fully evident in Peirce's meager published writings and not well represented by other pragmatists (1970 [1930]: 78). It is clear that he studied these papers closely. His writing teems with Peirce's language and thoughts. He adopts Peirce's pragmatist account of experience, meaning, and truth (if not precisely his account of belief), and he expands on how it might allow ethical beliefs to be responsive to experience and to aim at truth. He also had a Peircean, pragmatist, account of the *a priori*, on which

> we confront what is presented by the senses with certain ready-made distinctions, relations, and ways of classifying. In particular, we impose upon experience certain patterns of temporal relationships, a certain order ... It is by interpretation that the infant's buzzing, blooming confusion gives way to an orderly world of things.
>
> *(1970 [1926]: 250)*

As soon as one makes a statement or forms a belief about what one observes, the statement or belief contains much more than is given to us by our senses. Interpretation is constrained by what is given to us in experience, and it is 'subject to the check of further experience'. But this does not 'save' or guarantee an interpretation's validity, for we bring a wealth of concepts to what is given in experience. His students, Quine, Goodman, and Morton White, who did not much like him, wrongly accused Lewis of appealing to the myth of the given—to the idea that something is given to us with notion of certainty. But in fact they adopted Lewis's (Peircean) position almost in whole. (The exception is Quine, who retained the fact-value dichotomy and hence, in the end, can just barely be called a pragmatist.)

That is a tremendous influence on one side of the Atlantic. On the other, we have Frank Ramsey being introduced to Peirce by his mentor, C. K. Ogden. Ogden himself had encountered Peirce by Lady Victoria Welby, who we have seen was one of Peirce's rare intellectual correspondents. Ogden gave Ramsey the letters that Peirce wrote to Welby, and in 1923, when Peirce's first volume of posthumously published essays was brought out in America by Harcourt and Brace, Ogden simultaneously published it in England. Ramsey's diaries in early 1924 show him reading Peirce, and he was from then on to fully acknowledge Peirce in his work.

Ramsey adopted Peirce's account of belief as a habit, to be judged by whether or not it works, and by whether or not that working is connected to the facts. Indeed, Ramsey is famous for figuring out how to measure partial belief—by looking to how we act, especially in betting contexts. He was also coming around to other parts of Peirce's position, including his stance on truth. Had Ramsey not died in 1930, just shy of his 27th birthday and in the middle of writing a book titled *On Truth*, his brand of Peircean pragmatism would be much more in the public view. It is undergoing a renaissance only now.

Ramsey also put sustained pragmatist objections to the position that his friend Wittgenstein had articulated in the *Tractatus*. Truth, Ramsey argued, cannot be a one-to-one isomorphism between simple items in a sentence and simple objects in the independent world. For that position leaves out countless kinds of beliefs: scientific hypotheses, open generalizations, causal laws, counterfactual conditionals, ethical beliefs, and so on. We need a more human account of belief and truth. Wittgenstein was persuaded in 1929, the last year of Ramsey's life and the first year of Wittgenstein's return to Cambridge after his long exile after the Great War. He moved to the idea that meaning is to be explicated in terms of how we actually use language and concepts. So Peirce, through Ramsey, was responsible for one of the most significant movements in the history of philosophy, although I think that neither Peirce nor Ramsey would have liked the direction in which Wittgenstein took their pragmatism.

In any event, Peircean pragmatism is alive and well these days, in all of the accounts of truth and knowledge inspired by the Lewis/Sellars nexus and by the Ramsey/Wittgenstein nexus. John McDowell is but one example of the former and Huw Price but one example of the latter. It turns out that Peircean pragmatism, not always traveling under the banner of Peirce or, indeed, even the banner of pragmatism, remains one of the leading contenders for how we should see ourselves and our aspirations for getting things right in a world not of our making.

Notes

1 This paper draws on Misak (2013, 2016a) and Legg and Misak (2016).
2 References to Peirce's published material are as follows. *Collected Papers*, 'CP n. m', where n is the volume number, m the paragraph number; *Writings of Charles S. Peirce: Chronological Edition*: 'W n: m' where n is the volume, m the page number.
3 See Fisch (1964: 461).
4 See Misak (1991, 2013, 2016a).
5 See Legg and Misak (2016) for a more sustained discussion.
6 See Quine (1935) for the expression of this opinion.
7 See Sowa (1984), the articles collected in Lukose, Delugach, Keeler, Searle, and Sowa (1997), and Shin (1994).
8 The term 'subterranean' is from Thomas Uebel (2015). See also Misak (2016b).
9 See Misak (2013) for the argument, as opposed to what I do here, which is merely setting out Sellars's lineage.

References

Donaldson, Tom forthcoming. What Was James's Theory of Truth? in *The Oxford Handbook of William James*, ed. Alex Klein, Oxford: Oxford University Press.
Fisch, Max H. 1964. A Chronicle of Pragmaticism, 1865–1879, *Monist* 48: 441–66.
Goodman, Nelson 1955. *Fact, Fiction, and Forecast*, Cambridge, MA: Harvard University Press.
Hardwick, Charles (ed.) 1977. *Semiotics and Significs: The Correspondence between Charles S. Peirce and Victoria Lady Welby*, Bloomington: Indiana University Press.
James, William 1975 [1907]. *Pragmatism: A New Name for Some Old Ways of Thinking*, ed. F.H. Burkhard, F. Bowers, and I.K. Skrupskelis, Cambridge MA: Harvard University Press.
Legg, Catherine and Cheryl Misak 2016. Charles Sanders Peirce on Necessity, in Logical Modalities from Aristotle to Carnap: *Logical Modalities from Aristotle to Carnap: The Story of Necessity*, ed. M. Cresswell and E. Mares, Cambridge: Cambridge University Press.
Lewis, Clarence Irving 1968. Autobiography, in *The Philosophy of C.I. Lewis*, ed. Paul Arthur Schilpp, La Salle, IL: Open Court: 1–21.
Lewis, Clarence Irving 1970 [1926]. The Pragmatic Element in Knowledge, in *Collected Papers of Clarence Irving Lewis*, ed. John D. Goheen and John L. Mothershead, Jr., Stanford: Stanford University Press: 240–57.
Lewis, Clarence Irving 1970 [1930]. Pragmatism and Current Thought, in *Collected Papers of Clarence Irving Lewis*, ed. John D. Goheen and John L. Mothershead, Jr., Stanford: Stanford University Press: 78–86.
Lukose, Dickson, Delugach, Harry, Keeler, Mary, Searle, Leroy, and Sowa, John (eds.) 1997. *Conceptual Structures: Fulfilling Peirce's Dream, Fifth International Conference on Conceptual Structures, ICCS'97, Seattle, Washington, USA, August 3–8, 1997, Proceedings*, Berlin: Springer.
Misak, Cheryl 1991. *Truth and the End of Inquiry: A Peircean Account of Truth*, Oxford: Oxford University Press.
Misak, Cheryl 2013. *The American Pragmatists*, Oxford: Oxford University Press.

Misak, Cheryl 2016a. *Cambridge Pragmatism: From Peirce and James to Ramsey and Wittgenstein*, Oxford: Oxford University Press.
Misak, Cheryl 2016b. The Subterranean Influence of Pragmatism on the Vienna Circle: Ramsey and Peirce, *Journal for the History of Analytic Philosophy*. 4(5): 1–15.
Peirce, Charles Sanders 1931–58. *Collected Papers of Charles Sanders Peirce*, 8 vols., ed. C. Hartshorne, P. Weiss (vols. I–VI), and A. W. Burks (vols. VII–VIII), Cambridge, MA: Harvard University Press.
Peirce, Charles Sanders 1982–. *The Writings of Charles S. Peirce: A Chronological Edition*, ed. The Peirce Edition Project, Bloomington: Indiana University Press.
Quine, Willard Van Orman. 1935. Review of the Collected Papers of Charles Sanders Peirce, vol. 4: The Simplest Mathematics, *Isis* 22: 551–3.
Roberts, Don D. 1973. The Existential Graphs of Charles S. Peirce, The Hague: Mouton.
Rorty, Richard 1982. *Consequences of Pragmatism (Essays: 1972–1980)*, Minneapolis: University of Minnesota Press.
Rorty, Richard 2010. Intellectual Autobiography, in *The Philosophy of Richard Rorty*, ed. Randall Auxier and Lewis Hahn, Chicago: Open Court: 1–24.
Shin, Sun-Joo 1994. *The Logical Status of Diagrams*, Cambridge: Cambridge University Press.
Sowa, John F. 1984. *Conceptual Structures: Information Processing in Mind and Machine*, Reading, MA: Addison-Wesley.
Uebel, Thomas 2015. American Pragmatism and the Vienna Circle: The Early Years, *Journal for the History of Analytic Philosophy* 3: 1–35.
Venn, John 1883. Review of Studies in Logic, *Mind* 8: 594–603.
Welby, Victoria. *Welby Fonds*, York University Libraries, Clara Thomas Archives and Special Collections.
Wiggins, David 2002. An Indefinibilist cum Normative View of Truth and the Marks of Truth, in *What Is Truth?* ed. Richard Shantz, Berlin: de Gruyter, 316–32.

14
WITTGENSTEIN'S UN-RULEY SOLUTION TO THE PROBLEM OF PHILOSOPHY

David Macarthur

> Philosophy is a battle against the bewitchment of our intelligence by means of language.
> —Wittgenstein[1]

1. Introduction

The present volume is devoted to the question of what makes philosophers great. I would like to approach the question of Wittgenstein's greatness as a philosopher—which I shall take to mean his *originality* as a philosopher—by attempting to characterize his discovery of a new way or manner of philosophizing as we find it expressed in *Philosophical Investigations*, Part 1—a work that he prepared for publication and that is widely regarded as the most definitive presentation of his so-called later philosophy.[2] I mean this to be a response to the widespread sense, as Crispin Wright (1980: 162) puts it, that 'Wittgenstein's later views on philosophy constitute one of the least well understood aspects of his thought.' For present purposes I shall leave aside the question of how much continuity there is between early, middle, and later Wittgenstein; or, indeed, whether there is a final shift in his outlook expressed in unpublished notes written at the end of his life in the period 1949–51.[3] Moreover, I shall not be concerned with his diagnoses of particular philosophical problems.[4] The aim of the chapter is to explain why Wittgenstein's philosophy takes an unassertive form, a philosophy without theses.

We can summarize Wittgenstein's originality in philosophy like this: he found a novel way of continuing to do philosophy—that is, something that, while diverging from traditional philosophy, still merits the name of 'philosophy'—in the face of a perception (that metaphysics is an illusion of explanation) and a commitment (that philosophy is not science and not dependent on science) that jointly seem to make it impossible to philosophize any more.

In the first place, Wittgenstein had a keen sense of the unintelligibility, or partial intelligibility, of a good deal of traditional philosophy, which inspired in him a pervasive skepticism about metaphysics that he likens to an 'illness' requiring 'treatment'—a skepticism strikingly akin in many respects to ancient Pyrrhonian skepticism.[5] Second, Wittgenstein had an abiding commitment to the traditional idea that philosophy is a *conceptual* activity (hence, one involving norms of the correct use of concepts) that does not require or depend upon scientific inquiry concerning empirical facts about what causes what. He opposed any attempt to 'naturalize' the subject of philosophy by modeling it on scientific modes of inquiry or making it answerable to new scientific discoveries.[6] If there is no such thing as *a priori* metaphysics and no such thing as a scientific or science-based philosophy, then it seems unclear what could *possibly* count as doing philosophy in so far as this is not merely imagining doing philosophy.

As is well-known, Wittgenstein's solution to the problem of the very possibility of philosophy is the ingenious proposal that 'All philosophy is "critique of language"' (1961: 4.0031). Since traditional philosophical thoughts are expressed in language we can study these thoughts by studying the language that expresses them (cf. sec. 120). As we have knowledge of our native language, the language of which each of us is a master, independently of any empirical investigation, then reflection on this knowledge—at least as it bears on philosophical (that is, metaphysical) expressions—can plausibly count as a continuation of philosophy. But what is it to *know* our native tongue? And how is a 'critique' of that a fitting subject matter for philosophy?

Wittgenstein remarks (1998: 13):

> The limit of language manifests itself in the impossibility of describing the fact that corresponds to (is the translation of) a sentence without simply repeating the sentence.
>
> (We are involved here with the Kantian solution of the problem of philosophy.)

In this passage Wittgenstein refers to 'the problem of philosophy', which, I take it, concerns the traditional question of the relation between thought and the world. In effect, he proposes that this problem is superannuated by, or absorbed into, the problem of the relation between language and the world, since language is the expression of thought. The 'solution' (or, better, dissolution) is to show that there is an internal relation between language and the world. The 'limit of language' reveals itself in coming to appreciate that the only way to explain the relation between language and the world is in terms of our prior world-involving understanding of language; and that would not really be *explaining* it at all—certainly not explaining it as philosophers had hoped to do.[7] The 'solution' is Kantian (but not Kant's) in so far as there is an analogy between 'explaining' language's internal relation to the world and Kant's more metaphysically substantial explanation of reason's internal relation to the world, both of which are achievable by a method of self-knowledge independently of any empirical inquiry.

In Wittgenstein's case a philosophical study of 'objects' can be conducted by studying our *concepts* of 'objects', which we study, in turn, by investigating the logic of language ('grammar').[8] Hence, on this conception, philosophical investigations are grammatical investigations. And, as Wittgenstein remarks, 'Grammar tells what kind of object anything is. (Theology as grammar)' (sec. 373). In revealing grammatical (internal) connections between a concept of an 'object' and other concepts, we identify the kind of object that is in question. In surveying grammar, we survey the 'objects' that constitute the world.[9]

Thus philosophy, as Wittgenstein practices it, satisfies the two conditions that originally seemed jointly unsatisfiable. It is a conceptual (hence normative) investigation, and in that sense akin to traditional (*a priori*) philosophy—that is, in not being a form of empirical or scientific knowledge acquired by postulation and experiment. Yet, unlike traditional philosophy, it is not a form of *a priori* metaphysical assertion. Knowledge of language is, then, not a form of empirical knowledge nor a form of traditional *a priori* knowledge (since, for one thing, it depends on all sorts of empirical conditions of learning and training). One could think of it as an unheralded form of knowledge that replaces the *a priori*. But this simply returns us to the question: what (kind of) knowledge is that? And how does it relate to the activity of philosophy?

2. What Is 'Knowledge' of Language?

Knowledge of language, in the sense relevant to philosophy, is, as we have seen, knowledge of grammar (or what Wittgenstein calls 'the logic of our language': sec. §38). It concerns concepts (hence judgments), their interrelationships with each other, and background conditions for their application (for example, 'general facts of nature': sec. 143). If that is the subject-matter of philosophy, then how do we know or have access to it? One answer that Wittgenstein puts on the table for consideration is this: philosophy is concerned with knowing and applying what he is happy to call 'the rules of grammar' (sec. 497)—or, in the secondary literature, what are simply called 'the rules of language'—perhaps especially where these rules have been misapplied or otherwise misused. This rule-governed conception of language seems to fit well with Wittgenstein's comparing language to games played according to definite rules (for example, chess) and his talking, apparently in his own voice, of 'the system of rules for the use of words' (sec. 133).

Many passages suggest this rule-based conception of language, of which one example is this (sec. 372):

> Consider: 'The only correlate in language to an intrinsic necessity is an arbitrary rule. It is the only thing which one can milk out of this intrinsic necessity into a proposition.'

Furthermore, Wittgenstein speaks of philosophy as the attempt to understand the confusion arising from 'entanglement in our own rules' (sec. 125).

Unsurprisingly, a widely popular view holds that philosophy, as Wittgenstein intends it, is based on our knowledge of the rules of language and diagnosing how we go wrong in applying these rules in spite of this knowledge.[10] Of course, it will not do to think of this knowledge as wholly unconscious as in, say, Chomskian linguistics, since philosophy surely involves bringing this knowledge to mind through reflection.[11] But even if we suppose that by 'knowledge' we mean something of which we are aware, or can bring to awareness, there remains a problem since, in speaking, we are obviously not operating according to any rule book, for there is none.[12] Learning language is a mysterious kind of osmosis where, after being exposed to a few sample uses of a term (for example, 'dog', 'red', 'smile', 'two', 'and') in a relatively small number of contexts, infants are able to go on to apply the term more or less correctly to indefinitely many new cases to which they have never been exposed previously. It is somewhat surprising, then, that Peter Hacker, a notable Wittgenstein interpreter, writes, 'everything relevant to a philosophical problem lies open to view in our rule-governed use of words' (1997: 9–10). We surely must ask, with mounting suspicion, *how* are the rules of language supposed to be 'open to view'? *What* rules? 'Open', in what sense?

Clearly, learning a language is not a matter of memorizing fixed rules for the use of words. If we are asked what the rules are for the use of some common term (e.g., 'chair'), we have great trouble in formulating them and our efforts in doing so are easily demonstrated to be quite inadequate to explain our ability to use the term in question (e.g., 'an artifact made to sit on' does not distinguish a chair from a fence, or a bed). Moreover, there are conceptual difficulties in the very idea of philosophy as a matter of knowing the rules of language. If we think that we can explain language in terms of explicit rules of use, then presumably we must suppose that any rule of use itself requires a further explicit rule for its correct application; but that, in turn, requires a higher-level explicit rule for its correct application and so on *ad infinitum*—an intolerable regress.

Consequently, if we are to do justice to the phenomenology of language use—which is very *unlike* playing a game like chess according to strict rules laid down in a rule book—as well as avoiding the explanatory infinite regress of rules for the application of rules, there is available the move of supposing that, for Wittgenstein, the rules of language that are the subject matter of philosophy are *implicit* in practice. This contrasts with rules explicitly formulated in propositions. Brandom, a leading defender of this line of interpretation, sums up what he takes to be Wittgenstein's key insight (1994: 20):

> proprieties governed by explicit rules rest on proprieties governed by practice. Norms that are explicit in the form of rules presuppose norms implicit in practices.

Knowledge of the rules of language is, on this line, a kind of implicit practical know-how. But how helpful is *that* as a conception of what the philosopher reflects upon?

It is important to see that what is doing most of the work in Brandom's conception is not the misleading distinction between know-how and know-that. For one thing, it is not an exclusive distinction. Theoretical work (for example, academic research, science, devising proofs, drawing inferences) is also a practice, so we can regard knowing-that as a kind of intellectual know-how. The crucial move is the claim that the relevant linguistic know-how is *implicit* in practice, so not rendered in propositional form. But, from the point of view of Wittgenstein's vision of philosophy, this conception suffers from two major disadvantages.

First, since philosophy is rendered in propositions we now need to be told *how* we are to translate implicit know-how into explicit propositions—that is, how are we to 'make it explicit' (in Brandom's catch-cry)? This is anything but straightforward since we are not, for the most part, aware of how we speak and write correctly.[13] Clearly, we are typically not aware of appealing to rules in our use of language; nor do we normally think of ourselves as producers of isolable 'meanings' with their own distinctive normative structures. These are matters we are *only* required to formulate if and when communication breaks down (cf. Riemer 2016: 5).

Second, one might think that it is not true that our linguistic know-how is *entirely* implicit, since we might suppose that we can produce a few examples of explicit rules of correct usage. For example, it might be said that if one ascribes *knowing that p* to someone then that implies that p is *true*; or that if we call something *red all over* then we cannot also call it *green* in part or whole. But if we doubt such things—for example, in the first case suppose that p is 'This sentence is false'; and, in the second, why could we not call a substance reddish-green when it reflects light only in that part of the spectrum where the reflectance profiles of green and red overlap?—then how can we tell whether they are *correct* translations of our implicit know-how?

What is clear is that it is one thing to *use* language and quite another to *describe this use* for philosophical (namely, conceptual) clarificatory purposes, such as showing that the metaphysical use of words falls to pieces under close scrutiny.

We do the first as a matter of course; but the second is something which we have little or no idea how to do. As Wittgenstein puts it (sec 122, 1967: sec. 111, respectively):

> A main source of our failure to understand is that we do not *command a clear view* of the use of our words.—Our grammar is lacking in this sort of perspicuity.
>
> We are not at all *prepared* for the task of describing the use of the word e.g., 'to think'.

The key to understanding Wittgenstein's new conception of philosophizing is to understand how he approaches the task of describing our use of language.

3. The Rules of Language vs. Criteria for the Use of Words

I now want to argue that the overwhelming emphasis of Wittgenstein's interpreters on something called *the rules of language*, and of philosophy as centrally concerned with knowing and following the rules of language, is seriously misguided. Indeed, I suggest that it is much more fruitful and illuminating to read Wittgenstein as wrestling to free himself from a conception of language as rule-governed that he endorsed in the *Tractatus* and which continues to cling to his thinking like eggshells (as he puts it), even *after* considerable self-criticism.[14] In sections 81–85 of the *Investigations*, for example, the idea that we can put any weight on the notion of rules of language in the attempt to explain our use of language is under sustained and withering criticism. For example, consider this passage (sec. 82):

> What do I call 'the rule by which he proceeds'?—The hypothesis that satisfactorily describes his use of words, which we observe; or the rule which he looks up when he uses signs; or the one which he gives us in reply if we ask him what his rule is?—But what if observation does not enable us to see any clear rule, and the question brings none to light?—For he did indeed give me a definition when I asked him what he understood by 'N', but he was prepared to withdraw and alter it.—So how am I to determine the rule according to which he is playing? He does not know it himself.—Or, to ask a better question: What meaning is the expression 'the rule by which he proceeds' supposed to have left to it here?

I take it that the answer to that is: 'little or none'. Wittgenstein analogizes the problem of describing the putative rules of language with one of observing people playing with a ball where we may be able, from time to time, to discern commonalities with existing games; but at other times not. We may not be able to clearly individuate games according to rules; nor need there even be rules, for some of their 'playing' may be just messing around with the ball. But which parts are those? Can we clearly demarcate them? Furthermore, there are games where one makes up the rules as one goes along, or changes them every now and then without warning, and so on. Furthermore, if we are not aware of rules in our everyday linguistic practice and there is no generally established rule book to consult, it may be hard, if not impossible, to draw a usable distinction between play that accords with rules and play that accords with a *conception* of rules—but only the latter kind of case is usefully analogous to the conceptual aspect of language that is of relevance to philosophy in Wittgenstein's sense.

Wittgenstein's crucial insight is that, from the point of view of (what he calls) philosophy, we *cannot* say that in using language in such and such a way a person *must* be following such and such specific rules, according to a conception of them as such. He observes that (sec. 81)

> in philosophy we often *compare* the use of words with games and calculi which have fixed rules, but cannot say that someone who is using language *must* be playing such a game.

Just as we cannot say that someone who is using language must be doing so according to definite fixed rules, so, too, we cannot say they must be doing so according to *any* specific set of rules—even if we add that these are flexible, changeable, indefinite, and so forth. Indeed, making these sorts of qualifications threatens to make the difficulties of describing language in terms of rules even more obviously insurmountable, and it threatens to undermine the point of positing rules in the first place.[15]

Let me be clear that I am not denying that language use is a normative practice and that concepts have correct and incorrect uses. I take that to be obvious and undeniable. The point is that linguistic normativity is not well-thought-of in terms of the definite fixed rules of language of philosophical imagining (*contra* orthodox Wittgenstein interpretation and the Wittgenstein of the *Tractatus*). We have seen that there is a problem, on Wittgenstein's conception of philosophy, of ascribing particular rules of language to a linguistic practice as a matter of empirical or metaphysical fact. There is also the problem of authority. Given some candidate rules, who or what lays down that *these* are the rules of language? This is similar to the problem that we already discussed with regard to Brandom's project: how do we know what the implicit rules of language are?

In the face of such difficulties, it is reasonable to conclude that the notion of a rule of language is unusable as a general explanatory tool in acquiring a fruitful philosophical understanding of language use. Indeed, Hacker and many other interpreters have apparently missed the clear indications in the text that Wittgenstein does not take the philosopher to be capable of simply reading off rules of language (supposing that there are such) from observing the use of words. On the contrary, he proposes that the best one can do is to construct (or stipulate) schematic 'language-games' according to specified rules and then to use these constructed language-games as *philosophical tools of clarification* by *comparing* them with the highly complex and constantly shifting flux of ordinary language. Wittgenstein unambiguously explains (sec. 130): 'The language-games are set up as *objects of comparison* which are meant to throw light on the facts of our language by way not only of similarities, but also of differences.'

If one supposes, with Hacker, that the rules of language lie open to view, one inevitably falls into metaphysical dogmatism—since one would then be making the unobvious and unargued claim that, given the rules of language as one 'sees' them, one *must* use a word according to these rules (that is, those that, on this view, constitute the correct use of the word) if one is to express a certain concept.[16] But such a statement of what *must* be so is precisely the problem of metaphysical assertion that Wittgenstein is assiduously attempting to avoid.[17] As Wittgenstein himself remarks (sec. 599):

> In philosophy we do not draw conclusions. 'But it must be like this!' is not a philosophical proposition. Philosophy only states what everyone admits.

But now how are we to understand the phrase 'what everyone admits' in this passage? We have seen that this is not to be understood as saying that everyone must admit that correct language use is governed (or constituted) by such and such rules of language. What, then?

It is at this point that we need to introduce a fundamental feature of Wittgenstein's philosophy: namely, its careful avoidance of putting forth philosophical theses either to be accepted or rejected by its readers. Stanley Cavell has called this feature of the text its 'unassertiveness' (1994: 117). Philosophy, for Wittgenstein, is not in the business of saying that, as a matter of empirical or metaphysical fact, language is characterized by such and such rules. It does not concern itself with asserting or denying *any* matters of fact, as Wittgenstein explains:

> What I should like to get you to do is not to agree with me in particular opinions but to investigate the matter in the right way. To notice the interesting kind of things (i.e., the things which will serve as keys if you use them properly).
>
> *(Klagge and Nordmann 2003: 343)*

In a famous and enigmatic passage, Wittgenstein writes (sec. 128):

> If one tried to advance *theses* in philosophy, it would never be possible to debate them, because everyone would agree to them.

By 'philosophy' here, Wittgenstein is referring to *his* philosophy, not traditional philosophy (that is, metaphysics).[18] The only thing that he is willing to recognize as a 'thesis' in philosophy is something uncontroversial: indeed, something 'everyone' would agree to without further ado—no justification or argument being necessary to win conviction. I take Wittgenstein's italicizing the term 'theses' to indicate that what is in question is *not* theses at all. If something is such that everyone agrees to it then it cannot be a theoretical explanatory claim, since any such claim is inevitably controversial, hence debatable. Furthermore, Wittgenstein is committed to not making an empirical prediction about what we would or would not do under certain circumstances. In particular, he is not predicting universal agreement about a matter of fact, contrary to what his locution (namely, 'everyone would agree') perhaps suggests; but, as we have seen, neither does his locution mean what everyone *must* agree to if they are to say anything at all. He is not doing transcendental linguistics.

A better way to understand 'what everyone would agree to' is as a statement not about the world (or language) but, instead, as an expression of Wittgenstein's *method* for the clarification of concepts.[19] Unless we all agree on the tools of clarification—for example, that a particular language-game is defined by such and such rules—then we cannot satisfy the (ideal) aim of philosophy—namely, 'complete clarity', which is signaled by the complete disappearance of the philosophical problem (sec. 133). The interpretative shift from a substantive to a methodological claim completely removes the air of dogmatism from the remark. Not falling back into the dogmatism that characterizes metaphysics is *fundamental* to Wittgenstein's entire conception of philosophy (sec. 131).

Wittgenstein's subject-matter is, notoriously, 'grammar', which concerns not what is true or false—a matter for empirical inquiry—but rather those uses of language that are *candidates* for truth and falsity, that *mean* something as opposed to gibberish, or unintelligible marks on a page, or apparently grammatical nonsense words such as those appearing in Lewis Carroll's poem 'Jabberwocky'. Grammar depicts or expresses 'possibilities of phenomena', ways that things might be (sec. 90). How can we investigate such things without making any claim about how things are? Let us consider this remark (sec. 496):

> Grammar does not tell us how language must be constructed in order to fulfill its purpose, in order to have such-and-such an effect on human beings. It only describes and in no way explains the use of signs.

We must now ask: how do we describe the use of signs without indulging in theses (assertions)?

I suggest that a key innovation to introduce at this point is Wittgenstein's concept of a *criterion*, where this means, schematically, the basis upon which we apply a concept of an 'object' to the world. With the notable exception of Stanley Cavell, this notion has been widely overlooked or slighted in recent interpretations of Wittgenstein, for the reason that it has come to be seen as theoretically intractable.[20] But this supposed weakness is, when looked at from a different perspective, a strength, an insight into the workings of Wittgenstein's philosophy.

Cavell has argued that criteria in Wittgenstein contrast with ordinary criteria along at least five dimensions of difference (1979: ch. 1) (see Table 14.1).

In ordinary parlance, criteria are specifications in virtue of which those with the requisite authority judge something—a person, object, action, and so forth—to have a certain value or status. J. L. Austin provides the example of judging whether a bird is a goldfinch, or rather, I suppose, a European goldfinch (1970: 67–116). An ornithologist or an experienced bird-watcher is in a position to make such a judgment, since they have the requisite expertise. They know the relevant markings that are distinctive of the goldfinch, such as having a red face, black and white head, and black and yellow wings. With respect to such criteria, it is worth noting that standards can be introduced to determine to what extent they are satisfied. For example, we could speak of a standard European goldfinch as one that satisfies to a sufficient degree (perhaps defined by samples) all of the standard criteria.

Wittgenstein's notion of criteria is not the ordinary (or Austinian) one, but it is not a technical one either. It is best thought of as an *extension of*, or *projection from*, our ordinary notion. Wittgensteinian criteria are criteria of *identification* or recognition, as Cavell explains (1979: 45):

> Criteria are 'criteria for something's being so', not in the sense that they tell us of a thing's existence, but of something like its identity, not of its *being* so, but of its being *so*.

TABLE 14.1 Austinian vs Wittgensteinian Criteria

'Goldfinch'—Ordinary (Austinian) criteria	*'Chair'—Wittgensteinian criteria*
Criteria are for specialized objects: for example, a goldfinch, a Rembrandt painting, an F-16 fighter plane.	Criteria are for everyday things; for example, chairs, trees, shadows, people, emotional expressions.
Criteria are specific marks or features: for example, red face, black and white head, a painter's signature, a plane's wingspan.	Criteria are non-specific, often indicated by indexicals: for example, *that* look (of a chair), that it can be sat on like *this*, that it fits under a table like *so*.
These features could be catalogued in, say, a guidebook or dictionary.	These features are not appropriate for cataloguing: they are radically occasion-sensitive; not circumscribable.
Expertise and special training is required to know these criteria.	No expertise or special training is required to be capable of recollecting these criteria; any competent language speaker can do it.
There is a question of how well the criteria are satisfied in any given case. Standards might be introduced to determine this.	Criteria either apply or not; there is no question of how well they apply. There are no independent standards.

Given that criteria do not settle the question of existence (or reality), they do not refute skepticism. Cavell has built a powerful and far-reaching skeptical reading of Wittgenstein's work around this pivotal insight. A key implication of Cavell's reading, I take it, is that criteria are not to be thought of as doing *any* epistemological work. This reading finds confirmation in Wittgenstein's discussion of the difference between criteria and 'symptoms' (sec. 354):

> The fluctuation in grammar between criteria and symptoms makes it look as if there were nothing at all but symptoms. We say, for example: 'Experience teaches that there is rain when the barometer falls, but it also teaches that there is rain when we have certain sensations of wet and cold, or such-and-such visual impressions.' In defence of this one says that these sense-impressions can deceive us. But here one fails to reflect that the fact that the false appearance is precisely one of rain is founded on a definition.

We may begin unpacking this dense passage by noting that symptoms are a matter of inductive evidence. A doctor calls crushing chest pain a *symptom* of a heart attack, on the basis of a well-established correlation between past instances of each of these things—the pain and the pathology. Similarly, we can say that a falling barometer is a symptom of rain, given that a correlation between rain and a decline in barometric pressure has been previously established on the observational basis of noting the one in the presence of the other. Wittgenstein makes the point that, in order to establish that one thing is a symptom of another, we must not forget that we inevitably rely on *criteria* of identification, which tell us what kind of objects we are talking about. In order to establish the extent to which two things, x and y, coincide, we must be able to independently identify x and y. That is precisely what we need criteria for—identifying things.[21] In the present case, Wittgenstein means to call to our attention to the fact that there are criteria for rain: namely, our having certain sensations of wet and cold, and certain visual impressions that we might describe simply as its looking like it is raining. There are, of course, criteria for reading a falling barometer, too. It is on the basis of the application of these two sets of criteria—for rain, and for reading falling barometers—that we can establish that one is a symptom of (that is, inductive evidence for) the other.

Cavell's anti-epistemological reading contests the epistemological reading of John McDowell, who argues (1982: 470) that criteria are a kind of 'indefeasible' grounds for claims to know that such and such. But, *contra* McDowell, criteria are not 'ways of telling *how* things are' (ibid., emphasis added). They are, instead, ways of telling *what* things are. Criteria establish that a concept of 'object' is at issue, but they do not provide indefeasible grounds for a claim to know how things are with respect to the existence or reality of that 'object' (namely, a claim about its *being* so). Indeed, a key feature of criteria is that they only defeasibly establish what *actual* 'object' or reality is at issue.[22] For example, consider Wittgenstein's example of the disappearing-reappearing 'chair' (sec. 80), which we have good reason to refrain from calling a chair at all. As regards defeasibility, it is akin to Austin's example of the exploding 'goldfinch' (1970: 88), something that satisfies the criteria of goldfinch but that is not a (normal) goldfinch. It is important that in each case the relevant criteria—of a chair, of a goldfinch—are satisfied even though we do not know what 'object' we are dealing with in actual fact.

One important respect in which Wittgenstein's conception differs from the ordinary one is that what is being judged are not specialized things (such as goldfinches or high dives or ancient Greek pottery), but are instead ordinary objects or happenings (for example, chairs, rain, dreams, trees, smiles) and ordinary concepts (for example, of understanding, or reading, or the color red, or the truth of a confession): a whole raft of disparate things and abilities and statuses with which any competent speaker is familiar. Of course, it comes as something of a surprise to learn that we have criteria for such things. For one thing, we clearly do not, and are not required to, first observe that criteria are satisfied and then, on that ground, apply the concept (of an 'object') for which the criteria are criteria. Criteria must be rather be elicited, recalled, or be thought. Perhaps just because such objects and concepts are so familiar, we find talk of criteria for them quite unfamiliar; or, rather, we are in the uncanny position of discovering something right under our noses, which we, unwittingly, tend to overlook.[23]

Another important feature of criteria in Wittgenstein's work is that there are no expert judges to decide whether they apply or not. All masters of the language are equally authoritative both in saying what are criteria for what—identifying or recognizing the things of the manifest image of the world—and in criticizing such claims.[24] We have said that recalling criteria (in the sense of calling to mind rather than remembering) is not a statement of fact; it is rather a statement of what *counts* as a possible fact. If, say, one sees that criteria for another's pain apply (for example, grimacing, crying out, nursing the hurt part), then either the other person is in pain, or, if not, they are perhaps feigning pain, or perhaps they are acting the part of someone who is supposed to be in pain, or. . . . It is not a *fact*, we do not know, that this behavior counts as pain; rather, the application of the criteria for pain brings the concept of pain into play in one of an unbounded variety of ways. To recall criteria is to articulate what one goes on in calling or counting things under concepts in judgments.

It is most important to see, in the face of a barrage of secondary literature to the contrary, that criteria are *not* rules of language.[25] They do not have the authority of rules, which are presumably established by some instituting body with the requisite power to do so: for example, experts, designated authorities, the community, or its representatives. Nor do they have the generality of rules.

Criteria are not reflectively or introspectively available *en masse*; rather, 'one *bethinks* oneself of them' case by case, in the investigation of the sense of specific judgments (notably, metaphysical pronouncements) under specific current, remembered, or imagined circumstances (sec. 475). Nor do they form a framework of communal agreement. Cavell has stressed the contingent and unguaranteed (hence potentially 'terrifying') fact of our *mutual attunement* in criteria as a condition of our mutual intelligibility, but attunement here does not mean widespread agreement in criteria on a certain occasion (cf. 1969: ch. 2). Cavell says that we are in 'agreement throughout . . . [like] clocks or weighing scales' (1979: 32). But clocks and weighing scales have been *made* to agree by their manufacturers in the time or weights they measure. Cavell is fully aware that there is nothing—not rules, not universals, not foundations, not brain-states, not God, and so forth—that ensures that we agree in criteria;[26] so, the suggestion that we 'agree throughout' requires qualification.

In explaining Wittgenstein's vision of language, Cavell adduces what he calls 'two fundamental facts about human forms of life', namely (1979: 185)

> that any form of life and every concept integral to it has an indefinite number of instances and directions of projection; and that this variation is not arbitrary.

Consider the concept of a tree. In order to correctly use the word 'tree', one must apply the word in—or, in Cavell's parlance, project the word into—at least some present, future, or counterfactual contexts that we take to be the *same*.[27] In one's training in language as a child, one is taught that a finite number of things are called 'tree', and from that training one is expected to go on to call various other things, in many and various contexts, trees. Wittgenstein's account of the 'projection' of a concept or word is related to a number of central insights about language; which, let me remind the reader, I read as part of Wittgenstein's effort to free himself of a picture of language use as rule-governed: (1) 'that the application of a word is not everywhere bounded by rules' (sec. 84); (2) that there is no such thing as grasping every possible use of a word (sec. 191); and (3) that correct usage depends upon systematic agreement amongst fellow speakers in actual judgments and not simply in definitions (sec. 242). Agreement here is not a statistical notion; nor does it refer to a consensus in a particular set of opinions (for example, Moore's propositions of common sense). It is, rather, a pervasive agreement in the possible applications of concepts in judgment—something that requires that we, for the most part, understand each other's projections of concepts into new or different circumstances—which makes disagreement possible, as well as possible ways of supporting or criticizing judgments.

Since there is this open-endedness—'an indefinite number of instances and directions of projection'—in our use of language, and since there is no theory in terms of mental images, rules, universals, brain states, or anything else that predicts correct projections, there is always the possibility of *idiosyncratic projections* in which one projects concepts or words in a way that runs the risk of criticism or rejection by others. The external world skeptic's use of language is an instance of such idiosyncratic projection. In imaging his skeptical scenarios (for example, continuous life-like dreams, global hallucinations, brains in a vat), the skeptic relies upon what Cavell calls 'projective imagination', something that guides one's sense of what makes sense, what it makes sense to say, under certain imagined conditions. By itself, idiosyncrasy does not imply that a projection is incompetent or meaningless. It could be that the *naysayers* are wrong, that I have seen a new possibility of use, a possible extension of the term's established use that these others miss whether through a lack of a shared feeling, intuition, insight, or what have you. Of course, it could also be that *I* am wrong, that I only *imagine* that I have seen a new possibility of use, and that the others are right to reject this use and to find it, and so me, incoherent.

Criteria are, first and foremost, one's own, although they function to provide the basis of our mutual intelligibility. Criteria can be elicited or recounted in everyday settings or when one remembers or imagines what we would say in some actual or hypothetical situation—with the proviso that something only counts as a criterion if an actual or possible other could follow it for themselves by seeing the application of the concept that it secures as a reasonable projection from some of its past uses. Unlike the vision of the rules of language as open to view, criteria are *not* surveyable. So, if there is agreement in criteria, then, we cannot rely on any specifiable *prior* agreement on a wide range or list of cases (as perhaps the expression 'agreement throughout' suggests). Agreement, in so far as there is one, is constantly being forged in the projection of language into new or different situations by different speakers on different occasions for all sorts of purposes and interests. We agree, at best, in normal cases. As Wittgenstein puts it (sec. §142):

> It is only in normal cases that the use of a word is clearly prescribed; we know, are in no doubt, what to say in this or that case. The more abnormal the case, the more doubtful it becomes what we are to say.

And, 'we recognize normal circumstances but cannot precisely describe them. At most, we can describe a range of abnormal ones' (1969b: sec. 27).

For these reasons, criteria are only common property of a problematic 'we'—problematic, because it cannot be defined or secured in advance of the work of eliciting criteria and trying them out on others. In sharp contrast to the stabilizing role ostensibly played by rules of language, in standard Wittgenstein interpretation—something that supposedly establishes 'the bounds of sense'—criteria are exploratory, provisional, and contestable. Indeed, one can elicit different criteria for the same concept that come into conflict over its application (for example, notoriously, the bodily and psychological criteria of personhood can come into conflict as can happen after an accident that causes brain damage). Eliciting criteria is a useful tool of philosophical clarification precisely because it allows Wittgenstein to *explore* the extent to which one, two, or more people find themselves or each other intelligible or not and without having to agree on matters of opinion.

According to this Wittgensteinian vision of language, unassertiveness plays a crucial role in his *method* for investigating sense. The solution of the problem of philosophy is twofold. (1) We construct models (language-games) according to strict rules and then compare them to the shifting, messy, and highly complicated language of everyday life—what Wittgenstein calls 'the rough ground' (sec. 107). Unless we agree on our model of philosophical clarification, we can make no progress in attempting to achieve a perspicuous presentation of some misleading aspect of grammar that tends to lead us into philosophical conundrums (for example, treating statements about numbers as statements about 'queer' non-spatiotemporal non-causal 'objects'). So, if we are practicing philosophy in Wittgenstein's manner then, ideally, we would *all* agree on these issues of methodology as a matter of good practice. But to agree on the potential fruitfulness of a model in the context of a particular philosophical difficulty is not to assert anything. (2) We elicit criteria as another unassertive tool of philosophical clarification. It is a method of exploration that does not forestall the question of possible confusion. That depends on the character of the link between one's current criterion for X and (past) common or familiar criteria for X. Investigating the link between what one takes to be a current criterion for X (under the pressure of philosophy) and the common or familiar criteria for X (which one recalls from everyday life) calls for imagination and sensitivity; but it requires no metaphysics (no claims about how things *must* be) nor does it wait upon any empirical discovery.

Recalling criteria is a method of self-knowledge (which is a version of, but more radical than, the Kantian solution to the problem of philosophy: the Kantian 'we' of rational agents is universal; the Wittgensteinian 'we' of fellow speakers who share one's sense of what makes sense is a problematic first-person plural). It is crucial to the power of this method of winning conviction that the one who is philosophizing is not being told something new. The philosopher is not asked to accept the assertions of another about how language *must* operate but is instead invited 'to investigate the matter in the right way'. This requires the unassertive mode of self-examination, the freedom to 'look and see' whether one has made sense on various occasions, or not (secs 66, 93). Like psychoanalysis, one has to come to certain realizations about oneself *by oneself* if they are to significantly penetrate into one's psyche.[28] Only in that way can one revolutionize oneself, by which I mean 'change one's own way of thinking'.[29] Only then can one rotate one's philosophical investigations 'about the fixed point of our real need'—that is, not forcing ourselves to conform to an ideal (and alien!) system of rules but instead, on the rough ground of everyday language, finding a way, a method, to avoid ineptness and emptiness in our thought and talk (secs 107, 108, 131).

Coda: Resisting 'Scientific' Metaphysics

Wittgenstein's philosophy is at present cast in shadow. We live in an age of science, and scientific forms of philosophy are in the ascendancy—for example, physicalism, scientific naturalism, and its naturalistic reduction programs, claiming ontological primacy for the 'absolute conception' of the world, so-called experimental philosophy, and so on. It can be justly said that Wittgenstein's vision of philosophy provides the most sustained resistance to these and other (what he would think of as deleterious) influences of science on philosophy—which is not at all to say that he does not respect the work of scientists and the importance of the findings in physics, chemistry, medicine, and so forth.

Some significant portion of Wittgenstein's greatness attaches to his defence of our shared humanity, or of what Cavell calls 'the human voice' (1979: 5), in the face of the skeptical implications of 'scientific' philosophy.[30] These implications are rarely acknowledged by orthodox naturalists—which is one reason for Wittgenstein's current fall from grace. Quine is a singular and useful example of one who has taken such thinking to its inevitably skeptical conclusions: that, since there is no *a priori* as traditionally conceived, philosophy collapses into science; and, given that most matters of everyday significance such as art, action, morality, and the reality of (other) persons find no genuine foothold in the scientific image of the world, they are treated with suspicion.

Wittgenstein's discovery of a philosophy understood as a form of unassertive linguistic therapy that one primarily performs on oneself is a way of recovering ourselves from falling into a skeptical denial of the human.[31] Such self-annihilating skepticism is inspired in our time largely by our intellectual obeisance to natural science, most especially in those aspects of our thinking that are not about settling matters of empirical fact. Wittgenstein writes (1969a: 18):

> Philosophers constantly see the method of science before their eyes, and are irresistibly tempted to ask and answer questions in the way science does. This tendency is the real source of metaphysics, and leads the philosopher into complete darkness. I want to say here that it can never be our job to reduce anything to anything, or to explain anything. Philosophy really is 'purely descriptive'.

In our times, one of the most potent forms of the denial of the human is a consequence of giving science an illusory metaphysical significance—one that sees in the workings of scientific modes of intelligibility 'a *super-order* between . . . *super-concepts*' (sec. 97). In one notable version of this metaphysical fantasy, the language of physics (that, for example, lacks the concepts of color, chair, and person) is treated as an 'absolute conception of the world' with explanatory and ontological primacy over other, more parochial conceptions (Williams 1985: ch. 8).

Wittgenstein says, opposing that alienated vision of humanity, that (sec. 97.)

> if the words 'language', 'experience', 'world', have a use, it must be as humble a one as that of the words 'table', 'lamp', 'door'.

Here he is not only recovering words from their 'holiday' in science-inspired metaphysical assertion; he is at the same time recovering the everyday ('manifest') world itself—in which there are *people* who *talk* about and *experience* such things as *tables*, *lamps*, and *doors* within a shared form of human life (sec. 38). Wittgenstein finds a new and rhetorically powerful way of reminding us of that.

If there is to be a recrudescence of interest in Wittgenstein within mainstream philosophy, it will depend upon seeing his work otherwise than as concerned with policing nonsense from some imagined authoritative perspective of one who 'knows' the (supposed) rules of language. In order to begin to do justice to Wittgenstein's originality, I suggest that we compare his philosophy with both psychoanalysis (scrutinizing one's own utterances in order to free oneself of self-deceptions and illusions) and Pyrrhonism (wherein skepticism of metaphysical 'objects' and metaphysical explanations can become a way of life).[32]

Notes

1 Wittgenstein (1958: sec. 109). All references to Wittgenstein in the text will be to the second edition of *Philosophical Investigations* (1958), unless otherwise indicated.
2 That is not to say that I will not allow myself some judicious quoting from other of his works.
3 These have been collected and published after Wittgenstein's death in the book titled *On Certainty*.
4 I concur with Paul Horwich (2005) in seeing Wittgenstein's originality firmly rooted in his conception of philosophy rather than in any specific thesis about language, meaning, mind, or mathematics. Indeed, as we shall see, Wittgenstein's conception of philosophy requires giving up propounding philosophical theses.
5 'The philosopher's treatment of a question is like the treatment of an illness,' writes Wittgenstein (sec. 255). For further discussion of the relation between Wittgenstein's metaphysical quietism and Pyrrhonism, see Macarthur (2017).
6 For an example of appealing to science as a model of philosophical inquiry, see Russell (1914). For an example of making philosophy empirical by treating it as continuous with science, see Quine (1981).
7 The 'limit of language' is that we cannot stand 'outside' language to consider how it and the world are related. The hoped-for explanation of language is well illustrated by Michael Dummett's demand for a 'full-blooded' theory of meaning, which is capable of explaining *every* concept expressed by a language, including its primitive concepts,

to one who does not possess them (1993: 5). Dummett elsewhere calls this a demand for 'an account of language as from the outside' (1991: 247).
8 Let us say that a concept is a node or pattern in a network of inferences that essentially involves generality, of being such-and-such.
9 Wittgenstein remarks, 'the way of thought . . . as it were flies above the world and leaves it the way it is, contemplating it from above in its flight MS 109 28: 22.8.1930' (1998: 7). In knowing certain things about language we *thereby* know certain things about the world that language is of or about: for example, that the fact that we do not call anything that is red 'green' shows that the world does not contain any reddish-green—that is, there is nothing we are prepared to count as being that.
10 Leading versions of this dominant form of interpretation include Kripke (1982); Brandom (1994); and Hacker (1997). The view is even held by otherwise careful readers of Wittgenstein's methodological remarks such as Fogelin (2009: 2).
11 Another problem with the idea of unconscious knowledge of the rules of language is this: by appeal to this notion, all that one can say is that a speaker accords with the rules, not that she is acting according to a *conception* of the rules as such. But then what becomes of the idea that these are indeed the 'rules' of the language in the required normative sense?
12 Grammarians are in the business of constructing a grammar of the language, but it is unclear what the role of this grammar is supposed to be. Is it simply a description of the way in which we use words since, surely, native speakers establish the benchmark of correct use? Or is it a prescription of the way in which we ought to use words? And if the latter, how does the grammarian presume to have any normative authority over other masters of the language regarding how we ought to use language?
13 Brandom's route of prioritizing assertion and the giving and asking of reasons for assertoric utterance—which he speaks of as 'the downtown' of language (2009: 120)—is clearly a significant departure from Wittgenstein's teaching, which involves a sustained critique of such descriptivism. For more discussion of Wittgenstein's criticism of descriptivism, see Macarthur (2010).
14 Here I have in mind Wittgenstein's remark, 'It will be hard to follow my portrayal: for it says something new, but still has eggshells of the old material sticking to it. MS 129 181: 1944 or later' (1998: 51). In the *Tractatus* Wittgenstein regarded language as an exact calculus of fixed rules and determinate senses. For his later critical perspective on that conception see, especially, secs. 81, 97, 101-2, 114-15.
15 How, for example, would one individuate one flexible or changeable rule from another into which it blurs? If a rule is indefinite, how can it explain all possible moves in language, for that was surely the hope of the appeal to rules?
16 We could castigate this as the 'nonsense-policeman' reading of Wittgenstein, one that assimilates him far too closely to logical positivism and its authoritarian and contemptuous way of dealing with metaphysical and religious utterances. It is of supreme importance to Wittgenstein to avoid dogmatism in philosophy (see sec. 131).
17 For a compelling (if partial) reading of the *Investigations* that takes seriously the importance of the distinction between claiming certain rules characterize (or constitute) actual linguistic practice and claiming (or stipulating) that certain rules characterize constructed language-games, understood as objects of comparison, see Kuusela (2008).
18 Wittgenstein seems not to have epistemology much in focus until the notes that he composed in later life that make up *On Certainty*. Even there, his primary concern is, as always, the logic of language ("grammar").

19 In adopting this interpretation I am in substantial agreement with Kuusela (2008: ch. 6).
20 Cavell writes (1979: 6), 'It is, of course, not hard to make out that the notion of a criterion is "important" in the *Investigations*.' It is hard to read this sentence without irony today.
21 As Cavell puts it (1979: 76), '[criteria] establish the position of a concept of an "object" in our system of concepts.'
22 As we have seen, in sec. 354 Wittgenstein considers the case in which our criteria of rain apply despite the fact that there is no rain. Of course, one could say in such cases that criteria are only *apparently* satisfied—a move that McDowell makes—but that simply plays into the skeptic's hands, since he will now say that perhaps criteria are *always* only apparently satisfied. In any case, it is worth noting that Wittgenstein does not qualify the application of criteria in this way. He makes the point that, since criteria for rain can apply when it is not raining, we are tempted to misconceive criteria as symptoms (that is, inductive evidence), so that it can come to seem as if there are nothing but symptoms. Of course, this is absurd. Symptoms presuppose criteria as a matter of logic. It makes no sense to suppose we have nothing but symptoms of rain.
23 Wittgenstein observes (sec. 129):

> The aspects of things that are most important for us are hidden because of their simplicity and familiarity. (One is unable to notice something—because it is always before one's eyes.) The real foundations of his enquiry do not strike a man at all. Unless that fact has at some time struck him.—And this means: we fail to be struck by what, once seen, is most striking and most powerful.

24 Notice that I do not speak of *the* criteria for a concept. Criteria are open-ended and extendable: there are my criteria, your criteria, and our criteria. A fact of our life with language is how good we are, most of the time, at keeping track of each other's criteria for the use of words.
25 The failure of various misguided attempts to use the notion of criterion as a rule of language to develop a semantic theory aimed at explaining competent language use or to refute skepticism has led to a confusion about their function in Wittgenstein's text. See, for example, Wright (1984). Apart from forcing upon criteria theoretical and antiskeptical roles that they were never intended to satisfy, such attempts fly in the face of Wittgenstein's repeated protest that 'we may not advance any kind of theory' and his attempt to overcome the demand to explain in favor of providing purposeful (namely, problem-oriented) descriptions instead (sec. 109).
26 This agreement Cavell explains as a matter of (1969: 52)

> sharing routes of interest and feeling, modes of response, senses of humor and of significance and of fulfillment, of what is outrageous, of what is similar to what else, what a rebuke, what forgiveness, of when an utterance is an assertion, when an appeal, when an explanation—all the whirl of organism Wittgenstein calls 'forms of life'.

27 Wittgenstein notes (1969b: sec. 455), 'Every language game is based on words "and objects" being recognized again.'
28 This connects with Wittgenstein's image of throwing away the ladder (of metaphysical assertion) that one has climbed up in order to see the world aright (1961: 6.54).

29 I mean to recall Wittgenstein's remark (1998: 51), 'The revolutionary will be the one who can revolutionize himself. MS 165 204: ca. 1944.' Herein lies a potential solution to Plato's problem of the cave.
30 It is worth adding that Wittgenstein's hostility to 'scientific' philosophy and to the ideology associated with science in our culture (for example, the progressivist idea that technological advance is an advance in civilization and human well-being) is still largely uncharted territory.
31 Wittgenstein remarks (1998: 50), 'The philosopher is someone who has to cure many diseases of the understanding in himself, before he can arrive at the notions of common sense. MS 127 76r: 1944.'
32 For further discussion of metaphysical quietism as a way of life, see Macarthur (2017).

References

Austin, John L. 1970. Other Minds, in *Philosophical Papers*, 2nd edn., ed. J.O. Urmson and G. J. Warnock, Oxford: Oxford University Press: 76–116.
Brandom, Robert 1994. *Making It Explicit: Reasoning, Representing, and Discursive Commitment*, Cambridge, MA: Harvard University Press.
Brandom, Robert 2009. *Reason in Philosophy: Animating Ideas*, Cambridge, MA: Harvard University Press.
Cavell, Stanley 1969. The Availability of Wittgenstein's Later Philosophy, in *Must We Mean What We Say?* ed. Stanley Cavell, Cambridge: Cambridge University Press: 44–72.
Cavell, Stanley 1979. *The Claim of Reason: Wittgenstein, Skepticism, Morality, and Tragedy*, New York: Oxford University Press.
Cavell, Stanley 1994. *A Pitch of Philosophy: Autobiographical Exercises*, Cambridge, MA: Harvard University Press.
Dummett, Michael 1991. *Frege and Other Philosophers*, Oxford: Clarendon Press.
Dummett, Michael 1993. *The Seas of Language*, Oxford: Clarendon Press.
Fogelin, Robert 2009. *Taking Wittgenstein at His Word: A Textual Study*, Princeton: Princeton University Press.
Hacker, P.M.S. 1997. *Wittgenstein on Human Nature*, London: Phoenix.
Horwich, Paul 2005. Wittgenstein's Meta-Philosophical Development, in *From a Deflationary Point of View*, ed. Paul Horwich, Oxford: Clarendon Press: 159–171.
Klagge, James and Nordmann, Alfred (eds.) 2003. *Ludwig Wittgenstein: Public and Private Occasions*, Lanham, MD: Rowman and Littlefield.
Kripke, Saul A. 1982. *Wittgenstein on Rules and Private Language: An Elementary Exposition*, Cambridge, MA: Harvard University Press.
Kuusela, Oskari 2008. *The Struggle against Dogmatism: Wittgenstein and the Concept of Philosophy*, Cambridge, MA: Harvard University Press.
Macarthur, David 2010. Wittgenstein and Expressivism, in *The Later Wittgenstein on Language*, ed. Daniel Whiting, Basingstoke: Palgrave Macmillan: 81–95.
Macarthur, David 2017. Metaphysical Quietism and Everyday Life, in *The Cambridge Companion to Philosophical Methodology*, ed. Giuseppina D'Oro and Søren Overgaard, Cambridge: Cambridge University Press: 270–296.
McDowell, John 1982. Criteria, Defeasibility and Knowledge, *Proceedings of the British Academy* 68: 455–79.

Quine, W.V.O. 1981. *Theories and Things*, Cambridge, MA: Harvard University Press.
Riemer, Nick 2016. Introduction: Semantics: A Theory in Search of an Object, in *The Routledge Handbook of Semantics*, ed. Nick Reimer, Abingdon: Routledge: 1–10.
Russell, Bertrand 1914. *Our Knowledge of the External World as a Field for Scientific Method in Philosophy*, London: Open Court.
Williams, Bernard 1985. *Ethics and the Limits of Philosophy*, London: Fontana Press.
Wittgenstein, Ludwig 1958. *Philosophical Investigations*, 2nd edn., trans. G.E.M. Anscombe, Oxford: Basil Blackwell.
Wittgenstein, Ludwig 1961 [1922]. *Tractatus Logico-Philosophicus*, trans. Frank P. Ramsey and C.K. Ogden, London: Routledge and Kegan Paul.
Wittgenstein, Ludwig 1967. *Zettel*, 2nd edn., ed. G.E.M. Anscombe and G.H. von Wright, trans. G.E.M. Anscombe, London: Basil Blackwell.
Wittgenstein, Ludwig 1969a. *The Blue and Brown Books: Preliminary Studies for the Philosophical Investigations*, 2nd edn., Oxford: Basil Blackwell.
Wittgenstein, Ludwig 1969b. *On Certainty*, ed. G.E.M. Anscombe and G.H. von Wright, (trans.) D. Paul and G.E.M. Anscombe, Oxford: Basil Blackwell.
Wittgenstein, Ludwig 1998. *Culture and Value: A Selection from the Posthumous Remains*, rev. 2nd edn., trans. Peter Winch, Oxford: Wiley-Blackwell.
Wright, Crispin 1980. *Wittgenstein on the Foundations of Mathematics*, London: Duckworth.
Wright, Crispin 1984. Second Thoughts about Criteria, *Synthese* 58: 383–405.

INDEX

Albert the Great 91, 124n20
Anaxagoras 14, 15, 18
Aquinas, T. 7, 124n20, 173; aesthetics 86; agency 86, 87, 99; angels 98, 99; Christianity 87, 92, 94, 99–100; ethics 86, 87, 90, 91–4, 97; form 88–91; free choice 98–100; God 87, 92–4, 96–9; hylomorphism 88–91; imagination 98; law 86; matter 87–91; metaphysics 86, 87, 90, 100; moral psychology 94, 100; pedagogy 94–7; physics 87, 100; psychology 87, 90; self-knowledge 98–100; substance 87–91; substantial forms, unicity of 87–91; and theology 86, 90, 97; virtue, and Augustine's definition of 92–3; virtue, and function of 92; virtue, as a habit 92–4; virtue, infused *vs.* acquired 91–4; virtue and happiness 92–3, 99, 100; *see also* Aquinas's greatness; Aristotle; philosophical greatness
Aquinas's greatness: breadth 96; influence 87; system 87
Aristotle 1, 7, 21, 87, 88, 90, 91, 105, 107, 109, 110, 115–18, 150, 163–4, 173, 187, 222, 234, 237, 239; causation 49, 50–1, 52–8, 60, 62, 164; Christianity 164; conditional necessity 58–62; *De Anima* 64n15; definition 48, 49, 50, 56, 59, 63n3; demonstration 55–7, 59, 64n20; essence 50–63, 164; explanation 50; form 164; function 51, 58–62; matter 164; *Metaphysics* 28n4, 28n11, 29n23, 49, 52, 64n12, 95; natural kind 51, 54, 63n10; natural philosophy 164; *Nicomachean Ethics* 68; *Parts of Animals* 49, 58–62; per se accident 52, 54–9, 61, 63; *Physics* 50; *Posterior Analytics* 49–53, 55–6, 58–62; properties 51–61; science 49–52, 55, 58–63; subject, subject-kind 51–8; substance 164; *Topics* 63n3; virtues 165; 'what is it' question 48–53, 60; *see also* Aquinas, T.; Aristotle's greatness; philosophical greatness
Aristotle's greatness: breadth 48–9; continued relevance 48; influence 48, 52–3, 54, 62–3; rigor 48; as scientist 49; system 48–9, 63
Arnauld, A. 112, 117, 134
Astell, M. 130, 136, 137, 144; belief 134; Bible 134; certainty 133, 134, 140; custom 137–8, 140–4; education 135, 136, 143; error 134; faith 134–5, 140; God 133–6, 141–3; knowledge 134, 140, 141; marriage 143; mind 135; mind-body difference 140; moral conduct 135–6; passions 133, 134; Pauline texts 135, 143; Port Royal logic 134; rational minds 140; science 134, 140; self-awareness 135; self-knowledge 135–6; self-ownership 134; *A Serious Proposal to the Ladies* 133–4; testimony 134–5; truth 134; women's equality 133, 135, 136, 143; women's natures 133–6, 141;

see also Du Châtelet, E.; philosophical greatness
Augustine 91, 94, 95, 115, 222; *see also* Aquinas, T.
Austin, J.L. 255, 257
Averroes 91, 101n4, 101n11, 173
Avicenna 173

Bacon, F. 161
Bain, A. 229
Battacharyya, K.C. 71
Baumgarten, A. 189, 197, 199, 204
Berkeley, G. 129
Boethius 94
Boole, G. 70
Boyle, R. 110, 111, 123n3, 161
Brandom, R. 250, 252, 263n10
Brito, R. 91
Broad, J. 133, 145n13
Buddhaghosa 1; agency 73–9; analytical philosophy 73, 74; attention(alism) 73–5, 77, 78, 80, 81, 83; believing 74; bodily expression 80–1; Buddhism 71–3, 75–6, 77, 82, 83; cognitive science 75; concepts 82; consciousness 72, 74; embodied cognition 75, 77; embodied 'you' 79; empathy 74, 79–81; end-of-life experience 74; feeling 74; genealogy 75–6; insight 74; intentional action 76–7; introspection 74; knowledge 74; memory 74; mental action 76–8; mindedness 78–9; (Myth of) mediational mind 72, 73, 82; Myth of the given 82; perception 74; perceptual experience 74, 82; phenomenology 73, 74, 75; philosophy of mind 73, 75; reason 82; representation 74; self 73–5; self-control 75; stances 73; testimony 74; truth 74; virtue 74; volition 75; *see also* Buddhaghosa's greatness; Carruthers, P.; philosophical greatness
Buddhaghosa's greatness 78; originality 72, 74; strength beyond fashion 82–3; transformative influence 71–3, 82–3

Cantor, G. 156
Carroll, L. 254
Carruthers, P. 78–9
Carus, P. 228
Cavell, S. 253, 254, 255–6, 258, 259, 261
Chakravartty, A. 73
Chomsky, N. 249
Clarke, D. 129

Clifford, W.K. 234
Cohen, G. 174
Colebrooke, H.T. 70
Confucianism 30, 32, 37, 38, 41, 43n3, 44n17
Confucius 37, 38, 40, 42n2, 44n18, 149; *see also* Confucianism; Zhuangzi

Damascene 98
Democritus 23
De Morgan, A. 70
Descartes, R. 7, 94, 95, 129, 130, 145n10, 163, 171, 211, 222; action 105, 108, 109, 110, 117; attention 114, 119–21; certainty 118; Christ 114–15; *cogito* 124n17; color 118–19; doubt 113–14; God 105, 106–7, 108, 109, 111, 113–15, 118, 121; imagination 112, 115, 116, 118, 120; knowledge 104, 112–13; logic 112; mathematics 29n24, 106, 114; matter 104–9, 110–12, 113, 114, 115, 122; memory 112, 115, 116, 120; metaphysics 105, 107, 108, 109, 110, 111–15, 121–2; mind-body relation 104–6, 110, 113, 116–21, 122; natural philosophy 106, 107–12, 116, 121–2; perception 104, 113, 115, 116, 118–21, 124n15; physics 106, 108, 109, 110, 111, 112, 121, 122; properties 106–9, 110, 111, 112, 113, 114, 119, 122; qualities 104, 107, 108, 110–11; skepticism 107; understanding 112, 115, 124n19; will 107, 112, 113, 115, 117, 119, 120, 121; *see also* Descartes's greatness; philosophical greatness
Descartes's greatness 104–6; influence 104–5; method 112–16
Dewey, J. 231, 233, 242; *see also* Peirce, C.S.
Dignāga 71, 82; *see also* Buddhaghosa
Donaldson, T. 231
Du Châtelet, E. 8; best possible world 139–40; Bible 131, 141, 143; canon of Western philosophy 128–30; certainty 140, 141, 143; custom 137, 138–9, 140, 141–2, 144; *Discourse on Happiness* 137, 138–9, 144; education 128, 130–3, 137, 140, 142, 143, 144; epistemology 129; *Examination of the Bible* 141; freedom 129, 131; gender 129; God 129, 137–43; happiness 131, 138, 144; inquiry 138; *Institutions de physique* 131, 133, 138–9, 140, 141, 143; mathematics 139;

metaphysics 129; mind 128, 131, 132–3, 137; moral conduct 140, 141, 142–3; natural philosophy 131, 137; optics 131; passions 130; physics 141; prejudice 138, 142; Principle of Contradiction 139; Principle of Sufficient Reason 138, 139–40, 141, 143; quietism 144; reason 138; self-knowledge 135, 137, 142–3; self-ownership 130, 131, 132–3, 137; standard narrative 128–9; standpoint epistemology 145n9; theology 131, 142; truth 132, 139, 140, 141, 142, 143; women 128, 130–2, 136–7, 142; women's equality 142, 143; women's nature 137, 140; *see also* Astell, M.; Du Châtelet's greatness; philosophical greatness
Du Châtelet's greatness 128–31; creativity 131; precision 131
Dummett, M. 262n7

Elgin, C. 4
Elizabeth of Bohemia, Princess 123n11
Epicurus 23
Euclid 156

Fichte, J.G. 169–70, 173
Fodor, J. 117
Foot, P. 213
Frege, G. 156, 187, 200–1, 237
Freud, S. 211, 215, 216, 221, 224n15; *see also* Nietzsche, F.

Gandhi, Mahatma 71
Gandhi, 71
Gassendi, P. 111, 123n3
Goodman, N. 223n2, 224n9, 235, 242, 243
Gournay, M. de 130, 133

Hacker, P. 249, 252–3
Hall, E. 68–9
Hatfield, G. 129
Hawking, S. 171
Hegel, G.W.F. 23, 70, 170, 173, 211, 221, 240
Heidegger, M. 187
Hobbes, T. 111, 123n3
Hofweber, T. 200
Huddleston, A. 224n16
Hume, D. 25, 129, 214, 225n23, 235; aesthetic judgment 153–4; beauty 153–4; causation 151, 160, 163, 193–4; cognitive psychology 160–1, 163, 167; color 153–4, 159; concepts (abstract ideas) 154–5; constant conjunction 151–2, 157, 159–60; convention 152–3; 'custom or habit' 158; desire 158; *Dialogues Concerning Natural Religion* 160; empathy 166; empiricism 161–2; epistemology 150; ethics 150; God 151; God, and argument from design 160; God, and miracles 159–60; God, and religious belief 159–60, 161; human nature 26, 160–1, 165, 166; 'Hume's Fork' 155–6; ideas *vs.* impressions 161; Is/Ought 157; laws of nature 151; logic 161; mathematics 152, 156, 161, 162, 167; memory 157, 166; moral judgment 153–4; moral motivation 158–9, 162; moral psychology 166; moral sentiment 154, 158–9, 166; naturalism 25, 162, 165; natural philosophy 25, 161; passions 155, 158, 159, 161, 162; perception 157, 166, 190; probability 16, 159, 166, 167; reasoning 152, 157–9, 166; skepticism 151, 158, 162–3, 167; 'standard of judgment' 153–4, 165, 166; 'Of the Standard of Taste' 153–4; sympathy 152, 166; *A Treatise of Human Nature* 157, 194; uniformity of nature 151, 152, 157; vice 153–4, 162, 165; virtue 153–4, 162, 165; volition 155; voluntary action 158, 160, 161; *see also* Hume's greatness; philosophical greatness
Hume's greatness: field framework 150, 163–7; fundamental questions 148, 167; influence 148–50, 168; original arguments 155, 167–8; original theses 155, 167–8; significant concepts developed 151, 167–8
Hutcheson, F. 153, 175
Huxley, T. 105, 121
Huygens, C. 161

Irwin, T. 169

James, W. 105, 228, 229, 230–1, 233, 237, 241, 242; *see also* Peirce, C.S.
Jayanta 71
Jayarāśi 71

Kant, I. 4, 67, 96, 129, 150, 156, 248, 260; action 164; aesthetics 187; agency 175, 181–2; autonomy 164–5, 166; beauty 175; belief 201–5; categorical *vs.* hypothetical imperative 164;

Index

causation 195–6; concepts 193–7, 200–1; *Critique of Pure Reason* 4, 188, 190, 194–5; dignity 164, 181–3; end in itself 164, 181–3; enlightenment 182–3; ethics 187; existence 194, 197; fallibility 170; freedom 181–2; God 180, 198–9; happiness 164; intuition 175, 177, 207n4; logic 187; logicism 197–9; mathematics 197; metaphysics, immanent *vs.* transcendent 205–6; morality 171; perception 208n20; personal identity 194; philosophical inquiry 171, 172; philosophy of mind 187; philosophy of science 187, 188; *Prolegomena to any Future Metaphysics* 193–4; properties 198, 200–1, 203; racism 170–1; reality 180; reason 164; reference 191–2, 197–203, 205–7; religion 180; science 171, 202–3, 204, 207; semantics 207n2; sexism 170–1; substance 191, 194, 197–9, 200, 208n31; truth 192, 201–2, 204; understanding (*Erkenntnis*) 204–7; universalizability, moral 176–9; vice 175, 178; virtue 175, 178; will 164; *see also* Fichte, J.G.; Kant's greatness; Nietzsche, F.; Peirce, C.S.; philosophical greatness; Rawls, J.
Kant's greatness: by being misunderstood 173–4, 183; influence 169–70; new answer 187–9, 207; new question 187–9, 207; as transformative 71
Kierkegaard, S. 94
Korsch, M. 169
Korsgaard, C. 179
Kretzmann, N. 27
Kripke, S. 263n10
Kuhn, T. 8–9

Leibniz, G.W. 111, 112, 122, 129, 156
Lewis, C.I. 228, 242–3; *see also* Peirce, C.S.
Lewis, D. 151–2, 153, 204, 208n27, 209n35
Locke, J. 25, 110, 129, 130, 152, 156, 161, 166, 189, 190, 194–7, 202; *see also* Hume, D.
Lombard, Peter 96
Lotze, H. 173

Malebranche, N. 112, 151
Mandeville, B. 136, 142
McDowell, J. 28n2, 243, 256
Mersenne, M. 108, 110, 112, 123n7
Mill, J.S. 70, 131
Mohism 30, 32, 44n17; *see also* Zhuangzi

Monet, Claude 10n2
Moore, G.E. 258
Murdoch, I. 74

Nāgārjuna 71; *see also* Buddhaghosa
Newton, I. 104, 111, 122, 131, 161
Nietzsche, F. 9, 94; art 222; beauty 221–2; belief 214; *Beyond Good and Evil* 212, 214, 216, 218, 221; Christianity 212–13, 215–18, 219–21; compassion 212–13, 216–17, 220; creativity 221; drives 215–16, 219, 221; *Ecce Homo* 213, 214, 218; epistemology 212, 214; eternal return 213; existential meaning 218–21; genealogy/etiology 212, 213, 214; *Genealogy of Morality* 214, 215; God 212, 216, 217, 219; greatness 222; humility 212; identity 212; intuitions 211; and Kant 215, 216, 222, 224n17; metaphysics 212, 214; morality 212, 214–18, 220; narrative 212–13, 216, 219, 222; nihilism 218–20; philosophical autobiography 213; psychoanalysis 222n1; and psychology 213–14, 220, 221; reason 213, 215–16, 217, 221; resentment 215, 221; science 211, 222; skepticism 213, 223n8; sublimation 221; *Thus Spake Zarathustra* 211–12, 222; truth 214, 215, 222, 223n5; truth, value of 213, 214, 216–18, 219, 220, 224n13; truth, will to 213, 216, 219, 220; *Untimely Meditations* 220; values 212–14, 216–18, 219–21, 224n10; Western academic philosophy 212; *see also* Nietzsche's greatness; philosophical greatness
Nietzsche's greatness 222; philosophy as constitutive of being human 222; philosophy as life and death struggle 211–12
Noë, A. 9

Ockham, William 90–1
Ogden, C.K. 243

Parfit, D. 70
Parmenides 13
Peirce, C.S. 7; abductive inference 235; agency 236; belief 227, 229–34, 240, 241, 242, 243; certainty 232, 235, 243; doubt 232; empiricism 232; ethics 233–4, 243; explanation 234–5; fallibility 232, 240; induction 235; inquiry 227, 230–2, 237, 241; intuition 240–1; and Kant 229,

231–2, 237; knowledge 227, 232–4, 235, 240; logic 229, 231, 234–7; mathematics 233; meaning 230, 234, 235–6, 242; perception 237–40, 241, 242; probability 229, 235–7; reality 239, 241; science 233, 241, 243; semiotics 237–40, 241; truth 227, 229–34, 237, 240, 241, 242, 243; understanding 230; *see also* Peirce's greatness; philosophical greatness
Peirce's greatness: depth 227, 241; influence 241–3
Pennafort, Raymond of 95
Peraldus, William 91, 95
philosophical greatness: art 9–10, 222; knowledge 3–5; manifest image 3; metaphysical realism 5, 8; paradigms 8–9; philosophical image 2–3; possible criteria 5–8, 27–8, 48, 67–71, 82–3, 148–50, 169–74, 183, 187, 211–12, 227; scientific image 3, 261; *see also* Aquinas's greatness; Aristotle's greatness; Buddhaghosa's greatness; Descartes's greatness; Du Châtelet's greatness; Hume's greatness; Kant's greatness; Nietzsche's greatness; Peirce's greatness; Plato's greatness; Wittgenstein's greatness; Zhuangzi's greatness
Picasso, Pablo 9
Pinker, S. 171
Pippin, R. 224n11
Pissarro, Camille 10n2
Plato 1, 48, 49, 67, 70–1, 72, 90, 187, 200, 216, 222, 265n29; anti-Platonism 12–13, 21, 22, 25, 26; and Aristotle 12, 23, 26; atomism 23; causation 14, 23, 27; Christianity 22, 25; Demiurge 23; desire for wisdom (philosophia) 19; dialectic 17, 19, 20, 29n20; *Euthyphro* 50; explanation 14–19, 20–3, 27; Forms 14–15, 16–18, 21, 22, 23; and Hume, D. 25, 26, 193–4; Idea of the Good 14, 15, 17, 18, 20–1, 24; and the immaterial 14, 23, 24, 25, 26, 28; intentionality 21, 25, 26, 27; knowledge, empirical 19, 20, 22, 23, 25, 26, 27; knowledge, from philosophy 12, 16, 20, 22, 26, 28; knowledge, infallible 24; knowledge, representational 26; knowledge (episteme) 14, 19; materialism 14, 22, 25, 26; mechanism 14, 22, 24, 25; *Meno* 50; metaphysics 21, 22, 24, 27–8; naturalism 21, 23–5, 26–8; nominalism 13, 22, 25; objectivity 14; One-Indefinite Dyad 21, 22, 23; *Parmenides* 17–18; *Phaedo* 15–17, 26; Platonism 12–15, 20, 21, 22, 24–8; rationality 24, 26; reality 20, 23–4, 28n2; reduction 27; relativism 14, 22, 24, 25, 29n30; religion 28; representationalism 19, 26; *Republic* 15, 17, 18, 20, 28n9; science 12, 13, 15, 16, 19, 20–1, 22, 26, 28; skepticism 14, 22, 25, 26; and Socrates' 'autobiography' 15, 26; *Sophist* 28n4, 28n5; and Stoicism 23–5; *Theaetetus* 28n8; *Timaeus* 23; truth 14, 17–19, 26, 27; Ur-Platonism 13, 15, 21, 22; *see also* philosophical greatness; Plato's greatness; Rorty, R.
Plato's greatness: system 20, 26, 48; vision of what philosophy is (Platonism) 27–8
Plotinus 21, 72
Pollock, Jackson 9
Poulain de la Barre, F. 130, 145n10
pragmatism 29n30, 227–31, 233, 241–3; *see also* Dewey, J.; James, W.; Peirce, C.S.; Rorty, R.
Price, H. 243
Proclus 21
Putnam, H. 242
Pyrrhonism 162–3, 247, 262; *see also* Sextus Empiricus

Quine, W. 214, 242–3, 261, 262n6

Ramsey, F. 228, 242, 243; *see also* Peirce, C.S.
Rawls, J. 145n4, 170, 173, 175, 177, 179–80
Renz, U. 135, 142
Roberts, D. 237
Rorty, R. 12, 19, 20, 26, 28n1, 29n22, 224n13, 241–2
Royce, J. 228, 231, 242
Russell, B. 21, 262n6
Ryle, G. 117

Śale, G.76
Scheler, M. 80
Schopenhauer, A. 7, 211, 213, 216, 221, 225n23
Scotus, Duns 90, 101n7, 173
Searle, J. 117, 121
Sellars, W.F. 3, 241, 242, 243
sexism 8, 170–1; *see also* Astell, M.; Du Châtelet, E.
Sextus Empiricus 24, 25, 162; *see also* Pyrrhonism
Shaftesbury, (third) Earl of 153

Shapiro, L. 11n6, 129–30, 132, 144n1
Sider, T. 204, 209n35
Siedentop, L. 224n12
Smith, A. 94
Socrates 2, 15–16, 17, 26, 28n1, 28n12, 48–50, 53, 54, 94, 124n17, 149; *see also* Plato
Spinoza, B. 94, 111, 112, 129
Śrīhar 112.
Suarez, F. 91
Sunaitiai 23

Taylor, C. 73
Thomasson, A. 200
Tzu, L. 10n5

van Fraassen, B. 73
van Gogh, Vincent 9
van Schuman, A.M. 130, 145n10
Vanzo, A. 129
Venn, J. 234

Wagner, R. 213
Weil, S. 74
White, M. 243
Whitehead, A.N. 12, 21, 48
Wittgenstein, L. 7, 9, 94, 242, 243; action 261; art 261; *On Certainty* 262n3, 263n18; concepts 248, 252, 256, 258; criterion 254–60; experimental philosophy 261; 'forms of life' 258, 264n26; games 249, 251–3, 260; 'grammar' 248, 251, 254, 256, 260, 263n12; induction 256; know-how 250; know-that 250; language, critique of 247; language, knowledge of 247, 248–50; language, rules for 248–52, 253, 257–9, 261; linguistics 254; metaphysics 247–8, 250, 252, 253, 261–2; metaphysics, and quietism 262n5, 265n32; morality 261; pain 257; *Philosophical Investigations* 246, 251, 263n17; philosophy, and 'complete clarity' 254; philosophy, and science 247, 261–2; philosophy, *a priori* 248, 261; philosophy, naturalized 247, 261; philosophy, nature of 247–51, 252, 260–1; physicalism 261; physics 262; psychoanalysis 260, 262; scientific image 261; self-knowledge 248, 260; skepticism 247, 256, 259, 261, 262, 264n25; 'symptoms' 256, 264n22; *Tractatus* 243, 251, 252; voice 248, 261; *see also* philosophical greatness; Wittgenstein's greatness
Wittgenstein's greatness: defense of shared humanity 261–2; originality of method 246–7, 254, 262; 'unassertiveness' 253, 254, 260, 261
Wolff, C. 189, 197, 204
Wright, C. 246, 264n25

Zahavi, D. 79–80
Zhuangzi 1, 7, 9; certainty 34, 38, 39–41; doubt 34, 35, 38, 39, 42; empirical approach 35, 36, 37, 42; good life 30; habit 31, 40, 42; imagination 35–7, 42; knowledge-claims 31, 32, 36; language 31, 33, 35, 36, 37; mastery 30, 34, 39–42; performance 40; perspectives 31–9, 41, 42; relativism 32, 34, 35; responsiveness 30, 35, 37, 38, 40–2; skeptical questions 30, 34; skill 34, 40–1, 42; *see also* Confucius; Mohism; philosophical greatness; Zhuangzi's greatness
Zhuangzi (text) *see* Zhuangzi
Zhuangzi's greatness: approach to life 30, 42; continued relevance 30, 42; multi-perspectival 42; playfulness 9, 30, 33